An American in Gandhi's India

An American in Gandhi's India
THE BIOGRAPHY OF SATYANAND STOKES

Asha Sharma
WITH NANDINI SHARMA

FOREWORD BY
His Holiness the Dalai Lama

INDIANA UNIVERSITY PRESS
Bloomington and Indianapolis

This book is a publication of

Indiana University Press
601 North Morton Street
Bloomington, IN 47404-3797 USA

http://iupress.indiana.edu

Telephone orders 800-842-6796
Fax orders 812-855-7931
Orders by e-mail iuporder@indiana.edu

First published by Penguin Books India 1999 as *An American in Khadi:
The Definitive Biography of Satyanand Stokes,* copyright © Asha Sharma
1999

The paper used in this publication meets the minimum requirements of
American National Standard for Information Sciences—Permanence of
Paper for Printed Library Materials, ANSI Z39.48-1984.

Manufactured in the United States of America

Library of Congress Cataloging-in-Publication Data

Sharma, Asha.
    An American in Gandhi's India : the biography of Satyanand Stokes /
Asha Sharma with Nandini Sharma ; foreword by His Holiness the Dalai
Lama.
        p. cm.
    First published: New Delhi : Penguin Books India ; New York, NY :
Penguin Putnam, 1999, with title An American in khadi : the definitive
biography of Satyanand Stokes.
    Includes bibliographical references and index.
    ISBN 978-0-253-35158-6 (cloth : alk. paper) — ISBN 978-0-253-21990-
9 (paper : alk. paper) 1. Stokes, Samuel, 1882–1946. 2. India—Politics
and government—1919–1947. 3. Americans—India—Biography. 4.
Missionaries—India—Biography. 5. Apple growers—India—Himachal
Pradesh—Biography. 6. Social workers—India—Biography. 7. Po-
litical activists—India—Biography. 8. Gandhi, Mahatma, 1869–1948—
Friends and associates. 9. Hindu converts from Christianity—India—
Biography. 10. India—History—20th century—Biography. I. Sharma,
Nandini. II. Sharma, Asha. American in khadi. III. Title.
    DS480.45.S4674 2008
    954.03′5092—dc22
    [B]
                                                      2008003026

1 2 3 4 5 13 12 11 10 09 08

Dedicated to my mother,
Champavati,
Quaker by Heritage, Christian in Spirit,
Karmayogi in Life

CONTENTS

Photographs are on pp. 171–186.

FOREWORD

This story is a wonderful example of the natural give and take of good human relations. Samuel, later Satyanand, Stokes originally came to India from America, more than a century ago, with the intention of helping in a leprosy mission. He served there for a time and later worked hard to provide relief after the Kangra earthquake. But when he fell ill, he was sent to the hills to recuperate, as was customary.

I can easily understand how, once circumstances had brought him here, Stokes chose to settle in this attractive part of India. Like him, I too have had the privilege of regarding the green hills of Himachal Pradesh as my adopted home—for the last forty-seven years. It is a delightful place to be, the air is clean and full of birdsong, and the climate is pleasant, although I suspect that Stokes did not see in Kotgarh the kind of heavy monsoon rainfall we experience here in Dharamsala. What's more the people are friendly, straightforward, and welcoming.

Gradually Stokes began to realize that India, which is perhaps the one country whose civilization and culture have survived intact from their first beginnings, had a lot to teach him. Because India and her people have, from ancient times, cherished a rich and sophisticated philosophy of nonviolence at the core of their hearts, it has developed into a kind of natural reflex. Accordingly Stokes began to adopt a more Indian lifestyle, married a local woman, and settled down at Kotgarh in the hills beyond Shimla.

Of course, Stokes did not stay just because he was comfortable, but because he felt there was work for him to do. His stand against indentured labor and his joining the Indian freedom struggle are a tribute to his natural compassion and his urge to work against injustice.

While I share with Stokes an unflinching admiration for Mahatma Gandhi, he had the good fortune not only to be influenced by his ideas, but also to know the great man personally. Their correspondence about tackling contemporary issues seems to have been of great value to them both. Mahatma Gandhi had taken up the ancient and powerful idea of *ahimsa* or nonviolence and eventually made it familiar throughout the world. I believe that, following him, Stokes understood that nonviolence does not mean the mere absence of violence. It is something more positive, more meaningful than that. The true expression of nonviolence is compassion. Some people seem to think that compassion is just a passive emotional response instead of a rational stimulus to action. But to experience genuine compassion is to develop a feeling of closeness to others combined with a sense of responsibility for their welfare. This book makes clear that this is how Stokes felt about the people around him.

Finally, there are the apples that are his long-lasting bequest to the people of this region. Stokes is said to have been single-handedly responsible for introducing the *Red Delicious* strain to this region. Could there be a more commendable tribute to a man's life than that even fifty years after he passed away, wherever people bite into this sweet and juicy fruit, he is ultimately responsible for the pleasure they enjoy?

THE DALAI LAMA
AUGUST 29, 2007

PREFACE

I do not remember my grandfather Satyanand Stokes. He died when I was very young. But I have very fond recollections of frequent visits with my mother to his house in Barobagh, Kotgarh in the Simla Hills. It was situated on a hilltop with a magnificent view of the snow-capped Himalayas and the river Sutlej. The river was many miles down in the valley but we could see it clearly and hear the roar of its waters. The house was full of his memories. His *chupta,* a long traditional coat he wore, still hung on a peg behind the stairs in the small living room, and the little attic he used as his bedroom remained undisturbed.

As I grew older and heard snippets about his life from family and conversations with local villagers I became curious to know more about him. I started discussing the subject with my mother and reading whatever material came my way. Then, during a visit to Barobagh, my grandmother gave me a beautiful book to read, bound in red leather and with the title *Harmony Hall Letters* embossed on it in gold. It contained extracts of Stokes' weekly letters written from India to his mother in Philadelphia, which he had compiled for his wife and children. The letters covered a period of twenty-five years and reflected the close relationship between a mother and son. They not only narrated the extraordinary story of Stokes' life but also his evolving worldview and philosophy. These letters left a lasting impression on my mind.

His was truly a remarkable life, noteworthy for its fearless intellectual honesty, the strength of his convictions, and his sense of justice, equality, and fair play, and also for his immense contribution to the social and economic development of the hills.

He was born and brought up in America but India became his true home. He fought for India's independence alongside Mahatma Gandhi and other nationalist leaders, and was the only American who went to jail for India's cause. A legend in Kotgarh, Stokes was responsible for bringing about a sea change in the lives of people in the Simla Hills. He fought for and earned them freedom from the age-old tyranny of *begaar* or impressed labor. He transformed the economy of the region by importing apple saplings from America, distributing the saplings for free to the local farmers, and helping them plant and nurture them.

It is ironic that until a few years ago little was known about Stokes outside of his home state of Himachal, and there it was largely his gift of apples to the people that was remembered. Though his portrait hung alongside other stalwarts of India's independence movement in the Nehru Memorial Library in New Delhi, his role as a freedom fighter was not well known. The present biography, first published by Penguin Books India in 1999 under the title *An American in Khadi: The Definitive Biography of Satyanand Stokes,* helps to correct this injustice to Stokes and all that he stood for. There was an amazing response to the book—very warm and personal. Since the publication of the book, recognition of Stokes' life and work has come in different ways.

September 16, 2000, was a special day both for Indians and Americans in this country, when a statue of Mahatma Gandhi was unveiled in front of the Indian Embassy in Washington, D.C., by Prime Minister of India Atal Bihari Vajpayee in the presence of President Clinton. For Indians it marked the fruition of efforts that had begun fifty-one years earlier to establish a memorial for Mahatma Gandhi in the nation's capital. For Americans it was a reminder of the long relationship that Gandhi had with this country and its people, and honored the man who inspired the civil rights movement in the United States.

While the great American philosopher Henry David Thoreau was one of Gandhi's inspirations in "the science of civil disobedience," Gandhi was the guiding light of Martin Luther King Jr., who said: "The Christian doctrine of love, operating through the Gandhian method of non-violence, was for me the most potent weapon available to the oppressed people in their struggle for freedom."

Speaking about Gandhi's influence on ordinary Americans, Vajpayee singled out the life of Samuel Evans Stokes who, the prime minister said, became a "soldier in the Mahatma's army of Satyagraha in India . . . and had the rare honor of being the only American to become a member of the All India Congress Committee. . . . His recent widely acclaimed biography, 'American in Khadi,' shows how there has always been a natural affinity between India and America."

I had always wished that there should be an American edition of the book for the simple reason that Stokes was an American by birth and heritage and, despite his being so Indian, he never forgot his American roots. I felt it was only right that the subject should be known here and that many Americans would be keen to know about the remarkable life of one of their countrymen in a foreign land. I also believed the large Indo-American community in this country would take pride in the life of an American who, more than a hundred years ago, believed in India—its past, present, and future—as few Westerners did and who made an immense contribution to the development of the country.

Throughout his life Stokes worked toward building a more equitable world order. Upholding the democratic principles of his American heritage, he fought for similar rights for the Indian people. I have chosen to call the present edition *An American in Gandhi's India,* because Stokes was a true Gandhian. He found in Mahatma Gandhi someone he could admire and follow. "Gradually, as I grope my way from old conventional modes of thought towards the meaning and significance of his conceptions and methods," Stokes wrote in 1921 during Gandhi's non-cooperation campaign, "I become more and more convinced that the movement which he has initiated calls us to the deepest and noblest in our nature. It is that old call to victory by the path of utter self-renunciation, to purification by the path of self sacrifice." Gandhi in turn supported Stokes' campaign to eliminate *begar*—forced labor—in Himachal Pradesh, his home place. "You should continue with your struggle under the guidance of Stokes and suspend all . . . *begar*. . . . It is much better for you to undergo hardships and be ready to fill the jails for the sake of your faith . . . than to give *begar* to any official. . . . In your efforts I am with you with all my heart and soul."

Musing over his writings toward the end of his life, Stokes acknowledged that they were, in a sense, "a testament" and that he had "kept the faith" with his Quaker ancestors. "The struggle for right and fair play in the relations of men is a fight worth fighting. I shall never regret such part I have been able to play in it," he wrote.

He sometimes felt that few of his dreams of service had come to full fruition. "Very few of them have had more than the most imperfect realization," he admitted, "yet the dreams were something. . . . they were not ignoble, no matter how imperfectly they found fulfillment."

A remarkable odyssey, Stokes' life foreshadows a world prepared to learn from and embrace difference.

NOTE ON THIS EDITION

Stokes was a meticulous chronicler and record keeper. He painstakingly recorded his thoughts and views. He conscientiously preserved important letters and documents. But his papers are today widely dispersed and difficult to trace. Material for this book was collected over several years from old records and letters and interviews with family, friends, and contemporaries.

The American edition of the book is very similar to the Indian one. The response from those who read the book here convinced me that it would be best to leave the tenor of the book as it was—with its very Indian nuances. New material for the present edition consists of a foreword by His Holiness the Dalai Lama, a new preface, acknowledgments, and a glossary, as well as some revisions and additions.

Many changes have taken place since Stokes' lifetime in the names of towns and cities in India. In the interest of consistency of narration, the more popular names and their spellings have been used in the text. For instance, Simla, the venue for much of this story, is now known as Shimla. While there is a glossary attached to this book, an effort has been made to explain non-English words in the text itself.

An American in Gandhi's India

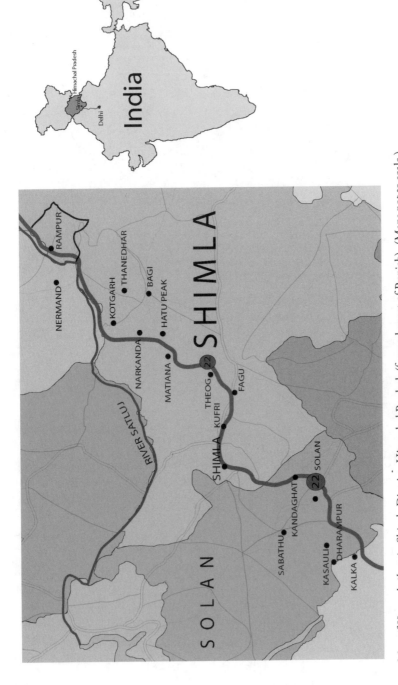

Map of Kotgarh *ilaqa* in Shimla District, Himachal Pradesh (formerly part of Punjab). (Maps not to scale.)

—— River Satluj

▬▬ National Highway (22), formerly Hindustan-Tibet Road

PROLOGUE

In the early hours of 3 December 1921, two policemen entered a first-class compartment of the Punjab Mail at Wagah railway station, near Lahore in British India, and approached a distinguished-looking American dressed in a khadi kurta and dhoti. They told him he was under arrest on charges of sedition and asked him to accompany them to the police station in Lahore. Six hours later, he was standing before district magistrate Major M. L. Ferrar, who magnanimously offered to release the man if he would provide a security deposit of Rs 10,000 for "good behavior." The terms were not acceptable to him. The American was in fact an Indian nationalist who, following Gandhi's principle of non-cooperation, had no intention of cooperating with the colonial government to obtain his release.

Samuel Evans Stokes Jr., formerly of Philadelphia, Pennsylvania, had made India his home some twenty years before and was now actively involved in the fight for India's independence from Britain. On the day of his arrest, he was traveling to Lahore to attend a meeting of the Punjab Provincial Congress Committee, of which he was a member. He was arrested on the grounds that he was going to Lahore with direct instructions from the "Central Congress Committee" for the nationalist leader Lala Lajpat Rai to start civil disobedience and hold mass meetings in Lahore in contravention of the Seditious Meetings Act. The charges were false. Stokes had come straight from his home in the Simla Hills and had not met any member of the All India Congress Committee (AICC) for days. His arrest was actually prompted by his articles published in Punjab's leading daily newspaper, the *Tribune*, which, according to the British, were likely to "spread sedition and promote hatred between different classes of His Majesty's subjects."

Even though the government tried to play down the arrest, it made news. Mohandas Karamchand Gandhi reacted to Stokes' arrest with a front page article titled "Reward of Adoption" in his weekly journal *Young India:*

> This is a unique move on the part of the government. Mr Stokes is an American who has naturalized himself as a British subject and who has made India his home in a manner in which perhaps no other American or Englishman has. He rendered eminent service during the War and is known in the highest quarters as a well-wisher of the government. No one can suspect him of ill-will. But that he should feel with and like an Indian, share his sorrows and throw himself into the struggle, has proved too much for the government. To leave him free to criticize the government was intolerable, so his white skin has proved no protection for him. The government is determined to quash the movement at all cost . . . When therefore Mr Stokes is put away, the strongest suspicions arise in respect of the bona fides of the government's case even in the estimation of an outsider.

That the news was not reported immediately by the Bombay press made Gandhi suspicious. "I cannot imagine that no wire has been dispatched about such a sensational arrest. My inference is that the wires notifying the arrest have been suppressed or delayed."

A couple of months earlier, Gandhi had convened a meeting in Bombay of the most prominent nationalist leaders of the time to discuss the future course of the Congress. Lala Lajpat Rai and Stokes were invited from Punjab. The meeting resulted in an important manifesto calling upon Indians to withdraw from government service. Stokes was the only non-Indian signatory to the manifesto. He was also the only American to ever serve on the AICC of the Indian National Congress.

Gandhi spoke highly of Stokes. "As long as we have an Andrews, a Stokes, a Pearson in our midst, so long will it be ungentlemanly on our part to wish every Englishman out of India," he said. "Non-cooperators worship Andrews, honour Stokes," he said on another occasion. For his part, Stokes felt his association with Gandhi was "the part of my life of which I am most proud."

The news of Stokes' arrest also appeared in several American newspapers and magazines of the time. The *Nation* of New York, describing Stokes as a "disciple of Gandhi and an apostle of non-cooperation," wrote:

> In what spirit he preached this national gospel appears from this extract from an article of his published just before his arrest: "If we fight with the ignoble weapons of pride and hate and prejudice, we are undone, even if we win a sort of unmoral victory. If we fight in the spirit of true nobility, God and eternal justice fight for us and the victory is certain. So fighting, even defeat is victory." By such a road has this son of well-to-do Philadelphia parents been brought to a British prison in the far-off land of his adoption.

It had indeed been a long journey.

A JOURNEY OF NO RETURN

When twenty-one-year-old Samuel Evans Stokes set out for India from Phila-delphia aboard the old *Haverford* on 9 January 1904, little did he know that this would be a journey of no return. His destination was Sabathu, a small town of Punjab in the Simla Hills, where he intended to work in a leper home run by the Leprosy Mission in India.

His plans were uncertain—he did not know how long he would remain in India, when he would return home, or how he would cope with the challenges of the life he had chosen. But right then he did not want to dwell on any of that. His heart had been set on going to India for so long that he could think of noth-ing else, and when the steamer was temporarily ice-bound a little way down the Delaware River, he became impatient, wondering whether he was at all des-tined to undertake the journey. It was nearly six months since he had first met Dr. Marcus Bradford Carleton who headed the Leprosy Home at Sabathu and who was home on a visit. Dr. Carleton brimmed with missionary zeal and com-passion. His enthusiasm for social work was infectious and gradually young Sam was influenced by the doctor's description of the work at the leper home and the dire need for dedicated workers. He was soon convinced he should go to India to help Dr. Carleton and join his small band of workers.[1]

Among the crowd of friends and relatives assembled to bid goodbye to Sam were his father, Samuel Evans Stokes Sr., engineer, holder of numerous patents, successful businessman, pioneer of elevators in America and founder-proprietor of Stokes and Parish Machine Company in Philadelphia; his mother, Florence Spencer Stokes, devout Christian, devoted mother, an American proud of her heritage and family values; his brother Spencer, twenty; and sisters Anna, nine-teen, and Florence, fourteen.

It was a cold and dreary day, ominous of an uncertain future, and Florence Stokes found herself shivering in her warm fur coat. When the steamer dis-appeared from sight and the family turned to go home without Sam, Samuel

Stokes Sr. put his arms around his heartbroken wife. "Don't worry too much, dear," he comforted her, "we had to let him go. He would never have settled down to anything else till he had tried this out, but he will be back in a year or two."[2]

For the family it had not been a happy parting. Sam's mother could not bear to think of him living so far away. She worried about his health which had often been a cause of concern. How would he survive working among lepers in the trying climate of India? His father, too, had not hesitated to express his disappointment. Samuel Stokes Sr. had always hoped that his eldest son would study engineering or medicine as was the family tradition and earn recognition in his chosen field. To him Sam's decision to go to India appeared rash and irresponsible, particularly as he did not seem to have any plans for completing his education or earning a livelihood.

As the steamer sailed down the Delaware, Sam was lost in thoughts of an age gone by. It was more than 200 years since his first American ancestor, Thomas Stokes, accompanied by his wife, Mary, and three small children, had sailed up the same river in the tough and rugged *Kent** in search of a life of freedom in the New World. Now he, an eighth generation descendent of Thomas Stokes, was setting off on a journey no less adventurous, motivated by a spirit no less aspiring.

Thomas Stokes was a contemporary of George Fox, religious reformer and founder of the Society of Friends, and of William Penn, founder of the Province of Pennsylvania. A "convert to their religious doctrines and tolerance, with the largest liberty for individual belief,"[3] he had spent considerable time in the White Lion prison in Surrey, England for his religious convictions. When the Society of Friends decided to found a new colony in accord with "Friendly" principles in the New World, he was eager to join it.

Sam had never tired of reading about the adventures and struggles of the early settlers and the stories of his own ancestors, many of whom, either in name or otherwise, were associated with the colonial history of America.

Thomas Stokes was among the signatories of the Concessions and Agreements of the Proprietors, Freeholders and Inhabitants of the Province of West New Jersey and was "a man of influence." He took a very active part in the affairs of the colony and during his lifetime the family acquired "an influential position in the country which it had never since lost."[4] His son, Joseph Stokes, was also a respected member of the Society of Friends in Chester County. The township records show that he took an active part in its affairs, and that the town meetings were often held in his house.

Joseph Stokes' son, Samuel Evans Stokes I, was a prominent member of the

---

* The *Kent* sailed from London in 1677 with 230 passengers aboard.

community and a member of the Colonial Assembly in 1758. He built the family home, Harmony Hall (now a historic landmark) in Moorestown, New Jersey, in 1753, where the family lived the simple and healthy life of the period, "patriarchal in its simplicity and bountiful in its hospitality." The tradition of friendly interaction with the American Indians continued to linger, and young Sam had heard how, often in the early morning, his forefathers would find a number of them wrapped in blankets, asleep on the kitchen floor with their feet toward the fire.

Sam's great-grandfather Dr. Hinchman Stokes I, who was Samuel Evans Stokes I's second son, was a "progressive" physician. He was among the first to adopt Jenner's discovery of vaccination. To convince others of its effectiveness, he vaccinated his little daughter and put her in bed with a smallpox patient. This won him the confidence and admiration of the community. The Stokes family were Friends (popularly known as Quakers) by inheritance and conviction, but Dr. Hinchman Stokes I and his wife, Anne Evans, who were cousins, were disowned for marrying within the prescribed degree of relationship. Though they lost their membership, in ideals, home life, and associations this branch of the family remained what was called a "Friendly Family."[5]

Sam's father, Samuel Evans Stokes Sr., was the second son of Dr. Hinchman Stokes II and was born and brought up at Harmony Hall. He was a bright student, and after graduating from Lawrenceville Academy in 1863 he joined the Isaac P. Morris Machine Works in Kensington, Philadelphia, to train as a mechanical engineer. In 1873 he set up his own business in Philadelphia with a friend, Alfred Parish, under the name "Stokes and Parish Machine Company." This was the beginning of twenty-four years of a continually enlarging and prosperous business enterprise.

In 1875, the firm built its first steam elevator for the Continental Hotel at 8th and Chestnut Streets, then the most elegant and fashionable hotel in Philadelphia. The elevator was among the first in any hotel in America and attracted much attention.

The firm's business and reputation were greatly enhanced during the Centennial Exposition, America's first World Fair, held in Philadelphia in 1876 to celebrate the centennial anniversary of America's independence. It was awarded a contract for erecting the woodwork for the display of various exhibits in the American and foreign sections, and also for the entire management of the machinery hall. It also put up a steam elevator in the main building to carry passengers to the roof. Each trip on the elevator cost ten cents and it was so popular that it showed profit within the first few days of the exhibition, and was bought by the Emperor of Brazil afterwards. From the following year, Samuel Stokes' business concentrated exclusively on manufacturing elevators.[6]

If Sam had reason to be proud of his father's ancestry, there was much to reckon with in his mother's family tree too. His mother's father, Dr. Jonathan John Spencer, was an unusually remarkable man who had worked with both Dr. Hinchman Stokes I and Dr. Hinchman Stokes II. He was born a Friend, but had to forfeit his membership for having served in the army—a vocation not in consonance with Quaker beliefs—as a surgeon in 1815. He took an active part in the politics of the state for several years and was offered the nomination for governor of New Jersey in 1846. After giving it serious thought, he declined the offer on the ground that a governor's "pardoning power was a responsibility which he, as a non-believer in capital punishment, did not feel he could assume." He was then appointed one of the six judges on the Court of Errors and Appeals—a higher court then peculiar to New Jersey. He was also one of the moving spirits in the early agricultural improvement of the state. Among his close friends was James Audubon, the renowned ornithologist. His wife, Sarah Lang, was the daughter of John Lang, editor of the *New York Gazette*, the city's first daily newspaper, for forty years. She was an exceedingly attractive woman, spoken of as "the most beautiful girl in New York,"[7] possessing a gentle dignity and courtesy of manner which endeared her to all.

Sam's mother, Florence Spencer Stokes, inherited her mother's beauty and charm. She also had her mother's deeply religious disposition along with her father's clear insight, rational mind, and sense of humor, qualities which sustained her during the personal tragedies that dogged her younger days. Within a span of four years she lost her father, mother, and her only brother. Then she herself was stricken with tuberculosis and was able to overcome the disease only after many years of suffering.

Happiness had eluded Florence for so long that it was with diffidence that she accepted Samuel Evans Stokes' proposal of marriage in the spring of 1880. She was already thirty-four and past all thoughts of marriage. After a long period of courtship they were married in 1881 and set up home at 5419 Wayne Avenue in Germantown, a largely Quaker suburb of Philadelphia. Their marriage proved a perfect one, and the birth of their first son, Samuel Evans Stokes Jr., on 16 August 1882 brought Florence a happiness she had not believed possible for her.

There was nothing in Samuel Jr.'s early years to indicate the unusual life he would find halfway across the world. He grew up in the finest American traditions. His home was beautiful and steeped in history. It abounded with artifacts collected from all over the world by his parents and ancestors during long travels abroad. Family portraits by famous artists lined the walls, and the library was a treasure trove of old books, papers, letters, wills, and deeds, which greatly fascinated Sam. His childhood was secure and comfortable. His mother spent much of her time in the upbringing of her children. The sense of honor and fairplay, truthfulness and integrity, love of fellow beings and of nature—qualities intrinsic to Sam's character—were the result of his mother's steady and patient devotion to her children in their early years.

Florence Stokes was devoted to all her children but was closest to Sam, her happy, robust eldest child who even as a toddler was full of the spirit of adventure and knew no fear. She always remembered how she witnessed his baptism at the Calvary Church with a "passion of dedication." She could never tell why, but it was a "much more intense feeling" than she ever had with the other children.[8] Sam reciprocated his mother's feelings; nothing made him happier than bringing her gifts—flowers, drawings, and later, little pieces of antiques on which he would not hesitate to spend his entire savings. When he was six, his parents presented him with his first watch. The same year he was admitted to the Germantown Academy. Later, he went to the Quaker Penn Charter School in Philadelphia and then on to Mohegan Lake Military Academy in New York State from where he graduated in 1900.

The family led a happy but hectic life. Samuel Evans Sr. was keen to have the same rapport with his children as his father had had with him. Despite his business commitments, he tried to get home early in the evenings so that he could spend time with them before they went to sleep. He played with them, told them stories, and taught them old songs from his schooldays at Lawrenceville. Holidays were spent in long walks, family visits, or outings to the countryside, and the summer months were passed at Cape May Point where the family had a cottage on the seafront.

While the family grew, Samuel Evans Stokes Sr.'s business thrived and became more and more demanding. Within a few years his company had become one of the leading concerns of its kind in America, only acknowledging as rivals the Otis Elevator Company, the Crane Elevator Company, and the Moores Williams, and for years he was able to compete with them on more than equal terms. The firm handled practically all the important elevator work in Philadelphia and Baltimore and much in the new Western cities, especially Detroit. It put elevators in the new State and the War and Navy Department buildings in Washington, D.C. Stokes Sr. invented and patented many safety devices and other improvements in elevator construction. He also designed the complicated window openings at the top of the Washington Monument.[9]

The Great Elevator Trust was being formed at this time and other elevator companies urged Stokes to join it. But he was unwilling to do so as a matter of principle. When his health broke down he was forced to make a decision. Then, still stoutly refusing to join forces with the bigger elevator combines, he sold his business to them and retired. The Stokes and Parish Company was sold to the Otis Elevator Company of New York in the winter of 1896–97.

The following June, the Stokes family started on a two-year-long European holiday. Sam, who had joined Mohegan Lake Military Academy the previous autumn, accompanied the family on his first ocean voyage. During this holiday, Sam had an adventure on the Madatch Glacier in Austria that nearly cost him his life. What started out as an early morning walk to get a better view of the glacier, turned out to be a nightmare for him. On reaching a vantage point, as he leaned over to see the glacier, he lost his footing and partly slid, partly fell down to the glacial ice some thirty feet below. Without climbing implements or proper shoes, he was unable to climb back up the steep slope and spent the whole day in a rock moraine among crags and precipices. He lay on the rocks, exhausted and without food, exposed to cold winds, occasionally shouting in the hope that he might be heard by someone searching for him. At last, just as the sun was about to set, he heard an answering call from a distance.

He was rescued by a party of six young guides, two of whom had to be lowered into the moraine to fasten a rope around him and pull him up. He was taken to a little chapel nearby where a passing physician gave him some brandy, and it was not long before he was comfortably in bed fast asleep. "He must have remarkable vitality; no rheumatism, no pneumonia, only stiffness and pain in the back resulting from his bruises," his father wrote in the family journal that night.[10]

In a few days he felt quite well, though it was some time before he wanted to look at a glacier, and even years later could not remember the experience without horror. His mother felt that though no immediate effects of the incident were apparent, his poor health in the ten years that followed—from rheumatism, neuralgia and nervous depression—was perhaps due to this day's adventure. While the family continued its European tour, Sam returned to America and school.

In June 1899, the family was back in Philadelphia. Samuel Stokes Sr. came home well and hearty. Though no longer in business, he kept in touch with community affairs. His name still carried weight in the business world of Philadelphia and he was greatly sought after for positions of trust and discretion. His name on a company's board of directors was a guarantee of its integrity and a source of confidence for the investors.[11]

Sam was now in his last year at school. He was captain of his company and president of the school YMCA. He was also on the school football team. Apart from school activities, he was devoted to books, especially to stories of old Greek and Norse heroes. He loved tales of chivalry and adventure. Among his favorites were the stories of King Arthur and his Knights of the Round Table, which had an influence in shaping his attitude toward life and his feelings as regards justice and honor. Giving presents to his friends and family gave him great joy, and the sight of anyone hungry or poor could always coax the last penny out of his pocket. As a small boy he once emptied his money box into the hands of an inebriated gypsy woman who came begging at the door. He was easily moved by the disabilities of the aged and the infirm, and could often be seen helping people to cross roads or carrying packages for the elderly.

As for religious matters, he did not have the slightest interest in them. Going to church seemed to him a "waste of good time and an extreme bore imposed by elders upon long-suffering young people—a time that could have been spent much more profitably in reading or play." Yet, this was the time when he had his first spiritual experience, he recounted later. "It was while attending church with my people while on a holiday that my spiritual awakening came to me. A hymn was being sung that I had heard and sung myself countless times without its making any impression. Its subject, the unrequited love of God for man and the divine plea that we open the door of our hearts to Him. It spoke of the patience of the divine love in the face of our hard-heartedness, and of a sudden the whole thing became intensely real and poignant to me, taking all my self-control to keep me from breaking down openly. From that moment all the interests and objects of my life underwent a complete reorientation."

After this experience, religion for him was never so much a matter of seeking personal "salvation from sin, or the attainment of some form of heavenly or spiritual reward," as it was a deep emotional response to the sense of divine enfolding love, and the longing to be able to feel "that tender presence" in his being and to give it all his love.

He had left school for his holiday with no more interest in spiritual matters than his schoolmates—which was nil. He returned brimming with new happiness and was eager to share his experience with others. A number of boys were taken in by his enthusiasm and would meet every day to pray for a spiritual awakening in the school. Some of them tried very hard to win over their friends to Christ. In this they got some initial response, but the results were not lasting, for their friends' attention could not be sustained for long, and they very soon got involved in other teenage activities which were of far greater interest to them.[12]

Sam was dismayed to learn that most of his schoolmates were "simply indifferent to religious matters." This troubled him. He had seen a new light and knew that the "Message of the Gospel" alone could save men, and yet his friends were not willing to see the "light." In his boyish simplicity, he accepted the "Message of the Gospel" as it then stood, and in which was inherent the irreconcilable Christian view that the soul had one single life in which to seek salvation, and if it failed to seize the opportunity it would be condemned to burn in Hell for ever. Many saw Hell as a vast lake of fire in the actual material sense, and the "tortures of the damned" as consisting of the scorching and searing of bodies for ever. Others looked upon the descriptions of Hell in the New Testament as symbolic of intense mental and spiritual suffering, and agonizing remorse for the chance of salvation forever lost. Whatever the conceptions, their one common belief was that this single human life was the only chance for the soul to earn salvation.

The apparent spiritual indifference of his schoolmates made him sad. In his mind he saw his schoolmates and friends passing through life careless of the call of Christ—and then passing out "into the everlasting fire prepared for the devil and his angels." The thought drove him to such desperation that he could not rest or sleep.

A broken collarbone in an inter-school football match that fall compelled him to go home to recuperate. Gradually his distress shifted from his friends at school to the crowds of his city, the hundreds and thousands of people absorbed in material interests and indifferent to the welfare of their souls. He saw them as "a great river sweeping over the precipice of death into the abyss of eternal damnation." Often, long after the rest of the family was asleep, he would steal out of the house and walk the six miles from Germantown into the center of the city, brooding over their fate and arriving home exhausted in the early hours of the morning. His feelings were so intense that he wondered how those around him, earnest Christians, could sleep in peace and be happy with this doom hanging over their fellows.[13]

Eventually, his health broke down under the emotional strain. Family doctors insisted upon a complete change of scene for him. His father took him out to New Mexico and stayed some weeks with him on a cattle ranch many miles away from the nearest town. There he slowly recovered. At seventeen he could hardly fail to be carried away by the wild open life of ranches, the companionship of the cowboys, the cattle round-ups, and the long rides upon the plains. Sometimes he had his dark hours, but the life about him helped drive them more and more into the background. With improving health, his mind grew stronger to cope with the horror that had almost overwhelmed him.

While in New Mexico, a dramatic incident resulted in a sea change in his views on Christianity. One day when he was riding alone, far out on the mesa, he found himself half unconsciously repeating the words, "until He find it . . . until He find it." At first he failed to place them, and then it came to him that they were from Christ's parable of "the lost sheep"—"will He not have the ninety and nine in the wilderness and go after the lost sheep until He find it?"

"The words struck me like a blow and in a moment swept away all the clouds of fear and horror that had so nearly been my undoing," he wrote many years later. True, there were all those verses in the Gospels that clearly condemned the unrepentant sinner to the fires of everlasting torment and banishment, but against them was this promise—"until He find it"—and many more. "What if there were a thousand verses in the New Testament that spoke of everlasting damnation. Obviously, both teachings could not be true, and if so, that one clearly should be accepted that was everlasting and consistent love," he reasoned. From that day, all fear and despair vanished for him, and he was never again troubled by any doubts.[14]

The improvement in Sam's health at the ranch was offset by an acute attack of pneumonia followed by inflammatory rheumatism. This left him very weak, and he was forced to give up his plans of returning to school to complete his final year's work and take his college entrance examinations. Instead he went back to New Mexico to recover.

After graduating from Mohegan Lake the following year, Sam joined Cornell University, but his studies were again interrupted when the university closed down in spring because of a serious epidemic of typhoid fever. He had intended to return to Cornell in the fall, but in the meantime got intensely involved with the YMCA in Philadelphia. A little later he, along with his friend Sanville, founded a club for the poor boys of the neighborhood in the old district of Southwark, the most densely populated section of Philadelphia. The money his father had given him to start a business was used in leasing a large house at the corner of Front and Ellsworth Streets. The house had been a saloon for many years and its proximity to the wharves made it a center of iniquity and a bad influence for the neighborhood.

Sam worked long hours with a group of friends to renovate the house, and in a few weeks had a gymnasium, a recreation center, and a bath for boys in a neighborhood where such amenities had never existed. Carpentry and other vocational classes were conducted to channel the energies of these youth. The club soon developed into an important institution and marked the beginning of the Southwark Neighbourhood House, which was to become one of the finest social service clubs of Philadelphia in a few years.[15] Sam practically lived at the club. He was so involved with it that he had no time for his family and for the first time became irregular and unpunctual at meals and careless about keeping his room tidy. His mother worried about him, especially since he often came home late at night, looking pale, tired, and overburdened.[16]

Sam retained his interest in religious matters. He read avidly and taught Sunday School at the Calvary Church in Germantown. He also became increasingly interested in missionary activities. Plans for a college education were held in abeyance and he now talked less about going back to Cornell and more about doing mission work.

At this time he met Dr. Carleton, a physician working in India, who was home on his first furlough in twenty years. Dr. Carleton constantly talked of the miserable plight of lepers in India and of his work at the Sabathu Leper Home in

Simla Hills, where he had been working since 1881. The home was founded by an American Presbyterian missionary, Dr. John Newton, in 1868 with a few huts. It was later taken over by the Leprosy Mission which was established in Ambala in 1874 by Wellesley Cosby Bailey of Dublin. The crusading efforts of the Leprosy Mission during the preceding decade had aroused considerable interest in the subject in England and in the United States,[17] and Carleton received a sympathetic hearing wherever he spoke.

Since there was no known cure for the disease, the only way to prevent its spread was by segregation. In India, the British government had passed a special Leper Act in 1898 decreeing that beggars with leprosy should be treated like criminals requiring compulsory segregation from society, and district magistrates were given powers to commit them to institutions. Consequently, lepers in India suffered not only because of their physical disabilities and lack of medical care, but also because of social ostracism. The leper homes were inadequate and understaffed. Few doctors cared to work for these hapless souls, and even social workers were afraid of going near them. Overcrowded homes with constant staff shortages put a great strain on doctors.

Sam was greatly moved by Dr. Carleton's account and decided to join him in his work. He had always been interested in helping those less fortunate than him. It was only at his father's request that he had not yet joined a missionary society. Dr. Carleton's leper home offered him the opportunity.

Samuel Stokes Sr. was not happy with his son's decision. He wanted Sam to complete his education first. Also, he was not enthusiastic about foreign missionary work and felt strongly that there were "immense needs" for social work in their home town of Philadelphia. In the final analysis, though, he conceded that it was his son's duty to follow what he felt was right. However, since Sam was going to India in an independent capacity without any means of support, he decided to make adequate provision for him. He arranged to give him $500 a year, in quarterly installments, for a period of five years. Samuel Stokes was certain that before the end of this period Sam would return home and find himself a living.

Sam's mother, too, though not unhappy about his ideals of service, was opposed to the idea of his going to India. She worried about his being so far away and about his working among lepers. The disease was then thought to be highly contagious and she was afraid that he would be exposed to a greater danger than he realized. Sam's argument—that Dr. Carleton had worked all his life among lepers and remained healthy, so why shouldn't he do the same?—offered no consolation to her. She finally yielded, hoping that Sam would change his mind and be back with them before long. But his parents were soon to realize that they had underestimated the depth of their son's conviction and the intensity of his purpose.

Sam's friends at Southwark were anxious too. He was the inspiration and motivating spirit of the entire project, and they wondered how they would manage without him. But Sam had no doubt about the future of the club. He was confident that there would be someone to take his place and the club would survive.[18] His immediate concern, however, was getting a steam bath installed on the premises. It would cost $150 and all arrangements for it had been made on the assumption that the money would be raised. Now that his plans had changed, it would be difficult to raise the money. He felt responsible for this payment and if all else failed, intended to make it from the $1,000 inheritance that he had received from his aunt Anne Stokes, who had died a few months earlier.

Christmas of 1903 was a sad event for the close-knit Stokes family. The coming parting cast a shadow over the festivities and beneath the semblance of normalcy was the fear that it could be many years before they would be together for another Christmas. They all tried to be cheerful, especially Sam, who made a great effort to be merry and bright and was the life of the Christmas party with his fun and nonsense.[19]

THE QUEST BEGINS

Sam's journey to India was full of surprises—a foretaste of what lay ahead. The hectic pace of events in the months preceding his departure had left him tired and listless. His parents had hoped that the forced rest on the passage across the Atlantic would help him regain his strength for his travels in England, his onward journey to India, and the work that lay ahead of him. But no sooner had the voyage commenced than he was down with high fever and a severe headache. For the next ten days he was restricted to his berth.

His stay in England was pleasant and stimulating. He spent a week in Edinburgh with Wellesley Cosby Bailey, founder-secretary of the Leprosy Mission in India. To his amazement, when he boarded the train for Edinburgh he found himself sharing the coach with Robert Clark, who was well known for his pioneering work in establishing Christian Missionary Society (CMS) missions in Punjab and who was closely associated with the Sabathu Leper Home. This chance meeting seemed to Sam a "special providence" and reaffirmed his belief that he was on the right path. For the first time he began to appreciate his father's generosity in enabling him to do what he thought was right.

His voyage to Bombay on the *Olympia* in early February was more comfortable than the Atlantic crossing. He was now well and cheerful, the ship was clean, and he had pleasant companions. Even so, he felt a great sense of relief when he landed in Bombay on 26 February.

Once he reached Sabathu in the foothills of the Himalayas, he plunged into the routine of the leper home, which he found to be just as Dr. Carleton had described. His first glimpse of the disfiguring disease came as a shock but he felt "no repugnance, only an intense feeling of sympathy for the affected." Working with the sick seemed to come to him naturally and he quickly learned the basic care of patients. Dr. Carleton was pleased to have him and within a couple of months of his arrival began to trust him with surgical work. In addition to his work, Sam spent many hours learning the local language. He was deeply moved by the suffering around him and was eager to communicate with the patients in their language.

His letters home were full of details about his work and of how well he was keeping and how much he was enjoying himself. To his sisters he wrote about his many humorous encounters with the local people. His description of the place and the diagram of his room, illustrating where his bed, books, and pictures were, made his surroundings very vivid to his family.

The gruesome details of working with leprosy patients, however, distressed his mother. She worried about his "reckless disposition" and urged him repeatedly to take adequate precautions—to always wear surgical rubber gloves when treating patients and to follow Dr. Carleton's instructions carefully. She was afraid that he might wear himself out with work and study. "Your greatest danger is in a willful zeal that does not realize that God does not wish us to do one thing more than He gives us physical strength for."[1]

But Sam did not find the work strenuous and was happy and healthy even though he was eating only lentils and rice twice a day. He liked the work he was doing. Moreover, he was getting closer to the local people, which gave him a greater sense of purpose. He started taking care of neglected and destitute children, and even adopted a four-year-old orphan, Kirpa Ram.[2]

In April, Dr. Carleton took Sam on a visit to the Tarn Taran leper settlement in the Punjab plains which was being looked after by the CMS missionary Rev. E. Guildford. In May, he sent him to Kotgarh, a beautiful little hamlet fifty miles beyond Simla, which had an old church and a small congregation of Christians. It was his first Indian summer and Dr. Carleton wanted him to spend the hottest months in the cooler climate of Kotgarh. He would also have greater opportunity to learn the local language there than at Sabathu. The Simla-Kotgarh road was not passable for motor vehicles then, so he had to walk the fifty-mile stretch in stages. Sam was instantly captivated by the charming ilaqa (a contiguous area of villages) of Kotgarh, called "Mistress of the Northern Hills" by Rudyard Kipling, nestled high in the mountains, which was later to become his home. He enjoyed his stay that summer. For the first few days he stayed at the mission house where he could look down at the deep valleys and across the Himalayas from his small room. Later, he pitched a tent in the adjoining grounds and spent his time in quiet study and contemplation, sometimes writing poetry or making sketches.*

Within a few months of his arrival in India, Sam had realized that the scope of his work could not remain limited to the leper home in Sabathu. There were

---

* The poem "Where Is Your Faith?" later included in Stokes' book of poems, *The Love of God*, was written in his tent at Kotgarh during a thunderstorm.

many villages without medical or educational facilities which he perceived had tremendous opportunities for service. On his return from Kotgarh he traveled to different missions in Punjab, trying to understand the work they were doing and helping out in whatever way he could.

By January 1905, he had been in India for almost a year and had not yet mastered the language. To resolve the problem he decided to live for a while in a place where no one spoke English, and moved to the predominantly Christian village of Zanaar, sixteen miles from Tarn Taran. It was a secluded place and his life was lonely with no familiar faces around him, but the six-week experiment proved a success and at the end of it he was quite fluent in Hindustani, the language commonly understood and spoken in the hills and plains of Punjab. It helped him in enlarging the ambit of his work, and during the next few years he not only worked in leper homes but also in smallpox camps and plague-stricken villages. In addition, he spent whatever extra time he had teaching children.

His base, however, remained Sabathu. He would return there often to a warm welcome at the Carleton home where his room was always ready and his place at the table kept for him. This was his home away from home. Dr. Carleton's wife, Marion Janvier Carleton, loved and cared for him like a son. On his first birthday in India, she made a special Indian meal for him and for the group of destitute children accompanying him.[3]

He led a very simple life, living as the villagers lived and eating what they ate. His father sent him $42 per month but he had schooled himself to live on only $10.[4] Despite the extreme climate of Punjab, the dust of the plains, and his simple diet, he remained well and happy. He felt even better when he was in the hills where he thought nothing of walking eighteen or twenty miles a day.

To add to his happiness and to soothe him when he was weary and lonely, was the wondrous splendor of the Himalayas around him. Every day he went for walks in the hills and each excursion brought new discoveries and new joys. The flowers, the foliage, the trees, the birds, the sunrise, the sunset, the fragrance in the air, the changing seasons, all unraveled a rare beauty for him. He longed to share each new experience with his family. He wrote to his mother each week and his letters arrived punctually in Philadelphia every Monday morning with the breakfast mail, making the four-week journey with unfailing regularity and bringing her comfort. She could almost see the "magic and mystery" of the wonderful hillsides, the pure mountain air, and was thankful that amid all the sorrow and suffering he had beauty too, for it helped him to keep strong and fresh for his work.

She, in turn, wrote to him every Sunday, never missing the Indian mail leaving London every week. Her letters were full of news of family and friends; she did not want him to lose touch with life at home in any way. Her steadfast support during times of trouble and uncertainty, and guidance when he had made a mistake and suffered for it, or when he felt people to be unkind or unfair to him, helped him to keep up his spirit. "It certainly does train and strengthen us if the weak spots in our armour are often attacked, that is if we seek and find the grace to bear and forbear," she would remind him.[5]

There was motherly advice on mundane matters as well. "Neatness in your room and punctuality at meals is due to a housekeeper," she wrote, urging him to show consideration to his hosts. "Nobody can be excused for making work around him as he goes through life, or from trying to help in little ways outside of his regular vocation."[6] Whenever he failed to write his weekly letter she was upset. "Ninety-nine one-hundredths of your duties in life lie right about you where you are, but the little one-hundredth part, your weekly letter to me, is your home duty—and just as positive a duty I think as any of the others."[7]

She also kept him informed of the developments at Southwark. His old colleagues were all there and a young medical student was doing Sam's work. The club was thriving. In May, a committee meeting adopted a scheme to set up a Southwark Neighbourhood Organization and asked all friends and relations to join it. The steam bath was installed and before the year was out, funds had been raised to purchase the building in which the club was housed and for which Sam had been negotiating. His mother, Florence Stokes, was now involved in the club's work. Later, she and Sam's sister Anna Truitt helped to start and run the Southwark House Day Nursery.[8]

Meanwhile, Sam was beginning to feel disillusioned with the manner of work and life of missionaries in India. After his initial euphoria was over he found few people who measured up to his ideal of a true missionary. The lifestyle of the missionaries contrasted greatly with that of the local people. They lived in large bungalows, had a number of native servants at their beck and call, dined well, and entertained frequently. On the other hand, the people they ministered, many of whom they had converted to Christianity, were the poorest of the poor. Sam could not accept the argument that the missionaries needed these amenities, that the comforts of bungalows were necessities, especially during the hot season, to those who had been brought up in the West. His criticism of missionary methods worried his parents more because they thought that he tended to be "so positive and argumentative" in his temperament.[9]

His differences with the established missionary practices were not confined only to these outward factors but were also theological, especially his position on the doctrine of eternal punishment. To him it was clear that no one could be condemned to hell for ever and that everyone would be eventually saved. He based this on what he believed was God's "love and justice." To him this was a "precious belief," but it was in contradiction with what most Christians believed;

few could read such a message in the Bible. The result was that he often got into arguments over the issue with the missionaries and other Christians he came in contact with. This did not win him many friends. He found it vexing to be reminded all the time of how young and inexperienced he was, and to be told that it would be better for him not to assert himself so much. Some of the missionaries went to the extent of telling him that if he did not believe in eternal punishment, he should go home and find something else to do.* Even Mrs. Carleton, who cared for him and tried to understand his views, found herself "hopelessly confused" when she tried to reconcile his views with the text of Christian scriptures and therefore gave up discussing the subject altogether.

Sam was now considering staying permanently in India. When he told his parents about his intentions they urged him to join some organized work. His mother wanted him to work under a missionary board—preferably as an ordained minister of their own Episcopalian Church. His father, who was earlier against his joining a missionary society, now encouraged him to do so. But Sam was now more than ever against the idea of organized work. He felt its positions offered temptation and were sometimes abused. The missions in India did not appeal to him at all. He also felt that if he were to join an organization, he would have to spend most of his time working for it and would not be free to pursue his own interests. Although his family argued that every unselfish, hardworking man who joined organized work helped to raise its levels, instead of increasing "discords and schisms as erratic and independent work so often does," he was not convinced.[10]

The path he wanted to follow was closer to the Franciscan ideal of service than to the existing missionary ideal. Within a year of his arrival in India he had begun contemplating a life of "poverty and absolute renunciation"—a selfless, Christ-like life lived simply in the service of others. Such an ideal, he believed, would bring him closer to the people among whom he was working and be of

---

* Though Christian belief on the subject became more liberal in subsequent years, it was only in November 1996 that the Church of England abolished hell-fire and the centuries of belief that sinners will suffer eternal punishment. The General Synod ruled that warnings of torment and damnation which had sustained preachers and frightened congregations for years were crude and sadistic. The Church's parliament report, "The Mystery of Salvation," stated: "In the past the imagery of hell-fire and eternal torment and punishment, often sadistically expressed, has been used to frighten men and women into believing." Appalling theologies which made God a sadistic monster had left "searing psychological scars" on many, it added. The decision, however, brought protests from traditionalists.

The Synod's meeting at York also accepted the doctrine that no one needed to be a Christian in order to go to heaven. The atheists and those of other faiths would recognize the truth of Christianity when they got to heaven, the Synod decided. This decision too was attacked by critics. ("Rejoice! They've Done Away with Hell"; *The Daily Mail,* 13 November 1996)

greater help to them. He spoke of having seen with "convincing clearness" a vision of Jesus Christ, "toilworn and travel-stained, trudging on foot along an Indian high-road."[11]* The vision affected him deeply and inspired him.

The extreme poverty around him contrasted with the privileges he enjoyed as a Westerner and, above all, his relationship with Indians influenced his thinking. While he had made many friends among British officials and missionaries during the past months, he had also made every effort to befriend Indians. He was young and enthusiastic, and with missionary zeal set out to win the hearts of the local people. But he found that he was unable to strike a rapport with them. The simple hill people reciprocated his greetings warmly but did not make an effort to go beyond that with him. Nor did he feel any spontaneity in his relationship with the educated Indians with whom he came in contact.

Indians came to see him but he was always conscious that they were on their "company manners," and could almost imagine that he heard them heave a sigh of relief as they went away. "If I visited their houses, they would always be most kind and polite, listening deferentially to what I had to say and insisting upon my eating some sweets or drinking some tea or milk before I went. If I passed through the bazaars they would courteously salaam me, but in all of my relations with them I felt that an invisible barrier was ever present, standing in the way of any natural unaffected friendship."[12]

Finally he was convinced that it was his Western clothes and customs which, above everything else, hindered his relationship with the local community. He had realized soon after his arrival in India that the Englishman's clothes were unsuited to the hot climate of India. More significant than the suitability of the clothes was the fact that to keep clean and dress properly, a large supply of clothes was required and a servant was needed to look after them. Servants were also necessary to maintain the lifestyle and food habits of the Europeans. As such, a man who lived as a European in India could hardly get along without a retinue of servants, even if he lived in the simplest manner. As a result, Sam realized, the European became an employer and all members of the serving community looked upon him as a master. He wondered how, under such circumstances, "brotherly" relations could be established between a Westerner and members of the Indian community.

---

* In his introduction to Stokes' book of religious poems, *The Love of God*, J. O. F. Murray wrote how this vision inspired Stokes to "give his life from the love of his Master to the service of his Indian brothers in literal imitation of the poverty, humility and self-sacrificing devotion of the earthly life of Jesus."

Stokes himself refers to having seen the vision in a letter he wrote to Fredrick J. Western of the Cambridge Brotherhood in 1911. "It was this vision which has so deeply affected my life, and which then made me set to work actively to realize the life of Imitation in Poverty." There are no references to this incident in Stokes' later writing.

"I greatly longed to overcome these hindrances," he recalled later, "and to arrive at a point where the relations existing between myself and the people would be unaffected by any material interest on their part. It grieved me to see that all the conditions of my life were such as made it almost impossible for me to understand or draw near to them. It made me feel as if 'a great gulf were fixed,' and that neither of us could draw near to each other, and I hated my Western customs and longed to cast them aside."[13]

When he first suggested to his mother that he felt it might be right for him to "give up everything beyond what was necessary for wholesome food and a garment to cover" him, she was stunned. She could not comprehend how he could think of living like a mendicant friar, dependent upon others for everything, when his father was ready to give him what he needed for a simple life. "Surely that would be a poor kind of Christianity."[14]

He had been dropping hints about his plans in his letters home, suggestions that he might take a step "no one will understand or approve of." She got a clearer picture when he asked her for some books on St. Francis of Assisi.[15] The realization that he was seriously contemplating giving away everything that he possessed to lead a life of self-abnegation and asceticism in conformity with the Franciscan ideal came as a great shock to her. Although she did not denigrate a life of sacrifice, she could not bring herself to agree with her son's plan. The attitude of a poor Franciscan seemed to her "unintelligent and unhelpful." To live moderately and give liberally according to one's means, and to give employment to honest, hardworking men was a sane and practical use of one's means, "saner and more practical I think—resulting in much more good in the end— than your idea of giving away everything."[16] She was also not sure if he was planning to take up this life because he felt it was God's will or whether it was the result of his own intensely idealistic temperament. She kept hoping, however, that nothing would come of it and that he would find a "more moderate and less fanatical" point of view.[17]

His father, too, utterly disapproved of the idea of his pursuing independent work. He wanted to see Sam occupy a self-respecting position and did not think that his differences with other missionaries were sufficient reason for him to neglect the fundamental duty of arranging his life in a way that would make him financially independent. Samuel Stokes Sr. did not grudge the money he sent his son, but he believed that no man of good mental and physical ability should be dependent upon his father after he had received an education that enabled him to provide for himself. He wanted Sam to join some organized work where he would be supported by a church, albeit modestly.

More important than the issue of money was Samuel Stokes Sr.'s conviction that Sam would benefit by working in an organization like a missionary board because he believed that no man could lead until he had learned to follow.

He now decided to give Sam the ultimatum that his allowance would continue only if he was working in accord with one of the church organizations within five years. On the other hand, if Sam were to join a board right away, he would help by adding an allowance equal to his wage. But when he learned that Sam was not considering his allowance at all, he was angry. "What will he do then? He must eat and have some clothes on his back. I suppose he will accept support from the poor natives he lives among, or from the missionaries."[18]

To his parents, the step Sam intended to take seemed unwise and impractical, to say the least. It was now becoming more and more evident to them that his ideal of work was so entirely different from theirs that it seemed hopeless for them to even try to understand it.[19] Sam, however, was determined to carry out his plan of leading a life of poverty and renunciation, and intended to embark on his new life in the autumn. He had used his stay at Zanaar as a test of his ability to live among the people as they lived and to survive on the food they ate. He did not speak much about the kind of work he intended to do. He spoke even less about continuing at the leprosy missions at Sabathu or Tarn Taran.

It bothered him that his family did not support his decision and it took all of his courage to do what he knew was contrary to the judgment of those he loved. He had no support from anyone; not even his loyal friends Dr. and Mrs. Carleton could see his point of view. He felt depressed and dejected. His sparse diet and frequent fasts resulted in a lack of stamina and he tired very quickly. He began to feel the strain of the exhausting heat, even finding it hard at times to keep awake during the hot, humid days, and for the first time since his arrival in India he complained about the monotony of his work.[20] His mother worried that his life of introspection was wearing him out both physically and emotionally. Mrs. Carleton too spoke anxiously about him—of how he was very thin, had sobered greatly, and had lost the old "fun and nonsense" that had been so charming. There was a sadness in his life which showed in his countenance.

That summer when Sam went to Kotgarh, he did not live at the mission house or pitch his tent in its grounds as he had done the previous summer. Instead, he found a small cave called Sudmu Garh in Rhoga Khad near Kotgarh where he spent his days and nights. It was a beautiful spot with exquisite greenery all around and the sound of falling water from a nearby stream was continually in his ears.

Sam's decision to lead a friar's life was deferred as a consequence of the devastating 1905 earthquake in Kangra in April. As soon as he had heard of the ravages caused by the earthquake he wanted to help in the relief effort and immediately rushed down to Lahore to offer his services to the Punjab government. Though the government took a long time to decide, he was one of eleven young men who were finally selected for the relief work.

He reported to the commissioner at Nurpur in Kangra district on 13 September. He was asked to go from village to village to assess personal losses suffered by the people and distribute small sums of money among them. Besides the responsibility of assessing damage, he was put in charge of the Palampur Treasury. Equipped with two tents, two clerks, and ten servants he plunged into his work with enthusiasm. The work was expected to take two months to complete. The government offered to pay all his expenses for the period but he declined. Sam's parents were gratified to know that he had even been considered for the work, given the fact that he had been in India for less than two years.

The job was demanding and Sam was busy from morning until night seven days a week—visiting remote villages on horseback to assess the damage and then issuing checks; bringing in coolie-loads of money under police guard and distributing it; and rushing thirty-one miles to Kangra almost every day to consult with officials in charge of the relief work.

His enthusiasm, however, soon waned when he found that since he had the money and the authority to distribute it, people's attitude toward him was different. "Everywhere I go all the people salaam me and fawn on me and want to give me presents, and I know it is not because they care a cent for me or what becomes of me," he wrote in a letter, "but only because they hope to get some more rupees out of me. Wherever I go they flood me with written petitions for aid. Some true, most full of lies. It is awful. I love Indians and so it is very hard to stand in this relation to them."[21] He also realized that distributing money was a thankless job. People either cursed him behind his back for not giving them as much as they wanted or else for not considering them in need of help. "I hate this work," he said, "I would not do this straight ahead for a thousand dollars a day."

Yet he did not regret having undertaken the assignment. He had been given charge of distributing about $100,000. As treasurer of the Palampur Treasury, he was also responsible for disbursing another $35,000 at his discretion, by assessing damage to property. He had to honor his own checks so the money was entirely in his hands. Since he had always hated the "sight of accounts," he took great pride in the fact that his accounts were absolutely clear and up-to-date.

Another reason he was glad that he had undertaken this work and completed it to his satisfaction, was that it proved to him that he was capable of doing any task if he considered it worthwhile. He knew that his father had wanted him to join a mission because he desired that there should be some indication that men considered him useful and trustworthy. "You can surely gather that such a work would not be put in the hands of one who was considered unworthy or incapable," he wrote to his mother.[22]

In the beginning of November, when Sam had almost completed his task, he was suddenly taken ill. Though his temperature was not very high, he felt unwell. But he was determined to carry on as best as he could. When he felt too sick to move, he lay on a bed and directed the clerks around him, little realizing that his extreme weakness was due to a virulent form of typhoid. The relief work was finally completed on 19 November and he submitted his report to the headquarters. He remembered nothing of the next three days even though during this time he paid off his servants, undertook a sixty-mile journey in a carriage, spent all night in a train, and traveled twenty-three miles in a rickshaw. All he could recall was arriving in Sabathu and going straight to Dr. Carleton's residence. Half an hour later he was violently delirious. His temperature rose to over 105 degrees Fahrenheit and his condition remained critical for many days.

During his illness Sam kept hoping that his mother would come to India to be with him. Day after day he looked for her, certain that when she learned of his illness, she would visit him. Her inability to do so added to his suffering and he felt hurt. But his parents did not think it was wise for Florence to go, especially since each cable from India gave them the impression that Sam was recovering. They felt that by the time she completed the month-long journey to India he would be well recovered. The knowledge that he was with friends who were giving him the "most tender, skilful care" also reassured them. Besides, Florence Stokes was hesitant about going because of an undertaking she had given to her husband when Sam was planning to go to India, that if he fell ill she would not insist on going out to him if he had someone to take care of him. But restraining herself at this time was hard for her. In a premonitional letter of 4 November, she had written to Sam: "While you are well and strong I do not worry at the idea of hardships for it is the life you have chosen for yourself, not one that has come to you through any failure on our parts—but it hurts me to the heart to think of you ever being ill and homesick and perhaps needing care and attention you do not get."[23]

The fever lasted for fifty-four days and a relapse on the day after Christmas gave Dr. Carleton many more anxious moments. "I feel as if I had been watching your bedside with every breath and prayer, as you hung between life and death," Florence Stokes wrote during the most critical days of Sam's illness.[24]

That year there were few Christmas presents for Sam. He had said that he would keep nothing and there were few things his family could think of sending him that he would care for. His younger sister, Florence, bought a book for him with her own money—a story she loved and which she hoped he would read. "Give it away later, but let it give you a few hours of relaxation," his mother pleaded.[25] After hearing of his illness, however, they wished they had not listened to him—a few more presents would have brightened his otherwise dismal Christmas. "For during your convalescence more books, at any rate, might have helped to while away the time and perhaps you may feel differently about giving up everything."[26]

The devoted care and vigil of the Carletons enabled Sam to pull through the illness, but it was nearly three months before he could stand on his feet. During this time Mrs. Carleton wrote to Florence Stokes almost every day, telling her of every symptom and treatment, and of the affection of the local people for Sam and their prayers for his recovery. Her "long, tender, minute letters" and the many cables informing them of Sam's latest condition saved the family much anxiety, but it was nevertheless a time of terrible distress for them.

Government officials connected with the Kangra relief work, who were full of praise for the way Sam had conducted and finished the work he was assigned, recognized that the illness had been a consequence of the terrible conditions in Kangra—the masses of unburied dead and polluted water—and offered to pay his medical bills. The offer was not accepted by Sam's father. However, it gave him great satisfaction as it was a recognition of Sam's services.[27]

Throughout his illness Sam constantly talked of going home to his parents—either of giving up India entirely or doing a theological course, studying for the ministry and coming back to India as an ordained clergyman under a board. He even asked his father to make arrangements for his return. But his father doubted the wisdom of such a hurried decision, taken when Sam was ill and feverish. He thought that when Sam was better, he might feel that the two years he had spent in India learning the language and getting to know the people would be, in a measure, wasted if he left now. In any case he did not think it was wise for Sam to embark on a mid-winter voyage before he had fully regained his health.

Florence Stokes agreed with her husband, even though the idea of Sam's coming home was very appealing. "You ought not, on your sickbed, with a high temperature, to make a decision which would change the whole tenor of your life work—after all the years that you were so absolutely sure that your call was to mission work in India," she wrote to him.[28] She also hoped that after this crisis was over Sam would be wiser. "Wherever you are, in India or here, I believe from this time on you will see this differently—will see that the highest service is not an ascetic one."[29]

And so, during his illness, Sam's parents, who had once tried their best to prevent him from going to India, were the ones who urged him to stay till he could make an unbiased decision. They also knew that it was futile to hope that once recovered he would still choose to come home.

In January, Dr. Carleton and the other doctors attending on Sam decided to send him back to the United States and his father immediately sent a check of $400 to cover his traveling and other expenses. By now Sam had changed his mind. Instead, he pleaded to be sent to Kashmir, Kotgarh, or Chini, on the borders of Tibet, where he could rest and recuperate. The doctors warned him that if he did not go back home he would never be strong or able to work. Reluctantly accepting their advice, he wrote to his mother, "My life has been given to this land and I must be able to work well for it so I am obeying them, but it is very hard."[30] He did not, however, return to America. His passage was booked for 15 March and all arrangements made for his travel, but when he grew stronger he quietly wrote to get it canceled. His family had never really believed that he would come back; they were certain that once he was well he would not even consider it. They were right.

THE ASCETIC

In early March 1906, Sam Stokes set off for Kotgarh. He had been steadily gaining strength but was still not fully recovered. Yet he chose to undertake the journey on foot, taking the seventeen-mile shortcut from Sabathu to Simla on the winding bridle path, and later traveling the distance from Simla to Kotgarh in short stages. The long, lonely walk on the hill tracks was, as usual, a balm to his spirit and provided him ample opportunity for reflection. His family and friends doubted if he had been wise to remain in India after his severe illness. His parents especially were afraid that he might slip back into his "old dream of poverty and self-abnegation." They hoped that after his grave illness he would see his duty differently and when his strength returned he would be willing to join an organization instead of working independently.

In Kotgarh, Stokes spent a month at Bhareri in the care of Emma Matilda Bates, the widow of an English forest officer, who greatly supported missionary work and assisted missionaries whenever possible. Under her competent care he regained his strength. During this period he came up with the idea of starting a small asylum in the mountains for the children of lepers and soon began searching for a suitable location. Finally he chose Kol-Koir, a small village situated deep in a remote valley with no proper roads leading to it and no means of communication. His little asylum would not only provide a carefree, happy, and healthy environment for the little children, it would also enable him to take the message of the Gospel where it had never been heard before.

The idea of a children's asylum appealed to his parents, who readily agreed to send him $500, which he asked for from his inheritance, for purchase of the land at Kol-Koir. It would be a life of utter isolation from all the people he knew, but they hoped that he would persevere and accomplish what he had planned to do. However, they were concerned about his health and urged him to start the asylum in stages until he was strong and well. They warned him not to make the mistake he had made over and over again—of undertaking more than he had the physical strength to accomplish—and which could mean a breakdown "far from home and friends, and, not improbably, a permanent invalidism."[1]

If he started the asylum before he was strong enough, he would falter in his plan due to fatigue and probably have to give it up altogether. This had happened a number of times earlier, particularly since he had the tendency of immediately pursuing a task to completion merely because he had undertaken it, regardless of his ability to do it. The result had been breakdowns and grievous disappointments. This had been the case when he tried to do all the YMCA work at school and keep up with his lessons at the same time. And now, he was again doing the same since his arrival in India. "Your four hundred miles of walking so soon after your illness has been another instance of the same trait," his mother reminded him.[2]

The plans of moving to Kol-Koir were changed when Mrs. Bates offered to sell him a part of her large estate at Kofni. This was a more practical proposal. The seven-and-a-half acres of land were near Kotgarh and would meet all his requirements—his scheme would remain the same, only the location would change.*

Stokes was in a hurry to start the groundwork for the asylum. He needed money to run the place and he could only hope to raise it in America where he had his family and friends. But before asking for financial assistance he wanted to get the work started. His plan was to start the asylum in the fall, run it for a year, then go home the following winter to raise more money. Eventually, though, he became involved in educational work and the asylum plans were dropped altogether.

During this period Sam had not given up the idea of leading a life of renunciation. As soon as he was stronger, he moved into the old cave in Rhoga Khad where he followed a harsh regimen of self-denial. He bathed in the cold water of a nearby stream and cooked simple meals for himself in a small earthen pot. His days were given to prayer and meditation. At night he lit a small oil lamp and read the New Testament. In early August 1906, he took the final step. He distributed his possessions among the poor and after "three days spent alone in prayer, donned a friar's robe and the obligations of a friar's life" as he understood them.[3]

The villagers were astonished by his courage. The cave was a good mile from human habitation in the heart of the jungle. Bears and panthers abounded. Villagers were afraid of going there even in the daytime. They never ventured on the Kotgarh road after sunset for fear of wild animals and the shira, an evil spirit

---

* The sale deed with Mrs. Bates for forty bighas and two biswa of land for Rs 401 was formalized the following October. A rough draft stated that the land was to be used only for an asylum for lepers, cripples, and destitutes. (*Stokes Papers*)

which was said to terrify and trouble passersby. Stokes was oblivious of his surroundings and was not bothered by loneliness or the proximity of wild animals. He had always been unafraid and could not understand the fears of the local people who were scared to go out after dark and mortified if they had to pass the cemetery after sunset. (To dispel their fears of ghosts and spirits he once slept in the Kotgarh cemetery and another time slept with bones he had brought from the cremation ground, under his bed.)

The story of a "sahib" becoming a "sadhu" (mendicant ascetic) spread in the mountains and people from far and near came to Kotgarh to pay homage to Sam. His appearance and lifestyle baffled them. He no longer looked like a sahib but every bit a young sadhu with a beard and a long saffron choga (long loose dress) and polas (hemp slippers) on his feet. He had few worldly possessions—a blanket thrown over his shoulder, a lota for keeping water, and a degchi to cook and eat in. Two pet snakes shared his dwelling.

His family was distraught to get the news of his new life. Even his mother, who supported his work and believed in it, found it hard to accept his way of living. How, by giving up everything, could he advance the cause of Christ? Making sacrifices to help others was understandable, but to "mortify himself continually for the sake of mortification" didn't make sense.[4] Sam was hurt by the admonition in their letters but it did not affect his decision. "I believe I have been doing my best but not always just what you would have approved of," he wrote home, explaining the unusual step he had taken. "I know that you both consider me unwilling to be guided, unstable in my purpose, extreme in my views. Be it so; I am not willing to be guided by any man. I wait constantly on Him that He may reveal His purpose to me and then do it with all my might. I am extreme in my views. As regards religious views this is the age of milk and water for the general mass of mankind. We are either 'agnostics' or 'liberal minded' as a race. I will not say that in both ranks men have not existed who are earnest and careful seekers after truth but I will say that the general run of agnosticism and liberalism is nothing more than spiritual indolence."[5]

Stokes' decision to lead the life of a sadhu had a deep impact in Kotgarh, a place of great interest and challenge to missionaries. It was one of the few small pockets directly under British rule surrounded by autonomous hill states. The government encouraged missionary activity there to enhance British influence in the area. In 1824, Captain Charles Pratt Kennedy, political agent to the Hill States, had recommended that a mission of the Unitas Fratum or Moravians be set up in Kotgarh as, in his view, they were the most suited for "the moral and political upliftment" of the local people. India was opened up to missionary activities of other nations in 1833, when the renewal of the Charter made the East India Company a "governing body" instead of a "trading company," and threw

India open to the whole world, allowing "any honest man who likes, to settle here."

The British first came to the region at the invitation of the local rajas to repel the invading Gurkha armies from Simla Hills. The Gurkhas were pushed back in 1814–15 by the East India Company, which then took over certain areas, including Kotgarh, directly under its control. In 1825, a small cantonment was established in Kotgarh. When the danger from the Gurkhas ceased, the British decided to withdraw their troops from the area and the cantonment was wound up. The civil administrator, Mr. Gorton, and the army commander, Major Boileau, who had been struck by the "extreme neglect, backwardness and poverty" of this area decided to hand over their buildings and property for the establishment of a mission station at Kotgarh. Subsequently, a school and a mission center were established in the former officer's mess. During the following years, Gorton, Boileau, and some other early residents of Simla raised funds for evangelical work in the area. They founded the Himalayan Missionary Union for this purpose in 1840. The group, called the Simla Friends, established the Himalayan Mission in 1843 and the Rev. J. D. Prochnow, a Prussian minister, was posted to Kotgarh. A year later the Christian Missionary Society (CMS) took over the responsibility for the mission. A missionary colony was also established at Bhareri about three kilometers from Kotgarh. The first conversion at Kotgarh was of James Kadsu from the village Mangsu. He was baptized in 1853 and later sent to Lahore Divinity School. He was to become the first native pastor of Lahore. In 1873, St. Mary's Church was built in Kotgarh. Funds for this beautiful church, which can accommodate up to 200 people, came not only from the Christian community but also from the Hindus of Kotgarh.[6]

The sixty-year-old mission at Kotgarh bustled with activity. Missionaries assigned to the Moravion Mission at Kyelang, the oldest of its kind, first came to Kotgarh to study the Tibetan language.[7] Visitors from Delhi and other missions came there every summer for long sojourns. The mission owned vast property and ran a small orchard at Kotgarh. The CMS also ran a primary school at Kotgarh and some branch schools in nearby villages.

But despite its best efforts, the Kotgarh mission failed to make an impact, and during the previous twenty years there had been only one or two conversions. The area was therefore described as "unfruitful" and the neighborhood often spoken of as "Gospel Hardened."[8] The main reason for this was the caste rigidity in the ilaqa where a conversion resulted in absolute social segregation. Converts were severely persecuted by their families and by the villagers. Many left their homes and settled elsewhere.

When Stokes began living in Kotgarh as a sadhu, the predominantly Hindu community began to take a greater interest in him and his faith. A wealthy Brahmin from the adjoining princely state of Kumarsain, on hearing of Stokes' transformation, came to Kotgarh and took Stokes with him, insisting that he stay with him in his house. "Now you are one of us," he told Stokes and treated him with the deference he would have shown only to Hindu holy men. Though an orthodox Hindu, he was impressed by the "fire of renunciation" and could understand and appreciate the life of a sadhu, even a Christian one.[9]

Stokes now had many opportunities of talking about Christianity with upper-caste Hindus. A number of people came under his influence and expressed their wish to convert. The most important of these was Dhan Singh, the son of a prominent high-caste Mian Rajput of Jahu.

Dhan Singh's father had great ambitions for his son. He wanted to educate him so that he could get a government job. Dhan Singh was first sent to the local primary school, and later to the Mission School at Kotgarh, where a Hindu cook was employed specially to cook for upper-caste boys. At the Mission School, Dhan Singh came in contact with Stokes and was intrigued by his life. Gradually, his faith and confidence in the American missionary grew. When Stokes gave away his possessions and went into retreat, Dhan Singh approached him and expressed his desire to become a Christian. As the boy was still very young Stokes advised him to be patient and think over his decision before taking a final step.

Once Dhan Singh had made up his mind, he fearlessly asserted his resolution of becoming a Christian. The entire ilaqa of Kotgarh was shaken by his announcement. Word of his impending conversion spread to the surrounding villages and caused much resentment among the people. Dhan Singh's father immediately withdrew him from school, beat him mercilessly, and swore that he would kill him if he dared to convert and bring disgrace to the family. Wherever Dhan Singh went, he was insulted and threatened.

Fearing for the boy's life, Stokes decided to take Dhan Singh to the plains. One night, they packed their belongings and fled the village. The journey was not one to be forgotten. They walked all night and arrived in Simla the next day at noon, with blistered feet and exhausted bodies, having covered more than fifty miles of mountain track. The same afternoon they left for Ludhiana. The following day, Stokes placed Dhan Singh in a mission school under the care of a friend and returned to Kotgarh to face the wrath of the community. Several weeks later, Dhan Singh was baptized. It was many months before his father was sufficiently reconciled with his decision and agreed to send him back to school at Kotgarh. For Stokes, Dhan Singh was "the first" and, as far as he could see, "the best gift" which God had given him.[10]

For Stokes' family, this incident was another period of trial. His letters arrived irregularly and all his mother had received in six weeks was a line written on the road, in pencil. Then Mrs. Carleton wrote to say that Sam continued to be "hard on himself, denying himself food and sleep," and had arrived in Sabathu "in a poor state—so footsore that he needed rest." Meanwhile, reports that he was "fleeing . . . in an effort to save the life of a Christian boy who was with him" reached Sam's mother in Philadelphia, causing her even graver anxiety. The news came as a great shock to her. So far she had been sure that he was surrounded by friends, both native and English. But now she knew he had enemies as well and was afraid for his safety.

Soon after Stokes became a sadhu, an Indian Christian, Sundar Singh, joined him. The son of an orthodox Sikh farmer of Punjab, Sundar Singh had converted to Christianity against his family's wishes. He was supported by the Presbyterian missionaries at Ludhiana, who sent him to Sabathu to get him away from all the excitement caused by his intention to convert, and there he came in contact with Stokes. Shortly before Sundar Singh's sixteenth birthday, Stokes took him to Simla where he was baptized at St. Thomas's Church on 3 September 1905.[11]

Sundar Singh was full of tremendous zeal and was determined to preach the Gospel among the people of his land. But he did not want to preach the Gospel in the manner of other missionaries. He wanted to become a sadhu, one who would be free to go from place to place, free to pray and meditate in a manner and time of his choosing, unfettered by the rules and regulations of a mission. Soon after his baptism he set out on an evangelical tour and reached Kotgarh in the summer of 1906, just as Stokes was preparing for the life of a sadhu. Sundar Singh decided to join Stokes. He took the vows and draped himself in the robes of a friar. Those who saw him described him as a very humble and quiet young man, full of earnestness and devoted to Stokes.[12]

In the succeeding months, Stokes and Sundar Singh went from village to village in Simla Hills, preaching their message of service to humanity. They looked every bit like Hindu sadhus except for the rosary and the cross worn around their necks. They worked closely together, with Sundar Singh preaching and Stokes taking care of the sick.

During this period, Stokes was also involved in the conversion of several young Hindus. He had observed how almost all proselytization by missionaries was concentrated on the poorer section of the society, who converted to Christianity for reasons of economy rather than religious conviction. He had come to feel that if Christianity was to have a lasting impact in India it was not enough to convert the lower castes. He therefore worked chiefly among those who belonged to the upper castes—Brahmins and Rajputs, a group who were least affected by missionary work carried out on conventional lines.[13] Converting high-caste Hindu boys to Christianity was dangerous, especially as the Arya Samaj, a progressive Hindu movement, was keeping a close watch on missionaries trying to do that. Stokes was not aggressive in his proselytizing, but whenever a young boy showed an inclination toward Christianity he did his best to help him. Consequently, he had to contend with not only members of the Arya Samaj but also with the law that forbade the conversion of underage boys. On some occasions, he was accused of "leading astray young men," and in one case he was even charged with kidnapping two young boys.

Many missionaries did not agree with Stokes' methods. His theology, lifestyle, and way of working were not generally acceptable to the Christian community either. Mrs. Carleton, who felt responsible for him, disapproved of his new life and made no pretence of hiding her feelings. She considered his methods extreme, which would do more harm than good to the cause of Christianity. She even wrote a severe letter to him in the hope that he might change his views. His friends, too, were anxious for him.

Stokes' parents' attitude, however, was changing. During much of the previous two years, his mother had felt sure that he was making mistakes and had spent her energy in trying to persuade him to see things her way. She now decided to leave it all to God's "never failing wisdom." "I have so much more peace of mind about you since I have given up trying to settle your problems for you," she wrote.[14]

There was also a change in his father's attitude. Though differences over some issues remained, his father had gradually come to appreciate his work, more so after what he had done in the Kangra earthquake. That summer, his father talked more proudly and affectionately about his son than he ever had before. He talked of Sam's work among the lepers, of the relief work in Kangra district, of his illness, and of his boyhood—his love of animals, his various adventures, his day on the glacier, and his canoeing trip. "I thought that you would like to know this and to realize that your father was growing more and more into sympathy with your life," his mother wrote to him.[15]

In the spring of 1907, Stokes visited the plague-stricken villages of Punjab. The plague usually started at the end of October and continued through the winter until the heat of May abated. Government efforts to check it had been unsuccessful. This was mainly due to the fact that people rarely cooperated with health officials whom they viewed with the suspicion universally harbored toward foreigners. In many parts of the country it was believed that the government was responsible for the spread of the epidemic, that the village wells were deliberately infected with the plague bacteria, and that this was a method the government was using to reduce the population of India. Such reports made people very suspicious of relief efforts and, in many cases, they openly refused assistance offered by the government.

Convinced that he would succeed where government officials had failed, Stokes decided to go out and work in the infected villages. Taking with him only bare essentials and a few medicines, he started out in early April to look for a village where he could work. After making enquiries he came to a village which seemed to be the most affected by plague. In two years, nearly half the population of the village had perished. Most of those who survived were living in makeshift huts outside the village. Many were sick and were dying.

Stokes did not go to the villagers directly. Instead, he spread his blanket on the ground beneath a banyan tree and started reading his New Testament. After some time, the headman of the village and a number of others came over to enquire who he was and what he wanted. He told them that he was a bhagat (devotee) and that he lived, as a rule, up in the mountains, but having heard that so many were dying in their village he had come to help them, and he had drugs which might be able to cure them. At first, the villagers were inclined to refuse his offer, but after some discussion they told him that they had no objection to his trying his drugs first on the sick chamars, and if they were not harmed by the drugs, the villagers would, perhaps, let him treat others as well.

He stayed in the village for a few weeks. Once the medicines proved effective, villagers began to come to him in large numbers and their attitude toward him changed. Now they came to make friends with him. Every evening, when work in the fields was done, men brought their hookahs to the banyan tree, where they sat and talked for hours, while the children listened or played about. They no longer gave him stale food in battered vessels; old women vied with each other to prepare food for him. Wherever he went it was, "Salaam, Baba, will you have some milk or buttermilk?" or "Salaam, Maharaj, can I not cook something for you?" They called him in to visit their sick and obeyed all his directions implicitly.

It was not long before the villagers started calling Stokes their bhagat and taking care of him. News of his work spread and people from the surrounding villages came to visit him with entreaties for help. Stokes could not help them, as he had to return to Sabathu. The villagers did not want him to leave. They offered to build him a small house beside a well near the village if he would stay, assuring him at the same time that he would never lack for food or other amenities of life. It was difficult for him to explain to them that he could not always stay in one place. When they realized that he was determined to go, they begged him to take a gift with him, an offer he would not accept. Finally, when he was leaving, five villagers accompanied him on foot to the railway station, eight miles away, and insisted on paying his fare.[16]

Stokes' work among the plague-stricken villagers gave him new confidence. He had won their trust in an environment of hostility toward foreigners. He was now more convinced than ever before that his decision to lead the life of a friar was the right one, and would be effective in the work he wanted to do. He felt a friar had better opportunities of coming close to Indians than did other Europeans. He was easier to approach and did not stand in a superior position. More-over, his mode of living was in accord with their ideas of what was proper for a man devoted to the service of God.

"The sadhu," he discovered, "finds doors open everywhere. He is entertained by king and sweeper, and comes in contact with men of every caste and school of thought." As a friar, he constantly received invitations from people he met in trains or other places to visit them. On some occasions he accepted these invitations and was always welcomed. He was able to come into close contact with many Indians and visited houses where no European had ever set foot. In the mountains he entertained "Hindu friends—Brahmins, Rajputs and Kanaits—for several days, calling in a Hindu to cook for them." He also made friends with the Arya Samajists who were critical of Christian missionary methods and propaganda. His becoming a sadhu overshadowed the fact of his being a Christian and he was even invited to stay at their schools, where he had long talks with Hindu scholars on Hinduism and Christianity.

This experience also altered his relationship with the people of the country. "Formerly I could see the faults of Indians and few of their virtues," he said, "now I know more of their faults, to be sure, but I had an opportunity to see the good in them in a manner which probably would have been impossible had I not been a friar."[17] He realized that, for a friar at least, such true and unaffected friendship was indeed possible between Europeans and Indians. It was a relief that the barrier which all earnest missionaries in India keenly felt, and which was formerly his despair, was at last removed for him. God, he felt, had given him "a hundred-fold for the little he had forsaken."[18]

Stokes' interaction with members of the Arya Samaj had one interesting result—he was inspired to establish a Christian school at Kotgarh on the same lines as the Arya Samaj's gurukul at Hardwar. The gurukul, founded by Pandit Munshi Ram (later to become famous as Swami Shraddhanand) in May 1902, was basically a revival of the old Brahamacharya ideal of student life, in which students and their teachers lived in close fellowship under a strict rule of ascetic discipline.*

During a visit to the gurukul, Stokes was impressed with its principles. He was full of praise for the idealism, dedication, and patriotism of its teachers. He believed that the purposeful atmosphere of the institution created the best environment for the growth and development of students. The idea so appealed to

---

* Munshi Ram later became a close friend of C. F. Andrews and Mahatma Gandhi. Gandhi described the gurukul as Swamiji's best creation. "It was his most original contribution to education, inasmuch as when we had lost our heads over Western education he decided that we should think and act and educate ourselves in the Vedic way" (*Young India*, 6 January 1927).

him that he soon worked out a practical scheme for a Christian gurukul to be established in the Simla Hills. His objective was to combine in this institution all the advantages of the ancient gurukul with those of a first-rate modern boarding school.

He wanted to establish an institution that would meet the needs of students of all religious denominations—Christians, Hindus, and Muslims. He found the state of education in the country to be very unsatisfactory. Government-aided schools were badly run. They did not educate students but merely provided them with a degree at the end of their schooling, enabling them to secure clerical jobs. He was quick to perceive that Munshi Ram's gurukul was not only a solution to the many ills pervading the educational system in British India, but also helped in building character. If a similar system of education could be adopted by the Christian community, it would go a long way in transforming its youth.

Stokes was not only looking at the prevailing system of education, he was also looking beyond, to the future needs of the country. There was hardly any national awakening at that point in time, though he had noticed a "spark of patriotism which had begun to burn in the hearts of the people." He feared that this spark would grow "dim and finally flicker out" unless young people of "high attainment and noble ideal" were found in ever-increasing numbers to devote themselves wholly to the nation's service. "Where and in what age has there ever been a nation more in need of men, true men, with ideals and earnest purpose, consecrated body and soul to the service of God and their motherland?"[19]

Stokes foresaw India as a dignified world power, a position he felt it could achieve provided its youth were given proper direction. If India was to progress and take its rightful place in the comity of nations, it needed to have men with high ideals and a sense of personal responsibility to God and the country. "They must be men whose ideals are as lofty as their patriotism is pure. They must be imbued with the vision of an India of the future, holding her place among the foremost nations in the world, contributing her share to the material, intellectual and spiritual advancement of the human race. They must be men who will realize that an ideal is a responsibility, and who will never rest until their ideals have become realities," he wrote in a paper outlining his scheme of a Christian gurukul.

The school he planned would be unique. Though it would be under an advisory committee of prominent and public-spirited Christians, and its general superintendent, principal, staff, and management would be Christians as well, it would also admit Muslim and Hindu children. Once they were admitted, the school would arrange for students at the facility to have their food cooked apart in accordance with the custom followed in their homes. All students would wear Indian clothes and eat vegetarian food. Regarding worship in the school, he emphasized that the order of service should not in any way be influenced by strictly European precedents, but should meet the requirement of the boys. Instead of hymns, the singing of the more familiar bhajans in Hindi would be encouraged. Indian musical instruments would be used in preference to the church organ.

The principal and teachers of the school would be capable men devoted to God and to India, and willing to work in an honorary capacity. They would strive to make the life of the students both simple and dignified, and implant in their hearts a "true, deep love for India, a pride in its past, sorrow for its fallen present, and a firm resolve to be of use in raising it to a glorious future." Though a Christian institution, the school would not be directly propagandist.[20]

To execute his plans Stokes got in touch with leading Christian families of Punjab and obtained their support. He received encouragement from another unexpected quarter, too. C. F. Andrews, of the Cambridge Brotherhood, Delhi, who was for some time acting-principal of the Lawrence School at Sanawar in 1906, had been pleading for a high school in the hills. Being conscious of the "mortal dangers of the great cities and the appalling risk to purity," apart from the health hazards which they presented, he gave the strongest approval to Stokes' scheme for a gurukul in the hills. "The present scheme fulfils my wish," Andrews said, "for it will not only be in the healthy hill air but will have the moral atmosphere also of noble self-sacrificing lives."[21]*

Stokes did not get to establish a Christian gurukul, but the educational work he did in future was guided by the principles of the Arya Samaj's gurukul system.

Stokes' life at this time was unusual in more ways than one. He was looking after five destitute children. Besides Kirpa Ram, there was Mirchu, whose parents were in the Sabathu Leper Home. Stokes was convinced that if the children of lepers were brought up in hygienic conditions, away from direct contact with their parents, they would remain unaffected by the dreaded disease, and he was determined that the two little boys he had taken under his care should lead normal lives. The third child he adopted was the almost blind six-year-old boy Nathu. Stokes had found him in the streets of Delhi wearing a velvet zaridar cap and with a laddu in each hand, crying helplessly. The boy's parents were dead and he had been apparently driven out of the house by his uncle. He appeared to be from a well-to-do family. There were eventually eleven children in this group, including Bodh Raj, Budhu, Dasi, Kokla, Phatti, Rupi, and Fazal-din Paul. While some of them were orphans, others were children of inmates of the Sabathu Leper Home. When they grew up, Stokes settled them in the neighbor-

---

* Charles Freer Andrews, an Anglican priest, came to India in March 1904 to join St. Stephen's College, Delhi, where he taught from 1904 to 1914. Later to become a close friend of Mahatma Gandhi and Rabindranath Tagore, Andrews (Charlie to Gandhi) was the most well-known Britisher to identify with India's aspirations.

ing villages. The girls were married and the boys were provided with small pieces of land. Nathu, the blind boy, drowned in the Sutlej in an accident in 1922 when Stokes was in jail.

Though the children came from diverse religious backgrounds, Sam brought them up as Christians. Their food and clothing did not cost much, but they were absolutely dependent on him for all their needs and he worried about their future. They lived with him in Sabathu. When he went to Kotgarh he took them along and for many months the cave at Rhoga Khad, where Stokes lived, was their home. They went with him to the Kotgarh Mission School where they studied with other children. He asked his mother to provide for them and take care of them should something happen to him.

When Andrews met Stokes, with his little wards, in Kotgarh in the summer of 1907 he found the small group, "a very strange company."[22] He was touched by Stokes' love for these destitute children, "all of whom he had brought up and loved as tenderly as if they were his own."[23] Andrews' famous book, *The Renaissance in India,* published shortly afterwards, included a picture of Stokes in his long robe with the children. "Everyone of them was a waif and stray of humanity. Stokes had fathered and mothered them all and taken them like a hen under his wing. But a merrier company you would hardly meet in the world. They hardly knew what sorrow was. They lived an abstemious life which hardly cost them anything at all," he wrote.[24]

Sham Sukh, kardar (administrator) of Mehlan temple, who was then a young boy, remembered how Stokes protected these children and took care of all their needs. He bathed them and washed their clothes. "He had no anathema to the poor—not till the end of his life."

VISIT HOME

In July 1907, after almost four years in India, Stokes began thinking of going home on a brief visit. His plans depended on his health which was still far from satisfactory. He wanted to earn his passage and would go only if he was strong enough to work as a deckhand. His father, who had offered to pay for his passage whenever he wished to come home, was not happy with this suggestion, for apart from the fear that he would tax his health by working as a deckhand, he disliked the idea of his son doing a menial job. His mother, too, urged him to change his mind and respect his father's wishes, especially as it was possible for him to find plenty of missionary work on the steamer. Besides, he needed rest and nourishing food. He had driven himself very hard of late and was often sick—the result of starvation and the hardships to which he exposed himself. He also suffered from rheumatism, sometimes finding it even difficult to write letters.[1] Though Stokes was at first adamant about working for his passage, he ultimately agreed to his father sending him the money for it.

Money was a constant problem. In September, his father sent him $200 for his passage and also his quarterly allowance. Soon afterwards, he wrote to his mother that he wanted another $200 to repay a loan he had taken from a friend a few months earlier. His father was sending him a handsome allowance, but he used most of it for charity and complained to his mother of the shortages he faced, not for himself but for his work. His payments to Dr. Carleton for his board had sometimes been delayed and there were misunderstandings with friends over money he borrowed and was unable to repay on time.

The question of money sometimes led to strained relations with his parents. Shortly before he left for India, he had told his mother that he hoped that whatever money he inherited would be left for him in a trust—he knew, he said, that with his temperament, any money that came to him would be spent at once, and that he ought only to receive the income from the trust. But when soon afterwards, he inherited $1,000 from his aunt Anne Stokes and his father put it in a bond with the provision of sending him only the interest, he asked for the capital for one reason or another. First he wanted to use it for the Southwark steam bath, then for the education of young Kirpa Ram. During the Kangra earthquake, he wanted to give away the entire amount to quake victims and was so desperate to have the money that he even threatened to force the issue, which made his mother wonder if he intended to go to court. "Legally you have a right to, but from every point of view . . . you would be wrong to take it."[2]

Later, when his parents had hardly recovered from the shock of his illness, Sam again wrote for his legacy, this time for the expenses of his illness which his father wished to pay for. There were also differences over how the family should repay its debt to the Carletons. While his parents wished to help with the education of Dr. Carleton's children in America, Stokes wanted them to donate an operation theater to the Sabathu Leper Home. Sometimes he even used emotional blackmail to get money from his mother. For instance, when he wanted to publish a short story of the Bible he had written in Hindi, he wrote to her that he would live on one meal a day to save the $20 he needed for publishing it.[3] His father was unhappy over his irresponsible handling of money matters, particularly his inertia in sending a full account of what he did with the extra money they sent him. He could not understand how, when Stokes used such a small part of his allowance on himself, he was always short of money. He also felt that Sam ought not assume obligations for which he did not have the money in hand.

Stokes wanted to make his visit as much of a pleasure for his parents as he could. He realized that his parents' happiness, especially his father's, would be marred on seeing the changes in him. He had decided to "sink all idiosyncrasies" during his trip and to live in the old way—to eat and dress as the rest of the family did and to interest himself in the life around him. The decision comforted and reassured his mother who was acutely aware that his home visit would prove to be a "blessing" only in this way. She believed that now perhaps Sam and his father would come to a better understanding of each other than they ever had before.[4]

This was the first time Stokes was leaving India. He was not equipped for the winter voyage across the Atlantic. He had given away almost all his possessions—his suits, sweaters, shoes, and overcoat. All he had left in the form of woollens was one warm sweater. His mother sent him £6 to buy a long, warm coat and other necessities urging him to use the money "*for this purpose and no other—not to give away, or to clothe anyone else with . . . I know it is easier for you to give away than to keep.*"[5]

By the end of the year Sam's plans of going home were finalized. He decided to take Dhan Singh with him. They were to leave in November from Karachi, in time to be home for Christmas.

En route to Karachi, Stokes' plans were suddenly changed during a stop-over in Lahore, when he learned that a young student of Forman Christian College, Marcks, was suffering from smallpox and the college authorities were unable to find anyone to take care of him. Stokes immediately offered to stay and nurse him.[6]

At first, Stokes was put with Marcks in a separate wing of the college and orders were issued that none of the students should visit them. But even this arrangement did not meet with the approval of the government health officer and they were moved to a segregation camp outside the city. The camp, located on a large barren tract outside the city, was run by an incompetent and dishonest doctor who was known for falsifying accounts and cutting the food ration of patients. Patients were lodged in small, dirty, reed huts and the nursing staff was comprised of two old men. The patients were, as a rule, those whose homes were far away and who had no family to care for them. Many died due to the poor conditions in the camp.

With Stokes' care and nursing, Marcks recovered rapidly. When he was well enough to move about, Stokes left the camp to resume his journey. Shortly before his train was to leave for Karachi, he went back to the camp to bid a final goodbye to Marcks. Satisfied that the boy was doing well and should be able to leave the camp in a few days, he went to look at other patients.

There were three of them. The first two seemed to be ordinary cases, not in too much distress, but as soon as Stokes got near the booth of the third, he knew that this case was different. An awful stench hit him as he entered the booth, the air was so heavy and foul that it was hard to breathe. A boy with his head covered by a blanket lay on the bed. Stokes lifted the blanket and a great swarm of flies rose up. What he saw sickened him so much that he almost fainted. The boy's skin was in a horrible state and it was difficult for him to recognize the pus-covered shape before him as a human face. The boy had arrived at the camp from afar five days earlier.

He had developed the most virulent form of confluent smallpox. In his delirium he further injured himself by bursting the pustules. His face was nearly torn to pieces and his mouth was little more than a bloody hole in his face. He was only half conscious and unable to do more than feebly moan and wave his arms about in a pathetic attempt to ward off the flies. He was dressed in the same tight-sleeved flannel jacket in which he had been brought in. No one had taken the trouble to remove it and as his arms had swelled, the sleeves got tighter hindering circulation of blood. The first thing Stokes did was to rip off the sleeves. He decided to stay back to look after him.

It was difficult to explain his change of plans to his family back home. "I am afraid you will never be able to understand me but if you cannot do this please bear with me and don't worry about me. I do not know how to write to you this morning; my heart is broken over what I have seen. How can you understand so far away? Were you with me, you would understand," he wrote to his mother.

Leaving Dhan Singh in the care of friends, Stokes moved back to the camp. For the next ten days he took care of the boy with the help of Sundar Singh, who was then in Lahore, nursing him, cleaning his sores, keeping the flies away from his infested body, and assisting him with the bedpan. As the disease progressed, the boy lost his eyesight and became incoherent. After a few days, gangrene set in on his arms and the stench in the room was so overpowering that even the doctor, standing as he did outside the room, was constrained to keep a handkerchief over his nose. But Stokes continued to be with the boy throughout, sleeping on a mat on the floor beside his bed. Despite his efforts he was unable to save the boy's life.

A few days later, Stokes penned down a detailed account of this experience. Describing the boy's last hour he wrote, "About half [an] hour before the end he seemed to regain all his faculties. He called me to him and told me to put my head down close to his ear. I did so and he tried to put his torn hands about my neck. For a moment I resisted, feeling that to put my face right over his own and breathe his breath and have his gangrenous arms about my bare neck would be wrong. But I think God put it into my heart that it was all right; at any rate I felt that I should let him do it, so when again I found his hands closing around my neck I put my face down by his and let him clasp me to him for as long as he desired. He kept whispering in my ear and I kept talking to him and comforting him . . . The end was very quiet. I was sitting beside him on the bed when suddenly he turned over on his side, opened his sightless eyes, and seemed to be free from pain. His face became quiet and peaceful in expression, his breathing gentle and regular: then in a moment he was gone."[7]

The repeated delays in his departure for home made Stokes weary and homesick, and were a great disappointment to his family. But they did not feel that he did "other than right" to stay with the second boy when he found him in the condition he did. Even his father, who still found it impossible to share his wife's views about Stokes' work, conceded that he could not have left the boy if there was no suitable person to take care of him. "I know you did right to stay with the boy—My 'Other Wise Man' could not do anything else," his mother wrote.[8]*

Word of Stokes' stay at the camp spread in the surrounding villages, and people began to visit him. They would come in the evening, bringing offerings

---

* This refers to Henry Van Dyke's book, *The Story of the Other Wise Man,* with its theme centering on "Service to Humanity" which made a deep impression on Stokes during his adolescence. In 1898 he presented a copy of the book to his sister Anna on her sixteenth birthday. He was then eighteen himself.

of food for him, and ask him for some message from God. Andrews, who was visiting Lahore, came frequently to be with Stokes and often met Sikh farmers, "seated in silent sympathy," at the nightly gatherings. For Andrews, seeing Stokes working at the camp was an experience never to be forgotten. "His intimate knowledge of the people, and their trust in him and devotion to him, have been an abject lesson and given me more food for thought than anything else I have seen in India," he wrote. "A spirit of sacrifice has sprung up both among Christians and among non-Christians wherever he has gone, and there has been an extraordinary response to the ideal. He is so little of a sahib that he has been roughly handled by that respector of persons, the Indian policeman. Hindus trust him as a brother and ask him into their homes. It is all Christianity, pure and simple, expressed in a language understood of the people."[9]

Describing Christian ideals in India in his book, *The Renaissance in India,* Andrews wrote about Stokes' exceptional degree of love for the Indians amid whom he worked and which he considered a privilege to have witnessed. "I have seen him at work in leper and plague camps, tending the dying, sleeping on the bare ground, and sharing in every way the life of his Indian Christian brothers."[10]

Reports of Stokes' work appeared in missionary papers as well. When he visited the Cambridge Brotherhood in Delhi, the *Delhi Mission News* reported:

We have had two very interesting visits from different parts of India itself. The first was that of Mr Stokes, a young American missionary, who for the last two years has been living the life of a sadhu, i.e. a monk possessing nothing, eating only the simplest food, and going about barefoot and bareheaded, exactly as religious teachers have done in India from time immemorial. He goes from village to village in the North Punjab and the lower hills, not actually preaching but ministering to the sick and talking to individuals as opportunity arises. His ideal is, in short, in many respects that of St. Francis of Assisi made Indian, and so far at least he has been wonderfully successful. Indians, whether Christians or non-Christians, feel at once that it is no foreign religion that he preaches, but one which appeals to their highest instincts and traditions, and doors and hearts are open to him as they are probably to no other European. He hopes that others, Indians and Europeans, may join him and form a sort of Franciscan Brotherhood . . . The life is, of course, a hard and dangerous one for Europeans, but for some, at any rate, it is not impossible, and it is earnestly to be hoped that he may find companions in a work which supplements ordinary mission work. . . .[11]

Stokes' work endeared him to the Indian community as well as drew the attention of the Europeans in India. A correspondent of the New York weekly the *Na-*

tion, who met him in Lahore, reported how, for days before, he had heard "little else among Americans and English than their stories of this odd American and his deeds," and of how the "sahibs," American and English alike, were inclined to be critical—"though they admitted the real sincerity of the man, they doubted his wisdom"—but from Sikhs he heard "praise of Stokes as the most religious white man they had ever seen."[12]

In December 1907, Stokes finally left for America accompanied by Dhan Singh. They traveled deck, doing odd jobs along the way. He used the cabin-class fare his father had sent to buy two deck tickets—one for himself and the other for Dhan Singh. The journey was significant because the brief stop over in England influenced Stokes' future plans, and it was then that the idea of the Brotherhood of the Imitation of Jesus took shape.

In England, he got the opportunity of meeting heads of missionary societies, members of religious orders, and young men from Oxford and Cambridge who were impressed with Stokes as a Franciscan Brother. Members of the high church Society for Propagation of the Gospel (SPG) were particularly inspired by Stokes and welcomed his ideas. So far he had only hoped that others, Indians and Europeans, would join him in his work and form a sort of Franciscan brotherhood. He already had the nucleus of this in the few Indians who were sharing their lives with him. The interest shown in his work in England raised his hopes. He could see in his mind a "great brotherhood, living according to rule, and winning India to Christ by its united efforts."[13] He was confident that if such an order was established, several English and Indian Christians in India would be prepared to join it at once.

He reached America with this ideal and the resolve to give a practical shape to what, till then, had only been a concept. One of his first tasks was to write about his experiences, his hopes, and his future plans. In a long article, "Interpreting Christ to India: A New Departure in Missionary Work," published in the SPG journal, the *East and the West,* he described his life in North Punjab during the previous two years, giving reasons for his entering upon such a life and the effect it had on the people among whom he lived. He gave details of his work in plague-stricken villages and in segregation camps; he wrote of the many barriers and problems which a European or American missionary faced when working in India and of the many opportunities that were open to the friar. No one had attempted a similar life in India and he tried to show by citing personal experiences that the line of work which he was advocating was a practical possibility.

He had not chosen the life of a friar as the solution to any of the difficulties in the Indian mission field. He had, in fact, "expected to be considered unbalanced, and to become the object of people's pity or the butt of their ridicule." But when he saw a thousand doors which had remained closed to him as a sahib joyfully opened to him as a poor religious man, he was certain that "God had a place for the friar to fill in the Mission work."[14]

He believed that the distressing lack of spirituality and enthusiasm in the Indian Church was largely due to the incomplete presentation of Christianity. What was lacking was "the vision of the homeless, suffering, serving Jesus." There was hence a need for a new Order having as its aim the imitation of Jesus in the service of the sick, and taking as its field the plague and cholera-infected areas, the segregation camps, the leper asylums of India. Unlike other mission-aries who were entrusted mainly with converting Indians to Christianity and were given positions of authority, the work of the mission of the friars was to in-spire, not to convert.

Stokes had no doubt that if the "novices" had the spirit of the friar, they would be able to endure the hardships such a life entailed. He himself had not been physically strong before he came to India and it was doubtful if he could have survived in the Indian climate. The typhoid fever he had contracted a few months before taking up the life of a friar had left him so weak that the doctors were certain that he would not live unless he returned home for a few months of rest and change. But he had remained and felt stronger than before.

"We are apt to conclude that many things are impossible before we have even tested their possibility. The man who suffers against his will speedily becomes a physical wreck; but if he suffers of his own free will, impelled to do so by his ideal, there is hardly any limit to his power of endurance. This I have seen in Brother Sundar Singh and in other Hindu bhagats, and know from what I have myself undergone," he wrote. "The ideal makes the suffering entailed by living up to it a privilege. At home I was placed by my doctor on a diet list, but as a friar I have often eaten food which some Indians were afraid to touch . . . A man's strength is commensurate with the work God gives him to do and his purpose and en-thusiasm in undertaking it."[15]

His article made a deep impact, particularly in England. Canon Charles M. Robinson, editorial secretary of the SPG described it as the "most striking" ar-ticle which had so far appeared in the magazine.[16] The Archbishop of Canter-bury, Randall Cantaur Davidson, recognized its importance and felt certain that it would "awaken widespread interest," and be of "immense practical good."[17]

Bishop George Alfred Lefroy of Lahore, who had seen Stokes' work in small-pox and plague-segregation camps, vouchsafed that "there was not one word of colouring in that article—that, so far from overstating what he is doing and the kind of life he is leading, he is rather understating." At the annual meeting of the SPG, Lefroy urged those present to read Stokes' article which "showed once again how God's spirit is calling His servants to fresh methods and to higher forms of self-sacrifice . . . I shrink from saying a word of commendation, I am so wholly unworthy to, in the case of a man who is leading so far higher and nobler a life—so much nearer to our Lord—than myself," he said in a glowing tribute to Stokes.[18]

During his stay in America, Stokes sought to find support for the proposed Brotherhood with the help of family and friends. He spoke a number of times in the homes of his friends. He also spoke at a Friends' yearly meeting, in a large city church, and before the Clergy Club in Philadelphia. His vision in every case seemed to make a deep impression and in several cases young men felt that the call to join him had come to them personally. Many present at these meetings felt they had never heard a more impressive missionary address.

In the summer of 1908, Stokes returned to England at the insistence of J. O. F. Murray, warden of St. Augustine College, to attend the Pan-Anglican Conference starting on 9 June in London. Murray was impressed by Stokes' Franciscan ideals and felt strongly that he should present his views at the conference. So, placing Dhan Singh for three months at the Mt. Hermon School in Massachusetts, he left for London. Again, unwilling to ask for any financial help from his father, he arranged to go on a cattle steamer, working for his passage as one of a gang of men in charge of the cattle on board.

The eight-day Pan-Anglican Conference was attended by thousands of representatives from more than two hundred dioceses outside Great Britain, many of whom were from India and the Far East. The objective of the conference was to discuss how best to interpret the life of Jesus Christ, both to the Western and native peoples among whom the Anglican Church was working.

In a crowded meeting at Caxton Hall in London on the afternoon of 19 June, Stokes spoke on "Presentation of the Christian Faith to Non-Christian Minds." He narrated his experiences in India and stressed the importance of presenting "the side and the character of the life of Christ, which perhaps a ruling race has too much left out of sight." Giving a short sketch of the new Order he was proposing, Stokes concluded by saying that "those who joined this band of friars would give their lives to the service of the sick and the suffering, dwell in segregation camps or similar places, never criticize the methods of others, and seek to represent Jesus by becoming the servants of all."[19]

Stokes' concept of the Brotherhood of the Imitation of Jesus, as he called the new Order, made a deep impression. He was praised for his "modest and telling manner"[20] and was described as one of the "most helpful" speakers at the conference.[21] His age—Stokes was not yet twenty-six—also made an impact on people. The secretary of the Women's Auxiliary to the Board of Missions of the American Church, Miss Emery, who heard him speak at the conference, was impressed by the respectful attention shown to him by men much older than himself and with many more years experience in the mission field. "I had the privilege of hearing your dear son in London at the time of the Pan-Anglican Conference," she wrote to his mother, "I think some must have had in mind the same thought that came to me—what might be the story he would have to tell thirty years hence."[22]

During his two-month stay in England, Stokes spoke several times at the conference and also addressed the Student Conference which followed the Pan-Anglican. He spoke at student gatherings in Oxford and Cambridge. Reports about his work were received with enthusiasm and several young men expressed their interest in joining the Brotherhood.

On finding so much interest in the new Order, Stokes began considering the possibilities of the Brotherhood working in conjunction with one of the existing missionary organizations. He realized that it could not work with both the high church SPG and the low church CMS, because of the many differences between them. Though he had received far greater support from the SPG and had more in common with them, he found it more realistic to join the latter. This was mainly because in North Punjab where the Brotherhood would work, most missionaries were from the CMS. Also, he believed that it would be dangerous to introduce here a body of high churchmen who would preach "the message which their consciences would force them to preach." For example, they would probably advocate use of the confessional—a concept with which he did not agree and which he thought was unsuitable in Indian conditions. Besides, he felt that the doctrinal position held by the high churchmen would make it difficult for them to have a friendly attitude toward the large number of non-conformist missionaries in Punjab.[23]

Once Stokes had made his decision, the next step was to approach the CMS. Anticipating obstacles, he sought the help of his friend A. G. Fraser, principal of the CMS Trinity College in Kandy, Ceylon, who arranged for him to meet the Rev. D. H. D. Wilkinson, candidate secretary of the CMS. Wilkinson welcomed the idea and saw no reason why the CMS should refuse Stokes.

However, Stokes' case was unusual. He wanted to be part of the CMS and yet have his freedom to continue the work he had been doing. The men who would work with him might or might not be CMS men and the CMS would have no control over them either. Though there were few precedents to the case, there was strong support for him. The Rev. E. Grose Hodge, chairman of the Candidate Committee found Stokes to be an exceptional man in every way and favored his acceptance. Hodge knew that to accept Stokes on his conditions implied the CMS allowing one of its missionaries to start a brotherhood in India over which it would have no control. But he also felt that this connection with the Society could be tentative and might be severed at the end of two years. "I see the difficulty in enrolling a man of such a temperament—so visionary, so emotional, and so determined—but have not these been the characteristics of the prophet in all ages? I think the danger of guarded acceptance is less than the danger of not accepting such a man."[24]

Stokes' meetings with individual members were positive. All his referees, including Bishop Lefroy of Lahore, the Rev. C. F. Andrews, Dr. Theodore Pennell, and the Rev. W. E. S. Holland were full of praise for him.[25] By the last week of July, Wilkinson had received a sufficient number of letters recommending the case. On 28 July, a special Candidates Committee met with Stokes and nominated him for acceptance. A week later, the CMS Committee of Correspondence nominated Stokes to the General Committee as a missionary of the Society.

In a formal proposal to the Society outlining details of the aims and objectives of the Brotherhood and its future relationship with the CMS, Stokes took pains to clarify his position on issues of dress, vows, and name. While declaring that he had no desire to be "medieval," he stressed that he and others who joined him would continue to wear the choga or long robe, which he and Sundar Singh had been wearing for the past two years. The robe was not like that of any other order and had been adapted for use in India, partly on hygienic grounds and partly as symbolic of Christian service; this dress had never been misunderstood in India. They would call themselves "Brothers of the Imitation of Jesus," but they would take "no vows," and would not call themselves "friars." Though he lived like a friar, he strongly objected to the word. "We have never done so (called ourselves friars), it has only been done by those who desired to advertise me since I came back from India, and has always met with my profound disapproval."[26]

Another condition in his proposal was that while he intended to live a life of absolute poverty as he had done in the past, he wanted the CMS to give him the maintenance allowance it gave to its other members. This was because his father continued to be anxious that his work should be recognized and still stood by his earlier offer of matching any allowance that Stokes might receive. Stokes planned to use the maintenance allowance for CMS work and the money his father gave him for his work at Kotgarh.[27] The CMS accepted his proposal.

Stokes sailed back to America on 29 July. He had intended to journey back home as an employee on one of the cattle steamers or in the steerage but changed his mind after his mother's relentless pleas that he needed a "quiet, restful interim" after his hectic stay in England. In the end he agreed to let his parents send him the return passage as a birthday gift.

On 27 August, Stokes wrote a detailed letter to the Archbishop of Canterbury, Randall Davidson, explaining at length the reasons why he had made the decision to join the CMS. Davidson, who was then in Italy, promised that he would study the matter on his return to England. "You have considered the subject so thoroughly that it can hardly be but that God has already been governing and guiding your resolves and arrangements," he wrote.[28] While Stokes' decision was a disappointment to members of the high church group, the CMS was delighted to have him in their camp. Many felt that if he kept his health and succeeded in training a like-minded group of helpers, his work would be a "valuable auxiliary" to that of the other existing missions. There were suggestions that he should not be tied too closely to any mission in the area in which he worked, but that he and his corps be treated as the "irregular cavalry of the main body." P. Ireland Jones, CMS secretary, Punjab, North West Frontier and Sind, who thought Stokes was an "excellent young fellow whose heart was better than his head and who needed plenty of training, though he possibly did not think so,"[29] now hoped that Stokes would "learn to take care of himself so that he may last longer."[30]

The Carletons were especially glad to learn that Stokes had accepted a CMS appointment and was to at last work for an organization. Andrews also welcomed the step. He had always felt that the missionaries had failed to reach the hearts of educated Indians, because of their presenting Christianity in a purely Western form and their neglect of the ideals and customs of India. "I cannot too warmly recommend Mr Stokes' effort to begin a new type of missionary work and development more in accordance with the highest ideals of the Indian people themselves in the purest and noblest form." Already the effect had been remarkable, he observed, for while in most missions the subject of discussions among workers was increase of pay, Stokes' workers voluntarily and joyfully relinquished their stipends.[31]

Stokes' visit home brought only fleeting joy to his family. It was now certain that he had made India his home, for he had declared more than once that he did not intend ever to return. While his mother took comfort in the thought of his life of service, his father still found it hard to accept his position. Stokes was saddened by his father's lack of sympathy but by the time he left, his father had begun to take a more kindly view of his work and way of life. Now sometimes Stokes Sr. talked warmly about his son, showing that at heart he understood him "at least in a measure." An off-beat remark made by his father, that Sam was a "real Christian, . . . it showed in his face," meant much to him.

Stokes and Dhan Singh sailed for India on 3 October 1908, working for their passage on the ship. Wilkinson's offer to pay his fare from London brought the reply, "Do not bother about my passage, I shall go deck, I am a 'poor-man'." They made a two-week stopover in England where Stokes again addressed groups of students at Oxford and Cambridge, and met with the secretaries of the CMS in connection with his future work and relationship with it. He also spent long hours with Canon Robinson and Bishop Montgomery of the SPG, who were not convinced of his decision to join the CMS and thought his action was a mistake.

On 31 October, Stokes and Dhan Singh left London for Trieste from where they sailed to Bombay on 3 November. Two days before they left, Archbishop Davidson invited Stokes for dinner at Lambeth Palace.[32] The archbishop was satisfied with the "intention and the proposed conditions or attitudes" of the Brotherhood. He believed it was "fraught with large possibilities" and commended it warmly to bishops, clergy, and laity of the Church.[33] Hearing Stokes speak a few words at the Prayer Meeting before dinner, CMS secretary G. B. Durrant was moved. "I think those who heard him could not fail to be deeply impressed with the spirit of Christian sincerity and simplicity, and absolute devotion to our Lord, which characterizes him and which we believe will characterize all his work," he remarked.[34]

Judging by the response he received during his stay in England and America, Stokes had hoped that he would return to India with other young men with similar ideals of service, but despite all the interest expressed in America and England in his work, no volunteers had finally come forward to join him and he returned to India to carry on his work alone.

Soon after his arrival in India, Stokes sought an interview with Bishop Lefroy of Lahore. Though the Bishop approved the idea of the Brotherhood, he advised Stokes not to adopt a Rule (guidelines which its members must follow) in full, until it had been further tested. It was best not to define any obligations for those who wanted to join, but rather to let those who entered upon that life first acquire by experience a practical knowledge of what they needed, and then frame their Rule in accordance with it. As a guideline, Stokes drafted a statement regarding the purpose of the Brotherhood which was approved by the Bishop.

In November that year, Stokes' book of religious poetry, *The Love of God,* was published. The poems, with the exception of one which was written during his voyage to India in 1904, were all written in the Himalayas or the plains of northern India. In Stokes' words, they were the "outpouring of the heart of one who, in the midst of so many hardships and many perplexities, was trying to serve God." J. O. F. Murray, who wrote the introduction to the book, predicted that it gave promise of a yet richer legacy to come. "All lovers of sacred poetry would find in this book the root of the matter in a genuine simplicity, depth and intensity of spiritual feeling."[35] The book was popular not only in India and England, but also in the United States and five editions were published during the next three years. The poems were seen as coming "straight from the heart of one who was following in Christ's footsteps," and, as one reader put it, beyond literary merit there was a "genuine ring about them that proves the author is 'the real thing'."[36] The book continued to hold the interest of select readers. Geoffrey Maw, well-known Quaker worker of Madhya Pradesh who lived as a sadhu for many years, read it on his way to India in 1917 and admitted the deep impact it made on him.[37]

5

THE BROTHERHOOD IN INDIA

The Brotherhood of Imitation of Jesus attracted much attention in India. Two important persons drawn to the new Order were Charles Freer Andrews and Frederick James Western, both members of the Cambridge Brotherhood in Delhi.

Andrews had come to India just about a month after Stokes' arrival and was already well known. He was a revered teacher and had endeared himself to people with his selfless and humane approach to their problems. Having no desire for worldly comforts and possessions, he was often seen in the slums of Delhi, happy and at ease amid the poor. He also had the "invincible" longing to live among the poor and experimented with living in the Sabzi Mandi area of old Delhi among the chamars. He had to give that up due to persistent attacks of a malignant form of malarial fever. But the desire to be close to the poor remained.

Andrews had heard of Stokes and his work and was keen to meet him. An invitation from Emma Bates to visit Kotgarh in the summer of 1907 provided the opportunity. It was at her house that Andrews met Stokes for the first time. Through Stokes he also met Sadhu Sundar Singh who was still comparatively unknown outside Punjab. Stokes and Sundar Singh were already living like friars and serving the local community. Andrews was fascinated by their lives and the work they were doing. This was the kind of life which he wanted to live but had been unable to.

The foundations of a strong and lasting friendship between Andrews and Stokes were laid at this time. The malarial fever from which Andrews suffered repeatedly left him so weak that it became necessary for him to go to the hills to recover after each attack, a time he spent in the company of Stokes and Sundar Singh. "To meet these two in the hills and to share their life with them at such a time of bodily weakness was a benediction," he said.

"Both of these shared to the full all the longings I had in my mind to live among the poor," Andrews wrote in his autobiography, *What I Owe to Christ*. "They had already done this themselves in a very practical manner. For in a literal sense they had set out to follow Christ like St. Francis of old, taking neither purse nor script, nor two coats apiece, but embracing poverty with joy for the Gospel's sake. In leading this simple Christian life, they had brought back into the distracted Church of the Punjab something of the pure happiness of sacrifice which we read of in the first century of the Christian faith, when men and women's hearts were filled with the Holy Spirit."[1]

Even before he had met Stokes, Andrews was drawn very strangely along the same line of inner experience as him, "whatever might be the case with others, we were being called not to preach about Christ, in the conventional missionary sense, but in some way—we neither of us quite know how—to live Christ among the people."[2] Andrews was a strong supporter of the Brotherhood ideal. Like Stokes, he was not satisfied with the state of the Church in India. In an article, "Indian Missionary Ideal," he denounced the earlier missionaries' endeavors to bring their personal experience of Christianity to India, including the Sabbath school, the kirk, the ministry, and the worship, which meant transporting all the missionary practices of England to the Indian congregation. This had resulted in innumerable problems, making the converts "hybrids," dependent on, and imitative of, the West. He also did not think that this was the right time for the newly evolved assimilative ideal which, in order to become indigenous in India, sought to "clothe Christianity in Hindu dress and be adapted to Hindu ways of thought."[3]

The Brotherhood of Imitation, whose work was not based on the Western or Eastern model, but instead on the primitive model of the earliest Christian days, represented a third ideal which had the strongest appeal for Andrews. The Brotherhood did adopt Indian customs of food and dress but "its main strength, as its name implied, rested in the imitation of the life of Christ in literal poverty and humility and renunciation . . . it has come . . . to rouse us from an over-trust in the busy activity of organizations and institutions, . . . It has come at a time when we were all feeling that something was wrong with our missionary work, and yet were in doubt and perplexity as to what reform was needed," he wrote.[4]

While Andrews' association with Stokes and Sundar Singh grew, another young member of the Cambridge Brotherhood, Frederick J. Western, was becoming increasingly influenced by the life and work of Stokes. Western, a graduate of Cambridge University, was a professor at St. Stephen's College in Delhi and had been in India for the past six years. He, too, shared Stokes' ideals of poverty, and the life of renunciation had a strong appeal for him. Therefore, when Stokes returned from America with his plans of starting the new Order, Western was anxious to join him.

Western was convinced that the proposed change was "absolutely necessary" for him. S. S. Allnutt, the head of the Cambridge Brotherhood, regretted the loss of such a capable and devoted worker, but he could well understand the reasons which impelled Western to seek a life with Stokes. The Cambridge Brotherhood insisted on celibacy as an essential element in its organization, but it allowed considerable latitude to its members in other matters and, according to Allnutt, it adopted a mode of life of which self-abnegation was an insignificant part. Many members of the Cambridge Brotherhood felt that Western could perhaps lead a life of renunciation even as a member of their brotherhood, but Allnutt thought it was best to leave him "wholly unfettered" in the pursuit of his aim. It was then decided that even though Western had opted to join the Brotherhood of Imitation, he would remain a member of the Cambridge Brotherhood for a while since the two Brotherhoods were not incompatible despite their ideals and methods being distinct.[5]

In September 1909, Western went to Kotgarh to be initiated into the Brotherhood of Imitation. He could not, however, start working with Stokes immediately as he was temporarily in charge of St. Stephen's High School in Delhi in the absence of its principal. After Easter he left for England intending to return to India a few months later, when he hoped to devote himself wholly to his new work and mode of life.[6]

Many others showed interest in the Brotherhood. The *Mission Field* of August 1909 reported in its editorial that four Englishmen had been accepted as members of the Brotherhood and hoped to go out to India shortly. Six Indians were also reported to be interested in joining the Brotherhood.[7] Among these were two learned sadhus. The first, Swami Dhar Tirath, a sanyasi for forty-two years, came up to Kotgarh in May 1909 and was later baptized there. The other was Swami Isanand, who had earlier converted and now intended to join the Brotherhood. Subsequently, a Christian Sadhu movement emerged in the hills, which grew quite strong during the next twenty years. These sadhus wore saffron clothes, wooden slippers, and carried a kamandal but preached Christianity.

Two months later, Stokes was joined by W. G. Branch, an enthusiast from England. Branch had been keen to join the Brotherhood ever since he met Stokes in Islington. Though he was not very strong physically, he was preparing himself for the work by learning Hindustani. Stokes had looked forward to Branch's coming and went down to Delhi to receive him. But soon after his arrival at Kotgarh, Branch told Stokes that he could not agree with many sections of the tentative Rule of the Brotherhood—mainly abstention from "flesh foods" and the taking of "obligations and pledges." He intended to be "completely independent" for the first year and did not make any commitments even for the future.[8]*

During the next year, while Stokes spent time in a plague camp at Multan and at the Sabathu Leper Home, he became more and more involved in the cause of education in the hills, a subject in which he had become interested before he left for America. Immediately on his return, he took up with the authorities the question of raising the Kotgarh Anglo-Vernacular Primary Boys' School to middle level. Such a school would become the educational center for the Kotgarh ilaqa and adjacent districts and be instrumental in raising an educated Christian community in the area. It would help, too, in training young Christian men to act as evangelists and teachers.[9] The need for such a school had been long recognized, but a decision was continually deferred.

In England, Stokes had pleaded for support for the school; if the school could get an additional Rs 100 a month, it would be possible to raise it to middle school level.[10] He also addressed the General Committee of the CMS on the subject.[11] Though he had the moral support of many, nothing ultimately came of his campaigning in England. It was felt that however desirable the step may be, they could not get the funds nor could they get Christian teachers to live and work in the hills.[12]

Stokes' efforts to persuade the authorities in India to change their position were also of no avail. Ultimately he decided to offer the CMS an alternative—if the CMS could not provide the educational benefits of which the ilaqa was in dire need because of lack of resources, then he would be willing to provide the funds for it. He intended to utilize the enhanced allowance which he was now getting from his father for this purpose. Very soon he put together a proposal which the authorities in India and in England would find hard to turn down. He offered to meet the additional expense of about Rs 1,200 per annum, if the school was raised to middle level, and to work as its principal without a salary until someone suitable could be found for the post. He also suggested that the mission's educational work in Kotgarh should be separated from the Pastoral-Evangelistic and offered to take full charge of it till Western's return.[13]

On 9 April, Stokes placed his proposal before the Himalaya District Mission Council (HDMC) with details of arrangements, income, and expenses. The pro-

---

* The real reason for Branch's unwillingness to take any vows was that he was engaged to be married, though no one knew about it. He was so intensely interested in what Stokes was doing that he was afraid that if he gave any such reason to Stokes, he might refuse him the work. He greatly valued the time he spent with Stokes and later was full of remorse for failing him when he most needed support. "I was a great trial to him but he was always generous and bore with me—he had no malice and gave me free forgiveness," Branch wrote to Florence Stokes several years later.

posal, seconded by H. F. Beutel, resident CMS missionary at Kotgarh, was welcomed by the HDMC, which resolved to appoint Stokes as the principal and put him in charge of all the educational work in Kotgarh and the branch schools in the vicinity, that is, at Khuni, Thanedhar, and Delan.[14]

Before Stokes could start working at the school, his proposal had to be approved by a number of bodies, such as the Punjab Educational Committee, the Punjab Central Mission Council, and also by the CMS Educational Committee and the Committee of Correspondence in England. As the CMS delegate from Kotgarh at the annual meeting of the Central Mission Council at Lahore at the end of April, Stokes pleaded earnestly for making Kotgarh an important educational center of the hill district. Members of the council were in favor of raising the level of the Kotgarh school. Stokes' plan was subsequently sanctioned by the CMS Educational Committee in England as a "tentative arrangement for two years" on the clear understanding that the "Parent Committee will not be called upon to make any grant for this school from the General Fund."[15]

Though there were inordinate delays, the new upgraded school began functioning in the fall. The raised standard, with a boarding house for boys coming from a distance, provided an educational facility not available anywhere else in the area. Students now flocked to it from the adjoining states as well as from areas high up on the Tibetan border. Within a couple of months there were more than 200 boys, including two little princes, in the school.[16] Forty boys were living in the old but spacious Nala Kothi, which was being used as a boarding house. The number of teachers, several of whom were graduates of Punjab University, increased to thirteen.

Stokes and the other teachers also lived in the boarding house and were hence able to be in close touch with the students. The boys trusted them and the barrier of suspicion and fear disappeared. A significant spiritual influence was also perceptible. The boys came of their own accord to the morning and evening prayers, and were most interested members of the daily Bible study classes at the school.[17] Many of them considered conversion. The evangelical purpose was also, therefore, being served through the school.

Stokes again ran into monetary problems. He had to shoulder almost the entire financial burden of the school, especially since most of the boys studying in it were too poor to pay the school fees. He could not expect more help from the family since, in addition to the allowance his father was sending him, his mother and sister Florence together were sending him another $45 per quarter for extra tuition for Dhan Singh, who was due to go to St. Stephen's College the following year. Money also came from unexpected sources—friends and members of the family who sent small sums of $5 or $10 to support his work. But he was still short of funds. Though he cut down his own personal expense to as little as $1.60

per month, he was still not able to meet the expenses of the school which were continuously rising.

As per his arrangement with the CMS, Stokes could not ask the Society for help. The only option open to him was to try to raise funds in America. During his visit home, many people had asked to be allowed to help but, with the exception of a few donations, he had refused. Now he decided to ask for help and printed an appeal giving an account of the work the Brotherhood was doing, and containing details of the school expenses. His immediate requirement was for $360.[18] His sister Florence undertook to send the appeal to family and friends, and follow up with correspondence and other formalities. Within a month Florence had received the amount Stokes had asked for. It came in varied sums, starting with as little as $1. Two orphan girls, working for their living, sent $2 each. The old family cook, Ellen, gave $4, nearly a week's wages, saying, "It is the widow's mite for Mr Samuel." The boys of his old school, Mohegan Lake, made a handsome contribution of $83, with the principal suggesting that some of the Kotgarh School boys could perhaps be supported as Mohegan boys.[19] Stokes was gratified that so many people shared in his work in little ways.

The school was expanding rapidly. It was the Brotherhood's aim to make it among the best in North India. The CMC reported satisfaction with the school's progress, and in the summer when Stokes asked for assistance for building additional accommodations, it agreed to sanction Rs 1,000 for the purpose. As Stokes pursued his goals he had full sympathy and support from CMS representatives in India, particularly from Joseph Redman, resident missionary at Simla, and Ireland Jones, CMS secretary, Punjab, North West Frontier, and Sind. "I think we shall be wise to trust Stokes fully to do what he considers best for the interest of the great work he has at heart," said Jones. But the reaction in England was different. There was general dissatisfaction with Stokes for taking up educational work which, it was felt, would take him away from the real work of the Brotherhood.[20]

Stokes himself did not see any conflict between the work he was doing and the aims of the Brotherhood. In any case, he had taken up the educational work only temporarily until Western joined him at the end of the year. He was impatient for Western, who was more experienced and qualified, to take charge of the school. "Then I shall feel free to devote myself to that form of work which especially draws me and for which I am best fitted—the service of the sick, I mean."[21]

Months of preparation and devoted work finally bore fruit when Bishop Lefroy of Lahore formally approved the Brotherhood in 1910. On Tuesday, 22 February, Stokes and Western, dressed in new robes designed by Western's sister, Mary Western, were admitted as the first two members of the Brotherhood at a solemn and beautiful service in Lahore Cathedral.[22] Bishop Lefroy was enthusiastic and "looked upon the founding of this new order as the greatest event that had happened to the Church in Punjab during his episcopate."[23]

Stokes was admitted as a full member and was temporarily appointed the minister general of the new Order—till the formal election of one at the annual convocation to be held in 1913. Western was admitted as Novice. Andrews, an ardent admirer of the Brotherhood and who had wanted to join it, was unable to do so. He continued to suffer from bouts of fever which made it quite impossible for him to even think of such a step at that time. But as chaplain of the Order, Andrews was a member of it in a way.[24] Sundar Singh, who had worked intimately with Stokes for a number of years, chose to remain free and did not join the Order. While he had no official connection with the Brotherhood, Sundar Singh remained very friendly with both Stokes and Western. William Branch did not join the Order either.

The Brotherhood was now firmly established and its Rule approved by the bishop. The Rule covered a great deal of ground, yet it was simple with a spirit of "joyous asceticism."[25] Andrews and Professor Sushil K. Rudra, principal of St. Stephen's College, Delhi, were made trustees of the Brotherhood and remained closely associated with it.[26] Home Committees for the Brotherhood were formed in England as well as in America to guide those interested in joining the Order.

The final approval of the Brotherhood was a welcome step. Though no new members had come forward to join it, the Brotherhood continued to be held in esteem and had the support of many eminent churchmen. Stokes' life and work were frequently written about in missionary journals such as the *East and the West, King's Messenger, Mission Field,* and the *Punjab Mission News.* In January 1909, the *King's Messenger* had started serializing Stokes' manuscript *Arjun, The Life-story of an Indian Boy.* The story, largely based on Dhan Singh's life, generated a great deal of interest, especially as most of the descriptions and customs of the people among whom Stokes was working had never before appeared in print. The serial continued till the end of the year and with each installment of the story there was a brief update of Stokes' work.[27]

In January 1910, the SPG published *Arjun, The Life-story of an Indian Boy* in book form. Later that year Stokes' book *The Historical Character of the Gospel* was published by the Christian Literature Society for India, Madras. (This was subsequently published by Longmans, Green and Co. London and by the SPG as *The Gospel According to the Jews and Pagans.*) It was dedicated "To the Boys of Mohegan Lake School" and was written with the aim of demonstrating from non-Christian sources that the life of Christ and his crucifixion were a historical fact.

The Brotherhood of Imitation of Jesus represented by Brother Western received further attention at the World Missionary Conference held at Edinburgh in June 1910. Western's comments on the future relationship between Christianity and a reformed Hinduism made a deep impression,[28] and his plea for the training for the "commonplace missionary" was strongly reinforced by other speakers.[29]

There was interest in the United States too, especially in Philadelphia, where a large number of people knew Stokes personally or knew of his work and were willing to help the Brotherhood in different ways. Florence Stokes received many requests for copies of his books, especially for *The Love of God*. At first, she hesitated to distribute them because of the very personal preface, which included the articles Stokes had written about his experiences as a sadhu in India, but changed her mind after the encouragement she received from some of her very devout and respected cousins. She now ordered them from England, and sold them individually or put them up for sale in charity fairs.[30] The profit from the books went to St. Augustine's Mission College in England.

Dr. Carleton, John Carter, and other missionaries during their visits from India were so full of praise of Stokes' work that it warmed his mother's heart. The Rev. George A. Johnston Ross, professor of Practical Theology in Union Theological Seminary, New York, told her, after he had delivered a sermon at Bryn Mawr College, that Stokes' was a "very wonderful call," and that her son had helped him as few men had.[31]

ALTERNATE PATH

During the summer of 1910, Andrews, Sushil Rudra, and his son Sudhir all came to spend a quiet summer in the hills. But instead of being a period of rest for them, the summer turned out to be a very hectic one. The outbreak of a severe cholera epidemic in Kotgarh and the adjoining villages kept Stokes, Sundar Singh, and Andrews fully involved in nursing the sick and caring for the dying. Since medication was scarce and ineffective, it was essential to carry out preventive measures and the small group spent all their time assisting the villagers in maintaining a minimum standard of hygiene.

No sooner had the epidemic subsided than there arose another crisis of magnitude. The conversion of seventeen-year-old Sukh Nand of Himtala resulted in a violent confrontation between the local Hindus and the Christians, the like of which had never been seen in the ilaqa. It was an incident similar to that of Dhan Singh's. The boy had fled to the plains with the support of Christian missionaries, been converted secretly, and then placed in a school in the plains, beyond the reach of his family. The villagers were furious but felt powerless. They did not understand the law; in their view it was futile to go to court with a complaint, because then, as in previous cases, the judge would take the side of the white missionaries.

A student of the Mission School, Kotgarh, Sukh Nand had become increasingly interested in Christianity. He urged Stokes to baptize him, but Stokes advised him to wait for some time. Sukh Nand, however, wanted to go through the formalities immediately. He managed to get away with the help of Wilfred Jacob, who had earlier been a master at Stokes' school. Jacob took him to Karnal where he was baptized as James Sukh Nand.[1] Since the boy was studying in Stokes' school, Stokes was considered to be responsible for the incident. He explained to Sukh Nand's disconsolate mother that the boy had acted against his wishes. At her entreaties, he went to Dehra Dun, where the boy had been sent, to bring him back. Stokes and Sukh Nand arrived in Kotgarh on 1 August, unsuspecting and unprepared for any confrontation.[2] They were accompanied by a group of young Christian men who were coming up to Kotgarh to spend their vacations and had decided to travel up with them from Simla. Meanwhile, the people of Himtala and other nearby villages had formed a rescue party of about forty men. Armed with sticks, they lay in wait for Stokes, intending to forcibly take away Sukh Nand.

Sukh Nand's mother, his stepfather, and his uncle met Stokes' party at some distance and walked back with them. Near Bhareri, the mother suddenly clutched her son and his uncle whistled for the other men, who clambered down to the roadside. The villagers demanded that Sukh Nand should denounce Christianity and ask his parents for forgiveness. Sukh Nand refused and looked to Stokes for support. This infuriated the people and a struggle ensued. In the commotion, Sukh Nand was taken down to Bhareri by a member of Stokes' group. Now there was violence. Suddenly Sukh Nand's uncle hurled a big stone at Stokes, which hit him on the forehead. He suffered a deep cut and fell to the ground bleeding profusely. The sight of the gaping wound and blood alarmed the villagers and they ran away, fearful of the consequences.[3]

The shouting attracted the attention of Andrews, Sushil Rudra, and Mrs. Bates, who were all in Bhareri. They rushed up the hill and found Stokes lying on the ground, his face deathly white and blood streaming from a gash on his forehead. He seemed to be dead. Rudra's son, Sudhir Rudra, and his friend Dina Nath managed to catch the man who had thrown the stone at Stokes.

For one whole day and night Stokes remained delirious, while Andrews and Sushil Rudra, helped by Mrs. Bates and others, took turns to sit by his side and bathe his forehead with iced water. All this while he kept moaning, a pitiful sound full of suppressed pain. Then he uttered one sentence which he kept repeating in Hindi, entreating Andrews not to let any action be taken against the people who had attacked him.[4] The deep wound and the loss of blood had left him extremely weak. The attending doctor, Dr. Jukes felt that Stokes would not be able to regain his strength from his meager vegetarian diet of dal and rice. He wanted him to take meat soups for nourishment, but Stokes refused as it was against the Brotherhood Rule. He finally relented when Dr. Jukes and Andrews argued that if he did not recover and died, the man who attacked him would be held responsible for his death and punished accordingly.[5]

Some of the villagers who had attacked Stokes were arrested and taken to Simla to be tried for assault. The district forest officer, Mr. Gibson, and other members of the Christian community advised Stokes to file a case of attempted murder against the villagers, but he would not hear of it. "I want to live among these people," he said. "I don't blame the boy's relatives for anything, even a bird attacks an aggressor for the sake of her little one."[6]

When he recovered a little, he insisted on being carried to Simla to plead with the deputy commissioner for forgiveness for his assailants.[7] "I shall do what I can to get them off, but fear that some of them may suffer," he wrote to his mother on reaching Simla. "I do not at all blame them. What do they know of the laws of 'underage' and 'over-age'? All they thought was that he was their boy, and as they had always controlled him, so it was their right to control him now. And they could not for the life of them see what right I had to keep him from them. When they saw the boy and saw that he was obeying me rather than those who had born and brought him up it maddened them and they forgot themselves."[8]

The men were charged with "assault and riot" but when the case came up for a hearing in the Simla Court, the "riot" charge was withdrawn at Stokes' request and insistence that such a course would not be conducive to peace in the district and to the termination of the present bitterness.[9] Finally he was able to get a pardon for all those who had attacked him. On 25 August, he returned to Kotgarh. The villagers of Himtala who had till the previous day been in police custody for assaulting him accompanied him on this journey.[10]

The incident had long-term repercussions. A shuddhi (purification ceremony) was performed for Sukh Nand's reconversion to Hinduism. At least ten or twelve children were withdrawn from the Mission School for fear that they might also be converted. The fathers of some children came to the school and said that all the boys should be taken out.[11] Stokes was deeply shaken and the incident greatly influenced the future course of his life. The scar on the left side of his forehead was a permanent reminder of the event, both to him and to the people of the ilaqa.[12] His efforts at coming closer to the people suffered a serious setback and he was on the verge of being driven away from them.

Andrews, who was witness to the incident, believed that it was this event which "more than anything else hitherto bound up the life of Stokes with the people of the Kotgarh Hills." In the long run, the incident and its aftermath was to bring the people of Kotgarh much closer to Stokes; it was also to raise questions in his mind regarding his role as a missionary in the hill community. He had been responsible for a number of conversions in the area, and encouraged to see that despite the opposition from village elders, many other young high-caste boys were ready to convert. But now serious doubts arose in his mind over the question of converting young Hindu boys to Christianity.

Social norms of the hill community presented insurmountable problems to Hindu converts. Earlier conversions in the area had been only from the poor low-caste kolis or of destitute or orphaned high-caste children. Since the kolis were considered "untouchables," their conversion did not much affect their relationship with the rest of the community—they were outcastes, and they remained so even after their conversion. But the conversion of high-caste Hindu boys of influential local families was a sensitive issue. High-caste Hindus made no concession for those who dared to violate the sanctity of their religion. A convert was ostracized by his own community. Social interaction with him was taboo for his family, relatives, and friends. Even if his family accepted the conversion, he could no longer visit them or invite them to his house in the customary manner. If his family accepted a meal in his house it had to be cooked by a Hindu cook of high caste and served in a separate place in the house in new utensils or in utensils unsullied by usage by the converts. If he was to visit his erstwhile home he would not be allowed to enter the inner courts but be made to sit in the outside chambers. His meals would be served to him separately and outside the kitchen which was now out of bounds for him, and in utensils kept apart for the outcastes. A violation of the rules meant the entire family would be ostracized.

Sukh Nand's case raised additional questions—were conversions of this nature helping the missionary cause or were they creating more problems by generating hatred for Christians in the local community? And should young boys be converted against the wishes of their parents? A few months earlier Stokes was involved in a conversion which required sheltering two young Brahmin boys from Bombay. It had caused much agitation and a charge was brought against him in the Bombay courts. The boys were from wealthy and powerful families and Stokes had a very hard time keeping them away from their families.[13]

At the same time Stokes was also facing anxieties regarding the school. As had been the experience of the CMS, finding suitable staff was difficult. Recruiting teachers remained an uphill task and Stokes was still unable to find a principal. Western was ill in England and could not return to take up the responsibility of the school as planned, which meant Stokes had to continue to manage it.[14] Problems with the CMS also persisted. It did not approve of Stokes' involvement in educational work, and there were some misunderstandings over the Brotherhood Rule. Also, the CMS head office in London was unhappy with a proposal to place educational work in Kangra under the Brotherhood of Imitation, apparently with the concurrence of the CMS representatives in India.[15]

In addition to all these problems, Stokes was also worried about the future of Hari Singh, a twelve-year-old fatherless boy who had lived with him for the past six years and for whom he had a great deal of affection. He wanted his parents to educate him in America, but they were not responsive. His father, particularly, would not hear of it, but Stokes continued to plead with his mother.[16]

It was amid such preoccupations and anxieties that Stokes received the news of his father's death in Philadelphia on 12 November 1910. Though he had been certain that he would not return to America for many years, he left for home immediately, giving charge of the school to Branch until Western returned. It was a great shock and a sad loss. His father was aged sixty-four and while he was not in the best of health, there had not been any cause for alarm. In fact, during the preceding months, he had been enthusiastically planning a trip to India to spend some time with his son and see the work he was doing.[17] Now Stokes was suddenly reminded of the last words he had spoken to his mother when he left America two years earlier, "Something tells me that it won't be too many years before we see each other again," he had said, little realizing the reason that would bring him back.[18]

His arrival in New York with Hari Singh, in the steerage of the White Star liner *Cedric*, attracted attention when the authorities refused to allow Hari Singh to disembark. Under the regulations, a child under sixteen years of age could not enter the United States. The authorities wanted to send Hari Singh to nearby Ellis Island to determine his case, but Stokes would not leave his young charge to face the examining inspectors alone and insisted on accompanying him. This was just as well, for Hari Singh did not understand English and none of the government inspectors could understand him, and finally Stokes had to act as his interpreter.[19]

He was not allowed to stay with Hari Singh at Ellis Island, but he visited him every day till the case was decided. "The detention of the boy has been a source of pain to me perhaps more than to the boy," he said. "The little fellow is lonesome in a strange country, sitting all day long with people who do not understand his language."[20] He told a reporter of the *New York Times*, "I am more lonesome in crowded New York than I was at the school in the Himalayan hills, where from our door we can look away into Tibet. If by any chance the boy is deported I will give up all business and sail with him. I took him from his native land, and I am going to see that he returns to it." Eventually, Stokes succeeded in obtaining permission for Hari Singh to enter the United States.

Stokes' unusual appearance, too, attracted attention. The *New York Times* observed, "He is a tall, thin man with a spiritual face adorned with a bushy brown beard. He wears a long brown soutane falling almost to his ankles. On his feet he wore rough low shoes and coarse woollen hose. The gown was covered with a long black cape."[21]

Stokes' visit home was a source of strength to his mother and of comfort to him, but he remained disturbed and unsure of the future course of his life. In his own heart he knew that "troublous times" lay ahead of him—"that something was going to happen, which would lay the Brotherhood open to misunderstanding and remove from it the sympathy of many whom it numbered amongst its friends."[22] He spoke of this in some detail to his mother, to his clergyman, Dr. Perry in Philadelphia, and to the Rev. C. C. Bardsley, honorary secretary of the CMS. It was this premonition which made him refuse to talk about the Brotherhood in India, or Indian missions in ordinary conversation while at home. In England, where he stopped for a short time on his way back, he was welcomed as the head of the Brotherhood of Imitation, but the believers looked at him in vain for the spark that had led to the founding of the Brotherhood two years earlier.

Meanwhile in India, there were more problems during his absence. Western, who returned in January 1911 and who now looked after the school, faced a predicament. Kotgarh had not yet recovered from the after-effects of the Sukh Nand case, and there were practical difficulties over finances of the school and the futile search for a principal. Reports that the Kotgarh Mission might be transferred to the Canadians created tensions. By the time Stokes returned to India at the end of May 1911, the future of the school had become uncertain. A meeting of the Educational Committee held in March had recommended the closure of the middle section of the Mission School since the Brotherhood was unable to provide a managing principal for it.[23]

Andrews, who was then visiting Kotgarh, became concerned at the state of affairs and, surmising that the Brotherhood could not continue as it had until then, suggested major changes to resolve the problem. He was also convinced that Kotgarh was not the right place for Western, whose work, he felt, was in Christian education in the plains. Western was by far the ablest educationist in the province, but his talent was being wasted at Kotgarh unless the mission was really going to develop. If Western could be set free from Kotgarh, he could ideally take charge of the Baring High School at Batala in Punjab.[24]

Stokes agreed with Andrews. He was fully aware of Western's abilities and was gladly willing to let him go if the CMS wanted it.[25] "His [Stokes'] position on the whole now is that God's leading to particular pieces of work for himself or for me should determine the working out of the Brotherhood scheme, and not that we have a Brotherhood scheme into which proposed work must fit," Western wrote to E. F. Wigram, Jones' successor, on 10 June.[26] A week later he informed Durrant, secretary of the CMS, that he was willing to take up the principalship of the Baring High School, Batala.

In Stokes' case, Andrews knew that he had his "very heart in the place" and whatever might be the future of the Kotgarh school or the Kotgarh mission, he would not leave the ilaqa. "I believe Stokes will more or less hover around Kotgarh, whatever happens. He has got so many ties here; but it is useless even to think of planning for him."[27]

Andrews could not have been more right, for a few days later, Stokes confided to Andrews that he had decided to leave the Brotherhood and intended to marry a local girl and settle down in Kotgarh as an ordinary householder.

AN INNER STRUGGLE

Stokes' declaration came as a shock to Andrews. For Stokes himself, it was the culmination of a thought-process that had preoccupied him for many months—the solution to a problem that had till then seemed to be insurmountable.

Though he felt he had achieved some of his goals during the last few years, he had a lingering sense of unease about the future relevance of the Brotherhood. His close association with the Indian people made him realize that it could never be the answer to the many problems besetting the Indian Christian community.

He was also concerned about the attitude of the local people toward the Brotherhood and how it affected his relationship with them. While the Brotherhood ideal expressed a very real side of the Gospel, it was misinterpreted by the Indians—both Christians and non-Christians—who saw in it only the message of an ascetic life. He felt that to them it seemed to be a pattern of the true Christian life and thus it confirmed their mistaken conviction that the truly religious life is to be attained only by freeing oneself from this "net" of worldly affairs, which in the eyes of most included all the relationships of normal life, home, family, and friends.

Stokes also felt that among the local people for whom he had deep affection, there was a "fundamental misunderstanding" about his asceticism. They mistook the true motive of his Christian service, regarding it as self-seeking and as something done for his own spiritual advancement.[1] They began to look upon him with superstitious awe, as a kind of holy man who was rapidly accumulating spiritual merit for himself by his severe penance and austerities. They regarded him as bent upon obtaining salvation for himself by these deeds. This attitude troubled him and he often complained to Andrews about it.[2]

A few months earlier Stokes had tried to explain his dissatisfaction with the life he was leading: "Indians, generally speaking, have two standards of righteousness—a high one for the man who has freed himself from all the problems of normal life; and a lower one for those who live in an ordinary way. This latter standard is—to all intents and purposes—a compromise with righteousness, and it is very generally accepted that a man living in a normal manner cannot be expected to govern his life by the highest standards. Even the Christians here have, for the most part, accepted this double standard, hence they do not feel that God can expect the same things from them as He does from me. Consequently they listen gladly to what I say, and admit that it is right, but they say, 'You can live up to this, for you are free from all the cares and anxieties which beset us. If we were free, we could do so too, but we are all entangled in all these lower ties.'

"With all my heart I hate this double standard. If what I preach can apply only to those who are free from home and other earthly burdens, then I am not preaching them a gospel which will help them. I must be—and they must know that I am—tempted with their temptations and burdened with their burdens, not others, however heavy, which will take the place of these . . . I must prove to them that there are not two standards, but one only, and that it is possible for them to attain it."[3]

Another issue that distressed Stokes was the white man's deep-rooted prejudice against Indians. Even the missionaries were not free from it. Racism was so blatant that there were several Christian churches in India to which admission was restricted to Europeans. In Simla, the Christ Church on the Ridge was exclusively for the Europeans and the St. Thomas Church for the Indians. In other cases, Indians were admitted, but only in separate pews at the back.[4] Stokes was so dismayed to see the unequal treatment accorded to Indian Christians as compared with European Christians that he sometimes wondered if intermarriage of foreign missionaries with Indians might not be the best way to get rid of these prejudices and bring about the unity of the Church in India. Marrying an Indian was a possibility that he had on occasion considered for himself and discussed with Andrews.

Racial prejudice was anathema to him. In a letter to Western about his change of plans, he wrote, "I have come to hate it so passionately that you have no idea how I hate it. On the one hand I am carried away by the thought of the oneness of the Church in Christ, on the other, I see the dividing lines and the separatist tendencies of the world brought into Her. I wish not only my words but my life in its very essence to be a fierce protest against this. It is not easy to make men whose hearts are filled with racial prejudice believe that there is none in our own, until we prove it to them. I think that, so far as I am concerned, this will be proof."[5]

Interracial marriage was a sensitive question. Even some of the most open-minded missionaries found it difficult to accept a Western missionary marrying a native from his congregation. Referring to the issue at the Pan-Anglican Conference of 1908 held in London, the Rev. Bishop Montgomery had wondered whether the various nations, for all their perfect equality, should intermix their blood or not? "The great strains of mankind—white, yellow and black—were meant to be great persistent streams, which God Almighty had meant to keep separate, because each had its own task to work out," he said, and further suggested that marriage should be prohibited not only between those "too nearly related" but also between those who were "too far off from each other," and told his bemused audience that "To the prohibition, 'a man may not marry his grandmother,' they might add, 'nor an Australian aboriginal woman.'"[6]

In an article, "Race Within the Church," Andrews had advocated intermarriage between the races as an effective way of fighting the growing evil of racial prejudice, and had pleaded that the Church should welcome and not boycott the occasional marriage of an English Christian to an Indian Christian.[7] His article raised a storm of protest and there was strong reaction to it in the London papers and elsewhere.

Though Stokes had been preoccupied with issues of racism for some time, his decision to marry an Indian and settle down in the Simla Hills was quite sudden. Throughout his six months' stay in the United States, he was engaged in work related to the Brotherhood. In February he had written to A. W. Nott, his friend and publisher, about the need for "the right men" for the Brotherhood[8] and when he met Cyril Bardsley, the CMS secretary in London, on his return journey, he entreated him to support his work.[9]

When he started back for India in April 1911, Stokes was full of new plans and renewed hopes for the Brotherhood. In addition to the work in the villages, he, Andrews, and Western were planning to devote the coming summer to younger missionaries, training and preparing them in the right spirit. This was the kind of personal work for which Stokes felt he was particularly suited.[10] There was now a substantial increase in his income from his father's estate and an inheritance from his grandmother as well, which he intended to use for new buildings for the school. He wanted to build a small church too and had placed an order for stained glass windows for it while he was in London. The windows cost £600 and his mother had offered to pay half of this amount.[11]

Evidently at this stage he had not thought of abandoning the Brotherhood and, as he said, it was only after his return to India, when he was on his way to Kotgarh from Simla, that the idea of marriage to an Indian came to him as a sudden "realization."

At first he was panic-stricken at the thought, because he had for long thought that he would lead a single life, and because he saw clearly the widespread misunderstanding such a step would arouse. "I pictured the destruction of the

Brotherhood ideal, and the distress and bewilderment of those who had been its most enthusiastic and earnest advocates here and in England."[12] For a while he tried to persuade himself that he was mistaken in his thinking and succeeded, but then his earlier conviction returned with even greater force.[13] He knew it would be hard to leave the Brotherhood—his name had become widely associated with it, and many people were helped and inspired by the ideal it represented. His dilemma was whether he should continue to lead a life which had become unreal to him, for the sake of the inspiration it was to others. The Brotherhood life was also becoming less of an expression of his own inward spiritual need than it had once been and he felt compelled to make a choice—either to continue leading the life of a Brother, when it had ceased to be a reality to him, or to put it behind him and make his outer life the true expression of what his inner being yearned for.[14]

In this time of mental turmoil he turned to his friend Andrews. He told Andrews of his anguish over being identified with ordinary mendicants who went begging from village to village, seeking to acquire merit on their own account, often through the avoidance of worldly duty. He also told him that though he had been fighting to rise above racial prejudice, he had not been able to entirely do away with racial barriers.

Andrews watched Stokes struggle with the problem night and day, earnestly praying to God for an answer. Stokes would consult Andrews frequently as they went for long walks together in the hills, faced with these "insoluble problems."[15] Andrews could understand that for Stokes, a practicing Christian, the people's perception of his work was a fundamental issue. The idea of "acquiring merit" was the very last thing he wished to encourage. Yet his actions seemed to do just that. Knowing Stokes as he did, Andrews could see that this issue made the change of life he contemplated inevitable.

He could also understand Stokes' dismay and outrage at the racial discrimination prevalent in every sphere of life. Andrews had himself been concerned about racism. In certain places, the two races were not allowed to be buried side by side. In Punjab, too, racism had a stranglehold on the Church. "The arrogance of the white race and the bid for a white race supremacy in every continent of the world stirred in both of our minds the deepest anxieties and fears," Andrews wrote. By marrying an Indian Christian, Stokes was ready to make his protest in a most drastic way[16] and show in a "most direct way that there was no 'race' or 'caste' within the Christian Church, if the Church were only true to its Founder, Jesus Christ."[17] Andrews considered this a noble ambition and though his immediate reaction to Stokes' declaration was one of shock and bewilderment, he felt that if Stokes was ready to make the experiment, then he, for one, would wish him "all God-speed." His only reservation was that the "Order of

Imitation would be in that way abandoned after such long and prayerful preparations."[18]

While Andrews did not approve of "reckless and ill-conceived" interracial marriages, he believed that the absolute refusal by the English to marry their fellow Indian Christians meant that Christianity was "tainted with caste." He strongly approved of cases like Stokes', as he told his friend Mahatma Munshi Ram. "For it is really a breaking down of *our* caste system just as your nation has seen the breaking down of yours."[19]

Within the next few weeks Stokes crystallized his future plans in confidence with Andrews—he would marry a local Christian girl, buy property in the region, and settle down to the life of a hill farmer. His marriage would be proof of his belief in the equality of races. Moreover, the step would help him to become a member of the community. For Indians, blood relationships were the most sacred of all bonds, and by marrying a local woman he would become related to almost all the Christians and a large number of non-Christians in the area. This would bring him closer to the people of the land like nothing else could.

The last was very important to him. "Other ideals have seemed as important for a time—but not one had so truly from the first until then affected all my life. In a way, I should say, that it was the ideal which I had least of all defined, just as one often neglects to define that which is the most natural and obvious part of one's life."[20]

He was well aware that many marriages between Europeans and Indians had failed. The reason for this, he believed, was that when a European married an Indian, instead of becoming a member of the community into which he married, he almost always separated his wife from it. People did not look kindly upon the Eurasian community, but he felt certain that if this community would only claim its right to be called Indian, and identify itself with the Christian Indian community, it could become an important factor in the formation of the Indian Church. "What we need then is not that, in the event of such a marriage, the Indian wife should become Europeanized, but rather that the European husband should absolutely throw in his lot with the community into which he is marrying."[21] This was what he proposed to do.

His decision to marry, therefore, not only entailed his resignation from the CMS but also his disassociation from the life of the European community in India, for he not only intended to marry an Indian, but in so doing proposed to discard the European way of life and customs, and become one of the Indian community.

"I shall as far as in me lies become an Indian, marry an Indian girl, and, if God gives me sons and daughters, bring them up absolutely as Indians in manner of life, language, dress and education . . . I shall try to make my home life, in all its aspects, a gospel of what Indian home life should be, and as a Christian farmer and landowner in Kotgarh, shall devote the rest of my life to building up and developing the communal life there."

The change in Stokes' plans did not mean that he had doubts about the ideal of the life he had been leading for the past four years, or that he doubted the positive role of the Brotherhood of Imitation. The Brotherhood, he affirmed, "had cast new light on the possibility of intimate and human intercourse between missionaries and Indians. It had demonstrated that it was possible to live upon terms of equality and real personal friendship with their Indian brothers, and not suffer by doing so. And it had proved that, to say the least, some Europeans were able to live a similar life out here in India and not be hurt by it." Moreover, it was a life which rendered "access to Indians more possible—all other conditions being equal—than any other adopted in India at that time . . . (it) has had an important message for both England and India. The essence of its value was that it put us in a position to get much closer to the people of this country, but no more than any of the older forms of work has it made us one with them.

"I need hardly say that I have come through many fears and much anxiety to my present position. It is not easy to take any step which involves the loss of friends, and causes those who have trusted to think that one has been untrue to one's ideal," he wrote to Cyril Bardsley. "And yet I am certain that I never have been truer to my ideal than now, and that I am aiming exactly at that which made me take to the life of poverty years ago . . . I cannot be true to Him or to myself unless I take this step, and so I am going to do it."[22]

Stokes' drastic change of plan was a bitter disappointment to many of his friends, particularly in England. They were surprised and shocked. The Franciscan ideal, as he embodied it, had a reality and a charm which had raised high hopes and proved its power to attract Indian sympathies. His departure from the Brotherhood would be a very serious setback to the kind of work Stokes had undertaken. The fact that he was contemplating marriage to an Indian woman—a native and a Pahari—did not make matters easier in an environment in which race was an important factor.

Stokes' decision to resign from the Brotherhood was a great blow to Bishop Lefroy, who had witnessed the birth of the Order and watched it grow to what he believed to be a significant milestone in the history of the Church in Punjab. Lefroy had been filled with "thankfulness and hope" at Stokes' work.[23] That the Brotherhood should come to such a sudden, unnatural end within a short period was something he did not anticipate and, even though Stokes went to Lahore to explain his position, Lefroy could not reconcile himself to his point of view and very strongly opposed him all through.[24]

Stokes' resignation also put the Church authorities in a quandary as to what the official stance should be to this new development. Since Stokes and Western were the only two full members of the Order, Archbishop Davidson felt that it would be unwise to give "overmuch publicity to its dissolution," and advised Lefroy that if anything was published it ought to be only "a brief paragraph." He also felt that if Stokes should propose to make any public statement of his own on the matter, he should be perfectly free to do so "without restriction or criticism on our part."[25]

The step which Stokes was about to take was so radical and, in its outward expression, so far removed from the life he had been leading for the last few years, that he himself did not feel justified in taking it without at least trying to make those who had been his friends understand his reasons for doing so. Therefore, he decided to publish the letters he had written to Cyril Bardsley, Alexander Hadden, and Brother Western, explaining the change in his plans and the reasons for it.[26] In a brief note to the letters, he wrote, "Personally I have no doubt that in taking it, I am following God's leading me, but I can hardly hope that all who have known me will feel the same." The introduction to the letters, written by his old friend, J. O. F. Murray, who was now Master of Selwyn College, Cambridge, showed his confidence in Stokes and helped to clear misgivings. "No one who reads these letters can question the utter sincerity of the writer . . . Whether we approve of his reasons or not, and in spite of the possibility that the result of his action may fall short of his anticipations, men who follow the call of God without flinching are not so common that we can afford to pass one by, or stand without as he takes us simply and frankly into his confidence."

Describing the letters as the fruit of strenuous thought and first-hand experience, Murray asserted that Stokes had a right, at least, to a patient hearing. He also did not believe that there was room for any charge against Stokes of unfaithfulness to his vows. The Rules of the Brotherhood gave any member freedom after a year's notice to sever connection with it and to be released from all obligations to it.

Stokes sent a copy of the published correspondence along with a personal letter to all his missionary friends in India, England, and the United States. While many sympathized with him, to others his change of plans remained unacceptable. They believed that the step he was about to take was a "grave mistake," and that his objective could not be attained by the means he was contemplating.[27] Anne and George Gleason, who were doing mission work in Japan and who were among the closest of his American friends, found it very hard to believe that such a marriage would be acceptable to the people of the country. "It would be impossible in Japan—equally distasteful to the Japanese and the Europeans."[28] B. K. Cunningham had been wary of Stokes joining the CMS three years earlier. He now considered this step a "real calamity" which had caused "deep distress" to his friends.[29] Even Stokes' friend Holland did not agree that interracial marriages would provide the solution to the Indian problem.[30] Others wondered if his marriage would "cut him off from his friends."[31]

There were some who, while agreeing with his objectives, did not consider his methods the proper ones, but were still willing to offer him a sympathetic hearing. This was particularly because the prevalent racial discrimination was causing concern to a number of missionaries who wished to be closer to the ministries they served. Apparently, the idea of marrying Indians had been considered by some of them, especially those who believed that it was time to revise their Western prejudices on the subject. A member of the CMS's Medical Mission at Peshawar admitted to having spent sleepless nights over the same issue in his early years in India and expressed his "intense interest and sympathy" in what he described as Stokes' life-experiment. "What you are contemplating seems to be far more the logical outcome of your ideals, as you yourself express them, than the brotherhood life could ever be . . . I absolutely and sorrowfully agree that in no other way than this can we Westerners hope to attain that closeness of contact with the Eastern which can for an instant be described as *union,* and yet how one yearns for closeness in place of the present impassable 'gulf'."

Arthur Davies of St. John's College, Agra, who had once urged Stokes to lead a normal life instead of an ascetic one, saw this step as the "most logical result" of his principles. But he feared there would be "difficulties and perplexities and disappointments" ahead of him. "We need to keep very high and noble ideals of the relation of a man and woman in Christ . . . I write as one who has to your face shown that he cannot follow you or your methods all along the line, but who feels at least something of the tragedy of the yawning gulf which by whatever means you are trying to bridge," he wrote. Davies had all along been convinced that Stokes' seeking "after oneness with the people" seemed almost "unattainable as a text for preaching missionary methods" and he had strongly disapproved of the "unwise publicity" which had been given to Stokes' projects. He now urged Stokes not to let his letters or articles get into the newspapers or magazines—"only time and experience, not articles to any papers, will prove your sincerity and wisdom."[32]

Douglas Downes of S.P.G. College, Trichinopoly, who had been a great enthusiast of the new Franciscan Brotherhood welcomed Stokes' decision. "I believe you are being led *by God* to 'break the ice' just as you were a few years ago when you first took up the 'life of poverty'."

The views of members of the Indian Christian community varied. While those in the hills welcomed Stokes' change of plans, particularly his decision to permanently settle among them, the reaction of the Christians of Punjab was mixed. But there was support from important quarters. Leading educationists like Bihari Lal, the principal of Mission School, Ludhiana, believed it "would augur well for the Indian community."[33] A letter from Sushil K. Rudra, one of the most prominent members of the Indian community, was especially welcome to Stokes. "Your recent action implies full brotherhood with us all—who are of this country," he wrote. "Though with portions of your printed letters I do not agree, there is no question that the equality has been asserted in a most striking manner. For marriage and Christian marriage implies equality."[34] He was happy that Stokes' friends had rallied around him. "They have done so because they know you—and believe in your Christian thoroughness."

Stokes' resignation from the Brotherhood in August 1911 sounded the death knell of the infant movement. While Andrews sympathized with his friend and supported him throughout, there was no doubt that he was also disturbed about the fate of the Brotherhood. The extent of his feelings can be gleaned from a note he wrote to Bishop Montgomery in England shortly afterwards. "I had almost made up my mind not to write about Stokes and I will not write about him personally except to say that I have full trust in him still. But I am more sad than I can say about the Brotherhood of the Imitation and his hasty withdrawal from that which he had founded."[35]

For a time, Andrews even contemplated reviving the Brotherhood with Western. "We are trying to see how, after this death blow, it may rise again. We both feel that it may be, it had to die in order to rise in a form more true to the Christian ideal." Andrews thought the Order could continue with some changes "to make it much less naturally visible to the world by doing away with the dress etc. but keeping closely to the inner spirit of poverty and devotion to the poor."[36] Archbishop Davidson too hoped that the Order would continue in some way and therefore did not favor its formal dissolution.[37]

The Brotherhood of Imitation did not however survive after Stokes left it. Though it held a powerful attraction for Western, who was the only other full member of the Brotherhood, and its Rule provided that he could continue with it with full freedom if he so wished, he did not feel that he could do so. In November, Western wrote to his bishop and told him that he did not feel capable of carrying on[38] and, in February, he returned to his former position at the Cambridge Brotherhood.

Short-lived as the Brotherhood was, it left a mark on the history of Christianity in India. The influence of the Brotherhood ideal, and of Andrews' preaching of it, spread far and wide. In April 1912, at a meeting of the National Missionary Society, Andrews declared, "There is a great future for Christian ashrams." His suggestion brought about the formation of new brotherhoods throughout the country.[39] Reminiscing about these events many years later in his autobiography, *What I Owe to Christ*, Andrews used a biblical analogy to describe Stokes'

Brotherhood of Imitation. "Except a grain of wheat fall into the earth and die, it abideth by itself alone; but if it die, it beareth much fruit. So it is possible," he wrote, "to regard this great experiment of the Imitation which Stokes and his little band sowed in the fruitful soil of India. While the Order itself died a natural death when Stokes married, the germinal idea has risen again with the Indian Christian Church in many singularly beautiful forms. The Christian ashrams at Tiruppatur, Almora, and other places; the Christa Seva Sangha at Poona—these, and other ventures of faith, have shown that Christ is still calling forth those who will follow Him to the ministry and service of the lowliest and the lost."[40]

Andrews had realized much earlier that Stokes could not be happy as an ordinary CMS or SPG district missionary, "with all the paraphernalia of a mission station about him—he could not be a conventional Padre."[41] And though Andrews could not speak with full confidence about all the consequences of the dissolution of the Brotherhood, he had no doubt about Stokes' personal decision. In the years that followed, he visited and stayed with Stokes and his family a number of times and could vouch for this. "Looking back now, after twenty eventful years, it is possible to say with truth that the very drastic step which Stokes took has been fully justified by the results as far as he himself and his own life service are concerned," he wrote.

Andrews also admitted that Stokes' actions had caused him to think afresh many things in his own "Christian life" and influenced to a very great degree his future actions. The brief existence of the Brotherhood was an intimate part of his own life-history. "Wherein," he said, "the presence of the living Christ was made known to me, in India, in wonderful ways that made my heart beat high with hope that I had found the true part of service at last . . . For in every detail of the movement I followed earnestly the thoughts and ideals of the chief actors, and was ready, if illness had not prevented me, to join them under Stokes' leadership as a member of the new Order."[42] In a letter to E. S. Talbot, Bishop of Winchester, he confessed, "Only once I was really tempted to change my life; and that was to join Stokes."[43] The Brotherhood had detached him from the conventional routine of college work, for which he felt he was not specially suited, and gave him a "sense of freedom and a desire, as it were, to try my wings in flight." In 1914, three years after Stokes left the Brotherhood, Andrews resigned his Anglican Order. He had met Rabindranath Tagore in London and decided to make Shantiniketan his new home.

Stokes himself had no remorse over his decision. "I have never for a moment regretted this step of mine, for I am convinced that our supreme duty is to be true to the guiding of the light within, and that no inspiration founded upon misapprehension can be of great lasting value. As long as the Brotherhood was a true expression of my inner spiritual life, that life would be a real inspiration to others; when the inner spiritual outlook had so changed that such a life was no longer a true expression of it, it would have been mere hypocrisy to have continued to live it."[44]

Stokes, however, had a lasting impact on the missionary field. Twenty years later when the missionary years were far behind him, an Indian student attending a conference at the Union Theological Seminary, New York, was asked whether E. Stanley Jones was not the most famous missionary in India. "He is the second most famous," was the reply. The finest and the best he said was "a Mr Stokes, little known in America but widely known and beloved in India." The student then talked of the marvelous work Stokes was doing, describing him as a very able man who had endeared himself to the people as no one else had succeeded in doing.[45]

Stokes' resignation from the CMS put the educational work in the Kotgarh ilaqa in jeopardy. Although he was an honorary missionary of the Society, he was looking after all the affairs of the schools as well as providing financial support for the middle school. But under the changed circumstances the CMS hesitated to have a permanent arrangement with him and were quite willing, if necessary, to revert the Mission School at Kotgarh to a primary school on a reduced budget, or completely withdraw from educational work at Kotgarh.[46]

Stokes, however, wanted to safeguard the educational development of the ilaqa. He was willing to continue to finance the middle school classes at Kotgarh— provided he was appointed principal and correspondent of the school, as he now was, and the CMC continued its grant for the primary school as well as let him use some of the rooms of the boarding house. While the CMS was willing to put the Kotgarh school in Stokes' charge, it did not want to commit for an indefinite period the support it was now giving the primary school. The CMS was short of funds and probably had the impression that Stokes was a wealthy man and would be able to run the school from his own resources. Stokes, on the other hand, did not wish to take over the entire educational responsibility of the ilaqa. He felt it would not be right for him as an individual to be responsible for the school without anyone to fall back upon should anything happen to him.[47]

The school had become a point of contention, with the CMS holding on to its interests and Stokes and his friends fighting for its survival. Both Andrews and Western were keen for an amicable settlement. Andrews was in touch with CMC members and advised Stokes at each step. He also took up the matter with Bardsley during his visit to England a few months later.[48] Western, who was now at Cambridge Brotherhood in Delhi, was even more concerned and was quite ready to go to Lahore and talk to the Educational Committee or the CMC about the future of the school. He was extremely unhappy at the state of affairs. He agreed with Stokes that it would not be advisable for him to have the sole responsibility of the school and found the CMS attitude "very unsatisfactory and ungenerous." He felt that the CMS did not want to have any connection with Stokes that would compromise the Society. They were "distinctly callous" about the welfare of the school and could go to great lengths both in "disregard of the interests of the school and its masters." He also felt that the CMS was taking advantage of Stokes' feelings on the subject—knowing that if he could help it he would not allow the lowering of the standard of the school or let its teachers suffer.[49]

Finally a more or less amicable understanding was reached, and Stokes continued to be in charge of the school with limited support from the CMS. Stokes' friends and well-wishers, however, were disappointed with the CMS' general attitude and with what Western felt was their "shameless abuse of his [Stokes'] generosity." Sudhir Rudra was sorry to learn about the issue. "I do think the CMS should for once play the game!" he wrote to Stokes. "However, it seems in whatever affair you have a hand, God does direct it aright."[50]

HOME AT LAST
A FAMILY MAN

Having made a final decision, the next step was to select a suitable bride and make arrangements for the marriage. As some friends observed, in his direct and downright way Stokes was ready to go forward at an "almost headlong speed." To them it seemed that the idea had "so got hold of him as a principle that the person whom he married seemed to him of secondary importance." Andrews had to urge him not to be too hasty.

Stokes intended the proposed marriage to be strictly in accordance with hill customs. Unlike the practice in most parts of the country, where the girl's family approached the boy's family with a marriage proposal, in the hills it was the boy's family that made the first move. Every marriage was arranged by a bishtu or "go-between," a responsible, reliable man known to both families. In this case, Ramsa, who worked at the Kotgarh mission, acted as the bishtu for Stokes.

Stokes wanted the girl he married to be simple and cultured, and a good Christian who shared his ideals. The final choice was fifteen-year-old Agnes, daughter of M. J. Benjamin, a first generation Rajput Christian. Benjamin worked as a printer in the Government Press at Simla. He had a small house in Bhareri where his family lived. His three children, two girls and a boy, studied at the Mission School. As was then usual, Benjamin allowed his son Emmanuel to continue with his studies, but he withdrew his two daughters, Ada and Agnes, from school when they completed the third standard. "That was enough education for the girls," said the elders of the family. "If they spend all their time studying how would they learn to do the housework and who will marry them then?"

After completing the third grade, Agnes, like the other village girls, spent her time helping in the home—fetching water from the khad, tending the cattle, cutting grass, and collecting firewood. During the winter, when it snowed and no work could be done outside the house, Agnes cleaned the pasham (pashmina wool) painstakingly and learned to spin fine wool and weave it into shawls. She was not fair and light-eyed like many of the other hill girls but had a distinct charm. Dark-brown in complexion, her beauty lay in her fine features, high cheekbones inherited from her Chinese grandfather (her grandmother had married a Cantonese settled in Kotgarh) and big black eyes. Though five-feet-one-inch tall, she seemed even smaller because of her tiny build. The full-length buttoned-up, long-sleeved rezta which the women of Kotgarh wore became her and she retained her slim figure till the end of her life.

Agnes was full of energy and enthusiasm, always eager to take up new chores. She was strong and agile and nimble-fingered, uninhibited at home but shy and reserved among strangers. By village standards, she would make any man a good wife. She had seen Stokes around since she was little and, like the other village girls, would sometimes give him a gift of flowers at the church. Though she had full confidence in her father's judgment, her first reaction to the proposal was, "Why should I marry such an old man? Why should I marry a bhagwa [a sadhu in ochre robes]?"[1]

When Benjamin was approached with the proposal, he was in a dilemma. For, though Stokes was an ideal match for his daughter in many respects, he was a foreigner. Also, she was a little too young for him[2]—fourteen years younger than Stokes, who had just turned twenty-nine. It was Dhan Singh, now married to Agnes' cousin, Georgia, who finally convinced Benjamin that Stokes was indeed the best possible match for his daughter and there was no reason for him to hesitate. "Wherever you marry her, she'll be carrying grass and wood and cleaning the khud [cowshed]—if you marry her to Stokes she'll be like a queen, she'll even be carried to the church in a palaki [palanquin]," he told him. Besides, everyone knew Stokes—he had been in and out of Kotgarh for the past eight years and his life was an open book. He was a God-fearing man. People loved and respected him. His being born a foreigner was of no account as he was now completely Indian in his ways and was going to live in Kotgarh permanently.

Benjamin's initial doubts were soon dispelled and he accepted Stokes' proposal for his daughter. But he and his family did not want Agnes to be married before she was sixteen. The marriage date was consequently fixed for the 12th of September of the following year, the day after Agnes' sixteenth birthday. The engagement was announced immediately. This arrangement suited Stokes, for by then he would have completed the one-year notice period he had given to the CMS when he resigned from the Brotherhood of Imitation.

Florence Stokes received the news of her son's decision to leave the Brotherhood of Imitation and live the life of an ordinary married man with mixed feelings. Even though it had been extremely hard for her to have her son so far away from home, she had come to accept his life of service and was grateful for the opportunity he had been given to follow his ideal. For nearly nine years he had led a very lonely life, often a very sad life, in a foreign land, and entirely separated from his own people. In the years that he had been away from home, the thought of him marrying had never dawned on her as a possibility. Throughout this time, his strongest feelings seemed to be that he had no right to simple, normal happiness—that constant, voluntary pain and suffering was what was required of him. But through all his hardships and travails, she had never urged him to give up his work. His decision to do so now of his own accord came as a shock.

At first, he did not write to her in detail and only indicated something of the change that he felt lay ahead of him. She was totally unprepared for the suggestion hinted at in his letter. She was bewildered and upset, shrinking from the thought of his giving up the Brotherhood and losing his friends by it.[3] When he explained his position to her more clearly, she began to realize that he was right in what he was doing, that God was leading him and making his way plain before him, and that he would "never be allowed to go far wrong."[4]

Andrews' letter to her, written from Kotgarh, which arrived at the same time, was a great comfort. It meant much to her to know not only that the step her son was contemplating was not losing him anything of Andrews' friendship, but that he "fully and unreservedly" approved of it in every detail.[5] Soon after that, she received a letter from Western which brought her even greater solace. While Western was the one most affected by Stokes' change of plans, like Andrews he, too, could understand the reasons for it and empathized with his friend. "His [Western's] attitude towards the step you were going to take meant more to me than that of any one else. His conviction seemed so clear and positive that you were called to do this, and that it must bring blessing with it, that it made me very thankful that your friend was in such close sympathy with you."[6] Another encouraging letter was from Bihari Lal, principal of the Mission School at Ludhiana, who told her in the most enthusiastic terms of all he hoped from Stokes for his people.

Though she was grateful that those whose love and friendship her son valued stood by him in this matter, Florence hesitated to speak about it in her circle of friends and relatives in Philadelphia, and, apart from confiding in the immediate family members, she said very little to others. The one person she did speak to was Stokes' old friend Alexander M. Hadden, who was a member of the Home Committee for the Brotherhood in America. During a visit from Hadden, she told him briefly of her son's change in plans, reading out parts of Andrews', Western's, and Bihari Lal's letters. Hadden sat quietly for some time, and then said that he did not think that "anyone could doubt the guidance—that a man of his [Stokes'] temperament and his vision would undoubtedly have advancing outlooks as he grew older, that the work or manner of work that God gave him to do at twenty would be different from what He showed him at twenty-five, and that again at thirty he would probably be given a further vision."[7]

Stokes' brother and his sisters did not deride his decision. "I see your point of view, which seems to be perfectly reasonable, although of course very unusual—your great familiarity with the East has doubtless revealed many things hidden from our Western eyes and minds and doubtless you are doing the right thing," Spencer wrote.

In the meantime Florence Stokes, anxious to know her future daughter-in-law, started making plans to visit India. She also wanted to be with her son at this time and to try to see through his eyes what he was undertaking. During Stokes' visit home the previous winter they had discussed the possibility of such a visit, but nothing was finalized. Now she was determined to make the trip. The fact that she was a frail sixty-seven-year-old did not worry her. The time she would spend in India would be a cherished memory for her as long as she lived— "a blessed realization of your life and work."[8]

Her other children did not discourage her. It seemed a long trip for her to take, but since Stokes would now be entirely separated from the family in the future, they felt that this was probably the best time for her to take it. Hesitating to undertake the arduous journey alone she decided to take her cousin Margaret Jenkins, who was a good friend and companion and was also interested in Stokes' work in India, with her. The two sailed from New York on the *Corona* on 18 November 1911, in time to be in India for Christmas.

Florence Stokes needed no introduction to Kotgarh, she knew all about it from her son's letters. What she did not anticipate was her instant attraction to the place. She loved it from the moment she arrived. She was also impressed with Mrs. Bates' property at Thanedhar in Kotgarh which Stokes intended to purchase. The 200 acres of land consisted of derelict tea-gardens, grasslands, and pine forests. Barobagh, the highest point in the property, stood atop a sprawling hill flanked by the majestic Shilajan peak to the north. It offered a stunning view of the snow-covered Himalayas. Standing on the Barobagh grounds one could also see the Sutlej rushing down eight miles away, the roar of the river clear and loud. To the west were scattered villages on the hillsides and terraced fields dotted with tiny huts of mud walls and slate roofs. Florence could not agree more with her son that Barobagh* doubtlessly, would be the perfect place for building the family home. Fortunately, the land could be sold to Stokes, a non-farmer, be-

---

* Barobagh, so named because of the unusually large size of one of its fields in which one "bhar" or 32 seers of seed could be sown, a rare phenomenon in the hills where fields are very small.

cause the Simla district was still exempt from the provisions of the Punjab Alienation of Land Act.

Plans for purchase of the property and final arrangements for the deal were
made in quick succession. The Deed of Sale between Stokes and Mrs. Bates was
signed on 6 February 1912 with both his mother and aunt Margaret Jenkins as
witnesses.* The price—Rs 30,000—was steep by prevailing standards for un-
developed land, far from any railway station or passable road. Stokes considered the offer reasonable.[9] He had no money, but he intended to take a loan of
Rs 14,000 from his father's trust. His mother promised to advance him the
balance.**

Florence Stokes had some misgivings about what her son and his wife would
do with such an enormous estate. He had very little business sense and his future wife was still a teenager. Florence was also concerned about the girl Stokes
had chosen to be his wife. Her son was not in love with the girl because he had
hardly ever seen her. The girl certainly was not in love with her son; she had given
her consent as required by her father. For her son, marrying a native girl was a
part of his mission to merge his identity with India. "Everything in your birth
and environment had made for a very different ideal," she told him.[10] No doubt
Agnes was a charming young girl, but Florence Stokes was not sure if she was the
best choice for her son. There seemed so little promise of companionship which
to her was an essential part of a happy marriage. Also, while Agnes seemed gentle
and lovable, she was such a child; Florence felt that if her son married, it should
be to a "strong, level-headed, brainy woman."[11]

The few weeks she spent with Agnes allayed some of her fears. Though Agnes
knew very little English and could not communicate with her directly, Florence
perceived that she was bright, receptive, and eager to learn. If her son continued
to be as earnest to teach her and remained as patient as he was with her then, there
was hope that they would become good companions in the years to come.

Florence Stokes' visit to Kotgarh also acquainted her with the people among

---

* The sale deed was for all the land and houses belonging to Mrs. Bates at Thanedhar, Kotgarh, including the properties of Nainidhar and Dugar Jubar below the Hindustan–Tibet
Road, and all her land lying above the road and to the back of the mission property, comprising in all one thousand twenty six bighas and fifteen biswas of land. In June 1911, Stokes
also purchased two small pieces of land in Mehlin and Chah villages from the CMS. He
did not believe in buying from fellow farmers and consolidated his main holdings almost
exclusively by purchase from non-farming owners. In 1918, he purchased the CMS estate in
Chuan near Kotgarh for Rs 450. (*Stokes Papers*)

** Stokes' loan had two parts—$6,000 from the Trust and $5,000 from his mother. Both
were repayable over a period of time failing which the amount and the interest would be
deducted from Stokes' final share of his father's assets. His mother had already spent $3,500
on her trip to India and had to deposit some of her bonds and securities to raise the amount
for him. (*Stokes Papers*)

whom her son had decided to settle. She visited the homes of a number of Christian families, many of whom were related to Agnes, and found them warm and friendly. She was glad to see that even though as a Christian Stokes was restricted in his relations with the Hindus, he had many friends among them. They came to the mission house and had long conversations with him. It was apparent that they liked him and welcomed the idea of his settling in their midst. He was also a friend to the low-caste kolis, who were ill-treated and despised by many.

Florence Stokes returned home with her mind at peace. She had had a wonderful visit which enabled her to see her son's life in India, an image she would carry for the rest of her life. "This one beautiful gift has come from my visit to you. I can see everything, and hear everything and feel everything you tell me in a way that would have been impossible if I had not been there," she wrote.[12] She also had no doubt now that in his "home life" among the Kotgarh people he would be able to do finer, and more enduring, work than he could ever have done as a friar.[13]

After his mother's return to America, Stokes became busy with the planning and constructing of his house at Barobagh. He designed it himself in the best traditions of Himalayan architecture, where buildings blended with their surroundings. He sought the best craftsmen to execute the job. The three-storey house would be spacious and comfortable, made of finely chiseled stone and beams of cedar wood. The doors were to be carved, as would the supporting pillars and the front paneling of the balconies on the second floor. The roof was to be of slate, like the other houses in the area. The ground floor was to be used for storing grains and farm implements and also as a cowshed; the first floor would have a large lounge and guest-rooms. The second floor was exclusively for the family. The kitchen, in the hill style, would be in the darak (a small attic).

In May, the cornerstone of the house was laid in the presence of Agnes and her family. Christian families from Kotgarh were invited for the simple ceremony. Special prayers were said and halwa distributed to workers and guests from the neighboring villages. On 1 June, Stokes personally supervised the laying of a very special stone into a wall of the first floor. This stone had a cavity, into which was placed a glass jar in a brass pot covered with a brass lid which contained a long written account of the Stokes and Spencer families, how they had come to America and also of how Stokes came to Kotgarh and his life since then. He also put a copy of each of his books into it before he put a stone lid over the stone's hollow and sealed it with cement.[14]

Stokes was anxious to have the house completed as soon as possible. He, Dhan Singh, and some other young men from the village gave a helping hand to the masons and carpenters. Agnes came to Barobagh once in a while to see how the house was shaping up. At times all the young people including the group of children living with him would get together at Barobagh for a picnic. Agnes was no longer as shy as she had been previously; she did not run away whenever she saw Stokes but talked to him. Also, according to the local custom, every morning she made a garland of pink and white wild roses and gave it to him when he came up to their house to give his salaams on the way to school. Stokes wore the flowers proudly, "not caring a rap what people may think about it."[15]

His letters to his family in America exuded happiness. They were full of little details of what he was doing and how his relationship with Agnes was developing. "I thank God that Agnes is to be my wife," he wrote to his mother, "I think that I have very truly fallen in love with her and am looking forward to our marriage with great eagerness . . . you would find it hard to understand how much more close I am coming to the real inner life of India since I have taken this step. I thank God for allowing me to do it."[16] A month later he was to write, "God has been very good to me, as I told you would be the case. He has put into my heart a very real love for the girl He is giving to be my wife. I can truly say she is always in my heart and thoughts and I am never so happy as when sitting and watching her at work or playing with her little niece."[17]

Meanwhile, the school work kept him busy. He had been under heavy strain for several months, teaching nine classes a day, and looking after the administration as well as maintaining all the accounts. The new teacher he had engaged was not up to his expectations, which added to his burden.

That summer, Stokes had very little time for old friends, particularly the young missionaries he had known. But the few he was able to meet wholly approved of his actions. Andrew's letter from Cambridge—"It is wonderful how what a large number of those here are sympathetic with the step you have taken and are making your life and work the subject of their prayers"—was heartening,[18] even though this was not in any sense vital to his happiness. In August, Bishop Lefroy was in Kotgarh for a confirmation service, which gave Stokes the opportunity to have another long talk with him. The bishop was one person he was keen to see, not because he thought that such a meeting would convert him to his point of view, but because he hoped that at least their old affectionate relationship might be re-established. He was happy too that Agnes was to be confirmed by him.[19]

On Thursday, the 12th of September 1912, Stokes and Agnes were married in St. Mary's Church in Kotgarh amid great rejoicing and fanfare.* Both Christians and Hindus had been preparing for the wedding for many days. They had even decorated the house in which the newlyweds were to begin their married

---

* The British priest was reluctant to preside over Stokes' marriage to an Indian, so it was solemnized by an Indian priest, Fazal-ud-din.

life. Stokes insisted on following all the local customs, including the baja (the hill band). He went in a palaki for the wedding ceremony wearing the traditional dress of churidar and achkan. A typical fare of rice and meat was served to the 250 guests who had gathered for the wedding. Since a large number of them were Hindus, the cooking was done by the upper-caste kanaits.

The villagers of Kotgarh had perhaps never witnessed such a grand wedding. And there were many warm greetings for Stokes and his wife from family and friends. Stokes had just one regret—his mother was not there to share this moment of joy and it made him feel "just a little lonely."[20]

"I shall try by His help to be worthy of my little wife and love her as few men have loved their wives,"[21] Stokes had pledged a week before his marriage and he was determined to keep his promise. In October he and Agnes went to live in Barobagh. It would be another two months before the main house was complete, but a smaller house was ready and they moved into that.

A month later they set off on a long holiday, Agnes' first trip to the plains of India. They went to Delhi, Agra, Benares, Mt. Abu, and Bombay. Stokes prepared himself thoroughly for the trip, reading extensively about each place so that he could make it interesting for Agnes. Though she found the heat trying, Agnes enjoyed every moment of the holiday. By the end of December they were in Bombay, staying at the "swanky" Taj Mahal Hotel. Agnes was fascinated by the city and its people but most of all by the saris worn by Parsee ladies and declared solemnly that henceforth she was going to wear only saris. Stokes was only too happy as he himself liked the dress far better than the long gowns worn by the Christians of Kotgarh, and immediately bought half a dozen saris for her.[22]

An evening with Elizabeth Wistar, a family friend from Philadelphia who was living in Bombay with her diplomat husband, revived old memories of home. Elizabeth had not met Stokes for a long time and was pleased to see that he looked better and stronger than she had ever seen him—"as well and happy as one could be." She noticed how gentle and considerate Stokes was toward Agnes and how he took every care of her. "I never knew—and felt I had no right to ask—if he had married her because he loved her, but I know now that he does and he shows it in every way by the happiness and the contentment on his face," Elizabeth Wistar wrote to Florence Stokes. "It is so intensely interesting to hear him talk of India, the people and the work out here. His ideas are so sane and reasonable and he knows so entirely what he is talking about that it is a great pleasure to hear him . . . We have enjoyed seeing them very much and I never felt that I knew Stokes so well before, nor could appreciate his work and thought so thoroughly. . . . He is as keenly interested in 'Current Affairs' and all that is going on as ever, and evidently enjoys talking of them and about home, but he also seems perfectly satisfied, happy, and content with his life and work—and it is certainly one that is well worthwhile."[23]

Before returning to Kotgarh, Stokes took Agnes to Sabathu so that she could spend a few days with Dr. and Mrs. Carleton. By now he was already contemplating taking her to America during the coming winter instead of two years later as he had originally planned. The trip to the plains had been very good for Agnes and she had taken a very keen interest in all that they had seen. She was also now more accustomed to being amid strangers than she had been before she left Kotgarh. He realized now that the sooner she came to have a command over the English language, and the earlier she had the mental stimulus which a trip to his home and a year among his people would give her, the more power it would exercise in molding her life. It was also his most earnest desire that Agnes have a chance to be with his mother while the latter was still strong and well.[24]

During the ensuing year the young couple learned to understand each other, to share experiences, and to organize their lives with care and discipline; much time was spent on long walks and on Agnes' study lessons, mainly English and arithmetic; social relations were developed and social customs followed.

At the same time Stokes gave serious attention to the development of the property, clearing the forests and tea shrubs, cutting terraces, and laying out fields for wheat, corn, barley, and potatoes. He worked with the laborers whenever he could. On Sundays and holidays, schoolboys came to work on the land and were happy to get two paise as daily wage. He was also exploring ways to increase returns from the land. The poverty of the region worried Stokes. The growing population was putting pressure upon the limited means of subsistence available, and now a situation had been reached when, with a few exceptions, the farming population of the ilaqa were unable to earn enough from the land to last them through the year. As a result, the majority of the Kotgarh people lived in abject poverty. The small, traditionally cultivated landholdings of the farmers, continually fragmented with each successive generation, could not provide them with even the basic essentials. Wheat and maize, the major cash crops of the region, barely earned enough even for the middle-class farmer. Life was hard—plowing was done by oxen and the hilly terrain made cultivation difficult. The long winter months forced farmers to remain idle and let their fields lie fallow. Small hill cows yielded no more than a liter of milk. People learned to subsist on plain rice and dal for one meal, and roti and salt and onions for the other. Even tea was usually taken with salt instead of sugar, which was out of reach of the common man. Without cash people had no means of buying essentials like clothing, shoes, and household goods. Kotgarh had, in fact, been declared the poorest of all the British-held hill territories. The Government Settlement Reports noted the incredible poverty, the alarming levels of indebtedness, and the inability of the villagers to improve their condition. People were so poor that revenue officials were compelled to take smaller increases in revenue in nearly every village.*

"If I can find anything which will yield the farmers here a larger crop per acre, I shall be doing the people a real service," Stokes wrote.[25] He realized the need for getting more out of the soil. Tea plantations had not proved to be successful in Kotgarh, as the experience of Mrs. Bates and others had shown. Wheat and maize also did not bring in adequate returns. As an experiment, he planted a new variety of potatoes in a number of fields and after harvesting a very successful bumper crop distributed the seed potatoes to his neighbors. The results were so encouraging that he decided to look for new and better strains of wheat, corn, and grass during his visit to America and to try to introduce them in Kotgarh.

After pondering over different alternatives, Stokes came to the conclusion that the answer lay in growing fruit. The soil and climate were ideal for growing apples, pears, cherries, walnuts, chestnuts, peaches, and strawberries. Kotgarh had the potential of becoming a miniature Kashmir with Simla as its captive market. Meanwhile, his mother was following developments in America, where there was a growing interest in scientific farming. The new "intensive farming" resulted in a 100 percent increase in yield. The neighborhood around Moorestown had been transformed by it and there were glowing accounts of enormous yields and handsome profits, especially from peaches and apples.

After his marriage Stokes had also begun a serious study of Indian history, literature, and culture. In 1913, he published his first article on India, titled "India of the Future," in which he discussed the social and economic future of the country. The article outlined measures that would help regenerate the country and enable it to "again rise to a position of dignity and honour among the nations of the world." India's hope of economic progress did not lie in the development of her vast natural resources for the building up of an industrial civilization like in the West. The concept of Western industrialization was unsuited to Indian conditions. India could become truly great not by emulating the West but by "quiet internal development, and by reforming, building up and perfecting its existing civilization." He did not want India to lose the "precious heritage" of

* According to the 1915–16 Final Settlement Report of the Simla district, the indebtedness of each family was Rs 90, while its income ranged from Rs 30 to Rs 80. The combined miscellaneous income of the ilaqa at Rs 28,010 was less than that of any other region. It also did not convey an accurate picture as about one-third of this amount consisted of earnings of a few families who had taken up government service, and of the Christian masters at the Mission School. The remainder was mostly the wages of casual laborers on the Hindustan–Tibet road and of postmen in Simla. The income of the bulk of the farmers in the area was therefore inconsequential.

simple living, which the West had unfortunately lost. "Let her cling tenaciously to the ancient traditions of family and village life . . . Let her look upon the simplicity and frugality of Indian home life as a treasure which she cannot afford to lose, and understand that simple living is in no way inconsistent with the very highest education and culture."[26]

He had also begun studying the writings of Rabindranath Tagore and was overwhelmed by the beauty and sensitivity of his poems. "Surely those who have read the poems of Tagore even in English must, whether they will or will not, come to see that the general feeling in the West of vast superiority over the East is at certain points open to question . . . It is of course not possible to institute a comparison between the two; this much can however be said—that though the East as a whole still lacks much that in the West makes for character, there are, generally speaking, elements lacking in the atmosphere of the West which make themselves felt here, and on account of which I have come to love this land of my adoption."

Agnes was expecting a baby in late December and looked forward to the day with hope and joy. Stokes was apprehensive for his wife's health and safe delivery of the baby.[27] The birth of their first child, a big, fair, brown-haired boy, on 7 December at the Mission Hospital in Ludhiana led to complications. Despite all the care, Agnes caught an infection which resulted in high fever for several days. Her condition was so critical that doctors doubted whether she would pull through. To Stokes it was the most agonizing experience of his life, to see his "love slipping away" from him just as the joy of parenthood had been granted to them. For two years now his life had found its "calm joy and its anchor" in Agnes. If he could "talk or walk with her or teach her or laugh with her," he was happy and now the thought that "she was going . . . and going in great suffering"[28] was more than he could endure and for days he could neither eat nor sleep. When Agnes finally recovered, it seemed to him that she had been given back to him from the grave and the very sight of her brought "a prayer of thankfulness" from his heart.[29]

On 23 February 1914, Stokes sailed from Bombay with his wife and son and reached New York in the first week of April. This time he was not traveling steerage but was booked in first-class accommodation all the way through, and in London he and Agnes were special guests of Archbishop Davidson.[30]

The homecoming of the young couple was marred first by an unfortunate brush with the immigration authorities and then by the extraordinary interest shown by the press. While the *Ancona* docked at New York, Stokes wanted to first come ashore so that he could go and meet his mother at Philadelphia. He was not permitted to disembark without his family. The incident provided good copy and received widespread coverage in the newspapers, which also published reports about Stokes' marriage and of his earlier visits to America as a "monk" or "friar."

Agnes was annoyed and upset when reporters surrounded and questioned her. She had never experienced anything like this before. The intrusion of the press into what to Stokes was a strictly "personal matter" distressed him. He was very reluctant to talk about Agnes, whom the reporters insisted on calling his "East Indian bride." To repeated questions from reporters, Stokes only replied that his wife was a Christian from the Rajput clan and that he had met her through his "acquaintance with her father." Finally, however, he felt compelled to make a public statement. He denied that he was ever a "friar" of the Episcopal Church but only a member of a brotherhood which did missionary work and which was not bound by any vows which the term "friar" implied. The designation had been conferred on him against his will. "I have never been a 'friar' and membership in the Church of England Brotherhood to which I was privileged to belong implied none of those obligations which the name 'friar' implies. In fact, in spite of constant opposition on my part, it was the press which conferred that title upon me during previous visits."[31]

The news of his marriage to an Indian girl had been received with much interest and speculation in Germantown as well. Memories of his earlier visits were still fresh and few had forgotten the image of the zealous young missionary seeking support for his Brotherhood of Imitation. Now he was bringing his Indian bride home to meet his family. As the *Ancona* entered the Vine Street pier in Philadelphia on 8 April 1913, a crowd waited excitedly for a glimpse of the young man and his Indian wife. Also waiting in the crowd were Stokes' mother and his sister Anna Marshall Truitt. Both hurried aboard the moment the vessel docked. The family waited in the stateroom of the ship till all the passengers had left, hoping that by then the crowd would have dispersed. But when they finally stepped down from the liner after four hours, a large crowd, including a number of reporters, was still waiting.

The next morning's papers carried news of their arrival with the photograph of a somber-looking Stokes walking out of the cabin with the baby in his arms, followed by his wife, wearing an overcoat over her Indian dress, her head and face partially covered, and his mother in the rear.

Stokes arrived in Philadelphia harassed and exhausted. The illness of his wife after the birth of their child and the long and tiring journey, during which he had taken full charge of the baby and looked after his wife's needs, had put a tremendous strain on him. Jhudoo, the servant boy he had brought along, was more of a liability than help.* The old Wayne Avenue home provided a haven to

---

* Jhudoo, who later took the name Dugar, did not return to India with the Stokes family. He became an American citizen and ran a small service-oriented company in Philadelphia.

both Stokes and Agnes. Very soon he regained his spirit and vitality; Agnes, too, learned to relax and enjoy her new surroundings and to speak English as it was spoken in America. She also got acquainted with members of her husband's immediate and extended family, who were all charmed by her.[32]

Amid the calm of life in the family home, Agnes remained busy, looking after the baby and attending her lessons, from which her husband never gave her respite. Their second son was born on 13 January 1915, and much to Stokes' delight, in the same house and in the same room in which he himself was born thirty-two years earlier. Both boys were baptized and christened in the Calvary Church where their father had been baptized and christened. The elder boy was named Prem Chand and the younger, Pritam Chand.

During his visit home, Stokes became interested in his family history, a subject which had fascinated him since his youth. The immediate cause of this renewed interest was the discovery of a packet of old letters, written more than a hundred years earlier, by his great-grandmother Anne Evans Stokes, wife of Dr. Hinchman Stokes I. He discovered them by chance in an old trunk in the attic of Harmony Hall, the old Stokes residence on Chester Avenue in Moorestown.* They had been lying there for more than half a century among other documents[33] and so impressed Stokes that he felt that "they belonged in a sense to all her descendants."[34] He decided to publish a selection from them.

At first, he intended to publish the letters without any comment or introduction, but later added a lengthy historical note. *Letters of Nancy Evans Stokes of Harmony Hall with a Historical Note on the Stokes' Family of Burlington County* was published by Stokes in 1916 after his return to India. The preparation of the note aroused Stokes' interest in genealogical studies and he started to research the lives of his ancestors in greater detail. The result was a three-part, 500-page comprehensive genealogical history of the Stokes and allied families including the Evans, the Hinchmans, and the Harrisons. The book, *Stokes of Harmony Hall and Some Allied Ancestry*, written by him in longhand, was carefully documented with photographs of all important records. (Parts 1 and 2 of the book were completed in 1923. Part 3 was written in 1942 as "Notes.")

During his stay in America, Stokes visited some of the prosperous apple orchards in the suburbs of Philadelphia which convinced him that apple cultivation was the answer to the economic ills of Kotgarh. If every orchardist in Philadelphia could have a bumper harvest of good quality fruit, year after year, why could not the Kotgarh farmer? He made a careful study of apple cultivation in the United States. He read books on the subject and subscribed to farm journals. To gain practical experience he visited apple orchards at different times of

---

* The house had long since passed from the hands of the family but Stokes was allowed to remove a number of valuable heirlooms from the attic, and among them the letters, by the kindness of the then owners.

the year, learning how farmers planted and tended trees, how they picked and packed the fruit, what fertilizers they used, how the saplings were grafted, and the trees pruned. It was a demanding task but one in which he felt compelled to become competent since, on returning to Kotgarh, he would have to rely entirely on his own skills. To his surprise, he found himself enjoying learning to be a real farmer.

After an eighteen-month stay at home, Stokes left for India with his wife and sons, sailing from New York for Liverpool on 27 October 1915 on the *H.M.S. Baltic.* It was a sad parting; perhaps he had a premonition that this would be his last visit home. His mother was nearing seventy and it was hard to leave her. He wondered if he would ever see her again. It would also be a long and indefinite parting from his brother and sisters.

His visit home had, however, done him a lot of good and he felt refreshed and invigorated both physically and mentally. He was taking back with him to India not only loving memories of his family and friends, but also something of the land and the home which was so much a part of him. His baggage contained bundles of old family papers—valuable letters and documents, diaries, paintings, trinkets, books, photographs of portraits of his ancestors, and a number of heirlooms given to him by his mother. He also carried a large number of books and journals on apple cultivation and the latest farming techniques, a variety of farm implements, quality wheat and grass seeds, and dozens of apple, pear, and peach seedlings and seeds of all his favorite flowers.

The journey back to India in the middle of World War I was eventful. The *Baltic* was presumably carrying not only its 600 passengers but also a rather "unusually valuable" cargo for the Allies. The greatest care was therefore taken to keep its course secret. But as the ship entered the "Danger Zone," passengers were warned of impending emergency. Everyone was supplied with a life belt and instructed how to fasten it; even little Prem was given one.[35]

While the *Baltic* reached its destination safely, the travails of the family were far from over. At Liverpool they boarded the *S.S. City of Marseilles,* which was scheduled to reach Bombay in early December. The journey was an anxious one. German submarines were active in the Mediterranean. The *S.S. Ancona,* on which they had sailed to America two years earlier, was later sunk with a number of women and children on board. On 24 November their ship was attacked. Fortunately, it was not hit, but it was a great trial for the passengers who were asked to quickly assemble in the dining room and prepare for abandoning the vessel. Agnes remained calm and collected throughout the attack, getting the babies ready and selecting what she would attempt to take with them with absolute calm. When the crisis was over, a number of people came up to Stokes and congratulated him for the exemplary courage shown by his wife.[36]

The ship docked in Bombay on 8 December and a week later the family was back in the hills, to a warm welcome from Kotgarh residents. On crossing Bhareri they found the road lined with teachers and boys of local schools; the boys all carried colorful flags and welcomed the party with songs. On their way to Barobagh, three large wooden arches, decorated with ferns and flowers, had been erected for their welcome. A special feast was held at Barobagh, after which the villagers sang and danced joyfully late into the night.[37] The Stokes family could not have come back to a warmer and more affectionate welcome.

The next few weeks were busy ones for Stokes. He would not rest till he had sorted out the treasures he had brought with him. The large living room of the Stokes home was soon transformed. Family portraits and valuable paintings now hung above the bookshelves lining the room. It seemed to Stokes that a bit of the spirit of his home in Germantown, thousands of miles away, had been transported to this small Himalayan household and, as if to keep that spirit alive and sacred, he now decided to name his house in Barobagh "Harmony Hall." Stokes had always had a strong affinity with his ancestral home. "Beneath the changed exterior the old house is there in which my great-great-grandfather lived and died, and my great-grandfather and grandfather also, and that there my father was born and passed his boyhood, and though I have spent less than an hour in it—and that through the kindness of strangers—I feel that 'Harmony Hall' is in some sense my home, and love it from afar."[38]

In July that year their third son, Tara Chand, was born and in December, when Stokes planted around the house a large number of apple, pear, apricot, and cherry trees, the foundations of the economic prosperity of the region were laid. The following July, they were blessed with their first daughter. They named her Champavati, after the "beautiful Champa flower—a delicate white blossom of wonderful fragrance."[39]

As the children grew, they developed distinct individualities of their own. In appearance they were all brown-haired with dark eyes, and as Stokes described, with skin "about the shade of the peasantry of southern Italy" and with a nice color on their cheek. "We think them very pretty children," he informed his mother with obvious paternal pride.[40]

9
WAR ON TWO FRONTS

Ever since his return to India, Stokes had been keen to join the war effort. As the war progressed he felt more and more strongly about it. He was convinced that the war signified the end of an era, and on its outcome hung the future peace of the world. In India, men were enlisting in large numbers and Gandhi, who had just emerged on the Indian political scene, favored India's support to Britain in "her hour of need." Stokes, too, felt that Britain's victory would be in the interest of India and considered it his duty to participate. "I should consider it a great dishonour, and myself a coward, if I held back now when *every man* is needed."[1]

But all his efforts to join the army were futile. While many senior officers viewed his application favorably, the deputy commissioner of Simla feared that Stokes might eventually become a seditionist because of his close association with Indians and rejected his application for enlistment. Stokes' offer to become a British Indian citizen if that would facilitate his enlistment was also turned down.

His letters of this period reflected his preoccupation with the war. He felt that England's role in it was admirable. It was fighting a life and death struggle for the interests of personal freedom for all humanity. He was anxious for all nations, particularly America, to support it. He was disappointed over America's reluctance to join the war and was dismayed to see that while the "very principles upon which America as a nation had been founded were being attacked—and defended—the Americans floundered about, clinging to the letter of the law and worrying about little things." If America did not now help to destroy Germany, it would be a "traitor to the cause of individual freedom and personal responsibility."[2]

Momentous issues were at stake. Germany had thrown the world into war in order to realize its political ambitions. The country was being destroyed by its newly acquired ideal of military conquest for commercial purposes. He hoped that the age of material conquest by force of arms was nearly over. "A nation's *true* conquest now must lie along the lines of a higher achievement than that of arms—in art and letters and religion and science and industrial progress."[3] He was certain that, in future years, the desire of nations to seek the opportunity to rule over alien people would be looked upon as one of the departed aspects of ancient barbarism. "It is as long as we remain partly civilized that one nation will consider it has a right to acquire the country of another and rule over it."

America's entry in World War I in April 1917 was joyful news for Stokes. He could never forget that by birth, blood, and tradition he was an American and he wanted America to act in such a way as to deserve the respect of the world. He rushed to Simla to meet the deputy commissioner to once again plead for his enlistment. This time his case was considered more amicably and he applied for naturalization as a British citizen—a prerequisite for enlistment. He was naturalized in July, and in October he was in uniform. To his disappointment he was not sent for active duty but was made a recruiting officer, a job for which he was considered ideally suited because of his knowledge of Hindi and his familiarity with the countryside. He joined as a second lieutenant and by the time he had reported for his first assignment at Dharamsala in Kangra district at the end of the month, he was already promoted to captain.

Though Kangra was his first choice for a posting he found life there difficult at first. Being away from his family was a strain. He was lonely without his wife and waited for her letters with impatience. He wrote to her almost every day. "It seems as if I were with you for a time when I write." He did not like living among strangers. "I have become such a pukka Pahari that I do not like being among the English,"[4] he confided to her. He was also not comfortable with the Western trappings in which he once again found himself. He was a total stranger, too, to the army way of life. He did not own appropriate clothes to wear for dinner at the officers' mess where he was expected to dine from time to time. Nor was he enthusiastic about formal dinners with the deputy commissioner of Kangra but found these necessary in order to maintain a close contact with him to facilitate his work.

Gradually, he became accustomed to this new way of life. During the day he was extremely busy, but in the evenings he would change into his mountain clothes and relax with a hookah. His two personal servants, Shaama Nand and Heeru, who had accompanied him from Kotgarh, took care of all his personal needs. Dharamsala was a beautiful place with the towering snow-covered Bagsu peak only a few kilometers away. The bungalow he shared with a British officer was surrounded by pine trees. His salary of Rs 550 a month was a luxury and it was a pleasure for him to send almost all of it to Agnes each month.

In February, he was sent to Kotgarh where, despite the government's efforts, people were reluctant to join the army. His tour of Kotgarh turned out to be very successful and a month later he was ordered to take up his headquarters there and work among the hill tribes. Nothing could have made him happier. He knew he could do much more in these hills than anyone else and he would be closer to his family. There was intense activity in and around Kotgarh during the next few months. With his encouragement a large number of young men volunteered for recruitment. He allowed the government free use of his property at Thanedar and erected a special camp on it for the training of local soldiers. He built barracks and stables and a baoli (a small reservoir of spring water) at Nainidhar. The baoli had an exceptionally beautiful view and came to be popularly called rangruton ki baoli (baoli of the recruits). It continues to be associated with Stokes even today.

Throughout the war, Stokes remained certain of Germany's defeat and did not lose heart over early reversals. "We have too strong a cause and our plans are too closely allied to the good of the world for the Germans to beat us."[5] At the same time he wanted America and the other Allies to keep their balance as far as Germany was concerned and did not for a moment agree with "all the violent talks of pulling her to bits." After the Armistice, Stokes sought his discharge from military duty. He was released from regular service but was retained as an officer in the Indian Army reserve with the honorary rank of captain. His confidential report was exemplary and he valued it as a "recognition that I too have done my bit."[6]

Though officially released, his military work was not yet over and for the next few months he was involved in winding up various recruiting camps in the hills. During this time he also looked after the interests of discharged soldiers belonging to all the twenty-eight hill states. He wanted to ensure that the men got all the concessions promised them by the government. Since they were neither fully aware of their new entitlements such as exemptions from begar and allotment of land, nor in a position to plead their case, he acted as their advocate.

The end of the war brought new hope to the world and a possibility of long-lasting peace. Like many others, Stokes believed a new era was dawning on the world and saw the draft of the constitution of the League of Nations as a "most wonderful political" document. "An age which has created it has the right to be proud even if it has accomplished nothing else. If the vision at the back of it is that of Wilson I cannot but give him the most profound admiration . . . I am indeed proud to have been an American, . . . I rejoice at the noble place America is taking in this affair."[7]

But his effervescence was short-lived and very soon he became disillusioned with the great and powerful nations of the West. He was distressed when the peace treaty, signed in Versailles on 28 June 1919, assigned the German and Turkish colonies to individual powers for administration. He felt bitter, too, about the Allied betrayal of China when Japan won its claim to extensive control over the Shantung province in northeastern China. The treaty, he felt, was a "sad comment upon our progress towards light. National selfishness, national pride and vengefulness seem written large over the whole business." In a severely critical article, "Unsatisfactory Peace," he contended that the conditions imposed by the peace treaty went against the cause of permanent peace; that it was a punitive document which aimed to weaken Germany to an extent that it would cease to be a danger to future peace in the world. He did not so much fear a strong Germany as he did the universal hatred and dissatisfaction upon the continent of Europe that the present settlement would engender. "Canker spots have been created which will grow into festering wounds," he warned, "and the atmosphere will not be one in which peace and goodwill among the nations can thrive." The peace treaty he felt "betrayed the trust of mankind." It only showed that selfish international politics had again won a victory at the expense of the welfare of the world, that "justice and the higher ideals have been sacrificed to expediency." He was quite certain that in a future and more enlightened age the "makers of this peace will be found to have failed the world in its need, and that men will say that our leaders proved unworthy to utilize for the good of the race the great opportunity which God has ever granted to a group of men."[8]

With the victory of the Allies, Indians expected an overwhelming change in the attitude of the British toward them. Many even believed that freedom for India could not be too far. One of Gandhi's motives in supporting the war effort had been "to qualify for Swaraj [self-rule] through the good offices of the statesmen of the Empire." The services rendered by the Indian soldiers to the Empire at "critical moments" of the war were duly acknowledged and the British admitted, "without India the war would have been immensely prolonged, if indeed without her help it would have been brought to a victorious conclusion," but Swaraj remained a distant dream.

In recognition of India's loyal services, major constitutional reforms were proposed for the country which laid down for the first time Responsible Government, and not Dominion Status, as a goal. But before the reforms were introduced, the government in early 1919 suddenly announced a set of new coercive measures—the Rowlatt Bills, which spread a feeling of anger and despair among the people and threw the entire country into turmoil. These bills sought to introduce laws which would do away with ordinary legal procedures and authorize imprisonment without trial. They gave the government the power to arrest and convict a person, based on the secret report of another person, whose identity was not to be disclosed in a court of law, and without giving the accused the opportunity to defend himself through a lawyer of his own choice or by calling witnesses. It was claimed that the bills would protect people from violence and had the support of the European community. But the Indians feared that they would be used by the government against its political opponents and there was universal opposition to them.

Stokes, who until now had identified himself only socially with Indians, suddenly found himself drawn into a national debate on the proposed legislation. Being convinced that the bills would do more harm than good, he criticized them severely, denouncing them as savoring "more of the period of Henry VIII than of our own." If the bills were to have any positive result it was essential to have "omniscient and unerring" officials for their implementation which was then not possible in India. The procedure laid down in the Rowlatt Bills was "an edged tool unfit to be administered by those who could only see through dark glasses," he declared.[9] "There are few countries where judges labour under such great disadvantages as they do here in getting at the truth," he wrote in the *Times of India.* "Members of a foreign community, cut off by their position and the traditions of Anglo-India from intimate association with the common life and thought of the people, the officials are largely dependent for information on intermediaries if they desire any inner knowledge of the people and their doings. And by and large these intermediaries are unworthy of such trust."[10] Through the spring he met with several officials to convince them that the bills were "retrograde legislation" and the plans to pass them must be abandoned.[11]

Gandhi, who had returned from South Africa in 1915 and had already become a political force in India, decided to oppose the notorious Bills with all his strength. "I have passed sleepless nights over it but I cannot find justifications for the Bill," he wrote.[12] The Indian political situation took a turn for the worse when Gandhi's final appeal to the Viceroy, asking him to withhold his consent to the Rowlatt Act, was ignored. Consequently, taking the lead in his first All-India agitation, Gandhi started the Satyagraha Sabha. Members of the Sabha pledged to disobey the Rowlatt Act if it was applied to them, as well as other objectionable laws, thus courting arrest openly and deliberately. Within days there were Satyagraha Sabhas in all major cities and a wave of mass demonstrations, strikes, and protests spread across the country. There were riots in several large towns in Punjab in which six or seven Europeans were killed and a British woman, Miss Sherwood, was molested.

The administration reacted with brutal force. On 13 April, fifty soldiers of the Gorkha and Baluch regiments under General Dyer fired 1,600 rounds of ammunition into a large unarmed gathering at the Jallianwala Bagh in Amritsar. General Dyer had used the violation of his order prohibiting public meetings as an excuse for the firing even though not everyone was aware of the ban. There was not a single call for dispersal before the commencement of the firing, which lasted for ten minutes. The exit from the park, which was also its entrance, was blocked by soldiers, allowing no means of escape for the trapped people. According to official estimates, "379 persons were killed, and 1,200 wounded were left unattended." Instead of placating the people's feelings, the government declared martial law in the state and heaped innumerable indignities upon the people. Indians were made to crawl while passing the street on which Miss Sherwood was attacked and they had to salute any British officer they saw. A public whipping post was put up on which violators of the orders were flogged.*

Even before details of the atrocities under martial law in Punjab were made public, Stokes had pleaded for restraint on the part of the British. "It behooves each individual to 'do his bit' by refraining from any act or word which would complicate things," he wrote. The situation was "extremely serious" and he urged journalists and administrators to work not only toward restoring order in Punjab but also restoring confidence and goodwill among the people, without which relations between the two races would suffer a great change for the worse in future years.

He was convinced it was the "short-sighted statesmanship" of the imperial government in unnecessarily forcing the bills upon the country and then following it up with a policy of repression in Punjab which had led to rioting in the state. The horror of Jallianwala Bagh, he believed, would remain a blot upon the name of the British administration in India which could "never be effaced and which no amount of whitewashing could in the least degree palliate."[13]

While he still hoped for good sense to prevail and for a change in the British attitude, he felt he could no longer be a silent spectator to the injustice imposed by the ruling race in India. Criticizing the government's methods of repression, he urged government members and non-official Englishmen to refrain from any action or expression of views which could be construed as implying "contempt or a sense of racial superiority." The Indians were an extremely sensitive people. "If any of them are rebels, treat them as such, but treat them as rebel equals." The changing times demanded a complete rethinking in the attitude of Anglo-India. British extremism would beget Indian extremism, he warned. "By temperament India is inclined towards moderation, and her best men at present are moderates. Let us not, by our inability to change with the times, drive them and the masses with them into the extremist camp."[14]

But the government went ahead with its policy of repression in Punjab. The methods used to quell disturbances there shocked Stokes profoundly. They showed how "utterly lacking in its understanding of India's mind and thought and feel-

---

* There was widespread reaction to the government's decision. Rabindranath Tagore renounced his knighthood in protest against the treatment of Punjab.

ing the bureaucracy was," and brought about an irreversible change in his thinking. He now bitterly condemned the administrators of martial law in the press and wrote personally to the lieutenant governor of Punjab, Sir Michael Francis O'Dwyer, and to various officers of the army expostulating in the strongest terms against the treatment of Punjab. He objected strongly to the Indemnity Act of 1919, which would protect government officials from the consequences of their role in the events of Punjab, and questioned the propriety of the Punjab Administration Order, which made professors and students alike responsible if any defaced papers and pictures were found in their institutions. This was harassment of the educated classes and a blow to their self-respect. Such measures would permanently alienate the majority of educated Indians from the administration. He also criticized the Anglo-Indian press which openly insulted Indians by alluding "exultingly" to the successful administration of "doses of Dwyer's Mixture."

The "very courteous" reply that he received from the lieutenant governor's office showed that his viewpoint was "poles apart" from that of the "custodians of the British Empire."[15] But his efforts were appreciated in other quarters. Bengal's prestigious journal *Modern Review* did not fail to point out that Stokes was "one of the very first to draw the attention of Sir Michael O'Dwyer to the grave danger of the policy of repression and humiliation on which he had launched."[16]

Though Stokes was troubled by the state of affairs in the country, he held no personal ill-will toward the British. "The English are a wonderful people, one of the finest ever, but they lack the capacity to put themselves in others' place and look at things from the others' point of view . . . They are very conscientious as rulers but are intensely distrustful of the capacity and good faith of any but themselves," he wrote in a letter during the summer. He concluded, however, that insofar as any race was unfortunate in being governed by aliens, "those which Britain governs are fortunate."[17] It was difficult for many of his English friends to understand his viewpoint. To them he was a Westerner and presumably should have looked at things their way—the more so as he had held a position of responsibility under the government and also the King's commission. But Stokes was now very Indian. "First, last and always in my hopes, my love and my efforts, India and the Indian people must stand first, and their rights and interests first. I served the Empire and the government because I believed that in loyalty to them lies India's hope . . . Loyalty to the Empire is one thing, and acquiescence in every policy of the bureaucracy is quite another,"[18] he declared.

His very strong stand in opposition to the government policy and the public expression of his views evoked the displeasure of the administration. "This does not render me more popular with the government out here, and I know that certain officials are far from pleased with me. Indeed I had an 'official warning' yesterday from one of them. I told him, though, that he might be certain I should never take issue with the government unless I were certain that I was in the right, and that when I was certain I should not give snap of a finger for anyone official or otherwise—as regards what I said. He seemed rather surprised at my reply and it may have sounded rather conceited to him, but in reality it was not. I should be stupid indeed if after my life out here I did not know more about the life and thought of Indians than other foreigners do. And even for one ordinarily situated knowledge is responsibility; how much more so for me who has cast my lot with Indians, and whose wife is Indian."[19]

The excesses and outrage continued in Punjab and Stokes grew more and more resentful and bitter, as did the rest of India. When the state of affairs did not improve, he found it unsuitable to be associated with the government any longer. "I am not so hopeful for my honorary title of captain as I was—nor in fact so eager for it."[20] His resignation from the army was not accepted at first but the government changed its stance after the publication of his critical commentary on the peace treaty and he was allowed to leave the service shortly afterwards.

The events of the summer of 1919 brought a complete change in Stokes' thinking and attitude. Up to that time he had hoped and worked for a reconciliatory relationship between India and Britain. In fact, until then, as he admitted, he had been "pathetically anxious" to see "some ray of hope for better relations between the peoples of the West and the rest of the world." But the passing of the Rowlatt Bills, followed by the treatment of the people of Punjab—coming as it did shortly after the moral debacle at Versailles—started in him a "train of thought which ended in a strong conviction of the necessity for the non-European peoples to get out of the clutches of the West."[21]

The "orgy of repression and calculated humiliation" of the Indian people in Punjab under martial law instilled in him a feeling of "hatred for imperialism." He saw the "wider significance of the motives behind such actions" and reached the conclusion that the "imperial nations of the West depended for their very existence upon keeping the non-European races in perpetual subordination and under white domination." He realized that "even the best of men could not transform into a blessing what was in its very nature evil and unjust—the domination of one people by another in its interests and against the will of those it held down."[22]

Stokes never believed that Western civilization was in any way superior to that of the East—the two were only "different." The trouble arose because of the conviction of the overpowering industrial civilization of the West that "everything Western was per se vastly superior to anything else to be found in the world," and that because of this infinite superiority the "great civilized nations of the West were quite justified in annexing, governing and exploiting the rest of the world for their own advantage irrespective of the wishes of the people in the countries concerned." He was afraid that if this attitude did not change, the world would be thrown into chaos.

"If the East is ever to win the political position which will make national self-respect possible, she will have to insist upon the recognition of her just claims. There is no other way when one considers the attitude of Europe and America to the Orient," he wrote. "These nations have built up a system of their own in the last 250 years which they consider far superior to anything else in the world. With an astonishing self-confidence they consider this so clearly demonstrated that they feel justified in demanding that the rest of the world fall in line, and judge the right of any nation to govern itself entirely by the standard of whether its civilization coincides in ideals with their own. Over those nations which have other ideals and standards they claim the right to rule, or more or less control them. The 'Mandatory'[23] system [which provided for international supervision of colonial areas] evolved in the Peace Conference is an excellent example of the Western viewpoint. But this will have to go. Western civilization has its own good points but is *not* the only possible civilization."

Stokes was concerned about relations between the East and the West. The growing racist policies of Britain, Australia, Canada, and the United States made him angry. "How can one keep quiet at a time when so much is at stake?" he asked, and protested vehemently against the selfishness and policies of exploitation of the Western nations, declaring that "the world will have to learn to live with some more definite ideals—more definite goals for its endeavours . . . In the past its opportunism has been its undoing." "The time will come though not till my old age when the smouldering resentment of the East will rise into a flame, and her nations will demand of the West a justification for her attitude. They will say, 'We refuse to allow your claim to interfere with us and exploit us,' and if the West refuses to admit her mistake there will be a world conflagration beside which the recent war was as a child's play. And the West will be to blame. God grant that before that time Europe and America may wake up to the real nature of the attitude and change it. The thought of my sons ranged against the West harrows me but if for such a cause such war should break out, I should wish them to be on the side of the East."[24]

A letter to Andrews revealed the extent of his feelings: "I feel that the one great question that the world must face and face now [is]—are the Western nations to go where they like, do what they like, demarcate any section of the world they take a fancy to as 'white' territory and evict from it foreigners of other races, or put them in a position of political inequality? It is the question of the 'superman' doctrine all over again. For my part I am quite disgusted with the nations of Europe and with America. I was proud to take my commission in the army because I felt that with all their faults the Allies would work for a better and a freer world. It has not turned out to be the case, they have proved themselves only less bad than the Germans in their selfishness and pride . . . Really, it is maddening. Where can one find the honest nation? I suppose they don't exist as yet. God knows! I have always tried to be a moderate but it is awfully hard to be one in the face of what one sees going on today."[25]

Letters to his mother continued to be full of the same concerns. "If we could only get it out of our heads that we have a sort of racial right to whatever we need in the world—more of a right than others, I mean; that the others have the same right in the world as we have and just as much right in our countries as we have in theirs, it would overcome all the danger. Unless we do so there will be a grand smash-up some day—and there ought to."[26]

While he strongly condemned the white community in South and East Africa and the Australians for their efforts to exclude Asians from certain territories, he did not spare America for its role in the affair either. This was a subject that had interested him for a long time. He was deeply concerned about the state of affairs in Africa and indignant at the treatment meted out to Indians there. "I am filled with shame when I consider the actions of the white people of South Africa and Canada," he wrote. "The Indian people have not asked for much. All they have asked is that in those countries into which they have been in the past years invited to immigrate, they may be given the same rights as their fellow settlers . . . what they do claim is that when once they have been admitted, allowed to settle down, build up business and even acquire land, it is unjust in the extreme to grant them none of the rights granted to other settlers and to continue to treat them as foreigners."[27]

"Personally I would go further and deny the right of a country settled, as America, Australia and South America have been settled to restrict immigration upon race grounds. Yet on what grounds could they restrict them? For those who immigrated into Canada or the USA are as intelligent and industrious—and superior in cleanliness and general morality—to almost any class of immigrants. In this I think I should be a better judge than most for I have come into more intimate relations than most people do with both.

"Nor can we say that America is less guilty than the others, for are not the laws that we have enacted in the past, and those we are at present intent on enacting, founded upon exactly the same standpoint as the Australian, though perhaps expressed not quite so badly? Indeed in some respects we are more to blame than the other Western nations for we have more than they, and we ourselves took our land from a coloured race and have always spoken and thought of it as a land of refuge for the oppressed and needy."

"I know you will bear with me in all this," he wrote to his mother. "For we are the descendants of the Quakers and have a right to be proud of our inheritance.

Our fathers founded their faith upon the equality of men, and consequently of races. We only of all the founders of the American commonwealth can claim a fairly clean record in our dealings with non-white races. Now, for the sake of the world, we should prove true to our spiritual ancestry."[28]

FOR THE RIGHTS OF MEN
BEGAR

In 1920, Stokes came into direct confrontation with the government over begar or "impressed labour," an ancient custom of the hills under which villagers were required to transport state material and luggage from one village to another with or without remuneration. He had witnessed begar first hand as a recruiting officer during the war and its injustice had weighed on his mind ever since.

Begar services were claimed as a right by the chiefs of the hill states for hundreds of years. When the British took over the affairs of these states after the expulsion of the invading Gorkhas in 1814, they availed themselves of the existing system of forced labor. It was made obligatory for the states to supply a specified number of begarees throughout the year to transport baggage of government departments, army regiments, and officers on duty. Separate agreements were made for Kotgarh, which was one of the strategic forts retained by the company. The practice presumably was a result of the exigencies of hill life where all goods had to be carried either by men or mules in the absence of railways and motor vehicles.

Under the provision of Wajib-ul-Arz or "record of rights" of Kotgarh ilaqa, farmers of the area were obliged to carry the luggage of travelers as they passed through Kotgarh and also carry government dak (mail), in lieu of which they were given certain revenue concessions. But within a few years of this settlement, begar in Kotgarh acquired a wider implication. With the completion of the Hindustan-Tibet road, Simla became a popular hill station for the British. Officials and non-officials on sporting trips also were permitted to use begar. Englishmen living in the hills too were given the same privilege. Construction of dak bungalows at ten-mile intervals encouraged summer travel into the interior. Narkanda and Baghi near Kotgarh, in particular, were popular locations. The number of travelers passing through Kotgarh increased. There were now more hunters and holiday-makers than officials on duty. These visitors received permits from the authorities in Simla entitling them to obtain coolies at various "stages" at government-approved rates; the onerous task of carrying the luggage of these multitudes of visitors fell on the poor, simple hill men. (The docility of hill people had been one of the factors that had made John Lawrence, Viceroy of India, choose Simla as the country's summer capital in 1864.) Wages paid for forced labor were so low that they were inadequate for the subsistence of a single man, let alone an entire family. They got what Andrews called "a pittance, which was often an insult and indignity."[1] Moreover, the laborer never received full payment for his work. If for some reason a farmer absented himself for a day he had to pay a fine which was more than twice his daily wage.

The injustice grew to vast proportions. The practice of begar, initially envisaged to be used only by the district administrative officers, spread to other departments. The Public Works and Forest Departments used them for developmental work in the hills. Not only did they employ begar coolies at nominal wages for carrying iron sheets, coal tar, and other materials, but they also permitted their contractors to avail of the service in spite of the orders of the deputy commissioner of Simla that, "no *begar* coolies should be given to contractors."[2] The Postal Department, too, found it more convenient and economical to use begar coolies during the rush season and sought and received permission from the government to do so.[3] The dak-begar, which originally meant "carriage by hand of letters, parwanas and other articles of the darbar," became a means for the Postal Department to keep expenses down by retaining fewer mail-runners and relying on begar labor instead. The department demanded four coolies every day to carry mail from Kotgarh to Narkanda, Nirath, or Kumarsain, which implied a loss of two to three working days for each begaree and for which he was only paid one day's wage. The dak-begar was particularly dreaded because in several cases coolies had died in the snow while carrying dak on the higher reaches during winter months.

In 1863, the nearby Bushair forests were leased out by the government. It was a highly profitable venture for contractors, but one which increased the burden on the people of the area. The Forest Department, founded a year earlier to meet the demands of the expanding railway network, marked the trees and auctioned them to contractors. The people of Kotgarh, Keonthal, and Kumarsain made up most of the begarees deployed for cutting down trees but they derived no benefit from the operation. Since the total number of begarees at Kotgarh was defined in the last Settlement and was limited, the additional demands of the Bushair Forest Division greatly increased individual workload.

In theory, the obligation for begar in the Kotgarh ilaqa was for one man per chulha or kitchen—which meant one man per household—but in practice it came to be unevenly distributed among the community. Many villagers received sanads of exemption from begar for various reasons. By 1920, 371 homes out of 715 had been granted exemption, which left the remaining families to shoulder more than twice their share of the burden.[4] Under the Settlement, the villagers were also obliged to spend a specific number of days repairing roads which were not maintained by the Public Works Department (PWD). Eventually, the burden became so heavy that farmers were often compelled to be absent from begar and ended up spending more money in paying fines than what was granted to them by the government under the Settlement terms.

In addition to begar, the practices of kar—free service demanded by the State and rendered without question by the people—and rasad—which entitled state officials to free rations while on tour in the area—were also prevalent. Under kar, villagers were forced to serve administrative officials staying at dak bungalows when on tour. They were required to bring their own provisions and live at their own expense while performing free labor. Kar and rasad, though meant only for administrative officials on duty, were also thoroughly misused by other members of the officer's party. They took full advantage of the plight and ignorance of the villagers. The best cows were brought to the dak bungalows so that the entire party would have plenty of fresh milk free of cost. People living along the route were expected to supply ponies for the touring party—again, without payment. Villagers were even expected to give their pots and pans and bedding for use by the official party. Though many of these malpractices were carried on without the knowledge of the official himself, either way, the villagers had no way of redressing their grievances.[5]

This systematic exploitation of villagers over a period of time resulted in growing poverty in the Kotgarh area. In contrast, areas which carried a lesser burden of begar prospered. Even as early as 1850, William Edwards, the far-sighted deputy commissioner of Simla district, in comparing the parganas (a subdivision of a district) of Kotgarh and Kotkhai found the latter to be "highly prosperous" because, "being removed as it was from the chief lines of road, the people were seldom subject to the harassing and degrading duty of serving as begarees, and had their own time at their disposal for the cultivation of their general holdings."[6]

The Kotgarh people blamed the exploitative system of begar for their poverty. But government officials in general held the villagers themselves responsible for their pitiable condition.* Very few British officers and visitors thought begar to

---

* The Final Settlement Report (1915–16) of the ilaqa stated that begar was not an "unmixed evil, as it provides the only alternative to farming of which the kanait seems able to take advantage. Apart from his earnings on the road, with the exception of a few families, he has shown no ability to cope with the new situation caused by the increasing population."

be "unjust." When Edwards tried to reform the system which he saw as "nothing short of an insupportable and fearful system of serfdom causing extreme misery and hardship" to the hill villagers, there were many protests. In trying to limit the use of begar to the terms of the treaty, Edwards had ordered in 1851 that coolies were not to be supplied to any "private parties whatever, either in the station of Simla or travelling through the district, by the government officers, European or native. All such parties are to make their own arrangements." A notice to this effect, displayed by him at dak bungalows outside Simla, raised a furore and Edwards' efforts brought only temporary relief to the begarees. The British community found it impossible to comply with his orders, since "gentlemen and their Hindustani servants could not search for labour in villages." They also complained because wages for privately procured coolies were twice that paid to the begarees. "The English have inherited this system and instead of honestly recognizing it as being a necessity, and working it on the Oriental lines but with British fairness, they have mixed up with it Western ideas of the 'freedom and liberty' of the subject,"[7] reasoned one Englishman. More than fifty years after Edwards' attempt to reform the system, these views still prevailed among most Englishmen.*

To Stokes, begar was a gross violation of the rights of the people, reducing their position to that of "a beast of burden and a Helot." The villager's rights as a free man were denied, his work was seriously interfered with, and his relationship with those who forced him to serve them was demeaning in the extreme. He was often cursed and beaten. Being founded on injustice the system could only be maintained by resorting to further injustice and repression, a situation which was totally unacceptable to Stokes, who had vowed to ameliorate the conditions of the community he had made his own. The precedence set by his Quaker ancestors was a constant reminder of his duty to his neighbors and community,** and it was from them that he inherited his fierce conviction that all men were equal and must be treated as such. For a long time now he had patiently and consistently petitioned the government to alleviate the hardships imposed on the people by begar. The burden of the people could lessen considerably if authorities in Simla reduced the number of permits issued for the use of begar coolies and increased the remuneration given to them.

---

* William Edwards, deputy commissioner and superintendent of Hill States from 1847 to 1852, was keen to promote education in the Simla Hills and passed an order that those parents who sent their children to government schools would be exempt from begar. The school attendance subsequently rose steeply during Edwards' tenure. Edwards' schemes were eventually abandoned by his successor William Hay. (*Imperial Simla*, p. 29)

** In America the Quakers held an impeccable record in their relationship with native Indians. They were also among the first to fight for the welfare and freedom of slaves.

Soon after his release from the army, Stokes took up the issue of begar wages which had remained at four annas (a quarter of a rupee) per day for more than seventy years. Admitting that it might be difficult to get along without some kind of begar, he reasoned that it should be so paid as not to be a "hardship" and demanded the doubling of wages with immediate effect. Prices had risen sharply during the past years; 1918 had been a bad year for farmers, 1919 was worse. In addition, the high mortality rate from a ravaging influenza epidemic reduced available manpower and increased the burden of begar for each family.

In early 1919, he met the deputy commissioner of Simla, H. P. Tollinton, and told him about the "hardships endured by the coolies in the hills on account of the present rates per stage, and the injustice of them," and urged for immediate action. When it became apparent by spring that no relief was forthcoming, he became impatient. Delay meant another difficult year for the people who were made to carry, at an actual loss, the luggage of trippers and pleasure seekers. "In strict justice no demand can be made upon them to carry the luggage of such people against their will," he wrote to Tollinton on 16 April. "It is a form of helotism which would have to go absolutely, in British territory at any rate, if its legality were called in question." He warned that if any question in India justified agitation at the time, this was one. "Rather than have the people with whom I have associated myself subjected to another year such as last, I should be prepared to put the right of the government to exact this service to the test of the court and public opinion."[8]

But subsequent events in Punjab impelled him to change his position and he informed Tollinton that, considering the conditions of Punjab, he would not resort to any agitation just then. He reiterated, however, that delay in the matter meant great hardship for the community which was doubly hit by a combination of high prices and very great poverty. "It was not so bad before the War and a delay of a few months then would not have mattered," he explained. "Now that prices have gone up, and have been pushed even higher by the operations of the Forest Department in the hills, there should not be delay or another season of the same conditions. It is contrary to every idea of justice and right."[9] His sustained efforts paid off when, the following spring, he received the long-awaited news from the new deputy commissioner and superintendent of Hill States, Colonel A. C. Elliot, a "most sympathetic officer," that the proposals for raising all coolie rates by 100 percent were awaiting government sanction.[10] A few weeks later the wages of begar were doubled to eight annas per day.

While enhanced remuneration helped the poor villagers, it did not justify begar. They often lost entire crops because they were called for begar during the sowing period and suffered through the year. For Stokes, therefore, it was not only a question of wages, but, as he said to the deputy commissioner, of the injustice of impressing the farmers and taking them away from their work. The villagers "seemed to have no rights," he argued. "The fact that they belong to the hills seems to be sufficient excuse to impose on them." He also knew that as long as begar was a permanent right of those in authority, the status of the villager, who was ignorant and therefore unable to defend himself, would remain no more than that of a "chattel." Therefore, while his immediate aim had been to increase the wages of begarees, his long-term objective was the total abolition of begar.

The system had become so well-entrenched in the hill ilaqas and was of such advantage to the privileged classes that fighting it was a Herculean task. Few shared Stokes' belief that officers were not "rulers" but "public servants" and that they were for the people, "not the people for the officials." Even though there were some officers who believed that the Kotgarh people had a "legitimate grievance,"[11] the status quo was convenient to the administration, especially for the Forest and Public Works Departments. It was "easier to impress men than to arrange for them and a little injustice and oppression covers a multitude of difficulties." Stokes' dialogue with the authorities had little effect. Ultimately, he came to the conclusion that the only way to overcome begar in the face of official determination to maintain it was to first create unity of opinion against it and then challenge the authorities to prove their right to it by refusing to give it— the way of "passive resistance." He realized that this course would be hard and a long struggle was inevitable, but there was no other option. "I know that I am in the right and as the most educated and intelligent member of the hill community I should consider that I failed in my responsibility if I permitted the authorities to impose upon our hill men because the latter in their ignorance were unable to defend themselves."[12]

During the following months, Stokes mobilized the Kotgarh community and on 26 August 1920, sent a formal representation, signed by more than 200 farmers "subject to the disabilities of *begar*" and a large number of sympathizers, to the financial commissioner, the commissioner, and the deputy commissioner at Simla. The carefully worded six-page document contained a detailed statement of hardships suffered by the people, and with it the ultimatum that after four months the people of Kotgarh would discontinue to perform begar for private persons and officials not traveling on duty, as well as for the Postal, Forest, and Public Works Departments or their contractors, unless they could prove they had a legal right to exact begar.

The farmers would continue begar for administrative officers on duty until a practical alternative was found on the condition that they were paid proper wages, and a list of officials was published and posted in public places. However, they refused to "admit any permanent right" to their services, stating that,

"when private travelling has proved itself practicable without the use of *begar*
coolies, we shall expect even government officials on duty to do without our
forced services." They also objected to providing free wood and milk to officials
and asked for a fair price for these items. Other demands included payment for
kar at the same rate as begar and a day's wages to anyone who was summoned
for duty irrespective of whether he was actually put to work or not. It was common to summon more coolies than were actually needed and to send the extra
ones back after an indefinite delay with no compensation.[13] For instance, when
the deputy commissioner visited Kotgarh or Thanedhar one person from every
house in the ilaqa was expected to be present during his entire stay there in case
he needed their services.

When a copy of the people's representation reached Colonel Elliot, who was
now commissioner of the Ambala Division, he forwarded it to Stokes for his
opinion, little realizing that Stokes was the one who had drawn up and typed
the "objections" for the farmers. While he admitted he had helped the farmers,
Stokes denied reports that the farmers' agitation was "quite artificial" and only
the result of his personal efforts. "The feeling against *begar* system has been growing for years in this ilaqa . . . On account of their ignorance and poverty the hill
men have been so far unable to put their position in writing but there has been
a feeling of injury and resentment among them for a long time, and as one who
had thrown in my lot with them I felt it my duty to help them express it. The
representation is not, however, the expression of my feeling, or of that of a few
leading men, but practically that of the whole ilaqa . . . I am convinced that the
claims of the people are so just and so moderate that the time has come when
you will have to face the question," he wrote to Elliot.[14]

While Elliot remained sympathetic, officials at Simla were not happy with
these developments. All these years, the villagers of the area had carried the burden of begar and its related iniquities without as much as a whimper. Now the
entire community was up in arms against the government. The officer sent to
Kotgarh to negotiate with the people tried to intimidate them with the help of
lambardars (revenue collectors). A report that a police post would be stationed at
Kotgarh was circulated before his arrival to frighten the villagers but they stood
their ground with Stokes' backing.

Stokes insisted that the forms of begar in question should be abolished because they were unjust and an imposition upon a people too ignorant and in-
articulate to defend themselves. It was the simple Simla hill population which
could be coerced as it had been for so many generations, he argued. Such en-
forcement would not be possible in any locality where people were "less gentle
and submissive." He was anxious to see the people free from the excesses of petty
officials, mates, and lambardars, to whom the begar system gave license and op-

portunity to practice all kinds of oppression. "That the villagers by reason of their inability to articulate their wishes and on account of a lack of knowledge about defending their rights, are inclined to succumb to persuasion or sternness, does not alter the case," he argued. "For this reason I am glad that I am here and in a position to voice their difficulties and, if need be, to contend for their rights." He again denied the charges that he was "butting in" where he had no business. "Not only is Kotgarh my home, but through my children I am connected by ties of blood with the communities whose problem is under discussion. It is not as though I were an outsider in Kotgarh, or that the question does not affect my relatives or would not affect my descendants."[15]

These were not the only grounds on which he had taken up the issue. There were other more important motives. "When in order to join the Indian Army I became a British subject I felt that I was undertaking new responsibilities and obligations as one whose home had become India, especially as regards the locality where I was domiciled. These I shall endeavour to fulfil to the best of my ability, and one of them I conceive to be opposition to any unfair conditions to which my neighbours may be subjected. In pursuit of this conception I feel impelled to oppose the *begar* system as practised here, though it is entirely to my advantage to have coolie rates down and to maintain the *begar* system here."[16] He was convinced his fight was a "fair one." "I do not hate the British," he wrote to his mother. "Many of those against whom I am struggling are my old friends. All I can do is to fight them cleanly as a gentleman."[17]

In September 1920, when the Viceroy of India, Lord Chelmsford, made a trip to Baghi in the Simla Hills, thousands of poor villagers were called upon to serve him in the midst of the autumn plowing season, when winter wheat and barley had to be sown. Stokes spoke to several farmers and learned of the great hardships they had to undergo and then publicly denounced the Viceroy's tour. His article "The Viceregal Trip," which appeared in Gandhi's *Young India* on 13 October 1920, gave an account of the suffering and "acquired the reputation of being the first shot fired in the fight against forced labour in the hills."[18] Stokes blamed the Indian Civil Service, one of the most highly paid in the world, for the situation. "They are civil servants and if they cannot act in the interests of the people—instruments of their prosperity—they are of no use in India. The peasants of the hills do not exist to increase the comfort of His Excellency or any other official, high or low. The system of kar and *begar* in the hills must go and go at once. It is responsible for thousands of poor people being forced to minister to the comforts and pleasures of those who are supposed to serve them and to whom their interests have been entrusted. Indeed, if the government fails to do something about this evil system soon, other ways will have to be found to do so," he warned.

Another detailed article by Stokes, *"Begar* in the Hills," which was published in the *Eastern Mail,* also attracted much attention. These articles caused an immense stir in Simla and gave a countrywide impetus to the struggle. Andrews, who had just returned from Fiji, reacted sharply. The British government which made such a profession of virtue for upholding the freedom and liberty of oppressed people was caught "red-handed, employing the methods of slavery." Praising Stokes' efforts, he wrote, "The very things which the leading newspapers in London had been publishing with horror as being carried on in British territory in East Africa, were shown to have been practised, in a lesser degree, by the Viceroy of India. The age-long scandal of forced labour in India had never come before the public so glaringly. Only when Stokes challenged the Viceroy, the matter became serious for the government." Andrews was convinced that in England outside wartime, such a scandal would have led to the downfall of a ministry in power. Even in India, the bureaucracy could not face, for long, "the obloquy."[19]

During the time Stokes had been fighting the battle for the rights of the poor man in the hills, Andrews was preoccupied with the same cause in Fiji. His description of the conditions of Indians working there as indentured labor had sent shock waves throughout the country. Stokes now urged Andrews to come up to Kotgarh and help him expose in the press the iniquities of forced labor in the Simla Hills.

Andrews arrived in Simla in November 1920 and accompanied Stokes on a tour of villages on the Hindustan-Tibet road. He saw how begar was affecting the people and how it was turning the sturdy hill men into a race of timid serfs. It was a terrible experience for him to find "the hill men cowed down and brought into a pitiable state of subjection." Again and again they implored him not to divulge their names or give any particulars which would lead to suspicion falling on them. He heard of how respectable landowners were forced to carry a heavy load for ten or twelve miles and then tramp all the way back again, neglecting their own farms. If they refused they were summoned to appear in the magistrate's court and harassed for their act of passive resistance.

The villagers flocked around Andrews, once a familiar figure in the neighborhood, telling him of what begar had meant to them. He could see the "bitterest discontent running throughout the district and the people on the very edge of revolt against an age-old tyranny." The presence of Stokes in their midst, he observed, had however given them new courage and the will to act together.[20] It was evident that the peasants were determined to resolve the begar issue and if their problem was not solved there would be passive resistance. They were the real satyagrahis, Andrews told Pearson, not the "decadent" English-educated middle class.[21] "I am very thankful indeed that I have come up here," he wrote to

Rabindranath Tagore from Kotgarh. "The conditions of forced labour or begar are such that the villagers are sinking under them into a hopeless slavery . . . I have seen things now with my own eyes and I have had the details fully explained to me by Stokes on the spot . . . The time has come to strike at its very root and release these poor people from their cruel bondage."[22]

On their way down to Simla from Kotgarh, Stokes and Andrews saw "a long weary line of hill men and hill boys, with great heavy sheets of corrugated iron tied on their backs," trudging along, "tired and worn and wretched." Inquiries revealed that these men had been "press-ganged" by a Public Works Department (PWD) officer "to carry these heavy iron sheets to the interior for putting a roof over his bungalow." The "iniquity of the whole thing was manifest," wrote Andrews. "At that very time the yearly fair of Rampur was going on—their one big holiday—and they could not but miss it all. We had seen the hill women only a few miles further on, marching joyfully to the mela. If the Barrack Master Sahib had not been able to get his cheap sweated labour, can anyone suppose for a moment that he would have sent all that way into Simla for those foreign corrugated sheets?"[23]

The new superintendent of the Hill States, A. Langley, was fortunately sympathetic to the people's plight and came to Kotgarh himself to study the situation. In a five-hour discussion with Stokes and Andrews, Langley agreed that forced labor for the dak would cease immediately and that "pleasure hunters" from Simla would also not be allowed to use begar. He, however, wanted begar to continue for Forest and the PWD officers till 1 March, by which time he promised to have the whole system changed.[24]

On his return to the plains Andrews continued to campaign against begar. He praised Stokes' efforts. "I can hardly imagine stronger evidence than that of Mr Stokes," he wrote. "For, on the one side, he is a cultured man, accustomed all his life to sifting information, and also fully understanding the scientific method of exact statement; on the other side, he is a Pahari, who has lived for many years the life of a zamindar in the hills, and as such has kept in closest sympathy and touch with the hill people."[25] In a series of articles published in leading newspapers through the winter months, Andrews exposed the injustice of begar and demanded that it be abolished immediately. "This system of forced labour, which I witnessed in all its cruel beginnings in East Africa, is so widespread over India as to be one of the leading causes of Indian degeneration. If India is to become regenerated and to regain her full manhood and self-respect and her lost freedom and independence, then this system of *begar* must be entirely and absolutely abolished."[26]

Recounting the minutest details of the system, he wrote, "Perhaps no other single cause has brought the government of India into such 'hatred and contempt' among the village people as this perpetual insistence on forced labour . . . Every subordinate government officer takes shelter for his own exactions under the cover of the 'Barra Sahib.' The drama is too well known to be repeated, the milk, the eggs, the 'murgi,' the wood, the flour, the ghee that is needed for the consumption of the 'Barra Sahib.' Yet the sum total of these exactions, in a thousand details, is due to the original and inveterate evil of the *begar* system. It is this system which must be abolished and the rest will follow as a matter of course . . . The government of India must realize, before it is too late, that the people of hill villages are not in a mood, today, to put up with these iniquities any longer. The government may have a thousand treaties in the Secretariat, by which 'forced labour' is given a legal standing. Such treaties make *begar* not *less* iniquitous, but *more* so. There were times in England and America when slavery was legal, and when the slave traffic was regulated by law, but this did not make slavery any less inhuman. Man-made laws are not valid in the eyes of God. If the government of India will not take the side of righteousness and humanity, if they will not abolish the *begar* system, then there will be nothing left but universal passive resistance. And no civilized government could keep its self-respect for a single day, if it attempted to use force against those who refused to submit to *begar*."[27]

In the meantime, Stokes continued to battle begar in the Simla hills. The combined efforts of Stokes and Andrews drew the attention of the government to the seriousness of the begar question, but it was many months before the issue was finally resolved.

Once begar was settled, Stokes wanted to take up other issues such as the peoples' forest rights, which had been encroached in various ways. "I do long to have the satisfaction of knowing that my settling in their midst has been a blessing to them and a means of freeing them from unjust burdens."

JOINING THE FREEDOM STRUGGLE

While Stokes was waging a battle in the hills against the government, dramatic changes were taking place elsewhere in the country. The years 1919–21 were momentous in the history of India's freedom movement. Events in Punjab provided a catalyst for the struggle for independence spearheaded by Gandhi under the aegis of the Indian National Congress (INC).* People were no longer prepared to accept the iniquities of British rule as an inevitability and a sense of outrage permeated the atmosphere. Stokes, too, became intensely involved in the political activities of the country during the next few years, coming into close contact with nationalist leaders, many of whom—including Mahatma Gandhi, Madan Mohan Malaviya, Lala Lajpat Rai, Motilal Nehru, Sardar Patel, and C. R. Das—became his friends.

The Montague-Chelmsford reforms, condemned by a special session of the INC as inadequate, disappointing, and unsatisfactory, had created a rift in its ranks, with most members of the Moderate Party resigning. Mahatma Gandhi was at first inclined to try to make the reforms work and the Congress session at Amritsar in December 1919, described as the Gandhi Congress, decided in favor of this. However, a few months later Gandhi changed his views and, on 1 August 1920, launched the first non-cooperation movement against the British rule in India with the objective of compelling the authorities to keep their word on the Khilafat question and redress the Punjab wrongs.

The Khilafat movement was organized by the two brothers Muhammad Ali

---

* The Indian National Congress (INS) was founded in 1885 by a group of lawyers, doctors, and other intellectuals from different parts of the country at the behest of Allen Octavian Hume, a retired civil servant, with the aim of seeking greater rights for Indians and with the hope of achieving national unity.

and Shaukat Ali in support of the Sultan of Turkey. Britain was blamed for the defeat of Turkey and dismemberment of the Turkish empire in the First World War. Its main demand was that the Caliph or Khalifa, formally regarded as the temporal head of Islam, retain control of places sacred to Islam and be left with sufficient territory to enable him to protect them. Gandhi perceived the Khilafat movement as a rare opportunity of uniting Hindus and Muslims, an opportunity that would not easily come again. But Stokes was not convinced of Gandhi's position on Khilafat. He thought that if Gandhi hoped to make Khilafat a means of closer relations between the two major religious communities in India, he was building upon a very insecure foundation. "A largely academic question of this kind may be very well for the working up of a temporary excitement, but the differences between the Hindu and the Muslim Indians require a more permanent basis for cooperation to give any promise of lastingness," he wrote soon after Gandhi's announcement on Khilafat.[1]

The situation, he felt, would be more promising if Gandhi stayed away from the religious issues altogether and devoted his energies to the question of Africa and the status of Indians there, to fight for the principle of equality of status for Indians throughout the Empire. In that, all Indians and all Asians had a common ground for effort and sacrifice. This was the "one great question" that the world must face. "If we don't get it in the Empire we won't get it in the world, and surely in comparison with this the Khilafat question is of trifling importance. Yet this is being settled before our eyes and adversely while all the newly-awakened energy of India is being wasted to the question of whether the Sultan of Turkey shall or shall not continue to govern certain parts of his former empire. To me it is simply heartbreaking," he wrote agonizingly while asserting that even for the Turks the question of the status of Asians in the world was ultimately of greater importance.[2]

By now Stokes was also certain that India could not for long remain a part of the British Empire as it was then constituted, and must aim at real equality with the other free peoples of the world. When Andrews came to Kotgarh in 1920, Stokes told him that he had now become convinced that as far as India was concerned, the only respectable course for her was to strive for total independence from Britain. Andrews was not surprised to hear Stokes' views. He had been pondering over the same questions and had himself reached the same conclusion.

The two friends had been treading different paths. While Stokes had been preoccupied with problems nearer home, Andrews had spent much time in the distant colonies, where he had seen the treatment meted out to Indian settlers by the ruling white race and had shared in their humiliations. "It is surely no light matter that when, at the end of the best years of both our lives, we compare notes together, after long absence from each other, we find that we have come to the same conclusion as to the impossibility of India remaining with self-respect within the British Empire as it now stands," wrote Andrews. Their position was unique in that, up to this time, Congressmen including Gandhi, had not decided India's goal and were talking about "self-government within or outside the Empire."[3]

Stokes was happy to share his confidences with Andrews. "His views on political questions are more nearly mine than those of any other Englishman I know out here," he wrote.[4]

In a special session held at Calcutta in September 1920, the Congress adopted its famous resolution on non-cooperation and recommended the renunciation by all Indians of government titles and the boycotting of legislatures, law courts, and government educational institutions, gradually leading up to non-payment of taxes. The resolution, however, was not adopted unopposed; almost the entire Congress old guard was against it, as was the president of the Congress, Lala Lajpat Rai.

Stokes, too, was skeptical about non-cooperation as proposed by Congressmen. For years he had been "in sympathy with the aspirations of the moderate nationalists" and had always had "great hopes that this party be built up by sympathy and by cooperation between Englishmen and Indians." Despite his disillusionment with the British government over the passing of the Rowlatt Act and the treatment of Punjab, he still had faith in the reforms and wanted India to win her freedom through constitutional means. He had met Gandhi earlier in the year and had had a number of long conversations with him. The implications of Gandhi's program troubled him. He did not think that Gandhi's plan, to force the government to meet the people's demand by a process of progressive non-cooperation, would succeed. The line of action advocated by Mahatma Gandhi and his associates seemed to him "highly perilous" for India.

Subsequently, after discussing the subject with Gandhi himself and with several other leaders of the movement, he wrote a series of articles on the existing situation in which he tried to make what he believed to be "constructive" suggestions. "Most of the stuff we talk and write in India is either reactionary or destructive nowadays and there is nothing but danger in destroying without building at the same time."[5] He was not sure how his writings would be received, either by the government, or the people. "I have long given up writing with reference to what people want to hear or with reference to what may result to me from my writing." His outspoken articles were published in the *Bombay Chronicle,* in three installments, under the heading, "A Study in Non-cooperation."

In the first article, Stokes put forward his trailblazing proposal that the national objective for India should be nothing short of complete independence from Britain and not self-government within the British Empire as envisaged earlier. "My own conviction is that this cannot be our ultimate objective. It may, or may not, be a stepping stone to it . . . Our self-respect should make it impossible for us to think of a perpetual partnership with such a group of nations as compose the British Empire."[6] To those who were working for the welfare of the country, the "ultimate goal must be absolute Swaraj and their immediate aim the elimination of those aspects of the British connection which make for racial prestige in the rulers and racial inferiority of Indians."

He was aware that some of the worthiest Indians still clung to the thought of an equal position for India within the Empire. They hoped that in a "new awakening of the world" the white races would outgrow their racial pride, but he urged them to dismiss the dream of a permanent connection as incompatible with India's fullest life. India could never be in reality an equal member of the Empire. "The colour prejudice of the Germans, British and Americans is too deep-rooted to justify any hope of a change in the near future. These races honestly believe in their innate superiority, and consider it their right and duty to control the destinies of mankind. It does not even occur to them that they have no right to forcibly exploit the resources of the world, or to compel all other nations to adapt their political and economic life to the requirements of Western industrialism." To him the conception of the British Empire, as a comity of equal nations, seemed quite impractical if the non-whites continued to be discriminated against and the white British subjects remained the privileged racial minority. "The idea is preposterous, a disgrace to those who propose it and an insult to those to whom it is proposed."

He maintained that his proposals were not disloyal. "The question of justice aside, the most profitable course for Great Britain in the long run is willingly to give India her independence, and to start preparing her for it at once." If Britain could make a declaration based not on how little she would have to give Indians, but on how much she could immediately transfer to them, it would immediately bring about a "wonderful change" in the relations between the two races.[7]

In his second and third articles, Stokes expressed his reservations about Gandhi's non-cooperation program and suggested an alternate solution. While admitting that Gandhi and his associates were attempting to strike at the root of the evils of injustice and iniquities, he was quite convinced that the application of the principle of non-cooperation, as contemplated, was only justified if there was no other way as "efficient and yet fraught with less danger."

The success of the non-cooperation movement depended solely on the growth of that spirit of discipline, which would make it possible for the masses to progress stage by stage and at each stage, only as far as Mahatma Gandhi dictated. Whether the masses would remain disciplined was doubtful, especially since the speeches of many leaders were calculated to stir up strong passions. "To me, the weakness in his programme lies in the fact that so few of those on whom he has to depend are imbued with his spirit," he wrote. "One fears that unless this movement of non-cooperation is carried out with the spirit of its great leader it will degenerate into mere unintelligent disorderliness. If it does, it may be the means of severing the British connection, but I doubt if it will bring us to the Swaraj we desire."[8]

Stokes also expressed his apprehensions about the possibility of the instant success of the non-cooperation movement. Indians as a people were not yet prepared to run the administration or to defend the nation against possible foreign aggression from India's more militant neighbors. (C. F. Andrews, Bipin Chandra Paul, and others had similar misgivings about the country's security.) Before the British connection was broken, it was important for India to evolve for itself the power of self-defense with which the British had so far failed to provide it. He believed, therefore, that it would be in the interest of the country to cooperate with the British government if it agreed to transfer the entire administration of the country to Indians within a stipulated period of time. In the meantime, the country should prepare itself to reach a position where it could defend itself without the help of British troops, and the people learn to act together and take a conscious and positive part in the effort to achieve a national life. Both were preconditions for making Swaraj a possibility.

To achieve this, Stokes outlined an action plan in which he proposed the use of reformed legislative councils and a system of vigilance committees. The vigilance committees would work in closest conjunction with nationalist elements in the councils, to force the will of the people upon the British element in government. They would stand in the same relation to their representatives in the assemblies that the big unions in England did with the Labor members in parliament, in bringing pressure on the legislative assemblies and for countering any attempt by the governor-in-council to obstruct measures considered by the Indian members to be essential to national welfare. The Indian nationalists in the councils would be in a position to call the people throughout the land to passive resistance and non-cooperation with the administration, by means of the vigilance committees in every province and district.

The local function of the vigilance committees would be to rectify the strained relationship existing between the British and Indians, and specifically between the people and local officials. Just as the government had divided the country into provinces, divisions, and districts for purposes of administration, the INC might appoint national, provincial, and district vigilance committees, and set them to work, carefully studying the problems, disabilities, and abuses prevailing in each locality. Members appointed to the committees would necessarily be responsible men prepared to do their duty faithfully. The vigilance committee would not directly concern itself with quarrels and disputes of individuals; private disputes would be settled in a court of law, or better still, in the local panchayat. One of the functions of the committees would also be to encourage the development of a panchayat system along the lines recommended by Mahatma Gandhi. The district vigilance committees would work toward building the self-respect and initiative of the people by showing them how to stand collectively and individually against injustice and imposition. They would help them through the panchayats to grow in capacity for future self-government. As champions of the people against all imposition and injustice, the committees would gain an influence which would make people willing to follow their advice should the leaders in councils request the people to exert pressure for the passage of some needed measure. This would also develop their capacity to cooperate with their leaders and their consciousness of a unity of interest in the national life.

Stokes was convinced that, in the face of such an organized coalition of the people and their leaders, any attempt on the part of the British official element in the councils to obstruct political progress of the country would be doomed to failure. "If the system is thoroughly developed on a nationwide basis, the government would never be able to carry through an unpopular measure like the Rowlatt Bills," he asserted.[9]

By now, Stokes was fully involved in the national movement and was the delegate from Kotgarh to the All India Congress which met at Nagpur in December 1920. It was to be his first Christmas away from home but this was something he could not avoid—he felt impelled to join the national forces, and hoped that his proposals would have a modifying influence upon the current thinking, and that his presence at the Congress might help to "partly deflect" events from the course which they were now taking. His political position and policy was "not all fours" with the policy of Gandhi, and therefore, he did not know exactly what reception it would meet at the hands of the extreme nationalists, but he believed that it offered an opportunity of helping the country.[10]

"The present state of affairs in India is such that I feel I must throw what influence I have upon the side of sane politics," he wrote to his mother. "As a nationalist, yet one who feels the need to keep our balance, I have a special responsibility. Feelings are running so high at this time that there are very few non-Indians who could obtain a hearing from Indians. Andrews is one and I am another. I know of no others in exactly the same position. Indians know that we are absolutely with India."[11]

The Nagpur session opened on a note of optimism. Non-cooperation had proved a success. The boycott of the elections to the legislative councils held on 20 November had been more than effective, with nearly two-thirds of voters abstaining. A large number of students boycotted schools and colleges. Motilal

Nehru gave up his law practice as did C. R. Das. Many senior Congress leaders who had differed with Gandhi three months earlier were now prepared to work with him. In the prevailing atmosphere there was little chance of support for Stokes' program. The Congress simply would not consider the use of the councils on any terms (though they did so subsequently when the Swaraj Party was formed).

However, the Nagpur Congress which voted for Swaraj was marked by a change in the Congress creed. While the old tenet of the Congress was attainment of self-government for India within the British Empire, the new creed omitted all reference to the British Empire and stated in its objective "the attainment of Swaraj by the people of India by all legitimate and peaceful means." Though this did not fully meet with Stokes' and Andrews' demand for complete Swaraj for India, and its total independence from Britain, it was a step toward that final goal which made it possible for the two friends, who were the most important votaries for absolute independence for India, and its complete break from the British Empire at the time, to accept the resolution of the Nagpur Congress. Gandhi himself believed that there was room in the resolution for both, "those who believe that by retaining the British connection we can purify ourselves and purify the British people, and those who have no such belief."[12]

The resolution was adopted unanimously. While Stokes supported the creed in its revised form and agreed upon the main issues involved, he still differed in his views as to the best method of achieving them. He was not convinced that Gandhi's plan of non-cooperation with the administration was the right action at the moment. "I have argued with him (Gandhi) by the hour," he said after the Nagpur Congress, "but can no more convince him than he does me."[13]

Not only did Stokes believe in a totally different line of action which included the use of legislative assemblies, but he also believed that the Congress should take up issues like begar to fight the government. This conviction had grown as his fight against begar in the Kotgarh ilaqa progressed. The begar struggle in Kotgarh was a test of Stokes' political beliefs. The experiment was proving successful—the relationship between the people and the government had improved; the just demands of the people had been met and the principle of non-cooperation used effectively but briefly, and only when its use had become imperative. Begar was an issue, he tried to convince Gandhi, which would lead the Congress to certain victory. "To me it is one of the key questions, and if only Gandhi had made his point of attack upon the evils of the relations between the people and the government, I have not the slightest doubt he would have been far more successful than he was," he reflected. Andrews endorsed Stokes' views. "For the cause [begar] is one which if successful is certain to help forward Indian freedom and independence," he wrote.[14]

But despite such reservations, Stokes finally chose to support Gandhi. The shift in his attitude was not only because of a change in the Congress creed but also because Gandhi's program appeared to be succeeding and there was no other feasible alternative to it. Once he reached that conclusion, he tried to resolve any differences with Gandhi in private.

Stokes was now very much in the limelight. His articles had aroused considerable interest, with Gandhi himself responding with an editorial, "One Step Enough for Me," in his *Young India* of 29 December 1920. "He has adopted India as his home. He is watching the non-cooperation movement from the Kotagiri hills where he is living in isolation from the India of the plains," Gandhi wrote. He did not think Stokes' apprehensions about foreign aggression were justified. He refused to contemplate the "dismal outlook," stating that if the movement succeeded through nonviolent non-cooperation, "the English will go as friends and under a well-ordered agreement as between partners . . . I do not believe that the English will leave in 'a night.'"

While the program suggested by Stokes did not itself attract much attention, his contention that the ultimate goal for India must lie outside the British Empire generated a debate. He was one of the first nationalists to advocate such a view. His assertion was called into question by a number of moderate journals and when, sometime later, he wrote "The Failure of European Civilization as a World Culture," to elaborate and document his earlier theory, there was an incredible interest in the subject. The essay was published in full by all important English and vernacular nationalist newspapers throughout the country, as well as brought out as a booklet in English and in other languages.

"I am moved by no feeling of animosity against the race of my fathers. Indeed, I have been motivated only by my loyalty to the larger interests of mankind," Stokes wrote while describing the despairing situation as far as race relations were concerned by giving a number of examples, documentation, and quotations from the *Encyclopedia of Religion and Fables, Cambridge Modern History, Encyclopedia of Religion and Ethics,* and other sources. "Is it not a farce to talk of her (India) attaining to the position of *an equal partner* in the comity of nations known as the British Empire? . . . The British Empire and the United States are completely committed to this policy of shutting up the peoples of Asia and Africa within their own borders, while they populate at their leisure all vacant habitable areas with their own people . . . Can India afford to be permanently associated with a political unit which, with the United States, stands above all others committed to a policy of racial segregation upon the basis of colour? If the answer is in the negative, then surely it is useless for us to talk about our goal as being self-government within the British Empire."

Stokes' essay with a long biographical introduction by Andrews received much publicity. "His object is to show the absolute impossibility of India remaining with self-respect within the British Empire as it now stands," wrote the *Modern Review,* while commenting on the article and added tellingly, "He has every right to speak of Indians as 'we' as he constantly does in this book."[15]

The Nagpur Congress brought Stokes into the mainstream of Indian politics and, for the next few years, he remained fully involved in the country's freedom struggle. In a letter of 5 March 1921, he wrote, "I could take as prominent a part in the politics of this land as I desire to do, as I have the confidence of those Indians who are the most active. But to tell the truth I am more of a philosopher than a politician, and it is only when the dictates of my philosophy impel me to take a part that I reluctantly leave those things which to me are of far greater interest. I do hope that I shall shortly feel able to leave such questions alone."[16]

In May, when Lord Reading, the newly appointed Viceroy, accorded interviews to Pandit Madan Mohan Malaviya, C. F. Andrews, S. E. Stokes, and Mahatma Gandhi at Simla, it made news of national significance. "There are not four other men in India today of loftier character, nobler principles and with more distinguished a record," wrote the *Indian Social Reformer.* "They are all men of ideals, who place the spiritual above the temporal, and who are animated by the highest hopes for India, not for herself but for the sake of humanity . . . It is, in our view, a thing to be grateful for, that the highest representative of the sovereign has seen fit to take counsel with men of this type and calibre. We are especially glad that Lord Reading has so early in his career put himself in touch with Mr Andrews and Mr Stokes. They are living proofs of the falsity of the dictum, which has done an immense amount of mischief, that East and West are fundamentally irreconcilable. These two men, and several others less prominently known, have shown and are showing that there is another side of Western civilization and culture than that which happens to be most visible to India."[17]

Stokes was pleased with the report. "I am proud to have a Hindu paper speak of me in this way," he wrote to his mother. "It will give you an idea of the place I have, under God, been able to win in the hearts of the people I love, and though of course I am not worthy of the opinion they have of me there is no doubt that at a time when the Indians are so bitter against the West it is a matter of pride to have so won their confidence."[18]

THE FIGHT CONTINUES

Meanwhile, the struggle against begar again received a setback when A. Langley, the deputy commissioner at Simla, who wanted to settle the issue amicably, was transferred. He was replaced by M. S. Williamson, a much less sympathetic official whose one ambition seemed to be to "defeat" the people of Kotgarh and who seemed to think that the government's prestige would suffer from the acceptance of even their most just demands. His unreasonable attitude only cemented the people's unity and increased their determination.

By now the whole begar-bearing section of the community had placed the issue in the hands of the Kotgarh Panchayat and vowed to abide by its decision. On 7 March 1921, the Panchayat appointed a special committee to carry on all correspondence with the authorities on the subject. The seven-member Kotgarh *Begar* Panchayat Committee chosen from the contiguous areas of Kotgarh, Bhuti, and Kepu pledged to work together to put an end to the "unwarranted" forms of begar then prevalent in the ilaqa using every justifiable means.

Although he was prepared for a confrontation, Stokes was anxious that the issue be settled without becoming an "open contest" between the authorities and the ilaqa. "We are absolutely prepared for it, but the *begar* question is widely ramified and it would seem to me that it would not be opportune to settle the matter in that way." He felt certain that an open struggle would bring more struggles within a month, and being the result of definite hardship it would be far more real to those who took part in them than such faraway matters as the Khilafat or Swaraj. Begar and rasad were things which the most ignorant understood from bitter experience, and the unanimity with which they would join in an organized attempt to repudiate them would be as spontaneous as the struggle of the Indians in South Africa some years ago. There was already widespread interest in the issue. Stokes had received letters from a score of localities where the people were only awaiting a lead and were more than prepared to follow.[1]

"I am going to do my part to end the system," he wrote to Williamson on 7 March 1921, "but I am anxious that it should end as a result of the government's putting an immediate stop to it rather than as a result of a stand-up fight against the government all over India, over a matter in which justice would be on the other side. I do not think that such a struggle, if it is at all possible to avoid it, would be the best thing for us at this juncture. The only worst thing would be for us to submit any longer to *begar*."* He expressed the same opinion to Langley who was now in Lahore and on whose help he counted: "My own feeling is that the government frankly acknowledging that *begar* has been an unjustifiable development, should announce of its own accord that it has put an end to it. This would be the most graceful way, and I assure you that the trouble of forcing us to keep it up will be infinitely greater than the inconvenience of immediately making other arrangements."[2]

When there was no announcement by the government regarding the abolition of begar by spring, a reminder was sent to the deputy commissioner in Simla. It was ignored. When a further deadline passed without any response, the people of Kotgarh called off all forms of begar they had objected to in their earlier notice of 26 August 1920. There was great enthusiasm in the villages as farmers rallied behind Stokes, pledging to stand together and to furnish funds that might be needed for the defense of those who might be charged by the authorities. Passions ran high and many people took an oath in the village temple to support the cause, an oath that no Pahari would "dare to go back upon." The quiet hill villagers, described not so long ago as "simple-minded, orderly people, truthful in character and submissive to authority so that they scarcely required to be ruled," were now aroused to fight for their "rights as men."

At the end of March 1921, Stokes rushed to Dehra Dun to address a conference on begar. He spoke at length about the people's struggle and the steps he proposed to take to ensure their victory. While the conference gave him yet another opportunity to meet Andrews and exchange views with Indian leaders, it brought him under greater surveillance by the government which by now was keeping a close watch on all his activities. But this did not deter him. Doing away with begar was not merely a question of making things easier for those who suffered from it; it was a "matter of principle." He was convinced that it was "an impediment to the growth of the people in manliness and self-respect that such

---

* Stokes refuted Williamson's position that the people were bound by the clauses in the *Wajib-ul-Arz*. The *Wajib-ul-Arz* had no provision for giving sanads of exemption to zamindars, and yet without consulting the wishes of the remainder upon whom the burden would fall, more than fifty sanads had been granted since the Settlement. He claimed that the burden on the people was now not the burden about which the clause in the *Wajib-ul-Arz* was written and any reference to it in consequence was not relevant.

a relationship should exist between them and those who govern them. We see that in the working it gives all sorts of underlings the constant opportunity to insult and impose upon our people and we hold that while it continues no real growth in the only qualities worth having is possible."[3]

Knowing that his mother would be anxious, he tried to keep her fully informed of the situation. In a letter of early March, he wrote, "As you know I am neither a Socialist, in the accepted sense of the word, nor an Anarchist nor a Bolshevik. At the same time I have been brought up to expect fair play, and I should consider myself a traitor to my ideals if I did not take the stand I am taking now quite irrespective of personal consequences . . . Though everything is possible, I am not inclined to think that the government will dare arrest me upon this issue. I have placed my ground so high that such action upon their part would imply a terrible moral bankruptcy in political matters."[4]

He was also very confident of his stand and assured her that he was fighting on an "absolutely constitutional subject—impressed labour," and the strongest weapon he could think of using was that of passive resistance. "This is one which our ancestors have used in the past for the sake of their ideals," he wrote. "I should indeed consider that if I sat supinely to endure such a system I would be untrue to those of our family who came before me. But we shall win by enduring, not by force."[5]

In early April, Williamson came to Kotgarh along with the divisional forest officer with the aim of finding ways of maintaining the old system. The people of Kotgarh had completely stopped giving begar and kar and the officials were forced to re-open negotiations. Initially they tried intimidating the people into giving in. The villagers were ready for such a contingency and despite all efforts the officials could not influence them. The strike against kar was so effective that the staff accompanying the two officers had to gather wood and fetch water themselves.[6] After many rounds of discussions and long arguments the issue was finally resolved, and a "memo" of the terms of contract agreed upon by the Kotgarh Panchayat and the deputy commissioner was drawn up.[7]

But the final settlement of the issue was stalled when, a few days later, Williamson expressed his reluctance to comply with the contract clause limiting the number of coolies for an officer on duty and the subordinates accompanying him to six. Stokes, however, was not prepared to make any compromises and replied in his usual candid manner that while the people were prepared to accept their responsibility to see that the administration did not suffer due to lack of resources, they were not prepared to admit the government's right to any begar at all. Their position was that though there were situations when the ilaqa should recognize its responsibility to furnish men, such situations did not exist when other means of transportation were available. Negotiating on behalf of the people, Stokes insisted that the number of coolies for an official on duty and the subordinates accompanying him would be limited to six. "A man should never be forced to take the place of a mule when a mule will do just as well. People had been prepared to assume the responsibility up to six coolies, because this would be less than two mule-loads, and one mule would not travel alone. Above six coolies, mules could take the place of coolies, and the justification for impressed labour would cease to exist. Above this we would consider it to be *begar* in the most offensive sense of the word; below that we can look upon it as a responsibility which any self-respecting man could assume."[8]

In a letter of 28 April, Stokes warned the deputy commissioner that the people were firm in their resolve to give no begar to anyone at all after 20th May, unless the government treated them as a self-respecting community. "Unless you can see your way to meet our very reasonable wishes, we shall have to fall back upon the position taken in the representation of August 26th of last year—that we shall refuse to give unless you can prove your right in a court of law to impress the people. We are quite prepared to have you attempt it. Of course in the event we should hold ourselves free to make use of every fair and legitimate aid that public opinion could afford us in the Punjab and elsewhere."

But the officials continued to dither and Stokes became more suspicious of their intentions. Another meeting with Williamson in Simla on 10 May proved fruitless. Stokes was determined to persuade the Punjab government to resolve the issue. The following day was an unusually eventful one for him. In the morning, he had an interview with the Viceroy, Lord Reading, and explained the begar system to him. In the afternoon, he met Gandhi who had arrived in Simla only that morning and apprised him of the situation in the hills. In the evening, he met J. D. Boyd, the revenue secretary in charge of the begar question with whom he had worked in the Kangra earthquake more than fifteen years earlier.

In a final bid to reach an amicable solution, Stokes wrote a detailed letter to Boyd on his return to Kotgarh, describing it as the "last act in an effort to co-operate with the government upon an issue in which justice is absolutely on our side." He reiterated the position of the farmers. "Beyond that minimum absolutely necessary to make administration practical, self-respect forbids us to submit to *begar* (paid or unpaid for) any longer . . . When we have given you a practical constructive solution of a difficult problem, are you prepared to treat us like self-respecting people and enter into an agreement with us or must you order us in order to maintain your prestige?"[9] Wanting to preserve the dignity of the people, Stokes also insisted that the new arrangement between the government and the people should be in the form of a "compact" and not as "orders or concessions."

The tug of war with the government finally ended in early June when the superintendent of the hill states accepted almost all the terms proposed by Stokes. The only point of contention remaining was the condescending language in which the official agreement was framed and which Stokes sought to change. This was finally conceded and on 6 June Williamson wrote to Stokes, "There is very little difference between the eight clauses of my draft and the nine of yours, and if the panchayat really considers yours are better I will accept them."

Lately, Stokes had also been keeping indifferent health. A medical checkup revealed ulceration of the stomach and he was ordered several weeks' rest. But rest and relaxation were yet a long way away, for even before the Kotgarh struggle had concluded he was drawn into the people's agitation against begar in the neighboring hill state of Keonthal.

Peasants in other hill states bore a greater burden of begar than their counterparts in Kotgarh, for they were obliged to give begar to their local chief as well as to the British administrators. A considerable part of their labor was also unpaid for. The states had steadily increased their exaction under begar irrespective of the terms of the *Wajib-ul-Arz*. In a number of areas there seemed now to be no assigned limit to the number of days of free labor demanded from the people, "the only standard apparently being the measure of its requirements." In the smaller states where the chiefs cultivated the land themselves, the demand for free labor included not only the service of the men, but also that of women and children. The men here were required to plow the fields of the chief with their own oxen; their families were required to help in the hoeing of potatoes and maize as well as in the harvesting of crops. They were also responsible for cutting grass for the chief's cattle and for collecting pine needles needed for cattle-beds. All this labor involved more than three months of working days for one member of each household. Moreover, the labor had to be given to the chief when he demanded it, which always coincided with the time when farmers needed to plow or sow their own land. As a result, the farmers' fields suffered year after year from neglect at crucial times.[10]

The hardships endured by the people were more or less the same in all the Simla hill states, varying only in degree. Farmers in these states had, therefore, watched with the deepest interest the people of Kotgarh fight their way to victory against begar. If the Kotgarh farmer could fight the all-powerful British government, they felt they could at least attempt to seek justice from their chiefs. In early June, people of Keonthal under the leadership of Munshi Kapur Singh, a spirited young man, who had been Stokes' assistant when Stokes was a recruiting officer, organized themselves to put up a fight against begar. Like the people of Kotgarh, they planned to first petition the authorities and if no action was taken, they planned to go on strike. The leaders did not intend to offer any active resistance but they were arrested and imprisoned without warning. Soon after, an excited crowd broke down the lock-up and rescued them. This action led to the induction of a large police force into the state and more arrests aimed at intimidating the people.

Kapur Singh's associates immediately sought Stokes' help. He was tired and weak from his recent illness but now once again felt "compelled to stand in opposition to the will of the Punjab government."[11] The arrest of villagers and the repression of people made him angry and his immediate reaction was to proceed to Keonthal and start a "general strike against all *begar*." In an "Open Letter to the Viceroy" he stated the people's position and warned the government of his own intentions: "I can see now but one path of honour. We must refuse cooperation, until justice has been done."[12]

He was dissuaded from going ahead with his plans by Pandit Madan Mohan Malaviya, who was then in Simla and who strongly felt that it would be better to first give the authorities a "chance to do justice themselves." It was then decided that the people's position should be again put before the administration "respectfully and frankly," and if in spite of this no action was taken Stokes should go ahead with his plan and organize a complete strike from all begar.[13]

Knowing that "direct action" might become necessary in the hills, Stokes wanted his position to be "impregnable" so that in any eventuality it could be pointed out that "the authorities were given both time and the fullest opportunity to set things right." During the following days he tried every means to attain justice for the poor peasants. In response to his letters to the Viceroy he was told that he should put the matter before the governor of Punjab before the Viceroy "could with propriety take cognizance of it." However, Lord Reading did inform Stokes that he had "inquired" from the governor of Punjab what was being done in the matter.[14]

In an interview with Edward Maclagan, the governor of Punjab, Stokes stated in no uncertain terms that it was the duty of the government to release those in prison and immediately settle the question of begar to the satisfaction of the people. He was not making an appeal, he said, but simply stating the people's position as he was most anxious that no one should be able, subsequently, to assert that the government had not been given an opportunity to execute justice and sympathy through ordinary channels.[15] He then had a long talk with Sher Singh, naib tehsildar of Fagu and manager of Keonthal State, at whose instigation the arrests had been made, and suggested to him ways of solving the problem without "sacrificing either justice or the izzat [respect] of the durbar." Finally, in a meeting between the deputy commissioner of Simla, Williamson, who was also the head of the Court of Wards in charge of the management of Keonthal State, and Pandit Madan Mohan Malaviya, it was urged that the question should be looked upon from the larger perspective of "elementary justice and sympathy with an ignorant and much tried people." However, he did not trust the administration. "There are lots and lots of words, but mercy in its true sense seems a lost art to this government and its subordinates," Stokes wrote to Agnes after his meeting with the governor and others.[16]

Determined to leave no stone unturned in his efforts to get the authorities to act justly, Stokes had made plans to organize a big protest throughout the area where repression was actively practiced. "It may fail or it may succeed," he said, "but we will at least have shown that we are not prepared to sit supinely by while our comrades are being unjustly imprisoned."[17] "Don't worry about me for a moment," he wrote to his mother, "You see, you brought an idealist into the world and must bear the consequences. After all, we know that in the old days knights went out to right wrongs and protect the defenceless. In our days it is not done in the same way; we have no swords or armour but the duty remains to us. We may not be knights but I hope that we are gentlemen; there still is a road of honour."[18]

Meanwhile, in a series of public meetings, Stokes continued to draw attention to the iniquities of begar and the injustice of the recent arrests. Mahatma Gandhi's four-day visit to Simla a month earlier had aroused "unprecedented enthusiasm" in the town's Indian population. Public meetings addressed by Mahatma Gandhi, Lala Lajpat Rai, and Madan Mohan Malaviya drew large crowds. It was the first time that nationalist issues were addressed to the people of Simla. Local issues also gained importance and begar in particular came to be viewed in the national perspective.

On 26 June 1921, Stokes addressed a large public gathering in Simla. Speaking in chaste Hindi he condemned the arrests of Kapur Singh and others who were protesting against the system of forced labor in the hills. "No hill man with any sense of honour could submit quietly to this act of repression."[19] In another crowded public meeting three days later, he declared that if the state authorities did not settle the case of Munshi Kapur Singh, the Simla public would take the matter in hand and would see that "justice was wrenched out of the unwilling."[20]

It was more than a month since the arrest of Kapur Singh and his associates and still no charges had been brought against them. There were reports that witnesses were being "terrorized and tutored" to ensure prosecution of the accused.[21] Consequently, the agitation intensified and many prominent leaders took an active interest in it. Madan Mohan Malaviya extended his stay in Simla and Lala Lajpat Rai offered to come up and help if needed. Andrews came to Simla again to render what help he could.

The papers were full of news about the agitation and Stokes was gratified to see the widespread public response it had evoked in the hills as well as the plains, and the assurances of support he received from every quarter. On the evening of 10 July, at a crowded public meeting of more than 5,000 people presided by Pandit Madan Mohan Malaviya, at Edwards Ganj in Simla, Stokes spoke passionately on the begar issue. A resolution presented by him placing on record the deep sympathy of the people of Simla with Munshi Kapur Singh and his associates was passed and a pledge taken to work by every "legitimate and peaceful means to secure their early restoration to liberty."[22]

Stokes also had the support of Gandhi, who sympathized with those who were arrested. On 16 July Gandhi wrote to him: "I do not mind a bit if even you have to go to jail. But the poor leader who has been arrested must be set at large or the government must be prepared to imprison you all."[23] In mid-August Gandhi sent a special message to the people of the Simla Hill states, urging them to support those who were in jail:

> You should continue with your struggle under the guidance of Stokes and suspend all kar and *begar* to the government and to the States till your compatriots remain in prison. It is much better for you to undergo hardships and be ready to fill jails for the sake of your faith [dharma] than to give *begar* to any official. Remember that, if on this occasion you prove unworthy, you will perpetuate your slavery and for all time to come you shall continue to be treated as slaves. In your efforts I am with you with all my heart and soul.[24]

The message printed in Hindi was circulated widely.

Stokes intended to discuss the situation with Gandhi at the impending meeting of the All India Congress Committee (AICC) in Bombay. If Kapur Singh and the others jailed with him were set free without fine or security, then he would return quietly to his home, if not then he would attempt to bring all begar to a standstill in the hills. He knew that he could be prosecuted and possibly imprisoned by the British. He hoped not; nor did he think that the Punjab government would go that far. "But if so it can't be helped. For an Indian nationalist these days the path of honour sometimes leads through such difficulties."[25] To his wife he wrote, "It is for right and justice that I am fighting, and I shall take no account of victories or defeats. As the motto goes 'Brave because in the right,' I shall go ahead."[26]

Praising Stokes' efforts to free the hillmen from the tyranny of begar, Gandhi wrote in *Young India:*

> If proof were wanted that the movement of non-cooperation is neither anti-British nor anti-Christian, we have the instance of Mr Stokes, a nationalized

British subject and staunch Christian, devoting his all to the eradication of the evil of *begar* . . . No Indian is giving such a battle to the government as Mr Stokes. He has become the veritable guide, philosopher and friend of the hill men. The reader should know that *begar* is going on under the shadow of Simla, under the Viceroy's nose as it were. And yet Lord Reading is powerless to remedy the mischief. I have no doubt that he is willing enough. But he cannot carry the district officers and others with him.[27]

A lead editorial, "Forced Labour," published in the *Bombay Chronicle,* praised Andrews' and Stokes' effort in drawing attention to the "imperative necessity of putting an end to a system that perpetuates all the horrors of old-time slavery and serfdom without their compensating advantages."[28]

After three months of as intense a struggle as Stokes had ever experienced, the issue was finally resolved. Kapur Singh and his colleagues were released and the official responsible for their arrest removed from service. Stokes was also able to obtain from the administration a full and satisfactory settlement of the begar issue in the entire Simla district.[29] An official communiqué published by the Punjab government shortly afterwards stated, "In view of the complaints made regarding abuse of *begar* or paid statutory labour on Hindustan-Tibet road between Simla and Bushair, the government undertook last winter a complete revision of the existing system on that road. So far as the British territory of Kotgarh is concerned, the use of *begar* has been practically abolished, government officers on duty alone being entitled to secure coolies on *begar* system and that only on a very restricted scale. Similar arrangements have been nearly completed as regards the stage of road which lie in State Territory."[30]

Andrews' prediction on his return from Kotgarh the previous autumn, "Perhaps it is not too sanguine to expect that the death-knell of *begar* has already been sounded in the hills," had come true.[31]

On 3 September, Stokes wrote to his mother, "This is a vindication of my trust that one determined man can fight a government and make it give up if the cause is a just one."[32]

According to Sham Sukh, a land owner of Shatla village, Stokes' biggest contribution to hill society was his fight against begar. "People had to work for a whole month as *begarees*. I have myself lifted loads up to Narkanda as a *begaree* and received four annas for it," he said. "Stokes freed us from this burden. He used to say, 'I am only working for the good of the people.'"

IN KHADI

On 31 July 1921, a surging crowd of humanity wended its way toward the Sohani maidan in Parel, Bombay. They came on foot, by tram, by train, or any other conveyance. By evening there was not an inch of unoccupied space within a half-mile radius of the maidan. The gathering was "unsurpassed in recent memory."

Prominent nationalists had assembled to pay homage to Lokmanya Tilak, one of the country's greatest leaders and the fearless proclaimer of "Swaraj is my birthright," on the very ground where he had been cremated a year before. It was also the first anniversary of the non-cooperation movement, a major plank of which was discarding all foreign clothing and wearing khadi on all occasions. Gandhi had decided to commemorate Tilak's death anniversary with the biggest ever bonfire of foreign clothing at Bombay. The clothes collected by volunteers—foreign-made caps, hats, costly coats and trousers, embroidered vests, bright-colored saris and umbrellas—were now piled in heaps a few paces away from the dais. Thousands of people watched as Gandhi lit the bonfire, commencing the nation's "final stage in its march towards Swaraj."

Foreigners had been warned to keep away from such public gatherings, but Stokes, who had come to Bombay to attend the meeting of the All India Congress Committee, was not only witness to the event, his own Western garments were in the flames that leapt up into the sky. "He [Stokes] and an English nurse were the only two Westerners on the platform which was surrounded by more than three lakh men and women," Gandhi informed Andrews.[1] Stokes was dressed in a white coat and dhoti and wore a Gandhi cap, all made of khadi. He had decided to wear only khadi thereafter. "It is a very comfortable kapra [cloth]," he wrote to his family in Kotgarh.[2]

Gandhi had launched the swadeshi movement with the aim of persuading Indian people to burn all foreign-made clothing and to start spinning and weaving in their homes for their own clothes. The policy of sending India's raw materials to England to be returned as manufactured goods at vastly increased costs was progressively draining India of the little wealth now left in it. For Gandhi, a complete rejection of all foreign clothing was the only way this "bleeding of the country" could be stopped. But the issue was clouded in controversy. While there was general agreement among the nationalists of the necessity of discarding foreign cloth, there was disagreement about burning it. Dissenters argued that India should build up her own textile industry to the point where foreign cloth would automatically become dispensable. Moreover, they said, why burn foreign clothing when it could be given away to the needy?*

Stokes, though, had been quick to see the significance of Gandhi's campaign. By insisting on the burning of foreign clothing and the weaving of indigenous cloth, Gandhi was not only ensuring the country's independence from England for her textile requirements, but he was also ensuring the common man's independence from expensive cloth manufactured in Indian mills.

Two days after the bonfire at Parel, a party of four left Bombay for an extensive tour of the United Provinces to propagate the burning of foreign clothing and of wearing swadeshi. The party was led by Mahatma Gandhi, and his companions were Maulana Azad Subani, Maulana Mohamed Ali, and Samuel Stokes.

The ten-day tour of Aligarh, Bareilly, Moradabad, Lucknow, Kanpur, and Allahabad was a memorable one for Stokes, and one which brought him closer to Gandhi and to the heart of India. The journey was marked throughout by scenes of extraordinary enthusiasm. Whenever the train stopped there was a howling crowd around their carriage. Thousands of people greeted the small group wherever it went. Many came from distant villages. Some had camped by the roadside for days, in rain and sun, to catch a glimpse of the leaders. In cities, "verandahs were crowded and streets were packed to overflowing. Vehicles in which the visitors travelled were covered deeply with flowers, constantly showered on them,"[3] and the appeal to "discard Bideshi" (lit. of a foreign country) was met everywhere by an immediate response in the form of showers of imported caps, turbans, and other apparel. Women organized meetings in each town and cheerfully donated their jewelry and money to the national cause. "The whole country is aroused and I think we are certainly upon the verge of great happenings," Stokes wrote to Agnes on 4 August.

Their schedule was hectic—they traveled by night and worked by day. Be-

* Attempts at swadeshi (lit. of one's country) had been made by Swami Dayanand in 1878 and in Bengal in 1905 but neither was successful. At that time people were asked to wear swadeshi clothes made in Indian mills but not necessarily of Indian yarn. This did not have a major impact because it was the yarn that generated the most income. Gandhi wanted his followers to wear khaddar, i.e., cloth made in India of swadeshi yarn, and he wanted every man, woman, and child to spin. (Lala Lajpat's speech at Lahore on 13 August 1921, *The Tribune,* 17 August 1921)

sides two to three public meetings at each stop, there were meetings with Congress and Khilafat workers. Consultations were held with local leaders and merchants, and visits were made to schools and to homes for destitute women. There were stirring speeches by the leaders. For Stokes it was a new experience. Sharing the platform with Mahatma Gandhi and the two Maulanas at each meeting, Stokes impressed the audience with his deep convictions—expressed in a language they understood. The main thrust of his speeches was unity and support for Gandhi, a strict obedience of the Congress program, and restraint at each step.

At Aligarh, their first halt, Stokes emphasized the need for unity at all costs. Whatever the differences of opinion might be as regards details, it was necessary to strengthen the hands of Mahatma Gandhi whose personality was, without doubt, the most important political factor in India. "To weaken his influence by divided counsels would be madness," he said. At a crowded meeting at Amin-ud-Daula Park in Lucknow he declared that "nothing less than divine purpose could bring together upon a common platform people of such widely differing views"[4] as Mahatmaji, Maulana Mohamed Ali, and himself. The one thing which united them was the "deep conviction that Mahatma Gandhi had been chosen to show the people the true road to Swaraj." In Kanpur he congratulated the people for their spirit of order and restraint during Gandhi's visit to the city. The first step toward real Swaraj was self-control, he said—"Swaraj over one's feeling and emotions."[5] Allahabad's prominent daily, the *Leader*, noted how Stokes always appeared on the platform wearing the dress of the country and described him as a "youngish looking man, fair, with clear-cut features . . . very vigorous in his addresses to the people, speaking fluently in the vernacular and holding their attention with ease."[6]

The tour concluded on 10 August at Allahabad with a mass meeting held in the grounds of Pandit Motilal Nehru's residence, the Swaraj Bhawan. It was marked by a huge bonfire of foreign clothing to which Motilal Nehru and Jawaharlal Nehru alone contributed more than a thousand costly articles. "I had a nice time with Stokes," Gandhi wrote to Andrews soon after the tour.[7]

The tours and speeches did not end for Stokes as he bade farewell to Gandhi at Allahabad. He had promised Lala Lajpat Rai, with whom he had traveled to Bombay, that he would visit him in Lahore before returning to the hills. Even though he longed for the quiet of his home he now proceeded to Lahore.

During the next ten days he and Lala Lajpat Rai traveled throughout Punjab addressing large crowds in Lahore, Amritsar, and Ambala. While Stokes was a familiar name to the people of Punjab through his writings, this was the first time he was addressing them in person. They were astonished to see him dressed as other nationalists, in khadi and with a Gandhi cap, and whenever he rose to speak there were shouts of "*Bande Matram*" and "Mahatma Gandhi *ki jai*." His speeches in "eloquent Hindustani" won the hearts of the people, the *Tribune* reported.[8] Wherever he spoke, Stokes stressed the importance of following the instructions of Mahatma Gandhi. Describing his travels with Gandhi in the United Provinces, he said that Mahatmaji had great confidence in his followers and it was on their strength that he had determined to secure Swaraj within the next four months. It rested with his followers to make his words come true, and thus give force to his character.[9] He also talked of how the "life and soul of Mahatmaji were bound up in the longing for a Free India," and how failure to attain it would break his heart. "His life is in our hands because upon our loyalty and obedience depends the attainment of that which alone makes life worth living to our leader."[10]

On 16 August 1921, Stokes and Lala Lajpat Rai visited the Golden Temple in Amritsar. Later, they spoke at a large meeting attended by more than 12,000 people at Jallianwala Bagh. In a fiery speech Stokes denounced the Jallianwala Bagh massacre and the atrocities of martial law. When he finished speaking there were resounding shouts of "*Sat Sri Akal.*"[11]

Stokes' plans of returning home were put off from day to day. "I had the greatest trouble in getting away from the plains," he wrote to Agnes when he finally reached Kasauli on 19 August. "Everywhere I spoke, people wanted to take me to other cities." Though he was very tired and wanted more than anything else to be with his family, he could not make any definite plans about returning home. Now that he had plunged into the national struggle he was not sure if he would be able to stay quietly at home.

During this period, Stokes had also been reflecting upon how the swadeshi movement would help the people in his hill ilaqas. They were so poor that purchasing cloth was a financial burden for them. At the same time, no peasant family had full-time work on its hands all through the year. Agriculture involved periods of heavy work alternating with periods of comparative idleness. During these idle periods there was ample opportunity for each family not only to spin all the thread that it would need to clothe itself, but even in excess of its own requirement. The same was true of all other farming families in other parts of the country. Gandhi's program, if followed faithfully, would clearly solve the problem of clothing for Indians and Stokes decided to initiate it in his ilaqa.

Subsequently, in Kotgarh, the Stokes family burned all their foreign clothing in a big bonfire on the grounds of Harmony Hall. Logs of wood were gathered and fine suits, saris, and military uniforms were emptied out of boxes and cupboards and piled on a wooden pyre. Then Stokes' eldest son, eight-year-old Prem Chand, lit the fire.[12] It was indeed a "sacrificial fire" as Gandhi called it, for in it were thrown all the precious and sentimental possessions of the family, all but the children's hand-knitted sweaters made by their grandmother. "They did not come from America," Stokes assured his mother, "they came from love-land."

For Stokes the change in dress was to continue and he hardly ever wore Western clothes again. He only wore khadi spun by his wife, and wore out his clothes to the last, preferring to put a patch on them rather than discard them easily. He also took to spinning every day. And while he was completely at ease in Indian clothes, the English who saw him in his new attire "almost had a fit."[13]

He was now a firm supporter of Gandhi. Whatever differences of opinion he had with Gandhi about the best course of action for the nationalists were put aside and he urged others to do the same. His unconditional support for Gandhi surprised many, especially since he had previously outlined a different application of the principles of non-cooperation.

He had valid reasons for his stance. It was evident that a showdown between the government and the INC could not be long postponed and he felt that the only possible hope of such a struggle ending successfully for the nationalist cause lay in securing absolute unity of action and policy during the coming months. Consequently, he had begun—both in conversations with fellow Congressmen and in the press—to advocate the necessity for unity of command, and absolute unquestioning obedience during the approaching crisis, irrespective of differences of opinion with Mahatmaji as to the lines upon which the struggle should be carried out. "It is our duty at this juncture to prove to the government that Mahatmaji has India at his back, and that India is prepared to follow him step by step."[14]

In two important articles, "Unity Our Supreme Duty" and "Our Duty," published in the *Tribune* of Lahore and the *Bombay Chronicle* respectively, he suggested that Mahatma Gandhi should be appointed "Dictator" by the Congress and given absolute and unquestioning obedience for the period of the struggle that lay just ahead. While he considered permanent dictatorship a hateful thing, as a Republican he favored such appointments for a brief period in a specific crisis in public affairs, but not as a normal form of government—"At times of supreme crisis such a course is vitally essential . . . dictatorship meets the need of a crisis; when that has been passed, the sooner it gives place to responsible government the better." He did not think that an absolute adherence to one person in times of crises was necessarily subversive of the spirit of true democracy. "Roman republic was not less republic because it appointed a dictator upon occasions. In war too unity of command made for strength; many a campaign had been ruined through the refusal to put the supreme command in the hands of the most worthy."[15]

Stokes' views were not well received. The *Indian Social Reformer* was not satisfied with the virtual dictatorship then held by Mahatma Gandhi. C. Y. Chin-tamani, the editor of the *Leader* who strongly opposed Gandhi's non-cooperation and civil disobedience program considered Stokes' advice "ill-calculated." "The course of man-worship has lain heavily upon India and we cannot but look with grave disapproval upon any proposal to perpetuate it in a political garb."[16]

During his Punjab tour, when Stokes was asked how he found it possible to give his entire adherence to Mahatmaji, Stokes' reply was that there were vari-ous stages in a campaign but at the time of actual struggle "unity of action" was of *vital* necessity. "We are face to face with a bureaucracy which *acts as one man* when dealing with our demands . . . So must we, if we desire not to fail ig-nominiously in our aspiration of Swaraj . . . At this time, therefore, when unity of action is our most vital need, we should look upon the personality of Gandhi as our greatest national asset. About him, and him alone, can we pivot the unity of nationalist effort and aspiration at this juncture. He is, as it were, the living embodiment of that aspiration. In strengthening him we strengthen the capacity of the nation to enforce its demands."[17]

His own views on Gandhi, Stokes admitted, had undergone a change during the previous year. "Gradually, as I grope my way from old conventional modes of thought towards the meaning and significance of his conceptions and methods, I become more and more convinced that the movement which he has initiated calls to the deepest and noblest in our nature. It is that old call to victory by the path of utter self-renunciation, to purification by the path of self-sacrifice. There is no greater. The question is not whether his message is worthy of India, but whether we are worthy of his message." In his speeches and writings Stokes urged the people to show that they not merely recognized the advent of a great leader, but also knew how to obey him. "Let them show that, though disarmed and defenseless, they have a nobler weapon than any invented for human un-doing by the hand of man . . . No formal resolution in the Congress Commit-tee is necessary. Let us all, whether as individuals or members of the Congress, give our loyal allegiance to Mahatmaji and strengthen his hands by our implicit obedience until Swaraj is attained . . . The road in which he could lead us is one which cannot be followed half-heartedly; it is a question of all or nothing. India must choose."

By now Stokes was a familiar figure on the national scene. His name was well-known among the nationalists. The people of Punjab especially knew him very well. The *Tribune* described him in its editorials as "a gentleman of unimpeach-able veracity."[18] His articles appeared in almost all the major national newspapers and magazines in the country, including Gandhi's *Young India,* the *Modern Re-view,* the *Indian National Reformer,* the *Bombay Chronicle,* the *Servant, Current Thought,* and the *Tribune.* His writings, frequently translated into major vernacular languages, attracted much attention and were often the subject of national debate. They had also made him familiar to the intellectuals of Bengal and the people of Bombay. His book of essays, *National Self-Realization*, containing many of his earlier articles, published at this time was widely acclaimed. Professor Ruchi Ram Sahni, who reviewed it for the *Tribune*, praised Stokes' thoughtful historical studies. Recommending the book to all nationalists Sahni wrote, "Mr Stokes treats each subject as an ardent Indian nationalist where such an attitude of mind does not bring him into conflict with his citizenship of the world . . . Mr Stokes is one of those pure souls whose real home is the world, who habitually thinks in terms not of a race or a nation but of humanity, and who cannot help spreading a sweet fragrance around by acts of charity and goodness wherever they may happen to be."[19]

FOLLOWING THE NATIONAL TRAIL

All through 1921, Congress workers were arrested in increasing numbers. Stokes, who had returned to Kotgarh in early September after a three-months' hectic stay in the plains, was asked to come down again immediately by the Punjab Congress Committee to replace one of the arrested leaders. It had become evident that a showdown between the government and the Congress was imminent. Leaving Kotgarh on 22 September, Stokes quipped that he might have to join the other leaders in the "Government Hotel."[1]

He had been expecting such a call, but leaving home again was hard. He longed to lead a "calm and uneventful life" in the midst of his family, spending his days in his library and fields. He did not care for the noise and rush of crowds, and the atmosphere of politics. "If I did not feel it my duty, I should never have anything to do with them."[2] He was also worried about his family. There were five children in the house, all under eight, who needed constant care. Besides, the fields had to be plowed and fruit trees tended. Agnes was young and not quite as independent for the heavy responsibilities as he would have liked her to be.

There were serious problems in the ilaqa too. There had been no rain during the past year. Crops had failed and near famine conditions prevailed. It would be hard for people to make ends meet until the next summer's crops ripened. He had succeeded in getting the Congress to include Kotgarh in its relief work, which meant that most people could get limited quantities of grain at controlled rates and the absolutely poverty-stricken would get it free of cost, yet the arrangement was a temporary one. It also required close supervision to be effective. His quarterly dollar draft from America had just arrived. He used it for buying additional grains from Simla, carried them by mule loads to Kotgarh and stocked them in his godowns, a practice he followed during years of food shortages. The

stocks ensured that no one in the ilaqa starved. Agnes would now have to super-
vise the distribution of the grains if necessary, a task which Stokes himself had
always undertaken.

His mother's anxiety about him was also a matter of concern. The "terrible-
ness of being at odds with the government" and the thought of his being thrown
into prison frightened her. He wrote to her regularly and in great detail. Realizing that she would rather know everything than be kept in the dark, he tried
to prepare her for his possible arrest. "Try to get that bugaboo about jails out of
your mind; after all they are much like other places if one's conscience is clear."
He did not wish to necessarily invite an imprisonment and fully intended to ensure that any sentence imposed on him was undeserved, but going to prison in
the course of the struggle for self-government was all part of the game.[3] "We cannot do our part in the world at this time and still hope to escape danger. However, the only danger is that of not being true to our ideal. The rest is all in the
day's work."

Fortunately, the laws of deportation and confiscation of property as applied to
nationalists had been recently abrogated. Though he was prepared for any eventuality and ready to meet the government's challenge at any cost, the changes
made him much less anxious, both for his own sake and for that of his family.
He realized that he could not take his large family to America and the loss of
his beautiful home would have been a catastrophe. "Now you may be certain
that it is no longer possible for the government to send me out of the country,"
he assured Agnes, "and it is also impossible for them to touch our property. I
thank God for this, for I would rather be in India in prison than free anywhere
else. Also it makes one's heart happy that the house one loves is no longer in
danger."[4]

When Stokes came down to the plains, the nationalist movement was at its
peak. Swaraj, for which Gandhi had set the target date of December 1921, seemed
close at hand and there was a feeling of euphoric expectancy. The confinement
of the two Ali brothers had a catalytic effect on the movement. Gandhi's article
in their defense, "Tampering with Loyalty," published in *Young India* on 29 September openly challenged the government. "We must spread disaffection openly
and systematically till it pleases the government to arrest us," Gandhi wrote.

The AICC was to meet at Ahmedabad on 6 October but Gandhi wanted to
consult important national leaders before the meeting. Stokes, who was then in
Punjab, was one of twenty-three leaders to receive Gandhi's urgent note from
Trichinopoly: "In view of the arrests of Maulana Shaukat Ali and Muhamed Ali
and others, it is necessary for some of us to meet and consider the situation . . .
From your province I have only invited you and Lalaji. You will please bring any
other friend whose presence may be helpful."[5]

Tuesday, 4 October 1921 was a crucial day in the history of the Indian national movement. Leaders from all parts of the country gathered at Bombay's Laburnum Road for a high-powered meeting presided over by Gandhi. The issue to be discussed was the duties of soldiers and civilians under the existing government. It was a sensitive issue. Indian soldiers were being used to repress nationalist aspirations. They had been used to brutally put down agitations when the Rowlatt Act was passed; they were used for firing on innocent people at Jallianwala Bagh; they were used for furthering imperial interests outside of India—for exploiting weak neighboring countries to the advantage of the Empire. The nationalists wanted to decide if there was any justification at all for Indian soldiers to continue being tools in the hands of a foreign government for the repression of their own countrymen. Their decision was put down in unequivocal terms in a manifesto issued at the end of the meeting which called upon every Indian soldier and civilian to sever his connection with the government and find some other means of livelihood. The manifesto signed by Mahatma Gandhi and forty-seven other leading nationalists was to become one of the most important documents in the history of the freedom struggle. Stokes was the only non-Indian to sign the manifesto.[6]

The government reacted immediately. In a statement issued the following day, S. P. O'Donnell, the secretary of state to the government of India, declared that short of a proclamation of civil disobedience this manifesto constituted as direct and forcible a challenge to the government as it was in the power of Gandhi and his associates to make, and it was "highly questionable" whether the government could afford to refuse to take up the challenge. The manifesto hastened a showdown with the government and resulted in the arrest of almost all important national leaders during the next few months.

Even before the names of the signatories to the manifesto appeared in the press, the first targets for prosecution by the government were M. K. Gandhi, Lajpat Rai, Motilal Nehru, Yakub Hassan, and S. E. Stokes.[7]* The administration, however, was in a dilemma. While the Congress provocation called for immediate action, the government was afraid that prosecuting and imprisoning Gandhi at this point might enhance his popularity and "reinvigorate and intensify" the non-cooperation movement. It was also felt that this was not the most opportune time to prosecute Gandhi because of the approaching visit of the Prince of Wales.[8]

While the decision regarding Gandhi remained under review, the govern-

---

* As per government records of 7 October 1921 the most prominent among the signatories of the manifesto were Gandhi, Abdul Bari, Abul Kalam Azad, Motilal Nehru, Ansari, Jawaharlal Nehru, Kelkar, Stokes, Lajpat Rai, Ajmal Khan, Shyam Sundar Chakarvarti, B. S. Munjee, Yakub Hassan, and C. Rajagopalachari.

ment machinery moved swiftly to gather evidence against the other nationalists. Dossiers were prepared and police reports updated. Lala Lajpat Rai and Stokes were considered to be the most active leaders of Punjab and their prosecution was inevitable. The administration viewed Stokes with rancor. The Criminal Investigation Department (CID) had kept a record of Stokes' movements since his return from America in 1911 when officials had questioned his fellow passengers about his activities on board the ship.[9] He came under greater scrutiny in 1919 when he began writing about imposition of martial law in Punjab.* The Intelligence Bureau's director's report described him as an "unbalanced character. Married Hindu; lives like small raja in the Simla Hills. Grudge against us because he did not get a CIE for recruiting work in War. Raises all trouble he can over *begar*, and getting servants in Simla to strike."[10]

While pressing charges against other signatories of the manifesto was not difficult, taking action against Stokes, who was a white man, posed a problem. The government did not want to interfere with Stokes' legal position and rights especially since suggestions that Andrews should be sent to England and tried for sedition had not been looked upon favorably by the government in London.[11] O'Donnell felt that in the case of Stokes it might be preferable to seek the good offices of the U.S. Consul General in India who had been very helpful in the deportation of some Americans, even though it was doubtful whether Stokes "would prove amenable to persuasion."[12]

During the next few weeks concerted efforts were made to determine the nationality and legal status of Stokes and a series of telegrams on the subject—eight in a week—shuttled between W. H. Vincent, Home Member, and O'Donnell. The Intelligence Bureau director's reports, which stated, "He is said to be an American," were scrutinized. If that were so then perhaps the threat of deportation or deportation itself would bring a change in his thinking. But if he was an American citizen, how was he enlisted in the army during the war? Fresh investigations were carried out. Finally, on 19 October the government was able to ascertain the fact of Stokes' naturalization. The way for his prosecution was now clear.

While the government prepared its case, Stokes was busy in mobilizing support in the nation's cause. After the Congress meeting in Bombay he accompanied Gandhi to his ashram in Sabarmati where he wrote a comprehensive pamphlet, "The Economic and Spiritual Significance of Non-cooperation," in support of boycotting foreign goods and on the economics of swadeshi. Gandhi, who commended Stokes' "able essays" to the reader in a foreword to the book,

---

* Special mention was made of his article "The Duty of Government and Englishmen," published in the *Leader* of Allahabad on 20 May 1919 and in Calcutta's *Amrita Bazar Patrika* on 3 June 1919.

felt assured that his efforts "must prove useful at a time when there is a fierce attack being made against burning of foreign cloth."

On returning north, Stokes remained engrossed in nationalist activities. He was constantly on the move, traveling through the length and breadth of Punjab, addressing public meetings, holding discussions, and writing articles and comments. Disregarding his health, his comforts, and his family, he put every bit of his energy and concentration into a cause that was of utmost importance to him. "I have got a day's rest after a period of constant labour in the nationalist cause. My voice is gone from much over-speaking in the midst of the Punjab dust and heat," he wrote.[13]

Toward the end of the month, Stokes went to Multan to attend the Punjab Provincial Conference. After the conference he made an extensive tour of Ferozepore district and addressed large audiences at Abohar, Moga, Dharamkot, and Muktsar. He also toured and addressed meetings at Karnal, Ludhiana, Montegomery, and Bhiwani.

Stokes accused the British of taking away India's wealth. Formerly famines were unknown in India. It was false to assert, as the British did, that when they came to India the country was in a very bad state. He charged that ignorant and illiterate Englishmen had taken away crores of rupees from India and enriched their own country. India had now begun to show signs of poverty and Indians were finding it difficult to earn a livelihood. The situation would become worse in the near future, he warned. At the same time he stressed that he had no personal grudge against the government and did not desire to create hatred in the public's mind against it. What he hated was the treatment accorded by the government to the people of India. His emphasis was always on nonviolence and decorum. At a meeting in Ludhiana when a boy recited a seditious and abusive poem, he was angry and reprimanded him.

On 4 November he was in Delhi at Gandhi's behest to attend the AICC meeting. It was attended by almost all the leading nationalists, including Lala Lajpat Rai, Motilal Nehru, Jawaharlal Nehru, Sardar Vallabhbhai Patel, Sardar Vithalbhai Patel, Swami Shraddhanand, and Lala Duni Chand. The meeting was unique in that the nearly 200 members who were present were without exception in khadi; even visitors permitted to attend the meeting wore khadi.[14] The meeting sanctioned a limited form of civil disobedience, including non-payment of taxes to each province on its own responsibility, provided individuals and bodies strictly adhered to principles of non-cooperation. It was left to the Provincial Congress Committees to decide on a suitable course of action.

Stokes' involvement in the national struggle was absolute. "We who are working for India feel that we are fulfilling the will of God," he wrote. This was a belief he sustained throughout. "The English think we are all seditionists and anarchists. Nothing can be further from the truth. We are struggling to gain for India that which the English value for themselves more than life itself—the freedom to realize the fullest potentialities of our manhood . . . and I am certain that we shall succeed—as certain as that there is an eternal justice."[15]

He was outraged by the behavior of the British and their treatment of Indians. "The British have not been playing the game out here, and they have made the business immeasurably worse by trying to cheat piously . . . The greatest heritage of the British nation is not its Empire, or its victories over other people usually weaker than itself with which its textbooks are filled, but its tradition of its code of honour by which a British gentleman is bound—to speak the truth, not to cheat, to play the game. This ideal, which our forefathers shared with the British, is the greatest heritage of the race. In India these standards have been thrown overboard."

It was this standard of a gentleman, the "noblest" word he knew, which did not permit him to "acquiesce in what was unjust, cowardly and hypocritical," which sustained him during the struggle against begar. "I should have felt stripped of my self-respect if I had not taken a stand against those things which outraged all my standards of fair play," he said.[16] It was the same standard that egged him on now into India's freedom movement. "Our cause is a just one; our demands are just and reasonable. We are prepared for the British connection if it can be made compatible with the interests of India. The government must be prepared to see that it is; if not it must be prepared for our opposition. We should be slaves if we desisted for fear of what the government could do to us. Personally I was not born or educated to govern my life by fear of what a stronger power might do to me."[17] In October, he wrote to his mother, "In my efforts for India I shall never heedlessly run into danger. On the other hand I shall not try to avoid it, if by doing so I have to sacrifice anything which justice demands for India. I do not hate the English; many of those against whom I am struggling are my old friends. All I can do is to fight them cleanly and as a gentleman."

Knowing that his arrest was now only a matter of time, he also wished to clarify his position on certain national issues. Though he had given his unflinching support to Gandhi he still believed that the two issues on which the Congress had based its fight—the Khilafat and the atrocities in Punjab—were not the best and that the course of action chosen by Gandhi was not the wisest. In a letter to Andrews he wrote, "Now that I have thrown in my lot with the followers of Mahatmaji, and am in consequence in danger of arrest along with others, I want very briefly to explain my position to you, for I am most anxious that it should not be misunderstood or that I should ever be thought to have wholeheartedly accepted the whole of Mahatmaji's point of view.

"My own personal judgment does not lead me to feel that Mahatmaji's application of the principle of non-cooperation is the one I should have chosen. Though entirely convinced of the necessity for non-cooperation, I still feel that the line advocated by me in my recent booklet [*National Self-Realization*]—or some other similar mode of application—would have been far more valuable and better suited to the realities of the situation in India today.

"You may ask why—my position being what it is—I can throw in my lot entirely with this party. Briefly it is this: Mahatmaji is the *only* man who matters at present. He only can fire the idealism of the masses and unite people of all communities under one banner. Only he can make politics *spiritual* and induce the common people to take part in them with a proper spirit. I feel on this account that it is vital to strengthen his hands in every way we can. Even if I do not agree with some of his applications of the principle of non-cooperation I feel that it would not be right for any of us to weaken in the slightest his influence by showing any disagreement. To weaken him is to weaken India.

"Moreover, as my article entitled, 'The India of the Future,' written as far back as 1913, shows, my ideal of the nature of true prosperity for India runs much along the lines which Mahatmaji desires."

"I am not inclined to think that our efforts will bring such victory as would have been certain had Mahatmaji been prepared to proceed upon different lines. Yet, even if I thought our struggle doomed to absolute failure I should still throw in my lot with it, for it stands for all that is best in the heart of India today . . ."[18]

He wrote to Agnes as well in the same vein. "No matter how much I am dissatisfied with his programme I still feel that he is *the only man who matters* to the nationalist cause. Whatever progress we make in these days will be the result of his influence. The government fears him alone of all the nationalists. All that it allows the Moderates to win is out of fear of his party.

"I can see fully the perils of expecting to trust the destinies of the country to such indisciplines and erratic forces as are at present carrying on most of the nationalist work. It is only because I see a greater peril in permitting the waste of this new national aspiration that I give my support. If this movement should die out—if Gandhiji should cease to grip the minds and fire the hopes of the masses—I fear they would sink back into a sleep of slaves and that Western civilization would gradually bleed us to destruction."[19]

15 ARREST AND TRIAL

The Prince of Wales' scheduled visit to India in November 1921 precipitated an already charged political atmosphere in the country. While the administration made all efforts to see that the Prince would be accorded a welcome in keeping with the status of the Empire, the Congress announced a boycott of all functions connected with his visit. The Moderates who by now had nothing to do with the Congress were on the other hand prepared to loyally support the government in welcoming the Prince to India.

Stokes' position was unambiguous. He saw no reason why India should accord a welcome to the Prince of Wales, who stood for the Empire—an empire which was an international association of white and non-white races providing the best of life's opportunities for the white man and a corresponding restriction of opportunity for the rest of humanity. An empire which was built upon the conception that the interests of the vast majority of its subjects could only be considered insofar as they did not conflict with those of the small white minority. What ground did the Empire have for demanding Indian loyalty? It would not only be "unmanly and dishonourable, but the height of folly, for Indians to co-operate in strengthening a political arrangement by which the peculiar interest of the white race would be forwarded by the sacrifice of the rest of the human race."[1]

"The Prince stands for the Empire and all the Empire implies; we believe that the Empire exists in its present form by the sacrifice of its non-European peoples . . . It is here that the nature of the relationship which the 'dominant race' seeks to maintain between the Empire and the people of India must undergo its 'acid test'," he wrote in a critical article, "Acid Test of Loyalty."[2]

Before the Prince's visit to Calcutta on 1 December, Congress volunteer groups were declared illegal in Bengal and the United Provinces, a move that led Bengal's eminent leader C. R. Das to declare that the whole of India was a "vast prison."[3] In the United Provinces the Congress took up the government's challenge not only by announcing that its volunteer organizations would continue to function, but also by publishing lists of volunteers in the daily newspapers. The first name in the list was that of Motilal Nehru.

In Punjab, political activity intensified with each succeeding week. The agitation which had earlier been confined to cities now spread to rural areas. In every district volunteers were being enrolled. There was also an increase in the number of demonstrations: 100 to 150 meetings every week in each district. As far as the government was concerned, Lahore was particularly volatile because of the close connection between the Congress Committee, Khilafat Committee, and various Sikh organizations in the city.[4] The Punjab administration was becoming increasingly concerned about a spurt in anti-government feeling and activity. If the trend continued, Punjab would be uncontrollable when the Prince visited it in February. At the end of November, the government announced the extension of the Seditious Meetings Act to certain districts in Punjab and also declared the Congress and Khilafat volunteer organizations illegal.

The Punjab Provincial Congress Committee (PPCC) meeting scheduled for the afternoon of 3 December provided an excuse for the administration to act. Claiming that it was a public meeting, the deputy commissioner sent a notice to Lala Lajpat Rai, president of the committee, asking him for the agenda of the meeting and an assurance that any issues not listed in the agenda would not be covered in the talks. Lala Lajpat Rai refused to comply with the order, maintaining that the meeting was not a public one. The government prohibited the meeting under the Seditious Meetings Act. The committee members, however, decided to go ahead with it in defiance of the deputy commissioner's orders.

Stokes was the first member of the PPCC to be detained. He had just come down from Kotgarh after spending a week with his family, and was on his way to Lahore to attend the meeting when he was arrested in the train at Wagah railway station early in the morning of 3 December. He was taken off the train at the next station, Lahore Cantonment, and produced before the district magistrate, Major M. L. Ferrar, at 11 a.m. The charges against him were of sedition and promoting hatred between different classes of His Majesty's subjects. Ferrar asked Stokes to furnish a security of Rs 10,000 for good behavior which he refused to do. He also turned down Ferrar's offer of release on bail.[5] His friends were ready to stand guarantee for him and provide any bail that might be necessary, but he spurned the idea.[6] As a non-cooperator he had no intention of furnishing a security for good behavior and cooperating with the government to obtain his release. By afternoon, most key members of the PPCC—Lala Lajpat Rai, Gopichand, Santanam, and Lal Khan of Gujranwala—were arrested.[7]* News of the arrests

* Until then, except for a few restrictive orders, the government had only taken action against those persons who had deviated from the principle of nonviolence. But now the Punjab leaders had been arrested, not because they had departed from the policy and program of the non-cooperation movement, but because they were pursuing that policy and that pro-

spread through the province. In Lahore the PPCC passed a resolution congratulating the leaders on their arrest. On 6 December, a similar resolution was passed at a mass public meeting in Ambala. It was an emotional meeting, especially as those arrested were familiar public figures who had addressed the thousands now assembled on several previous occasions. Some speakers, including Stokes' friend Lala Duni Chand, could not restrain themselves and broke down during their speeches.[8]

The government tried to downplay the arrests and withheld telegrams carrying the news. When the Bombay press received no wire of Stokes' arrest, Gandhi, who was then in the city, inferred that the telegrams had been intercepted or delayed as they had been after the arrest of the Ali brothers. "I cannot imagine that no wire has been dispatched about such a sensational arrest," he wrote in *Young India*.[9] Despite the government's efforts to suppress it, the news spread rapidly. Agnes began receiving letters of sympathy. Andrews, whose confidence in Stokes and his loyalty and affection for him were plain all through, rushed to Lahore to meet him in jail.[10]

Gandhi viewed Stokes' arrest as a "unique move on the part of the government." On 8 December, he published a front-page article in *Young India* titled "Reward of Adoption":

> Mr Stokes . . . is known in the highest quarters as a well-wisher of the government. No one can suspect him of ill-will. But that he should feel with and like an Indian and share his sorrows and throw himself into the struggle has proved too much for the government. To leave him free to criticize the government was intolerable and so his white skin has proved no protection for him. The government is determined to quash the movement at any cost. But it is beyond its ability to do so. Mr Stokes' arrest perhaps demonstrates the weakness of the government's case as not even Lalaji's [Lala Lajpat Rai] does. Lalaji has no record of war service to his credit. Lalaji is known to be an "agitator." He is not a white man. When therefore Mr Stokes is put away the strongest suspicions arise in respect of the bona fides of the government case even in the estimation of an outsider.

During the next few months almost all the important national leaders and thousands of ordinary Congress followers were arrested in all parts of the country. Motilal Nehru and Jawaharlal Nehru were arrested in Allahabad. In Bengal, C. R. Das, his son, wife, and sister were arrested, as was Jitendera Lal Banerji.[11] For Gandhi, the imprisonment of nationalist leaders heralded the dawn

---

gram. As the *Tribune* reported, they were prosecuted on the extremely narrow issue of disobeying what they considered an illegal order issued by a district magistrate. (*The Tribune*, 6 December 1921)

of freedom. "We should cling to our faith that anyone who serves when outside the prison serves better still if, though innocent, he is imprisoned."[12] "That many of the best of us are in jail is Swaraj," he wrote in *Young India*. Publishing the names of fifty-five national leaders who were then in jail Gandhi wrote that the list was of the "biggest prisoners" he could think of "as having won their spurs during the past few days."[13] Stokes' name was on this list.

Commenting on the arrests of Lala Lajpat Rai, Stokes, and Santanam in Punjab, and of nationalist leaders in other provinces, the *Searchlight* of Patna reported that the arrests of "leading Indians, who, whatever the government may think of them, are held in the highest esteem by all classes in the country . . . show undoubtedly that the government have made up their mind to suppress, repress and crush the present manifestations of public discontent by applying their age-old, but absolutely discredited, nostrum of unmitigated repression and coercion."[14]

Stokes had been expecting his arrest for weeks. When he left Kotgarh on 28 November, he had told his wife that as a nationalist he was sure to find himself in jail before long. Two days later he told Dhan Singh in Simla that he would be arrested "before doing anything in the plains."[15] And on the afternoon before his arrest he had written to his mother, "What the month will bring no one can say. We have done our best but the whole affair is in the hands of God. My own feeling is that we leaders will soon be arrested. I am ready for it and so are the rest."[16]

Agnes, too, was ready to face the situation with fortitude. In a letter to Andrews she wrote, "I know it well that when my husband is in jail with many other sons of India, suffering for the sake of righteousness, he is sure to be happy."[17] She also had the support of her husband's compatriots. Dhan Singh's letter written immediately after Stokes' arrest was both inspiring and comforting. "This letter of mine is not to convey condolences but to congratulate you for having such a brave husband as bhaiji [meaning Stokes] of whom everyone of us has the honour and right to be proud . . . I know that every true Rajput lady will be ready to undergo all the perils in life for the sake of the welfare of her country . . . I want to assure you that I shall be ready for ever to sacrifice my interests in the world and even my life for bhaiji's family and children. I shall be ready to do anything for you and the family at any time whenever you order me. Please consider me to be one of your family members."[18]*

Stokes was in Lahore Central Jail, awaiting trial. He was not in the least sorry that he was arrested. What concerned him was that he was placed in the Euro-

---

* Dhan Singh was the only one who addressed Stokes with the endearing and respectful term bhaiji (elder brother). Agnes' nieces and nephews called him khalooji (uncle). To all other locals he was sahibji.

pean ward in the "midst of ordinary felons who were hostile to Indian aspirations." While the European ward had all the physical comforts, he was "most uncomfortable" in it and wanted to be put in the Indian ward so that he could share in the experience of Indians in similar circumstances. When his friend Professor Ruchi Ram Sahni came to meet him on the evening of 5 December, Stokes urged him to get him "removed to more congenial, if physically less comfortable surroundings." Through him he appealed to the entire press, nationalist as well as moderate, to help him in obtaining the same treatment in jail as was accorded to Indian nationalists. "He says he wants an Indian atmosphere for his soul . . . He would be happy to have Indian jail food and sleep on the ground, and do other things which Indians under similar circumstances were made to do. . . . I cannot give adequate expression to the mental agony which Mr Stokes is feeling on account of his treatment as a 'European,'" Sahni reported after his meeting with Stokes.[19]

When Andrews came to visit him, Stokes urged him to use "every influence" he had to get him removed to the ward where his Indian friends were quartered. "I have married an Indian, I am a zamindar, having property on Indian soil; I have brought up my sons as Indians. India is now my country as it is theirs. I have adopted the Indian national cause, the Indian national mode of life, the Indian national dress. Why then should I be compelled to live as a European? Why cannot I associate in jail with my fellow Indians? I have played the game straight with the authorities. I have been open and above board in everything. Cannot they play the game with me?" he told Andrews.

But otherwise he had no regrets. "I am very happy and proud to be allowed to take my share of the suffering which the nationalists will have to undergo so that India may have her rights," he wrote to his mother. "We all gladly go; our womenfolk send us with loyalty to the cause and in the spirit of true devotion . . . as to hardships—if there should be any—I am used to them . . . Do not be anxious; do not worry; thank God with me that He has granted me this opportunity."[20] Meanwhile he continued to draw inspiration from his ancestors. "I am only doing what my own Stokes and Spencer ancestors did for the sake of their conscience . . . Surely we have not gone so soft that we can no longer do the same for our ideals."[21]

After almost a week in prison he could say that the quarters were "not bad" and that he was "quite settling down" except of course for missing his family. As he was yet to be tried in court, there were not many restrictions on him. He could receive visitors and write letters even though these had to pass through the jail superintendent. Also, the American missionaries were sending him some light literature. His friends and fellow nationalists who visited him in jail found him "quite cheerful."

When Stokes was brought to the court on 8 December he was greeted by a large number of people assembled outside the court rooms, amid shouts of *Bande Matram* and *Mahatma Gandhi ki Jai*. Inside the court, too, a number of leading non-cooperators were present to watch the proceedings.

He had been arrested under Section 108 of the Criminal Procedure Code. The immediate grounds of his arrest were that he was traveling to Lahore to convey "direct instructions from the Central Congress Committee" to Lala Lajpat Rai to start civil disobedience and hold mass meetings in Lahore in contravention of the Seditious Meetings Act.

The main charge leveled in court against Stokes was that his speeches and writings tended to bring about a breach of peace and incited the people of India. It was loosely based upon intelligence reports received of his lectures, two articles entitled "Oppression in the Hill States" and "The Acid Test of Loyalty," and the general tenor of his articles, notably "Differences of Opinion" and "The Price of Swaraj."

The state's witnesses included the deputy inspector general of the CID, Isemonger; senior superintendent of police, Lahore, Lieutenant Colonel Eggregson; and assistant superintendent of police, J. A. Scott. Stokes, who had no lawyer to defend him, refused to cross-examine the witnesses. His reply to the magistrate's questions was that though he meant no discourtesy personally to him, as a non-cooperator he would not contest the case and would not answer any questions. "Beyond the statement which I shall subsequently file, as a non-cooperator I feel unable to reply to any question put by the court." And once again he declined to enter into a bond for good behavior.[22]

The venue of the next hearing remained uncertain till the last moment—a deliberate ploy on the part of the administration to ensure that the case got minimum publicity. The *Tribune* correspondent was misled. He was given to understand that the hearing would be held in the district magistrate's court whereas the trial was held in Central Jail itself. By the time the correspondent reached the jail, after having first gone to the district court, the district magistrate Major Ferrar, who conducted the proceedings, had already left after finishing the hearing.[23]

It had been agreed among the national leaders that in the event of their arrest none of them were to put up a formal defense in court, but that they might submit a written statement—not to help them avoid conviction but as a good method of further clarifying the issues between the country and the government in the struggle that was in progress. Though Lala Lajpat Rai and other members of the PPCC were arrested a few hours after Stokes, he was the first to be brought to trial and his written statement was one of the first in a series of trials which took place at this time. In his statement, Stokes emphasized that its object was not to evade imprisonment, for which as a non-cooperator he was prepared, but it was to categorically deny the charge that he had ever given a lecture or written an article that tended to provoke hatred upon the part of the hearer or the reader. "I have not shrunk from telling the truth as I see it," he stated, "I have used every effort of late to persuade the people of this land to strengthen by their support and obedience to the great leader who has been granted to India at this time of crisis; and yet I have lost no opportunity of making the people feel that their most sacred duty was to start the work of reformation in their own hearts by cleansing them of hatred and violence. Were I defending myself I could call witnesses from every place where I have lectured to vouch for the truth of what I say."[24] As to his writings, they were before the public in books, pamphlets, and newspapers. He was confident that not one could be found which might be justly said to promote hatred for government or for the British people. "On the contrary, while seeking to arouse the aspirations of the people of this land, they have consistently pointed out that our path must be one of self-sacrifice, never of hatred or violence."

At the same time he pointed out that the reports upon which the authorities had to rely for information about the movements and activities of non-cooperators, were most undependable. Their lectures were reported by ignorant police agents and could be "highly misleading" unless they were taken down completely in shorthand. "We deliver them [the lectures] in the vernacular, they are reported in scraps and bits by persons quite incapable of taking down verbatim reports, and are therefore turned into English sometimes with quite remarkable results . . . Where, as in my own case, there is a long and fairly consecutive series of articles over my signatures, there is no justification for making use of the very unreliable and fragmentary information (or misinformation) furnished by police and other agents. The same applies to irresponsible reports sent to newspapers which the writer may or may not see."

The authorities, he argued, were acting on "manifestly incorrect" information when they charged him of bringing instructions from the Central Congress Committee for Lala Lajpat Rai. "I was reported to be bringing instructions from a 'Central Congress Committee.' Was it assembled in Simla or Kotgarh, from where I was returning to the plains after a visit to my family? Lala Lajpat Rai had himself just returned from the South, while I was fifty miles above Simla at my house, yet I was reported to be bringing him instructions. Coming down from Simla, I had reached Ambala in the evening, spent the next day quietly with a friend; left at five in the morning for Ludhiana where I remained all day with an old friend who is an ardent cooperator. In the evening I went out for an hour in a tonga to see a loom and took the night train for Lahore. I was arrested on the way during the early hours of the morning, presumably to prevent my carrying the 'instructions' to Lahore."

Responding to the charge that he had asserted that formerly famines were unknown in India, Stokes explained that this was a statement by the famous traveler Megasthenes, and that the sentence was but a link in a chain of evidence by which he had often sought to demonstrate that Indians of the past were able to maintain prosperity in their land from the earliest times up to the occupation of India by the East India Company. Quoting from former commissioner of Assam, H. S. L. Cotton's account of 1890, he argued how India had lost its position as a foremost manufacturer of finished goods to only an agricultural country that now looked to the West for all its needs. The British administration was responsible for this state of affairs. "I have become convinced that those who hold the vital interests of India in their hands should be made accountable to the Indian people for their policies and activities."

With regard to the maintenance of law and order he asserted that no group of people in the country was more anxious for it than Gandhi and those associated with him. "While still at large, the greater part of our thought and effort were devoted to ensuring that order was kept; and since being jailed, probably our greatest anxiety is that the masses remain true to Mahatmaji's injunctions as to perfect non-violence." Throughout his trial he maintained that he had done no wrong. "We have striven to infuse new life and aspiration into the people and yet teach them to be non-violent and free from hatred." He refused to defend himself but expressed confidence in the verdict of the public when the proceedings of the trial were published.

Major Ferrar conceded that while it may be Stokes' "genuine belief" that he had "never written an article that tended to provoke hatred by the reader against anyone," he did not agree with him. Stokes was again asked to enter into a bond of Rs 10,000 with surety of good behavior for a year and to abstain from the dissemination of seditious matter through his articles, but he refused. He also turned down the offer of the magistrate to reduce the bond amount to a nominal sum.[25]

Since there was no defense, the trial was quickly concluded. Major Ferrar's final verdict was: "In the absence of his bond I am obliged to direct that he be detained in jail for a period of six months under section 123 CPC, the imprisonment to be simple, time to run from 3.12.1921." The *Tribune,* which had followed the case with great interest, immediately denounced the sentence as a "grievous failure of justice," and published a two-column editorial highlighting the flaws of the case.[26]

In America, the news of Stokes' arrest appeared in several newspapers and magazines, including the *Philadelphia Ledger,* the *New York Times,* the *American Nation,* and the *Beehive of Germantown.* A few days after his arrest, Stokes' mother received the first letter of congratulations from India. Stokes' friend Duni Chand wrote to her from Ambala:

> The so-called prosecution against him [Stokes] is the merest excuse to either break him away from the movement or to put him in jail. Hundreds of the best and noblest sons of India are being put in dungeons for the mere sin of patriotism and Mr Stokes is only one of them. Here in India on each arrest congratulations are offered to the relations of the arrested and in the same spirit I most humbly offer to you my most sincere congratulations on the noble sacrifice your son has made. His name is one of the honoured names in these days throughout the length and breadth of India. Since he was arrested on 3 December, several hundred of non-cooperators have been arrested, including the greatest names in India, namely Messers Lajpat Rai, Moti Lal Nehru and C.R. Das, and thousands are determined to follow them into jails. I am quite certain that without shedding a single drop of blood the country will be able to bring so much pressure upon the government as to make it bend its knees before the will of the people and your son will come out of jail soon to become immortal in the history of India.[27]

Duni Chand's letter was a great comfort to Mrs. Stokes, as was her son's letter assuring her that he was in "perfectly good health, was in comfortable quarters and in no real hardship." Although she was expecting his arrest for a long time, it nevertheless came as a shock to her. Now she felt differently. His cheerful letters from jail raised her spirits. She even thought that it may be well for him to have a few months of quiet and rest. "It must be in God's ordering for him and these prison months will surely have a vision for him, which might not be possible in the strain of hard work and constant speaking,"[28] she wrote to Agnes.

Despite her personal feelings on the subject, and the faith of friends like Mrs. Carleton who wrote to say that independence would surely come to India but Sam was "ahead of his time," it was not easy for Florence to make public her son's arrest. She had talked to everyone for the past year of his "warm sympathy with the national cause, his faith in Mahatma Gandhi, and his work for Swaraj," but she did not at first have the courage to tell people other than the immediate family and her closest and most intimate friends that her son was in prison. It would have been so incomprehensible to people generally. A political arrest was so unheard of in America that she knew that few would understand, and realized that it might become "a matter of gossip." "It may have been cowardly on my part, but I hated to have it talked about by those who could not comprehend it at all," she admitted. But when the news of Stokes' arrest appeared in the press all the family friends read about it and, to Florence Stokes' amazement, they seemed to "understand it intelligently." She now found many of them congratulating her on her son's "arrest and courage and perseverance of an ideal."[29] "Oh! how proud I would be if it were my son," said one friend. "Bully for Sam Stokes!" said another. "If more of us went to jail for what we believe, the world would soon be a better place," wrote Stokes' old friend George Gleason.[30]

It was not only friends; even strangers showed a keen understanding. When the *Nation,* a radical weekly magazine which was very popular among the Friends, published an article about Stokes' arrest and a short sketch of his life, the news spread rapidly. At an afternoon tea attended mostly by Friends, several of the women came up to Florence Stokes and spoke to her with the "greatest sympathy and interest."[31]

Philadelphia's *Evening Ledger* published a full-page article on Stokes and his work in India with the opening sentence, "If you know your Kipling, you have the atmosphere of this story. If you know your New Testament, you have its lesson by heart. For there is woven into it the romance of far lands and the humility of a lofty soul. It is a page of the past, set down in the book of the present."

GUEST OF THE
BRITISH EMPIRE

Once the sentence was passed several restrictions were imposed upon Stokes. Visitors were limited and he was permitted to write only one letter in six months which made him feel as though prisons were made to break up family ties by keeping a man entirely out of touch with them. However, he soon found ways of smuggling his letters out of the prison, sending them out through Andrews and other friends who visited him. He camouflaged the letters to his mother by addressing them to his sister Anna Truitt.

Life in prison was a new experience for him. He had always lived a free and independent life and to be confined within walls was almost unbearable. The first twenty-four hours were the worst. "There is a horror about the barred gates and windows, the cells and the high walls, that gives one a crazy desire to dash desperately against them and beat oneself to pieces upon them. I never could cage anything after that first twenty-four hours experience," he wrote after he had spent a month in the prison.[1]

To his relief he found that the feeling passed entirely in two or three days. He realized too that, given time, one could get used to anything. For instance, initially he would get very upset when a prisoner was taken to the gallows. Executions were held at dawn and though the other prisoners could not see the actual hangings, they knew when they were being carried out. The condemned men's cells were close to the room where Stokes was first confined and often during the day he saw the men who were to be executed. As a result, whenever there were to be any executions—twenty of them during his first month in prison—he would lie awake all night, "entering into the feelings of the poor fellows" in his imagination hour after hour as the dawn drew near. Yet, after a few days he did not lose sleep over the executions though he hated to know that someone was going to be hanged.[2]

Likewise, he who was so used to the cool climate of the hills that he dreaded the Punjab summer and waited for it with apprehension, found that he could put up with 110 degrees Fahrenheit, when even the paper on which he wrote became warm beneath his hands and the place swarmed with flies during the day and with gnats and mosquitoes during the night, without much difficulty.

The secretary of the CMS of Punjab and the North West Frontier Province, C. W. Gough, who held service for some Indian Christian prisoners in Lahore Jail on Sunday afternoons, met Stokes and conveyed his message to Agnes—that he was "well in health and had comfortable quarters." "I do not agree with your husband's political action," Gough wrote, "but that does not prevent my feeling sympathy with you in this separation, and I am glad to be able to tell you that all is well."[3]

What Stokes found most difficult to accept, however, was the jail authorities' insistence on treating him as a European prisoner rather than an Indian one. The board and lodging facilities for Europeans were much better than those for Indians and they could avail of many more amenities. Stokes resented being treated differently from his nationalist colleagues. He had already pleaded for a change in his status but despite all his protests he was kept in the European ward. As a result he could not have any interaction with other fellow nationalists. His one great regret was that though his cell was very close to Lala Lajpat Rai's he could not communicate with him. The only time they could meet was when there was a common visitor for both of them and they were allowed the use of a meeting room. When noted journalist S. Nihal Singh of the *Literary Digest* went to Lahore Central Jail he met both Lala Lajpat Rai and Stokes together in this meeting room. Such occasions were, however, very rare. Moreover, a jail official was always present during such meetings.

Stokes' initial reaction to the authorities' decision to segregate him from the nationalists, and as a show of protest against it, was to refuse to eat the special food served to Europeans and insist on eating the "coarse and half-cooked" food given to the Indian prisoners. Gandhi did not believe that Stokes was in any way bound to take the food served to Indians and urged him to eat properly. "In spite of your having Indianized yourself you cannot all of a sudden make radical changes in your food and expect the body to respond,"[4] he wrote. Gandhi also thought that it was quite "unnecessary" for Stokes to demand the same food that was served to Indians. "We could not expect the jail regulations to be so drastically altered for the convenience of one person, nor could the authorities be expected all at once to regard your husband as an Indian for purposes of the jail regulations," he wrote to Agnes.[5] Only after a few weeks, when symptoms of Stokes' stomach ulcers began to reappear, did he think it was more important to preserve his health than to spoil it for such an "unimportant thing as food." He then decided to ask for a special vegetarian diet, which was good but simple.

Stokes' insistence on being treated as an Indian was appreciated by the Indian press, and when some other distinguished nationalists were detained in Calcutta in the European ward of Alipur Central Jail, the widely read *Modern Review*'s editor Ramananda Chatterjee was quick to cite Stokes' example. "It would have been better if they had insisted on being treated as Indians, which they are, just as Mr Stokes insisted on being treated as an Indian though he is an American."[6]

Stokes was given a small room with a window. Occasionally, he had to share the room with a European prisoner. As per jail regulations, he was allowed limited reading material but the jail authorities generally overlooked this rule and he was able to get the books he wanted. The rules for bringing in newspapers were stricter but the problem was sometimes circumvented by friends who brought him sweets and fruits wrapped in layers of the latest newspapers.*

As soon as Stokes settled down in jail, he made a timetable for himself. He allocated time for meditation, writing, walking about the little prison yard, and for bathing and washing clothes. He asked for a corn mill to be put up in the prison and spent some time grinding corn every day. This gave him the exercise he would otherwise have missed. A visitor to the jail was surprised to find Stokes "half-clad, perspiring profusely and totally engrossed in grinding corn."[7]

While in jail, Stokes discovered that it was not the prison life which was a hardship, but the "nameless fears" his enforced absence from the family raised. The welfare of his wife and small children living far in the interior of the mountains was always a matter of concern. Dread of family illnesses and his inability to go to them in time of need was frustrating. Before he had entered the freedom struggle he was reluctant to go too far away from home for long. Once when he had gone to see Lala Lajpat Rai in connection with the begar struggle, he returned to find one of his little daughters desperately ill. Another time he had a similar experience with his wife. Now his own uncertain health, too, brought doubts to his mind.

His mother could not write to him in jail and instead wrote regularly to Agnes. Andrews remained a friend during the long winter months. He was not

---

* Duni Chand's son, Tek Chand (later Justice Tek Chand), who was then studying in D.A.V. College, Lahore, was one of those who reached newspapers to Stokes in this manner. Lala Lajpat Rai used to get newspapers by similar means—a doctor on his rounds deliberately forgetting his newspaper behind.

only in close touch with Stokes during this period but he also kept Agnes informed about her husband's welfare and wrote regularly to Stokes' mother in Philadelphia. He considered Stokes' arrest "very unfair" and the charges against him at the trial "very unjust." He tried to correct any wrong impression that might have been projected by writing about Stokes' life for the general public, particularly for those in the southern states who did not know Stokes so well.

Gandhi, too, remained concerned and wrote to Agnes at Kotgarh, "Need I reiterate the hope that you will not hesitate to look to me for any service that I am capable of rendering?"[8] He also kept up with news from the prison. "The reader will be glad to hear that Mr Stokes is happy and well in prison. He is occasionally seen by friends in prison," he wrote in *Young India*.[9]

As the weeks passed into months, Stokes fell into a routine which kept him from brooding. He no longer suffered from the loss of physical freedom which had "irked and oppressed" him during the first few days in jail. "Indeed the place is no longer a jail to me but an ashram, where in silence and peace I can cultivate a companionship with you all which gates and bars and walls cannot affect. They are but the shadowy limitations of those who refuse to surmount them," he wrote to Gandhi from his prison cell. "Intellectually I had always known that the real world of action and accomplishment is within, and that the world we see about us is but the poor shadow of that great reality—the canvas upon which we give imperfect objective form and colour to the conception which lies within us. Here, in a very peculiar sense, I have come to understand this, and to appreciate how independent of distance and bodily separation one may become for communion with those with whom one is united in spirit."[10]

He was grateful for the enforced period of quiet—he had all the time to read, write, and think. There were no interruptions, and there were times when he did not see an outsider for an entire month. Sometimes he thought that in many ways it was a very beautiful time for him. Forcibly cut off from the world for half a year he had the opportunity for quiet thought and meditation that he believed came to few. This was a place where one could learn the meaning of "*true quiet and true solitude*—independent of outward noise and external circumstances." He divided his time between his philosophic studies, history, and prayer, with some time given to reading novels which he had always enjoyed. "I cannot speak for others, but for myself I want to tell you that I am in no anxiety to be free until the proper time," he wrote to Gandhi.[11]

He found his imprisonment profitable in many ways. In the first place, he learnt to cultivate "the spirit of prayerful dependence upon the will of God" as never before. In the second, he had the opportunity to get the books he wanted (without permission) and to devote time to a systematic study of Indian history. During his six months in jail he completed reading nearly six thousand pages of

Indian history. Thirdly, he was able to continue the contemplation of the system of speculative philosophy which had engaged his attention for some years, and put it down on paper in correlated form. By the time his term neared completion he had a tremendous feeling of satisfaction, "I feel I go back to the world with the knowledge of having been faithful."[12] He also made many friends in jail. The jailers "loved him and tried to do him some little service." When Andrews visited the jail a couple of months after Stokes' release he was touched by the "beautiful spirit he had left behind him."[13]

Stokes decided that after going "back to the world" he would devote all his time to philosophical studies which had been his main interest before he started taking an active part in the nationalist movement. The solitude of prison provided him with the opportunity to meditate upon several problems and he felt that he had a message people needed. He also decided to retire from politics. He had taken part in the nationalist struggle out of a sense of duty; now he felt that he had said all that he had to say. However, he wanted to write one more pamphlet on the political situation in the country before he retired.[14]

Stokes was due to be released on 2 June 1922. He could hardly wait for the day when he would leave behind the heat and the dust and glare of the plains and go up to the mountains. "I cannot tell you with what longing my spirit reaches out to the Himalayas that I love. I have become a hill man and the thought of the cool fresh breezes, and the heights, and the cold spring and the shaded forest paths is very precious to me."[15] The last month in jail was one of nervous strain and impatient waiting. "God knows how I have longed during these months to see my wife and kiddies and the dear home. I have hungered for them, altogether I have not had three weeks in my home since last July."[16]

As Stokes awaited his release, he received a message that an important meeting of the AICC was scheduled to be held in Lucknow on 7–8 June. The meeting came within five days of his release, too short a time for him to make a hurried trip home to see his family. As a member of the Committee he felt obliged to attend; both the government and the people would misinterpret his failure to do so. It was extremely hard for him to make the decision, because he wanted, with all his heart, to leave for home without a moment's delay. "Yet it would not be honourable, and I must keep my honour intact for my children's sake, and Agnes', as well as my own. The government must not have the opportunity to think that the prison has cowed me, or the Party that I was prepared to let them down," he wrote in his last letter from jail.[17]

His release was as abrupt as his arrest had been. A day before he was due to be discharged he was taken from Lahore Central Jail to Simla under the charge of the police superintendent and a sergeant. On the noon of 2 June, he was released at the Simla railway station. Apparently, elaborate preparations were made in

Lahore to celebrate his release and the authorities decided to take him to Simla to avoid the demonstrations. This would have suited him admirably were it not for the fact that he was committed to attend the AICC meeting at Lucknow. Now he was in the mountains, only fifty miles away from his family, but he resolutely returned to the plains without seeing them. This "turning back" was one of the few acts in his life of which he always remained proud.[18]

When he finally reached Kotgarh on 16 June after the AICC meeting, the warmest welcome awaited him. Hundreds of people dressed in their finest attire had gathered at Sidhpur, a few miles short of Kotgarh. They had come laden with flowers and garlands and greeted him with showers of petals and *Jai-jai kaar.* They had also composed a special folk song on Stokes which they sang as they accompanied him to his home in Barobagh. This was their way of bestowing on him their highest honor.*

When Stokes came out of jail the political situation in the country had undergone a change. Earlier the atmosphere was charged with enthusiasm and hundreds and thousands of people had gone to jail joyfully. But now the vigor and vitality of the non-cooperation movement had been replaced by a feeling of disquiet and despondency.

During the period when many noted Congress men were in jail, Gandhi had remained free. He had decided to launch the civil disobedience program at Bardoli in Gujarat on 13 February. Then, suddenly, Stokes and his colleagues in jail had learned with bewilderment that the civil disobedience movement had been suspended by Gandhi. The decision was the direct result of violence at Chaura Chauri near Gorakhpur in the United Provinces where, on 5 February, a mob of villagers protesting outside a police station were fired upon. The villagers had retaliated by attacking some policemen and burning the police station with six policemen inside. Gandhi was shocked by this violence and decided to suspend the movement until people learned enough discipline to follow it with a true spirit of nonviolence.

There was a feeling of dismay at Gandhi's decision. The nationalists' dream of Swaraj was being jeopardized just when the non-cooperation movement was proving to be an effective instrument against the government and victory seemed imminent. But there was even more distressing news in the offing. On the night of 10 March, Gandhi was arrested at his ashram in Sabarmati. It was dismal

---

* In the hills, folk songs or Geet are made about exceptional people and extraordinary events. Two folk songs were composed about Stokes. One at the time of his marriage and the other at the time he was jailed.

news made worse by the length of the subsequent sentence. The authorities ensured that at the most crucial stage of the struggle the nation would be deprived of Gandhi's leadership for six long years.

Stokes was deeply disappointed at the turn of events. The suspension of civil disobedience at this point seemed to him "a tactical mistake."[19] People had fought a valiant battle; the leaders had gone to jail during the past two years; many of the best nationalists had suppressed their viewpoints for the sake of unity and adhered to Gandhi's plan of action unequivocally. He himself had supported "direct action" as a "short, quick effort to bring the government to terms and induce it to yield what the country justly demanded," and had been confident of success.

The AICC at Lucknow decided to institute a civil disobedience enquiry committee to gather information on the state of affairs in the country, and to advise the Congress about the feasibility of initiating mass civil disobedience at this stage. The committee headed by Motilal Nehru was required to submit its report in six months. Stokes, who had come straight from jail to attend the meeting took an active part in its deliberations. He warned that civil disobedience was not free from dangers and difficulties, and stressed that it was important that the masses be fully prepared for it. If they were not, then he was in favor of abandoning the idea. Once the program was adopted, it had to be done thoroughly— half-hearted measures were of no avail. It was for this reason that he strongly opposed the idea of limited civil disobedience proposed at the meeting, which would involve the disobedience of some laws and support of some others.

At Lucknow, Stokes' name was proposed for membership of the Working Committee to "enlist American sympathy," and to show that India appreciated the services of those foreigners who empathized with the nationalists and worked with them. But he expressed his inability to accept, saying that he was living in a remote mountain area and would not be able to come down to the plains to attend meetings.[20]

But in September Stokes was in the plains again. The Working Committee of the All India Congress wanted him to participate in a meeting at Amritsar to discuss the alleged police brutalities perpetrated on Sikhs at Guru-ka-Bagh. The Akalis had decided to purge their gurudwaras of many ills that had crept into their functioning over the years. In August there was a confrontation between the Akalis and the Mahant at Guru-ka-Bagh which was located thirteen kilometers from Amritsar. The government intervened and in the ensuing conflict the Akalis, who had modeled their movement on nonviolent satyagraha, faced the police stoically. Scores of Sikhs allowed themselves to be brutally beaten by the police without making any attempt to retaliate or flee. The encounters between the police and Akalis continued for nineteen days.

The Congress Working Committee which met in Amritsar on 17 September strongly condemned the police brutality and appointed a committee of enquiry to investigate and report on the police excesses at Guru-ka-bagh. Stokes was one of the members appointed to this committee. Other members were M. R. Jayakar, Maulana Mohammed Taqi, and J. M. Sengupta.[21] The chairman was S. Srinivasa Iyengar. At the end of its investigations the Enquiry Committee lauded the Akalis and censured the police for its atrocities. It examined more than a hundred witnesses and concluded in its report: "We are all clearly and emphatically of the opinion that the force used was excessive on all occasions and on some was cruelly excessive. Divesting ourselves of all political bias, we consider that the excesses committed bring the greatest discredit to the Punjab government and are a disgrace to any civilized government."

During the following months Stokes remained preoccupied with the problems facing the country. There had been vast changes in the situation in India during the previous months and he felt there was need for a review of the future course of the party, especially with reference to the application of the principle of non-cooperation.

Stokes did not think that non-cooperation had been a failure, on the contrary he was convinced that in "the deepest and truest sense the non-cooperation movement had been thrillingly successful." But now the leaders needed to consolidate their past successes and adapt their methods to the changing conditions. He was aware that any proposal which differed from Gandhi's position would not be welcome. The fact that many leaders would profoundly disagree with his interpretation of the situation and needs of the movement did not discourage him. "My attempt at constructive suggestion has been dictated by no conscious disloyalty to India, or the Congress, or to him [Gandhi] whom I love and revere as the pioneer of India's regeneration," he wrote.[22]

Even before the Civil Disobedience Enquiry Committee submitted its report, Stokes had completed a long memorandum on the existing situation in the country outlining what he considered to be the wisest course for the nationalists to take, which was to drop civil disobedience and adopt a constructive program upon constitutional lines by making full and effective use of the councils. "I am no lawyer, nor have I the slightest intention of ever entering the councils. Upon the contrary, now and always philosophy—not political life—is my work and happiness. If I have striven to present a political method it has been with the earnest desire that a path might be found wide enough for us all to walk in it as fellow non-cooperators, and at the same time practical as a means of our united action bringing us to the goal toward which we all have turned our eyes."

Civil disobedience, he argued, was an efficient weapon for short, quick campaigns, but a dangerous one for inclusion in a more permanent policy. He reiterated his fears that the civil disobedience program contemplated in the Bardoli Taluka, including the non-payment of taxes, was fraught with dangers. "It was one thing to prepare for a short, decisive struggle with the authorities under the leadership of a great leader and a saint whom the masses well nigh worshipped; to keep the ideal of civil disobedience and non-payment of taxes ever dangling before illiterate millions as a state to be looked forward to, was quite another."[23] The government represented law and order, even if not justice, and this fact had to be recognized and accepted. It was far easier to accustom ignorant peasants to the idea of giving up the payment of taxes, than it would be to persuade them of the necessity of resuming it again, he argued. "It is easier to bring about a general disintegration of all sense of respect for constituted authority, than it would be subsequently to build it up. And yet one could never hope to see any true Swaraj in India without it."

Also, he was afraid that an immediate adoption of nationwide civil disobedience could not be free from violence until the whole country had become both fearless and nonviolent in its outlook. If it failed locally, then it would do more harm than good, and if "successful," no power on earth could prevent it from spreading. And the less disciplined localities could even refuse to wait for instructions. He had seen this clearly in the hills during the begar struggle. The Kotgarh agitation had been won without violence because of their organization and discipline. But the result was that the neighboring ilaqa, not nearly so well prepared, refused to wait after seeing the success of Kotgarh. Their actions resulted in great suffering. This experience was one of many which had convinced Stokes that successful mass civil disobedience could not be confined to prepared areas, and the moment it got beyond them it ceased to be nonviolent.

By keeping the issue of civil disobedience constantly before the minds of the people, the nationalists were, he felt, contributing their share toward the gradual disintegration of that sense of order and discipline which was as essential to "swaraj" as to any other kind of "raj."

Instead of civil disobedience he proposed an alternative political program based on his earlier idea of vigilance committees, which could be carried on in conjunction with the Bardoli program. He was thinking of a mighty people's party, formed by a live and independent electorate, that would send its men into the councils to represent the will of the Congress-Khilafat joint committee and put through a program entrusted to them with the help of national, provincial, and local vigilance committees manned by responsible men. The party would have no communal leanings, for the people would elect their representatives to act under the joint committee. Hindus, Muslims, Sikhs, Parsis, Christians, Jews would all stand in the councils, irrespective of their religion, as the exponents and instruments of a common policy and program. Having one commission and being bound by one pledge they would vote solidly together on all questions.* The issues taken up by the People's Party would be placed before their constituents through lectures, handbills, posters, and other literature published in local languages and distributed simultaneously throughout the country. This, he was convinced, would help in educating the electorate and in developing a common viewpoint among the people throughout the country. "All this is constitutional, yet it is a form of constitutional non-cooperation which the countrywide influence of the Congress and Khilafat would make not only practical but also tremendously effective," he said.

He also considered as impractical the demand that the public should absolutely refrain from using law courts. It was all right to boycott the courts for a short period as was done during the previous year but it could not be continued indefinitely. Far from leaving the courts alone in this second stage of the struggle for Swaraj, he advocated their free use. While the system had many shortcomings there were times when a lawsuit was the only method whereby people could protect themselves from ruin at the hands of aggressors and oppressors. To deny even this one poor means of protection to the people before offering them a better system did not seem to him a logical approach. "Why should we cooperate any longer by silent acquiescence with what we feel to be utterly unjust and illegal misappropriation of the law?"

The issue was relevant in his own region, where people were able to settle disputes which arose among themselves but were defenseless against oppression from outside. "Since my return from jail I have found food for reflection and thought upon this subject in my own ilaqa," he wrote. "Such simple and ignorant, deeply poverty stricken people might under the influence of a lofty ideal dimly seen suffer such oppression for the limited period of a short, quick campaign . . . but they cannot afford to stand defenceless in these matters for a protracted period. Living, as they do, upon the verge of subsistence, to do so may well mean ruin—starvation to their children.

"Our farmers here in the hills must have their oak ploughs from the forest; our potters and blacksmiths must have their charcoal; our chamars must have the wherewithal to prepare their skins [leather for making shoes]. To demand that for the sake of the new hope that has come to India, they deprive themselves of the means of feeding their families, that is to put upon *them* a greater burden than they can bear. To advise them to civilly disobey in an attempt to obtain

---

* According to well-known educationist and C. F. Andrews' biographer, Marjorie Sykes, if
  Stokes' proposals had been accepted the partition of the country may have been prevented.

these necessities, is in effect to say 'Go to jail,' and that means 'leave your wives and children to starve next winter.' You can go to jail, I can go to jail—we can afford to do it, but what of these?" he asked.[24]

While Stokes was reluctant to continue to take an active part in politics, he had at the insistence of Motilal Nehru and C. R. Das decided to attend the Calcutta Congress in November and the Gaya Congress in December before finally retiring from it. He placed his memorandum in the hands of every member of the AICC with the confidence that anyone who read it carefully would be forced to admit the feasibility of such constitutional non-cooperation. While he was quite certain that his views would meet with strong opposition from the "firebrands," he expected a more positive response from the more "thoughtful" of the party.[25] He expected no immediate results, but political developments toward the end of the year gave him reason to believe that his memorandum had undoubtedly influenced the views of some of the most important leaders.

His old friend Andrews was happy to learn that he was again taking an independent stand and even though he had not yet seen the memorandum he felt quite certain that it would be "noble and frank and strong"—qualities which were greatly needed. "I am so glad of this because I never liked his position of waiving all difference in order to get unity, and accepting a virtual dictatorship of Mahatma Gandhi, giving him 'carte blanche' and thus allowing for political reasons a Muhammadan claim which went beyond justice," Andrews wrote to Florence Stokes.[26]

No decision on council-entry could be taken at the sharply divided Calcutta Congress (22–24 November 1922), and the subject was referred to the Gaya Congress. Stokes took an active part in both. At the Calcutta Congress he defended the use of councils for constructive purposes. He also insisted that the preamble criticizing those associated with the councils be dropped because it was not accurate and constituted unnecessary condemnation of a few honest patriots who were then in the councils. His amendment was strongly supported by M. R. Jayakar.[27]

Though nothing concrete was achieved at the meeting Stokes was hopeful for the future. "As yet the idea of going into them [the councils] for their *destruction* or 'wrecking' predominates, but I feel that if only the party can be got to accept the proposal to contest the elections we may be able to carry [the party] on to the idea of using rather than wrecking them,"[28] he wrote after the Calcutta Congress.

Stokes received considerable attention from the press. The *Tribune* published his sixteen-page memorandum in full while the Congress was in session. The paper's editor, Kalinath Ray, praised Stokes' "excellent memorandum" and supported his views on the "vitally important" subject of entry into the councils, affirming that there was substantial agreement between the views of Stokes and those upheld by the paper. In an editorial, "Stokes and Ourselves," Ray reiterated, "There is no difference of opinion between Mr Stokes and ourselves." The paper lauded Stokes' suggestion that the Congress and Khilafat members must be in the council on behalf of the Congress and the Khilafat and not on behalf of their respective communities. "The suggestion deserved more than passing notice . . . That this is the *sine qua non* of success, any one who gives a moment's thought to the matter will admit."[29] The memorandum was published in several leading newspapers in other provinces as well. It was not only published in English and Hindi but also in Urdu, Bengali, Gujarati, and Marathi and was hence read widely.

The logic and persuasiveness of Stokes' views and the publicity given to them led many to believe that he contemplated forming a separate group in the Congress to advocate the program he was suggesting. "They are mistaken," he wrote with reference to the number of letters he received after the publication of the memorandum. "I do not even intend to bring forward a resolution . . . For myself, I am a student, not a leader, and my own particular life work, laid aside for a time at Mahatmaji's call last year, awaits me in my library."[30]

In December 1922, Stokes was in Gaya to attend the All India Congress. This was the fourth year in succession when he would be away from his family for Christmas. This was also going to be the last Congress session that he would attend.

The All India Congress' 37th session opened at Gaya on 26 December. More than 20,000 delegates and visitors dressed in khadi gathered at the huge pandal, made of hand-spun and hand-woven khadi and decorated with paintings and photographs of Mahatma Gandhi who was then in prison in Poona. Chairs and benches were dispensed with to accommodate more people and everyone was seated on the floor. Stokes was a prominent member at the Gaya Congress. Dressed in a khadi kurta and dhoti he sat on the dais along with Pandit Madan Mohan Malaviya, Pandit Motilal Nehru, Hakim Ajmal Khan, Vijiaraghava Chariar, Dr. Ansari, N. C. Kelkar, Rajendra Prasad, Rajagopalachari, Mazharul Haq, Seth Jamnalal Bajaj, Lala Duni Chand, F. Abbas Tyabji, K. Santanam, M. R. Jayakar, Sarojini Naidu, and others. In his presidential address C. R. Das used Stokes' definition of non-cooperation and mentioned his name in connection with it.[31]

The Gaya Congress, however, was held in an atmosphere of strife and contention. It witnessed a show of strength on the question of "council-entry." There was a deep divide in attitude between the "pro-entry" and the "no-change" groups. One group reiterated its faith in the principle of Gandhi's nonviolent non-cooperation and did not wish Congress to have anything to do with the councils. The other group, led by Motilal Nehru and C. R. Das, stood for contesting the elections on the issue of the Punjab and Khilafat wrongs and wanted to push for immediate Swaraj in accordance with the principle of nonviolent non-cooperation.

Motilal Nehru's resolution in support of entry into the councils was, however, rejected by the Congress, which led to the birth of the Congress-Khilafat Swaraj Party at the close of the Gaya Congress. One hundred and forty Congress members joined the new party. Stokes did not become a member—he had already decided to retire from politics.

Though the Swaraj Party did not finally accept Stokes' proposals that the councils should be contested with the view to using them constructively, there was no doubt that, within limits, his memorandum exercised a considerable influence upon the question of whether the Congress should make use of the councils. "Where I differ from many of our party is in believing that, though we may feel we must work out *our own* salvation because of what the British Empire is at present, we can do so to the best advantage by utilizing certain factors in the present situation resulting from the British connection, to work for our just and legitimate ends. They say 'destroy, that building up may become possible,' while I feel that wholesale destruction would greatly retard the building up of what we so greatly desire and truly need."

"My suggestions have not been accepted yet," he wrote from Fagu on his return journey to Kotgarh after the Gaya Congress, "but day by day the more thoughtful nationalists are giving it more attention, and some of the finest entirely accept my thesis. Whether the country will remains to be seen."[32]

The new party planned to meet in Allahabad in February to frame its policy. There were already differences within the party between those who wanted to contest the elections with the aim of destroying them and those who wanted to contest them for more constructive purposes. Pandit Motilal Nehru urged Stokes to attend the deliberations but he was now determined to stay up in the hills. His health was poor and he had been advised complete rest. However, this did not deter him from making one last effort to influence the party leadership not to succumb to a compromise which many in the party were urging, and to formulate a plan which was in keeping with the goals it had set for itself. In a second memorandum to Pandit Motilal Nehru, Stokes expressed his fear that a compromise for the sake of unity within the party would compromise nothing but the party's "convictions." Those who believed that the councils could and should be used in conjunction with work in the country had no right to surrender. Their conviction was a trust, else why did they hold it in the face of an opposing majority? They owed it to the country, the Congress, and themselves to stand for what they felt the country needed. "If we do not firmly feel that the struggle must be carried into the councils, I personally can see no justification for the formation of a party in the Congress; nothing less than such a conviction would give the right of impairing its united front."[33]

It was his hope that from this new party might evolve a great "centre party" within the Congress which would be able to carry the war constructively into the very heart of the bureaucratic strongholds, both in the councils and in the villages. "If this should come about our national alignment would be complete and there need be no more ineffectual efforts to advance with a broken line of battle."

The villagers were victims of a "nationwide non-violent lawlessness" of government functionaries who most immediately touched their life. The concept of a powerful and effectual local Congress committee which he had been trying to promote for the past two years was a means to alleviate the hardships which the villagers were facing everywhere. He expected these committees to become champions of the people in fighting all existing evils in an organized manner. He wanted the new party to wage a war of law against official lawlessness. What he was proposing was not cooperation but "aggressive constitutional non-cooperation of the most compelling character," which he was convinced would in the long run yield greater and more solid results than any program of agitation and lawlessness. He also believed that it was in the interest of the country for the new party to "capture the best of the liberals"—the more patriotic section, who would be naturally oriented toward the new party as they became more and more outraged by the short-sighted activities of the bureaucrats.[34]

Though his proposals were not acceptable to the Swarajists, his views were given serious consideration. The outline of the Congress-Khilafat Swaraj Party programs was drawn at Allahabad. During the next few years Congress activities remained mainly in the hands of the Swaraj Party which emerged as a powerful instrument of national struggle under the leadership of Motilal Nehru and C. R. Das.* It obtained large majorities in almost all legislatures and carried the fight on the parliamentary front.

Stokes, who had played a vital role in forging the birth of the Swaraj Party, now remained aloof from all political activity. He not only declined the invitation to contest elections to their councils from his constituency the following

---

* Das had always favored entry into the legislatures for the purpose of carrying on the national struggle there; Motilal Nehru had more or less the same outlook. Jawaharlal Nehru wrote in his autobiography, "His [Motilal Nehru's] acceptance of the council boycott in 1920 was partly a subordination of his own viewpoint to Gandhi's. He wanted to throw his full weight into the struggle and the only way to do it then was to accept the Gandhi formula in toto" (*An Autobiography*, p. 99).

January, but he also refrained from canvassing for the Swarajist candidate from his ilaqa. He had already refused to do any public speaking or writing. He was determined to make a complete break from politics. He resigned his membership in the AICC and the PPCC and was now a simple member of the Congress. He did, however, continue to support the party through whatever contributions he could make to the party fund.

Samuel Stokes Sr.

Stokes shortly before he left for India in 1904

Stokes, Florence Spencer Stokes, and Dhan Singh in
Philadelphia

Harmony Hall in Moorestown, New Jersey

Photo by Asha Sharma

Harmony Hall, Barobagh, Kotgarh
Photo by Vishnu Datta Sharma

Stokes with the children he had taken under his care

Agnes and Prem with Florence Stokes in Germantown

Stokes with Agnes and Prem in Philadelphia, 1914

Stokes' young sons

Agnes in Barobagh

Stokes during World War I

Satyanand Stokes

Stokes teaching an outdoor class

The Paramjyotir Mandir in Barobagh, Kotgarh
Photo by Vishnu Datta Sharma

Stokes and Agnes with their youngest daughter, Satyavati

Lal Chand Stokes with an American visitor at his farm in Kotgarh

The eldest daughter, Champavati, with Agnes
Photo by Asha Sharma

Stokes' jail number in Lahore
Central Jail (1921)

The centenary celebration at Thanedar on 16 August 1982
Photo by Asha Sharma

DEBATES WITH GANDHI
TEST OF FRIENDSHIP

"It has always been my fate to deeply love and revere Mahatmaji, while finding myself in strong disagreement with many of his theories and the lines of action he has advocated," Stokes admitted with a hint of regret.[1]

When he put his position on council-entry before the AICC, Stokes knew that Gandhi would not agree with him. Yet this did not deter him. He was convinced that his proposals were in the interest of the country. However, he was keen for Gandhi to know his views and the reasons which led him to advocate contesting for the councils.

When Gandhi was unexpectedly released from prison on account of his health in early 1924, Stokes was in Kotgarh. "I cannot tell you what happiness and thankfulness I have been experiencing since I read in the papers yesterday that you are not going back to Yerawada (prison near Poona where Gandhi was jailed) . . . India has been like a half fragment without you," he wrote to Gandhi.[2] But while the nationalist leaders rushed to Poona to be close to Gandhi, Stokes remained in the hills. He was involved in completing the philosophical book he had started writing in jail, and much as he longed to meet Gandhi he did not feel he could get away from his studies just then. He was, however, keen for Gandhi to read his memoranda so that he would know his entire position in the matter. "As a practical recluse I do not care what others think but it would make me happy to be able to feel that you understood."[3]

Gandhi, who was then studying the situation, welcomed Stokes' letter. "Instead of tiring it soothes . . . It is my duty before coming to a final decision to understand thoroughly the viewpoint of those who advocated council-entry," he wrote back.[4] He was eager to know Stokes' views and read his memoranda as soon as he received them. "I found both to be useful and instructive as giving me the mentality of one whose impartiality I am certain of and whose opinions I value."[5]

Gandhi's comments were frank and unreserved. He endorsed Stokes' opinion that if there was any council-entry at all it should not be for "mere obstruction." He also accepted Stokes' reasoning on lawyers and law courts and agreed that the ban on their use should be lifted. But he did not agree with Stokes' views on non-cooperation. "If I could but accept your premises and your view of non-cooperation there is not much with which I should disagree . . . I think that perhaps there is a fundamental difference between us as to the interpretation and implications of non-violent non-cooperation."[6]

Stokes believed that it was not the actual form of the expression of non-cooperation which would determine whether it was nonviolent or not, but the spirit in which the people learned to carry it out. He therefore did not think that the program he suggested violated the spirit of nonviolence, provided it was carried on without a spirit of hatred or revenge.[7] But it was Gandhi's firm conviction that one could not enter the councils in the existing system without participating in violence of an extremely bad type. "You evidently seem to think that mystical and religious non-cooperation can run side by side with purely political non-cooperation in the councils. I hold that the two are mutually destructive," Gandhi wrote to Stokes. "I am almost impatient to express an opinion on council-entry and kindred matters, the more so after reading your memorandum . . . When I am free to say all that I have in view on this question and if you have time to spare from your writing, you will see the development of the outline I have sketched above."[8]

Stokes was touched by Gandhi's long letter and not in the least surprised by his views. Responding in a lengthy rejoinder on 25 March he wrote, "In whatever I do not agree with you, I believe you will be patient with me, and I trust that you know how profoundly I am convinced of the greatness of the work you have to do."[9] He perceived a basic difference between his and Gandhi's approach. "Our difference lies in your conviction that the moral victory resulting from *lovingly* accepting all suffering without giving way one step to that which is unjust, is the only way to really conquer those who are blinded by selfishness, prejudice and blindness. Be not overcome of evil, but overcome evil with good . . . It appeals to me with great power, and far more than any other way," he wrote to Gandhi, reminding him that he himself came of a stock (Quaker) who had suffered more for their conception of nonresistance than most, and many of his ancestors had spent considerable periods in prison, "And yet I cannot accept it, as far as my present experience carries me—the details, I mean rather, of its application—as a practical solution of the ills which inflict our race."[10]

In any event, it did not appear to him that, under the existing conditions, the masses were in a position to realize the ideal of perfect nonviolent suffering in a manner that would awaken the British and make them aware of the wrong they did India. Moreover, what the villagers needed was not to suffer unjustly with patience but to learn, instead of resenting silently, as they did at present, to get up like men and discover a way in which with mutual trust and helpfulness they might face and overcome whatever was unjust and hurtful. "The moral problem," as he saw it, was, "to teach them to do so in the proper spirit, free from spite and hatred."[11]

The areas in which the poor village people were called upon to refuse cooperation could not be ignored because octopus-like they extended their tentacles into every facet of the life of the people. There were only two courses open to them—to meet, face, and struggle against them, or to succumb to them. He felt that the people lived so close to the borderline of sheer subsistence, that the consequences that would follow their adoption of the program of suffering advocated by Gandhi would drive them over it and result in starvation for their children. "The vast majority of the peasants of India cannot afford to go to jail, and they fully appreciate it. Indeed if they are to keep body and soul together, they cannot afford the slightest interference in their agricultural work." It was for this reason that he did not want the national leaders to stand up as examples of suffering bravely, but as their leaders and teachers in an active, aggressive nonviolent struggle against every form of injustice, whether national or local.

But while Stokes wanted Gandhi to be aware of his exact position and the reasons which led him to his conclusions, he did not wish to influence Gandhi in any way. "I know I cannot and do not want to."

Within a few months, Stokes was faced with another situation in which he was again impelled to oppose Gandhi. The issue in question was Gandhi's proposal to make membership to the Indian National Congress (INC) dependent upon the submission of a certain quantity of personally spun cotton yarn, instead of the old four-anna membership fee. Stokes had strong reservations against the concept. Personally he favored hand-spinning and was convinced of the value of using cloth from charkha and hand-spun yarn, not only as an economic factor but as a means of moral discipline. Spinning was done in his home as in most Pahari homes, and when Gandhi called upon every Congressman to take to spinning, Stokes started doing so himself for at least half an hour every day. He intended to continue the practice, not because he agreed with Gandhi's views but because he appreciated its value as a voluntary act of discipline. However, he could not accept the idea of "compulsory spinning as the *sine qua non* of participation in the Congress." Such a step he believed would be subversive to the representative character of the Congress. "Everyone who sought to serve India honestly and faithfully, no matter what his particular views on spinning or any other subject may be, should be entitled to belong to the national body if India was his home," he argued.[12]

Stokes appreciated Mahatma Gandhi's position in proposing a change in the membership rules for the Congress so that its members would be only those who were ready to discipline themselves in order to belong. But while he agreed with the end, he could not agree with the means. Also, he believed that while the end could be attained by the voluntary acceptance of a discipline whose value was individually recognized, it could not be attained by bringing about the forced submission of the minority who wished faithfully to serve their country but did not approve of spinning as a policy. "It seems to me that by its introduction the national character of the Congress will be destroyed, and if there is one thing above all others that our people need to apprehend, it is the right of representation of every opinion. It is because they have not grasped this that those expressing unpopular views are refused a hearing," he wrote to Gandhi.[13]

As the debate on the spinning franchise continued, Stokes found himself more and more concerned about its implications. During a brief visit to Delhi in September to attend the "Unity Conference"* he expressed his reservations on the subject to Andrews. In a subsequent letter to Andrews he wrote, "Though I

---

* In September 1924 an attempt was made to bring Hindus and Muslims closer together through a "Unity Conference" called at Delhi. Stokes received a telegram requesting he attend. He had not taken part in any public meeting for a year and a half and was not inclined to, but felt compelled to attend. He did not participate in all the sessions of the conference but met with all the people who "really mattered" and discussed the subject with them. He had many Hindu and Muslim (including Hakim Ajmal Khan) friends and felt he was able to do a much better service to the cause in these private conversations. Stokes' assessment of the conference was that while everyone present tried hard to evolve a formula which would make unity possible, none was prepared to sacrifice communal selfishness which indeed would have made such a unity a reality.

The spirit of self-sacrifice in its larger sense seemed to him to be conspicuous by its absence among the people he met at the conference. The stress was on "conception of rights rather than responsibilities." There was far more keenness to point out the shortcomings of the other party than to search one's own heart for its share in bringing about the troubles with which they were confronted.

"However, I think it may do some good. Hindus and Muslims learned for a few days at least to talk together calmly and listen without expressing resentment to the views with which they had little sympathy. This too is a moral discipline," he wrote in a "Note to The Spinning Franchise," 1924 (*Collected Essays, Memoranda and Letters*).

As expected, the differences between Hindus and Muslims were not resolved and tension between the two communities continued. In 1926 following two outbursts of communal rioting in Calcutta during April and May, one Muslim leader proposed to Gandhi that Andrews and Stokes should invite on their own a few Hindus and Muslims and attempt a reconciliation. The plan was not pursued as Gandhi did not think this would resolve the situation. "I am afraid their efforts cannot achieve this task," Gandhi wrote to the Muslim leader on 4 June 1926. "Nor is the time ripe to bring the Hindus and Muslims together in this way. You alone can bring them together when the time comes" (*Collected Works*, 1926, p. 531).

should continue to spin, I should never be able to accept the fact that my spinning established my right to membership in the Congress, and rather than accept such a principle I should feel compelled to resign."[14] Gandhi was then fast-
ing but Andrews had the letter read out to him. Gandhi did not agree with what
he described as Stokes' "passionate protest" against the idea. He felt it was Stokes'
"excessive regard for the liberty of the individual" which disabled him from "dis-
tinguishing between voluntary acceptance and compulsion."[15] Elaborating his
views in his Notes in *Young India,* Gandhi asserted that compulsion meant submission of protestors to what they opposed under pain of being fined or imprisoned which was not so in this case.

But Stokes was not convinced and when Gandhi's note on the subject appeared in *Young India* he felt compelled to express his views publicly. Nevertheless, he was not happy about doing this. "Even now I would drop the matter were
I not convinced that a vital principle is involved," he told Andrews. "Not only
my reason but all my instincts, the result of a social heredity that has been associated with democratic ideals for nearly 250 years, rebel at the idea of a spinning
franchise."[16]

Gandhi's proposal to introduce hand-spinning as part of the franchise raised
up a storm. Stokes was not the only one to object strongly to the proposition.
Jawaharlal Nehru was so shocked by what he considered a violation of the Congress constitution that he offered his resignation as secretary to the Congress
Working Committee. Gandhi himself admitted it was an extraordinary proposal. "Even a conscientious man like Stokes opposes it tooth and nail, although
he is himself an enthusiastic spinner. Many of our distinguished countrymen
laugh at it," he wrote in *Young India.*[17] The Swarajists opposed the proposal out-
right and staged a walkout from the AICC meeting at which Gandhi had proposed changing the franchise and the rules for membership. The subsequent history of the "spinning franchise" vindicated the position Stokes had taken at the
time, for ultimately the old four-anna franchise remained and the spinning franchise became an alternative form for membership.

"I have been fated to love you for your truthfulness and fearlessness—and
also to differ from you in so many things. Accept the love and pardon the other
things," Stokes wrote to Gandhi as he vehemently opposed him on the question
of the spinning franchise.[18] After his United Provinces (UP) tour with Gandhi,
Stokes had written, "He is so fearless and noble in his conception that I bow in
reverence to the man."

A few days later he again wrote of his impressions of Gandhi. "I have sat
studying him day after day, night after night, have spent many days living with
him, and am convinced he is one of the greatest and noblest of men—both
simple and profound. I doubt if there is such another in the world today. He

stands for the noblest in our nature."[19] "His character and personality defy description," he said on another occasion, "I speak as one who has known him and spent weeks in the same room with him—one who has not come so completely under the spell of his personality . . . as to be unable to disagree from him upon many points."[20]

This was true, for even though the two men were alike in their ideals, their love of truth, and their absolute adherence to their principles, they differed in many ways in their thinking and methods, and Stokes never attempted to bury his differences with Gandhi on the grounds of expediency or out of respect or affection for him. But while he thought Gandhi had his "weakness of judgement," he admired him for fighting the British as a gentleman. "He is pure and true and brave, a knight *sans peur et sans reproche.* His great fault is this only that being born of a nation ruled on the assumption that it is inferior, he dares to think and act and feel as a free man and an equal of the English."[21]

Stokes had long been an admirer of Gandhi. He had followed his work in South Africa closely not only through the press but also through his friend Andrews who had come to know Gandhi intimately during his visit to South Africa in the last phase of the struggle there. Andrews became a close associate of Gandhi when the latter returned to India in 1915. Stokes was then in Philadelphia, visiting his family and it was many years before he got a chance to meet Gandhi in person. Stokes' struggle against begar drew Gandhi's attention and support and brought them together.

Yet, despite his deep regard and admiration for Gandhi, Stokes was unable to accept all his views completely. The basic difference in their thinking arose from their perception of what constituted violence—this was a subject on which they disagreed from the time they first met. While Gandhi believed in absolute non-violence or ahimsa, Stokes believed that it was the spirit in which a particular act was carried out which determined whether it was an act of violence or non-violence. To him the nature of an action lay not in the manner of its physical expression but in the thought of which it was the fruit. "Are not outward acts the shadows of inward realities? Does not an actual murder take place in the heart, while the action is only the shadow cast by it? It seems to me that many a murder or other violent act has taken place without any physical result following. In the same way, may not that which in the world of *nam-rup* [name and form] looks like an act of violence be in reality the expression of a thought free from all hatred and passion?"[22]

It was the old question involved in the problem of what a man should do if he found himself pursued by a ruffian intent upon abducting his daughter, a question which Stokes had put to Gandhi during an argument on ahimsa. "What would be your duty?" Stokes had asked Gandhi—to refuse force for the sake of adhering to nonviolence or to fight the ruffian by every possible means? "I hold that it would be the latter," he had contended, "and that, moreover, the act would have been perfectly non-violent provided that it was dictated by a pure sense of responsibility for the moral welfare of the girl and absolutely free from animus towards the assailor." While Gandhi did not then agree with Stokes, in a subsequent letter on the same subject which he wrote to Richard B. Gregg* in Kotgarh on 27 November 1926, he said that it would be one's duty to defend the ward under one's protection and in certain circumstances one would be bound to carry out the law of protection by resisting the assailant by force.[23]

Stokes could never fully accept Gandhi's principle of offering "the other cheek." Putting it simply, he would argue that if one of his daughters was kidnapped and molested, should he offer his second daughter for similar treatment at the hands of the kidnapper? It was for the same reason that he took up the fight against begar and involved the people of the ilaqa in it. To meekly submit to oppression was something he was not prepared to accept, no matter what policy the Congress adopted.

For Stokes, the need in India was not to "teach the masses to suffer injustice, but to resist it." Gandhi wanted them to resist injustice too, but his method was different. He would have them withdraw, as much as possible, from all contact with the government and suffer the consequences by a willing and cheerful submission to imprisonment and petty oppression. For Gandhi, the "battle of right" was to be won by suffering so accepted for the sake of an ideal. But for Stokes this could not be possible. "This conjunction of active endeavour for right combined with readiness to suffer passively at the hands of injustice, leaving the body in their hands while holding the spirit unconquered and unacquiescent, will not meet the moral necessities of the masses which compose the Indian people, or result in the laying of the foundations of individual and national character upon which Swaraj must rise . . . such a course of discipline only becomes a moral blessing after a man has reached a stage of moral advancement," he asserted.

But despite these differences of opinion, Stokes' devotion and love for Gandhi was deep and abiding. To him Gandhi represented the deepest and best in the spirit and instincts of the Indian people. His impression of Gandhi was the result of a "very critical though loving study" of the Mahatma's reaction to all sorts of differing situations and circumstances. Stokes held that Gandhi's response was "one of utter directness, complete truthfulness of thought and word, consciousness of moral integrity, absolute lack of animosity towards those whose actions

---

* Richard B. Gregg was an American admirer of Gandhi who taught at Stokes' school in Kotgarh from 1926 to 1928.

and ambitions he opposed and was prepared to oppose to the uttermost." There was always a "lovingness, tenderness, compassion combined with readiness to suffer" as he called upon "those he pitied to suffer to their farthest strength if truth to an ideal and justice demanded it . . . It is because he has, and is willing to suffer all things for the truth, that India is ready to suffer with him and her people have gone to prison by the thousands and undergone hardships which you in America do not even dream of," Stokes wrote to his cousin Eliza Nicholson, in Philadelphia.* In a pen picture of Gandhi, he wrote, "He is truly 'a man of sorrows' and acquainted with grief and the most wonderful thing about it is his complete naturalness in it all. There is no 'piousness' about him—no self-conscious solemnity. On the contrary he sees the humour of every situation where it is to be found, and one can see the laughter in his eyes though he rarely laughs. When he does it is a clear and ringing laugh that does one's heart good." During their UP tour Stokes had seen Gandhi day and night thronged by crowds which gave him no rest and only interrupted snatches of sleep. He had noted that at such times the strong men about him showed the strain in many ways, but Gandhi was always gentle, always patient, always calm and sympathetic. He always appeared the freshest of the party though never permitted to rest. Only the dark shadows under his eyes told of the strain. There was something "gallant and debonair about him," Stokes noted, "which added infinitely to the charm of his deadly earnestness, and made men feel that he was no far-off 'inhuman personality'."

"It is the appeal of this smiling, suffering man of invincible courage and sincerity, inflexible in his opposition to wrong yet full of goodwill and love for all alike, that has gone straight to the heart of India. His appeal finds its response because it is an appeal to the divinest instincts in human nature. It is, if I may say it with all reverence, an appeal to take the Cross by one who has mounted

---

* To illustrate the point, he described an incident that occurred in Kanpur during his tour of the United Provinces with Gandhi. As usual a vast crowd had assembled around the house where they were spending the night. In the morning Gandhi was being taken by a number of important nationalist leaders to a meeting. As they passed through the crowd, Stokes noticed a little girl of the poor Mohammedan classes standing with her father. She was about seven years old and had about her head a gaudily colored cheap silk scarf. Probably it was the loveliest thing she had and one could imagine her pride in it. "Mahatmaji saw it too. I well remember the very tender look in his face as he stopped and kneeling down took the child in his arms. Her poor father stood by overcome with pride at the sight of his little daughter in the arms of the greatest in the land. 'This is a beautiful scarf,' he said, taking it between his fingers, 'will you give it to me? . . . Our country needs it!'

"His words were so tenderly loving that the little one nestled up to Mahatmaji and placed the scarf in his hands." Stokes was deeply touched by the devotion in her face, and more so because he knew how fully Gandhi appreciated the fact that he was calling upon her in her poverty to give up what meant so much to her. "I knew he felt far more deeply than I, and yet did not falter in his request."

upon it, and speaks from it. It is an appeal to the brave by the bravest, and as such calls most powerfully to the young . . . When Mahatmaji calls the people of India to overcome evil with good, through suffering and pain . . . it is the call of the Cross, made by one who has accepted it."[24]

During the year before he went to jail, Stokes had not only got to know Gandhi more, he was also able to discuss with him his innermost thoughts which he could not easily discuss with others. When Gandhi was tired and resting during the long train journeys in the UP, Stokes would talk to him about spiritualism and his understanding of "the meaning of life," a subject which was of utmost importance to him. He remained very close to Gandhi thereafter. "Somehow I have never felt you far away, even when in body you were shut off from us,"[25] he wrote to Gandhi after his release from Yerawada prison. It was a sentiment which Stokes had expressed earlier when he himself was in prison. Dwelling on how he had come to understand and appreciate in a peculiar sense how independent of distance and bodily separation one may become for communion with those with whom one was united in spirit, he wrote, "Think of me therefore as living from day to day in closest association with you all [his nationalist friends] and sharing intimately in those inner realities of which objective phenomenon are only the manifestation."

Though he had been unable to go down to Bombay to meet Gandhi on his release from prison, he had longed to see him. "These are not things which can be easily said," he wrote. It was almost three years since he had last been with Gandhi. He was often reminded of the night when he and Rajagopalachari were having a long discussion on ahimsa at Sabarmati and of how Gandhi had come in and told them what he felt on the subject. "That night is the picture of you that I always carry with me. And as I said in my first letter you never seem very far away."[26]

Gandhi's health was a cause of concern and Stokes urged him to put the problems of India out of his mind for a time. "The fact that you are recovering and gaining strength will be a highly important factor in the next few months . . . Leave things to take care of themselves—or rather leave God to guide the destinies of the country—until you are in a position to do so without bringing your health in danger. Not merely India but this poor, disillusioned world is in no position to lose you at present. I spoke of what I considered my svadharma in my first letter to you; may it not be your svadharma at this moment to put the instrument of your service to humanity to the best possible condition to serve it? I earnestly hope that you may feel it your duty to banish these problems from your mind for a time."[27] A few days later he wrote to him again on the subject saying that it was important for him to relax. "In this, of course, I can only give my personal opinion with diffidence and humility, as I certainly do with deep affection. 'Brother Body' as St. Francis used to call it, must be considered if it is to do the work for which it was given to us."[28]

He expressed his sentiments in other ways too. He sent Gandhi precious hill honey and Gandhi was one of the first to receive apples from Stokes' orchard when it began bearing fruit in 1926.[29] He sent a special shawl to Gandhi made from wool spun and woven by the students of Tara School and, when he took his children down to the plains for the first time in 1928, he took them to meet Gandhi. To Gandhi's amusement, when he asked young Lal Chand what he would become when he grew up, the four-year-old replied enthusiastically: "gaddariya" [a cowherd].[30] Stokes always wanted Gandhi to come up to Kotgarh, to share with him the beauty of the quiet hilltop. He felt certain that his place would give him a quiet rest as no other could. "If in the summer your health should demand a period of absolute rest and quiet my home—your home—in Kotgarh, would I am sure afford it to you in a way quite impossible in the plains."[31] Gandhi's response was warm and affectionate. "If at any time I could go over to the north for rest, it would be a privilege to me to regard your house as my own and place myself under your and Mrs Stokes' care and attention."[32] In another letter Gandhi wrote, "Of course, I am longing to be with you even if it is only for a few days. When that time will come I do not know."[33]

Stokes was not easily prone to talking about things about which he felt deepest, but with Gandhi it was different. His letters to Gandhi were sometimes sentimental. He could confide in him and unburden his heart to him about matters which he knew few could understand. On one occasion he wrote, "Dear Mahatmaji, forgive this long letter. To tell the truth, it does me good to pour out my heart to you . . . This is a private letter, to you alone."[34] Gandhi too regarded Stokes with affection. He admired Stokes' courage of conviction and his love for India. "He has made India his home in a manner in which perhaps no other American or Englishman has," Gandhi wrote in *Young India* at the time of Stokes' arrest. He also valued Stokes' opinions. For instance, when Stokes sent him his long memorandum on council-entry, Gandhi read it immediately even though he was not keeping well at that time.

When the *Indian Interpreter,* a Christian journal, criticized non-cooperation and alleged that Gandhi had surrendered himself to common hate as a means to attain unity, Gandhi cited Stokes' views to counter the attack, "Mr Stokes, who has endeavoured to study the movement as an onlooker, says that it is not based on hate."[35] A few months later he again wrote, "If proof were wanted that the movement of non-cooperation is neither anti-British nor anti-Christian, we have the instance of Mr Stokes, a nationalized subject and staunch Christian, devoting his all to the eradication of the evil of *begar.* Mr Stokes is a convinced non-cooperator and Congressman."[36] Tagore's criticism of non-cooperators in London brought the instant response from Gandhi, "How much better it would have been if he had not imputed the rudeness of the students to non-cooperation, and had remembered that non-cooperators worship Andrews, honour Stokes, and gave a most respectful hearing to Messrs Wedgewood, Ben Spoor and Holford Knight at Nagpur."[37]

A few years later when Gandhi was asked at a meeting of the Indian Majlis at Cambridge, during his visit to England for the Round Table Conference, about how an Englishman going to India could cooperate with Indians and serve India, his reply was, "Well, the first thing he should do is to see Charlie Andrews and ask him what he did and what he has gone through to serve India. He has dedicated every minute of his life to the service of India, and done the work of several thousand Englishmen. Let the Englishman, therefore, have his first lessons from him. Then, he must go, not with a view to teach, but to learn how to serve India, and if he approaches his task in that spirit, he will certainly teach. But, in doing so, he will efface himself and merge himself with the Indians, as for instance, Mr Stokes has done in the Simla Hills. Let them all identify themselves with the Indians and try to help them. What cannot real love do? Let all those who are fired with love for India certainly go to India. They are needed there."[38]

In later years when Stokes had retired from politics and remained confined to his home in the hills, Gandhi continued to remember him with fondness and often alluded to his life and work in his conversations. "Tell Stokes I often remember him."[39] On receiving Stokes' letter after a long gap Gandhi "devoured its contents with avidity simply because it is your letter,"[40] and when he received Stokes' philosophical book, *Satyakama,* he set aside other reading in order to go through his book and completed it in less than five days.[41]

Gandhi did not agree with Stokes on several issues but this did not affect their relationship. As he told Stokes, "In spite of our intellectual differences our hearts have always been and will be one."[42]

JOHNNY APPLESEED
OF THE HIMALAYAS

Through the years of his political involvement and philosophical preoccupations Stokes did not once lose interest in his land or neglect it in any way. The land was dear to him not only for its beauty and the solace it provided to his spirit, but also because of its potential as a source of income. The Delicious variety of American apples which he introduced on his farm transformed the entire economy of the region, placing Kotgarh on the world map of horticulture and earning Himachal Pradesh the title "Apple State of India."*

Some British strains of apples were already being grown in the region but their production was on a very limited scale and the orchards were owned by only a few enterprising Englishmen.** The first apple orchard in the Punjab hills was established by Captain R. C. Lee in Kulu valley in 1870. Thereafter, other orchards were planted at Manali, Raison, and Naggar in Kulu valley by English settlers including Colonel Rennick, Captain A. T. Bannon, and C. R. Johnson. There was also Alexander Coutt's orchard, "Hillock's Head," at Mashobra near Simla, which he planted in 1887. In Kotgarh, there was the mission orchard, which was the first to be established in the area by a group of missionaries. There was also a small orchard of about a hundred trees owned by a local Rajput, Gudrumal, who was the tehsildar of Kotgarh in 1881.[1] The apples then grown

---

* Stokes is often mistakenly credited with introducing apples in the area. Some varieties were already growing in the region when he settled there. He, however, is responsible for introducing the American Delicious apples in the country. The credit for introducing scientific and commercial cultivation of apples in the hills rightly goes to him.

** All the British settlers in Kulu sold out their properties and left India well before independence in 1947. The two families that stayed on were Johnsons and Banons. Both men had married local women and embraced the local customs and way of life. Some of their descendents live in Kulu.

in Kotgarh were mainly the Newton Pippin, King of Pippin, and Cox's Orange Pippin. Their production totaled about a hundred mounds.*

These strains of apples were sour in taste and not popular. Also, apple cultivation in hilly terrain was extremely difficult and costly and not attractive to farmers. Besides, the local farmers, poor and often ignorant, were averse to change from their conventional crops of potatoes and maize. Therefore, to meet the demands of the local market, apples were imported from Japan.

All this changed in the 1920s. The Delicious apples which Stokes introduced were sweet in taste and grew easily in the climate of the hills. His novel approach and the scientific methods of cultivation which he practiced paid rich dividends. His involvement with the people and his determination to help them become economically self-sufficient had a deep impact. The rugged topography, difficult terrain, infertile soil, lack of means of communication, and sharp variation in climatic and geophysical conditions—all posing seemingly insurmountable hurdles—were gradually overcome in the Kotgarh ilaqa as people gained confidence and ultimately diversified to apple cultivation.

The saga of apple cultivation in the Simla hills is the saga of one man's determination and foresight. The foundation of Stokes' orchards was laid with a few saplings of apple, pear, and plum trees that he had brought from America and planted around his house in the winter of 1916. Soon he was contemplating commercial cultivation of apples in the region and in 1918 he imported the first saplings from America and Britain. On his visit to America in 1914 he had taken soil samples from Kotgarh for testing. During the succeeding years he continued to experiment, importing and testing more than thirty-three strains of apples to determine which were most suited to local soil and climatic conditions.[2] Finally, after extensive study he selected only five or six of these as commercially suitable for local conditions. Of these, the Red Delicious and its sub-varieties and the Golden Delicious became the most popular both from the point of view of the quality of fruit and its output. The expense and labor involved in this process of progressive elimination of unsuitable varieties turned out worthwhile.

Stokes' mother, Florence Spencer Stokes, played a significant role in the development of apple orchards in Kotgarh. She diligently followed the progress and the latest technological advances in the apple industry in America. After Stokes returned to India she kept him updated on all aspects of the industry, corresponded with different agencies, placed orders, and sent parcels of apple saplings to India. Finding suitable and reliable agencies to deal with, and ensuring that the saplings reached the remote area of Kotgarh safely and in good condition,

---

* 1 mound or 40 seers was equivalent to 0.37324 quintal.
  1 seer = 0.9331 kilogram.

was an onerous task. But she learned fast, and very soon established a rapport with the suppliers. The State Department of Agriculture in Washington proved to be efficient and helpful. The advice and guidance she received from their personnel, some of whom themselves got interested in her mission, made her work easier than it would have otherwise been.

The safe delivery of the consignments, however, was another matter. There were occasions when parcels were dispatched but did not reach their destination. A consignment of Black Bens and Raniers that she ordered from Tappanish in Washington and which was sent in November 1920 through the post office reached India, but could not find its way to Kotgarh. It was returned to the United States two months later without any explanation or apology. However, a parcel of Baldwins which she purchased concurrently from a private nursery and sent through the State Department of Agriculture, reached its destination in time to be set out during the winter.[3]

The Delicious apple saplings were imported by Stokes in 1921, under license from the reputed Stark Brothers' Nurseries in Louisiana, which had only recently developed and patented the variety in America. The Golden Delicious apples which even today hold a place of pride in the Indian market came to the country as Florence Stokes' gift to her son—"My Christmas gift to you must be the Stark's Golden Delicious. For the other apple trees I have ordered for you, you shall pay, but these, which they seem to consider so wonderful, must be your mother's contribution to your orchard," she wrote to him in October 1921.[4] While Stokes signed the guarantee required in further selling the Golden Delicious, she herself gave the company her assurance that he "will be faithful to his part of the contract."[5]

The first consignment of the Golden Delicious sent from Washington in early December 1921 reached Kotgarh six weeks later when Stokes was in jail and were planted and nurtured by Agnes, who had become conversant with the various operations of farming during the years when her husband was away for long periods. Stokes had also trained an assistant who was of help to Agnes.

The Golden Delicious planted in the orchard by their house in Barobagh began to bear fruit four years later. Stokes was so pleased with the quality of the fruit and its appearance that he declared he would make Kotgarh the headquarters of the Golden Delicious for India.[6]

While some of the trees had "one to a dozen fruit on them" in 1924, the first apples from Stokes' orchard were sold in the market in 1926.[7]* "As I sit writing I can hear outside my window the bells on the necks of mules which have come to

* While the Delicious apples were brought to India on license from the Stark Nurseries by Stokes, Gudrumal's grandson Amin Chand's orchard in Kotgarh had a crop of Delicious apples before Stokes' orchard. The Delicious cuttings had apparently been smuggled

carry away the first boxes of fruit that we have sold from the new trees in the orchard near our home," he wrote delightedly to his mother on 31 August 1926. The total output was twenty boxes of about sixty pounds each. "I may be wrong, but I think by next year this new orchard by the house, and the other new orchard down at the lower end of our property, should between them yield us about a hundred boxes for sale. These should bring at the least three dollars a box, so you see that even from next year we should begin to get help from the orchards."[8]

The full impact of the Red and Golden Delicious apples was felt the following year when his best apples arrived in the market wrapped in green printed paper. The quality of the apples and the novel packaging took the Simla market by storm and made these new varieties better known to the public, in a single season, than any of the older varieties that had been selling there for years. Stokes, who had never been interested in business and had little knowledge or experience in the field of marketing, was happy with the result. "After all, when you have good stuff you can afford to tell the public about it, confident that they will like it and ask for more," he said.[9] A year later he started selling his apples under the trademark H.H., an abbreviation of Harmony Hall, the name he had chosen for his orchard. The trademark, an encircled "H.H," was not only stenciled on the wooden boxes but was printed on the wrappers as well. "We shall make every effort to see that nothing short of first-class fruit goes under that mark." He wanted his orchard to have an impeccable reputation. "I intend, if I live, to make the name of this orchard so that when its boxes come on the market no one will dream of the necessity of examining their contents before buying them."[10] Also, all his boxes were marked as "Kotgarh Apples." This was a conscious decision on his part. He wanted Kotgarh's name to be associated with good apples in the Indian market.

Another departure Stokes made from the usual selling practices was to keep the price of his apples to the minimum. Supplying good quality apples at a reasonable price to the public was very important to him. Until now better fruit was marketed at higher prices, but the policy in his orchard was "Better fruit at the same prices." To ensure this he insisted that his fruit agent as well as the man who bought his crop should follow the same principles as far as his fruit was concerned. The rules were clearly laid. "After all, it costs no more to grow superior fruit than to grow inferior fruit and that being so the public has a right to demand the best we can give it at a reasonable profit."[11]

By 1928 there were about a thousand apple trees in Stokes' orchard, the main strains being Red and Golden Delicious, Rich-a-red, McIntosh, and King of

---

out from Stokes' orchard by one of his workers—Tushar—and grafted on mature trees in Amin Chand's orchard.

Pippin. He was satisfied with the development of the orchard and proud of the fact that he had nurtured the trees himself, doing every bit of pruning, thinning, and shaping with his own hands.[12] The proceeds from the sale of the apples was gratifying. Instead of being an expense without returns as in the past, it now held a promise of sustained income for the future. The Delicious variety which had turned out to be the most popular in the market, also fetched the highest price.

The success of the venture also brought to mind his father's business spirit and he wrote to his mother, "One of the things that gives me pleasure in all this is that I know if Father were here he would be much pleased, for he did not look at such matters so much in terms of money as of money as a sign of achievement. To me it appears as the substantial promise of income in the future for service—for the advance of education in our ilaqa. Each of us sees these things in the light and terms of his particular temperament. Both Father and I are idealists, but it finds its expression differently."[13]

When Stokes' experiment in apple cultivation proved to be financially viable he knew that he had found the answer to combat the growing poverty of the ilaqa. Income from apples was many times higher than from grains or other crops grown on the same size of land. If people planted apple trees even in a portion of their small land-holdings, they would be able to generate sufficient income to be able to meet the needs of their families. Stokes' attention was now turned to encouraging small farmers to grow apple trees.

The farmers' initial response, however, was not positive. The older farmers even taunted and ridiculed Stokes for his newfangled ideas. Their major reservation against apple-growing was its long gestation period. They would get no returns from their lands for five to six years till the trees started bearing fruit. They were now growing cash crops—wheat, maize, and potatoes—and even though the returns were small, they had something to live on. But Stokes was determined to change the farmers' attitude. He imported nursery plants at his own cost and distributed them free among farmers and even offered to plant their trees for them. People were afraid of losing their paltry annual income. "*Sahib ji, hum khainge kya?* [What will we eat?]," they would say, to which he would reply, "*Dhari me lagaao, dhari me lagaao* [Plant on the divider between two fields]."[14] He also encouraged them to plant saplings in the so-called wasteland where steep slopes and contours made conventional cultivation impossible. His attitude was that no Kotgarh man, including the poorest and humblest, should fail to get any of the fine varieties that he was growing. Anyone who wanted to plant apple trees in Kotgarh was given saplings of his choice. For the first five years he gave plants free to everybody and thereafter he charged a nominal price from those who could afford it, but to the poor he always gave free.

Stokes' determined efforts to influence and help the farmers paid off. Soon there was a visible transformation in Kotgarh. The terraced fields of wheat and corn were interspersed with apple trees and people waited with hope for their first apple crop. Once the trees began to bear fruit they brought an unprecedented prosperity to the region.[15] Within a few short years, Stokes' dream of making Kotgarh the center of the apple industry in India had come true and Kotgarh came to be identified with the Delicious apples he so loved. His name also became closely linked to the apples he was growing.

While Stokes encouraged the Kotgarh farmers to plant apple orchards and helped them in every way, he was initially reluctant to impart the know-how of the trade and give apple saplings to people of other areas. He refused to supply his saplings even to old friends in high positions in Simla and elsewhere. He wanted the Kotgarh farmer, who was among the poorest in the region, to establish himself in the industry first. Stokes' protectionist attitude gave Kotgarh farmers an edge over their neighbors in other hill areas, something which they have retained ever since. Even today, farmers of Kotgarh are reputed for the superiority of their apples and excellence in their grading and packing methods.

Also, Stokes was worried that unplanned expansion of orchards in the hills would lead to problems unless there was simultaneous infrastructural development for the transport and marketing of the fruit. There were no proper roads in the hills except for the Hindustan–Tibet road, a stretch of no more than two hundred miles. This road, which passed through the Kotgarh ilaqa, was motorable to a moderate degree up to Narkanda, beyond which it did not have the width or the strength to take heavy vehicles. Its use was restricted to the government and the army. Motor transport was strictly forbidden except for touring cars, for which permission was rarely granted.[16] The traditional mode of transportation of goods in the hills then was mules, surefooted, hardy animals capable of carrying heavy loads. Mules were used by the army and by the contractors to bring up goods and equipment from Simla, and by shopkeepers to stock their shops in the interior. They were also used for carrying back to the plains any marketable produce of the farmers which until then had been mainly seed potatoes, a specialty of the upper hills. Fortunately for the people of Kotgarh, mules, which carted goods further up to Rampur-Bushair, passed through their ilaqa, and when the apple trees started bearing fruit, mule owners were only too willing to carry down crates of apples on their return journey.

Carting apples on mule backs could not be a long-term arrangement. The number of mules coming into the hills was limited. Moreover, this mode of transportation was painfully slow for a perishable commodity like apples. It was imperative for the crop to reach markets soon after it was picked and packed. Stokes knew that during these initial years, when apple production was limited, the fruit could easily be transported by mules, but he also knew that if production increased disproportionately to the infrastructure, transporting of fruit would become difficult for farmers. It was this consideration which prompted him to limit the size of his own orchards and to use the rest of his land for traditional crops or let it remain under forestation.

Realizing that the apple industry could not thrive without adequate means of transportation, Stokes urged the authorities to pay attention to this crucial issue and improve the condition of the existing road. The government itself had for years been aware of the problem of transporting farm produce, mainly potatoes, the production of which was anywhere between three to four lakh mounds per year. There was a plan to lay a cable-car service which did not materialize. A proposal to have a ropeway between Narkanda and Simla was found to be unsuitable too.

The government considered extending the railway from Simla up to Narkanda, and there was a strong lobby favoring it. Stokes vehemently opposed the idea, arguing that there was no point in its extension at this stage since there was already a road in existence, and the nature and volume of the fruit produced would only require its utilization for four months in the year. Besides, the project was of questionable financial merit, with the cost of the survey itself being almost as much as the amount required to widen and pave the existing road to make it usable for trucks.

Stokes believed that motor transport, which was used by the Kulu fruit growers from Kulu to Kangra, was the obvious answer to the Kotgarh growers' problems. He was confident that with a little expense and some effort the problem of transport could be overcome. The Hindustan–Tibet Arterial Road No. 20 which ran from Simla through strips of British territory to the Tibetan border, passed right through Kotgarh. The road was on one level from Simla to Kotgarh, with no steep gradients and no bridges which could be swept away by floods. Motor vehicles with special permission plied on it, and made the journey—which took mules two or three days—in a matter of four or five hours. While most of the road was good the last stage between Narkanda and Kotgarh needed to be improved to make it suitable for regular use by trucks. The expense involved was worth undertaking in view of the rapid growth of the apple industry in the region.[17]

An opportunity for Stokes to put forward his views effectively before the administration arose when the governor of Punjab, Sir Malcolm Hailey, visited Kotgarh in July 1928 and expressed a wish to meet him and "talk over various problems connected with the development in the hills." Stokes looked forward to meeting the governor, hoping it would give him an insight into what the government intended to do toward solving the transport problem in the hills. "Though

I am not a government man, and am ready to scrap with the bureaucracy when the situation demands it, I am—and always have been—ready to appreciate and take advantage of any real help they are prepared to extend to our people," he wrote.[18]

In his meeting with the governor, Stokes stressed the urgency of providing suitable means of transporting the fruit, without which facility the growing apple industry could not flourish. He also explained why he did not agree with the railway project, and stressed that the government should concentrate on the road project which was more practical. The road was already there; all it needed was a little more widening and paving. Fortunately for Stokes, Malcolm Hailey shared his views about the railway project and appreciated the nature and value of Stokes' scheme for paving the road as a means of salvation of the inner hills. An aspect of the scheme which appealed to Hailey was the fact that it would solve one of the chief difficulties of the Kalka-Simla railway—that of goods vans returning empty from Simla to Kalka. Once apples arrived in Simla in bulk they would necessarily be sent further by train from Simla. Hailey suggested that while certain sections would have to be paved before such a service was started, the entire road need not be paved, nor would the work have to be done all at once. A few trucks could "feel out the weak places" and weaknesses gradually eliminated.[19]

Their frank and detailed talks gave Stokes confidence that the governor's visit would hasten the development of the motor road. Before leaving Kotgarh, Hailey assured Stokes that upon returning to Simla he would "immediately begin to exert pressure on those who had the motor project in hand."[20] His subsequent meetings with Hailey left no doubt in Stokes' mind about the future of the motor road and he continued to encourage more and more farmers to turn to apple cultivation. Very soon the entire Kotgarh ilaqa was covered with blooming apple trees.

A SCHOOL IN MY GARDEN

Besides concentrating on the orchards, Stokes turned his attention to the education of his children. They were now of school-going age but were studying at home because he was not satisfied with the teaching in local schools. The curriculum of the old Mission School at Kotgarh was inadequate—they did not teach science nor Sanskrit nor Persian. Like the Mission School, the Arya Samaj's newly founded Himalaya Anglo-Sanskrit Middle School at Dhadha was also many miles away from his home and it was impractical for his small children to trudge along such long distances every day. So far, the older of the Stokes children were tutored at home but with Prem turning ten and Pritam nine, the question of their formal schooling could not be put off for much longer.

Though he intended to eventually send his children to Shantiniketan in the trusted care of Andrews and Tagore, putting them in boarding schools in the plains at this stage was out of the question. Children from the mountains suffered in their health whenever they were removed from their natural environment of the hills. Besides, the better schools—missionary or others—were largely Westernized, whereas he wanted his children to have a completely Indian education. Like many nationalists he believed that education in India needed to be rid of Western influences and domination by foreign ideals.*

By the winter of 1923, Stokes had decided on a course of action that would solve the problem of educating not only his own children but also his neighbors' children. He would start a school of his own at Barobagh that would pro-

---

* Annie Besant's views on the subject epitomize the nationalists' sentiments: "Nothing can more swiftly emasculate national spirit or could more surely weaken national character than allowing the education of the young to be handled by foreign influences, to be dominated by foreign ideals . . . National education must meet the national temperament at every point, and develop the national character. India is not to become a lesser—not even a greater—England, but to evolve into a mightier India. British ideals are good for Britain, but it is India's ideals that are good for Indians" (Annie Besant on National Education; *The Modern Review;* April 1919).

vide an ideal education consistent with the national ideals. The school would be located in the grounds right in front of his house. He planned to start with the primary section and raise the classes by one level every year. With his determination and his old friend from the Brotherhood days, Frederick Western, who was still teaching at St. Stephens College, as one of the trustees, he aimed for the school to be the very best in the region. He intended to get the finest teachers for it from all over the country. He would pay good salaries with provident fund benefits and provide comfortable accommodation. The syllabus would suit the children of the village and yet meet the requirements of the Education Board. It would work toward developing feelings of love and fellowship among children so that they learned to work for the good of the community at an early age. As far as financing the school was concerned, Stokes had no intention of asking for government aid which would inhibit its free development. Instead, he planned to meet the entire expense from his own resources. He knew that this would be a strain. His family was large and consisted of his own children and some of their cousins as well. Other responsibilities included providing for the children he had adopted during his Brotherhood days. But financial constraints did not deter him from his plans.

Once the decision to establish a school was made, Stokes went ahead with its immediate implementation. The first building was ready by the end of March 1923, and on the first of April the primary section was opened with a dozen children including his three sons, Prem, Pritam, and Tara, who were in the fourth, second, and first standards respectively. While Stokes himself taught English and geography at the school, two young masters, Parmanand and Charya Ram, took charge of the other subjects under his supervision. Both were old pupils of his and he was pleased that they were now helping him to teach his children.[1] By the end of the year all boys of school-going age from the five or six villages around Barobagh were attending the school. The children were provided with free midday meals and spent the whole day at Barobagh, studying and playing.

In the second year the number of students increased to nearly thirty. A class for the village girls was also now added. At first it was difficult to get the girls' parents to agree to send their daughters to school, but when they found that Agnes was involved in teaching the girls' section, they felt reassured. Once a few girls began to attend the school, the parents got used to the idea and the number of girl students increased.[2] The school, named Tara School, grew rapidly in size and scope.* Within two years its strength reached sixty, one-fourth

---

* The school was named after Stokes' third son, Tara Chand, who died of acute dysentery in June 1924, at the age of eight.

of the students being girls. In 1926 there were more than seventy-five children in the school. By 1928 there were more than eighty.[3]

The children in the school were almost all from the neighboring villages. Stokes wanted to concentrate on the villages around Barobagh, and tried to enroll all the children of school-going age from them, rather than look for students from more distant villages. He felt that while one or two boys may gain much by coming from distant villages, the most of what he wished to see developed—"the spirit of manly self-dependence and self-respect"—could only be maintained if they subsequently lived among those with the same outlook. "If I can have the villages about us full of such boys they will together raise the atmosphere of their village and strengthen each other by their numbers. It is a matter of concentration as opposed to diffusion—of quality as against mere numbers."[4]

To this school, Stokes brought the best of both the East and the West—an emphasis on reading and independent thinking which had been so much a part of his own education and the discipline and values of the old Indian system for which he had great regard. He introduced many revolutionary concepts in this remote center of education. The school library was filled with a wide range of books. There was a discussion club which encouraged children to express themselves freely and fearlessly on a broad spectrum of topics in the presence of other students and teachers.[5] Sports were encouraged not only because of their recreational value but also as a means of building character and integrity.

Impressed by the ideals of the old Indian gurukul system, Stokes tried to incorporate some of its concepts in his school, especially its emphasis on the student-teacher relationship which was the cornerstone of the system. While the teacher gave his all to the welfare and spiritual, intellectual, and physical development of his students, the students in return revered their teacher, emulated him, and felt duty-bound to obey his instructions. Stokes tried to adopt a similar approach in his school. He selected his teachers not only on the basis of their academic qualifications but equally on the basis of their personal qualities—dedication, sincerity, and sense of honor. The student-teacher ratio of ten to one made a close relationship possible between students and teachers. The school was a day-school but the children and their teachers all lived close by. The proximity as well as the day-long involvement of students in various activities led to a feeling of cohesiveness and a sense of belonging among them. Great importance was given to character-building. Honesty was a virtue to be cultivated. The importance of self-help and self-discipline were stressed. Having found inspiration in Rudyard Kipling's poem "If," Stokes got the poem printed on special paper and distributed it among his students.

Former students of the school describe Stokes as a "true guru," who though a great disciplinarian, was entirely devoted to the school and his wards. "People trusted him; children loved him. His presence was a joy and cause of inspiration," said Fazl-ud-Din Ali, the son of Agnes' sister Ada and one of the first students to join the school. Recalling a school trip to nearby Mt. Hattu, Fazl described how Stokes carried a large flask of milk and a tumbler on the trek and when they stopped by a wayside stream, he gave milk to each boy turn by turn, washing the tumbler himself every time.[6]

A significant feature of the school was its emphasis on Hindi which was introduced for the first time in the ilaqa as the medium of instruction. So far in all other schools the medium of instruction was Urdu or English. Stokes was convinced of the efficacy of teaching Hindi to the hill children as a first language. He believed that Indian children should become proficient in their mother tongue before they learned other languages. "The mother tongue comes to a child naturally," he would say. He insisted that his own children followed suit and did not even encourage them to speak English at home till they started learning it at school.* In later life Champa and Savitri never spoke English though they could read and understand it. All other Stokes children were fluent in English. Though Stokes laid greater emphasis on the learning of Hindi and Persian in his school, the importance of English was not undermined. English was taught in the higher classes, from seventh standard onwards, and by the time students reached the tenth standard the medium of instruction changed to English. But since it was taught by the direct method as opposed to the commonly practiced translation method, children were able to pick it up quickly.

Morning assemblies of the school, always attended by Stokes, consisted mostly of singing religious and patriotic songs, all in Hindi. An American visitor present at one of the assemblies was impressed with the singing. "The quality of the children's voices was, on the whole, good, and the melody as fine and simple and stately as a Gregorian chant," he observed.[7]

There were a myriad of activities in the school. Sports included football, netball, tennis, badminton, boxing,** the ever popular tug-of-war in which the entire school participated, as well as local games such as kabbaddi and kho-kho. Inter-school competitions were held with local schools and with visiting teams from Rampur-Bushair, Agra, and Delhi. Debates and discussions were encouraged, as was classical music. Dramatics was another favorite with students, who were as confident and enthusiastic about staging dramas from the great Indian epics as they were about enacting scenes from Shakespeare's plays. To encourage

---

* Elsewhere too, the nationalist schools' ideal of spreading the knowledge of Hindustani throughout India was gaining support. Leaders like Lala Lajpat Rai advocated the use of Hindustani as the medium of instruction, in either Persian or Devanagari script (*The Modern Review*, December 1921). Gandhi criticized the use of English in schools because he felt it was calculated to make Indian children foreigners in their own country (*Mahatma Gandhi*, B. R. Nanda, p. 200).

** Boxing was taught during the summer months by Professor Fitch, a Cambridge graduate teaching at St. Stephen's College, Delhi (*Extracts from Letters*).

scientific inquiry, Stokes would borrow Dr. Jukes' telescope and take the students out at night to study the stars. But there were no Boy Scouts at the school. Though Stokes believed that one could learn much as a Boy Scout, he did not introduce it in his school because of the vows to the king which were an essential part of a Scout's training.[8]

The library had a large selection of books for children and for teachers. Some were specially ordered from England and America, each carefully selected or approved by Stokes. In addition to English books there were a large number of books in Persian and Hindi because Stokes wanted the students to be equally at home reading in languages other than English, and to inculcate a love for and knowledge of the best in these languages. He took a personal interest in directing the children's reading so that by the time they left school they had done a good amount of extra reading—starting from fairy tales and graduating to books of general knowledge and science. There was a healthy mix of books both from the West and the East. Many were selected from the idealistic point of view and children were encouraged to read books that would instill in them values like valor and honesty.*

It was Stokes' aim to develop a real "love of knowing" among the children. He regretted that in most schools in India the focus of attention seemed to be the passing of examinations. Children's lives were anxious lives, in which there was no room for any kind of initiative. He saw to it that this should not happen in his school. "We too have our examinations but life is not centred about them, and all our work in school is not with reference to them." While the children in his school developed far more originality, they were not a bit behind the children of other schools in the standard of their education. They led busy lives and worked hard but Stokes was certain that they would be able to look back upon "happy and unanxious boyhoods and girlhoods."[9]

Since most of the village children could not afford to go to a university, Stokes did not plan to prepare them for advanced education. Instead, his aim was to make the course at the school a real education, as complete in itself as possible, so that when they passed their tenth standard they might properly be said to be educated, with a broad and intelligent outlook. "I aim at a real education covering a period of eleven years from the lower infant's class to graduation. My purpose is to turn out men with ideas of their own, developed personality and character, a clear conception of the world in which we live and the problems which

---

* Some of the titles in the library were *Stories of King Arthur, The Story of Roland, Stories from Indian Chivalry, Indian Heroes,* Kingsley's *Greek Heroes,* Hawthorne's *Tanglewood Tales, Wonder Box, Robin Hood,* and various Norse and Gaelic tales. Books of science and general knowledge included *The Book of Knowledge,* Arabella Buckley's *Life and Her Children, Through Magic Glasses,* and *The Fairyland of Science (Extracts from Letters).*

mankind has to face, a clear idea of the problems and needs of the Kotgarh locality and a sense of their personal responsibility to do their part in solving the immediate problems of their neighbourhood."[10] In a letter he wrote: "Upon the whole, it seems to me that the ideal we have set ourselves is the true one. The primary meaning of life is to make those who live it able to *get the most of the best out of it. It is not merely to fit them for the acquisition of things.*"[11]

At the same time he wanted to ensure that when students completed the final level, they would be able to find employment if they so desired. To this end there were classes in carpentry and masonry from class sixth onwards for every boy in the school. There was a great demand for men who could do either of these forms of work, and even more for those who could do both. Skilled men could earn even more money than an average clerk. "Moreover the public will want them—which is a far more self-respecting position to be in than that of would-be clerks who have to go round begging for work and be grateful for what they can get." For his own children too, Stokes felt it would be a wonderful moral asset for them to know that they were skilled workmen. It would increase their self-confidence as well. "In this country, as in England, it has been looked upon as beneath the dignity of persons of position to work with their hands. I want them to be free from such bad traditions," he wrote to his mother.[12] "Our ideal has been that high thinking and simple needs are the noblest combination our boys can aim at. There is so much love of luxury and the tendency to look down upon simple things in the world today that we feel every effort in the direction of 'noble simplicity' has an especial value of its own."[13]

Most of the children were very poor and were unable to pay school fees. Stokes' resources were limited and expenses of the school were increasing. Fazl Ali related how one day Stokes took the children of the three senior classes to the fields and told them gently, "I want you to learn to work on the land. I want to educate you but I cannot take any fees from you since your parents are too poor. Therefore I want you to earn your fees. I want you to work in the orchards and learn every aspect of apple cultivation. Every day for one hour you must work in the orchard. Make a line and go to work and once the work is finished, fall into line and put away your tools neatly before you disperse . . . I have great hopes from you that you will change this ilaqa."[14] He also told them of his dreams for the ilaqa—apples would one day change the face of the hills, he said. This inspiring little talk was remembered by the children of the school for many years. The work was done, and in a manner which instilled a sense of discipline and responsibility in the children. It also combated the prevalent attitude that manual farm work was beneath one's dignity.

Both boys and girls worked in the orchard every day; they dug, they weeded, they cut the grass and carried manure. When the weather was bad they worked indoors, thrashing corn, or helping in carpentry on a learn-and-earn basis, or they sat in the verandah spinning wool. The first time they spun and wove wool, they made a shawl with it and sent it to Mahatma Gandhi and were thrilled to get an acknowledgment from him. Stokes' unique experiment of making the students work in his orchard had far-reaching implications. Not only did it help in the development of the orchard and enable the students to earn their fees, but it also taught the future generation of the ilaqa the techniques of apple cultivation and inculcated in them the spirit of dignity of labor.

A system of an eight-day autumn harvest holiday in September was also introduced in the school. The work of the farmers was the heaviest at this time and Stokes did not want to let the students' education get in the way of their work at home. He wanted his own children also to grow up with the idea that they should help bear the burden of the family as a whole. So they also worked in the orchard along with the others to earn their school fees. "At school we learnt to do manual work without any shame," said his son Prem. "We did the ploughing, the quarrying and carried manure too. During the harvest holidays we helped in packing apples."[15] When the divisional inspector of schools, Atma Ram, visited Tara School Stokes told him, "I do not take any fees from the children; the children run the orchard and the orchard will run the school."[16]

Thousands of miles away at Sabarmati, Gandhi learned of Stokes' unique school and was as impressed by the spirit of dignity of labor inculcated in students as he was by the beauty of the words of the hymns in Hindi which were an integral part of the morning assembly. "I am watching with considerable interest your experiment amongst the hill people," he wrote to Stokes.[17] Gandhi himself was against government schools, which he said "have unmanned us, rendered us helpless and Godless . . . They have made us what we were intended to become—clerks and interpreters."[18] He favored boycotting conventional schools and establishing national schools.

Stokes was successfully implementing many of Gandhi's ideas in his school and Gandhi was eager for information and suggestions from him for his own school at Sabarmati. He was impressed with Stokes' unique way of making children responsible for their education by working in orchards and at the same time learning the skills of fruit-growing. "I now understand the school and its purpose. I know that Stokes is doing great work and good work and gives his all to it," Gandhi noted.[19] Gandhi's own proposals at the Wardha Educational Conference ten years later, stressing that education should be imparted through some craft or productive work which should eventually enable the school to pay toward the cost of its teaching staff, echoed the principles practiced at Tara School.*

---

* "The process of education . . . shall centre round some form of manual and productive work and that all other abilities be developed or the training to be given should as far as possible be integrally related to the central handicraft chosen with due regard to the environment

It pleased Stokes to see his own children blossoming in the company of other children. Even the little ones who did not read in the school, Savitri and Satyavati, were under the influence of a joyful crowd of school children. The progress of the school and the happy, healthy environment at Barobagh convinced him that no other form of education could be of so much value to the children, his own and others. They were learning as well as they would in other schools—probably better than in most—but they were also doing so in the healthy moral and spiritual atmosphere of their home. Their neighbors were learning with them, and they were all growing up with common ideals, which he believed would vastly facilitate their relations with each other in the years to come.[20]

He made sure that other village children did not feel the economic disparity between themselves and his own children. His children were always dressed simply and soberly, mostly in hand-woven, home-dyed cottons. When his daughters expressed a desire to wear jewelry he told them, "If I want I can cover each of you with gold from head to toe, but how do you think the other village girls will feel when they see you like this—they are very poor and their parents cannot afford to buy even silver trinkets for them." They never raised the question of jewelry with him again.

The school was of great importance to Stokes. "After all, these are the years in which the foundations of character, intelligence and ability are laid by our children, and to help them lay them properly is surely our greatest duty."[21] And to his own children he wanted to give an opportunity, along Indian lines, to get the best which life could give them in terms of building up character, as he had when he himself was a boy. "What is the use of a beautiful home and a sufficiency of worldly goods for children if one does not fit them to get the highest good out of them? I should not feel that half my income was too much for the purpose . . . To merely leave one's children a house and lands and money, no matter what a blessing the power to leave these is, is not leaving them a complete inheritance."[22]

There was no isolation or loneliness in Barobagh. His children were always happy in the school as were their little neighbors from the surrounding villages. The happy, shining faces of children pleased him. "Surely this is a happy school and all the children love it."[23] It was a great joy for him to stand on his upper verandah and watch the youngsters at play during recreation periods, or at work sitting under trees and making an "awful racket about it."[24] "To make one's home and one's village the centre of so much happiness and so much opportu-

---

of the child; and that the conference expects that this system of education will be gradually able to cover the remuneration of the teachers." Gandhi's proposals at the Wardha Educational Conference held on 22 and 23 October 1937 (*The Indian Annual Register*, Vol. II; July–December 1937).

nity for the attainment of more 'fullness of life'—what greater privilege could one have?"[25] he wrote. "There is happiness in feeling that when life is over, there will be something to show in the lives and characters of many, of its having been lived."[26]

As the years passed, Stokes' appreciation of his father and all that he had achieved grew. He often thought of how greatly the fruits of his father's labors had improved the life of these simple hill people and made it possible for him to make his own life useful in a manner that would probably otherwise have been quite impossible.[27] "Had I been pressed by the constant necessity of attending to money matters, much of what I consider the most valuable work I have done would have been quite impossible!"[28]

In the summer of 1925, the Stokes home in Kotgarh had an American visitor from Colorado. Richard B. Gregg (Govind to Gandhi), had arrived in India only recently. He had been with Mahatma Gandhi for over a month and with Andrews and Tagore for three or four months. Andrews was anxious for him to put in some time at Kotgarh to learn something about Hindu philosophy and the economics of khadi from Stokes.[29]

Gregg, who was a graduate of Wisconsin and Harvard Universities, was impressed by Stokes' school and the children's development in it. He found in them the same liveliness, the same variations in ability, attitude, and character that he had seen in American children when he had taught at a school years before in Massachusetts. To him they were a considerably more attractive group of children than those he saw in the plains at Rabindranath Tagore's school at Shantiniketan—"much poorer of course in terms of material circumstances, but far more natural."[30]

Stokes, too, was impressed by Gregg's keen intellect and sincerity. After studying him closely for two months, Stokes made him an offer to join his school which the latter accepted enthusiastically. Gregg's sojourn in Kotgarh proved to be of great benefit not only to the students and teachers, but also to Stokes who found he could discuss with him problems that lay outside the ken of others in the ilaqa.[31]

When Gregg joined in the spring of 1926 there were already seventy-two children in the school and the classes were up to the seventh standard. The classes had been increasing by one level each year and it was expected that in four years it would become a full-fledged high school, which would prepare students for the Board matriculation examination. The subjects taught were Urdu, Hindi, English, Persian, mathematics, history, geography, and physics. The teachers were all Indians except for Gregg, and four of them had been Stokes' students at one time. The principal of the school was Dhan Singh, who had graduated from St. Stephen's College, Delhi. The new English teacher, V. Sundaram, hailed from Madras. He was with Gandhi at Sabarmati in the early days, and had been private secretary to Madan Mohan Malaviya, at whose behest Stokes brought him to Barobagh. There were two teachers from Punjab, Sardar Kishen Singh who taught Urdu, and Sardar Gian Singh who taught Indian classical music. There was also the poetic and free-thinking Munshi Fazal who pursued his studies while he taught at Tara School and later became Professor of English at the D.A.V. College, Lahore.[32]

Stokes, who had earlier taught the two upper classes, was doing no teaching now under doctors' orders. His work was being carried out by Sundaram. Gregg was given charge of teaching physics and mathematics, including arithmetic, algebra, and geometry to the seventh class. He found the books for teaching mathematics so good that he sent a list of these to Gandhi to be used at his school in Sabarmati.[33]

During this period, many innovative ideas were introduced in the school. Since most of the prescribed textbooks were unimaginative and unrelated to the children's experience, Stokes and Gregg decided to take on the task of writing new textbooks in their subjects. Stokes' *Background of History* was written with the aim of nurturing a love of history among children and bringing them to the realization that Indian history was the history of man as he had developed in India—it was *human* history. The history that he himself had learned at school was mostly about kings and their quarrels and very little of it was about the lives and customs of the people they governed. According to him, this was not the way history should be taught. To him history was the most interesting and valuable of all school subjects: "For history shows us the meaning of our lives, and if we study it rightly it will teach us how to live finely and nobly and usefully."[34]

Gregg, too, prepared new textbooks, in both mathematics and physics, which would conform to the students' experience. All English textbooks, and even the Indian ones, were apparently written for city-bred children and presupposed familiarity with machinery and manufactured apparatus of all kinds. "These children here have never seen automobiles, steam engines, electric lights, pumps, water pipes, or even bullock-carts. So the assumptions, pictures, technical terms and arrangement of the textbooks of physics, and even of much of mathematics can have no reality and therefore no interest or educational value for them. Gradually, therefore, I am putting together what will be in effect a textbook of science and mathematics for Indian village children. Since most of the children of India are in villages, I hope it will be useful," Gregg wrote to Gandhi.[35] These innovations in textbooks drew Gandhi's attention and he made a special mention of them in his "Notes on Indian Textbooks."*

---

* Gregg remained in Kotgarh for three years and left in 1928 because of indifferent health. He was close to Gandhi and spent all his vacations in Gandhi's ashram. *The Collected Works of Gandhi* contains his correspondence with Gandhi. Gregg wrote the book *Economics of Khaddar* in 1927 while he was at Kotgarh.

From time to time Gregg wrote to Stokes' mother in Philadelphia describing details of life in Kotgarh. In one letter he described how, at the end of an important event, everyone from the school, including teachers, would gather around and sing and dance in the hill fashion. After that, sweets were always distributed—an occasion the poor village children looked forward to. "It was all great fun to see the children's faces shine and watch them gradually forget their first shyness and self-consciousness. The littlest boys looked on with open mouths, only half understanding what it was about. The amusing little rascals, most of them in ragged clothes; some eager, observant, whispering and grinning; some apathetic; some wistful. The kerchiefs [dhatu] on the girls' heads were red or white, the clothing of all either gray or soft browns. A few had gold or silver earrings. All were bare-footed. I wish my slow pen could give you a real idea of how picturesque it was, and how much the young unformed personalities and their sensibilities appealed to me," Gregg wrote of his impressions of children at the Barobagh school.[36]

The school continued to prosper. Both teachers and students were enthusiastic and Stokes was satisfied with the work. Financially it was a burden; "I meet the difficulties gladly because I am ever more convinced that it is the best way to do justice to our children, and gives them the sort of education that makes for the fullest life at the same time ensuring that their social environment will be of a helpful nature."[37]

Though he had hoped he would be able to meet the school expenses from his personal funds until the orchard started generating an income, he found himself unable to do so after the first three years. The school was expanding and its expenses increasing. There were nearly a dozen teachers. The salaries and provident fund of the staff alone amounted to more than Rs 4,500 per annum. Consequently, in 1926, he was compelled to take a loan from a friend. Borrowing money was a hard choice but Stokes felt that it would be wrong for him to let shortage of money interfere with the children's education at a time when it was so essential that there should be no break or setback in their development. Depending on the requirement he intended to take a loan of Rs 2,000 to 3,000 every year for the next three to four years with a 6 percent interest. The total amount to be repaid at the end of that period would be Rs 10,000 to Rs 12,000. By that time, he hoped to get a substantial income from the orchard, from which he could begin to repay the loan. Not wanting to rely upon his own judgment exclusively in this matter, he consulted Gregg and Western. When both agreed that he was justified in taking the step, he formalized the loan agreement.[38]

This was the first time that Stokes had had to borrow money from someone other than his mother and it evidently bothered him. "The debt is incurred for a specific object—to tide us over the next four or five years in the work we have undertaken, and is to be used for nothing else . . . It is a debt of honour, and as such must take precedence over everything else," he wrote in the school's account book. He was determined, however, to pay back the loan independently without help from anybody. When Sardar Vithalbhai Patel visited him at Barobagh and offered to help him tide over his financial difficulties, Stokes declined the offer, even though Patel was a personal friend.[39]

In 1926, Stokes applied for recognition of the school by the Punjab Educational Department. The ilaqa was so poor that he felt the younger men would have to eventually look for jobs to augment their family's income. Since there were no jobs in the village, the only way out was for them to seek employment outside their homes. As most of them could not stand the heat of the plains they had to limit their search to Simla. The only jobs available in Simla, however, were government ones for which a certificate from a government-recognized school was essential. Applying for recognition was a difficult decision for Stokes, especially since he had never been in favor of dependence on government jobs but he felt weighed by these considerations. Obtaining it proved to be even more difficult. The general policy of the Educational Department was that recognized institutions had to follow the department's rules and regulations and a strict regime of curriculum and schedule. Stokes, on the other hand, wanted recognition on his own terms. He wanted to retain the school's freedom to experiment and to run it in accordance with his own ideas and ideals. He did not want any official pressure and interference. "We shall not move an inch from our position as to keeping our freedom of action," he said.[40]

Gandhi did not think that seeking recognition for the school was a step in the right direction. "How I should love to convince him that he does not need government recognition for his school," he wrote to Gregg who had taken great pains to explain the reasons which compelled Stokes to seek government recognition. "There must be some method of enabling the boys to earn their own living without government patronage. The path is not easy but it is the only one that he or shall I say we must tread. However, I must not criticize. He must work by the light of his conscience even though to an outsider he may seem to be erring."[41]

The year 1928 was a landmark one for the students of the ilaqa when Tara School commenced its new session with the ninth standard and became the first school to provide high-school education in the area. The occasion was one of tremendous satisfaction to Stokes, especially because the first middle school in Kotgarh had also been started by him twenty years earlier, and now there were three. Stokes brought Bihari Lal, an experienced educationist of Punjab, to be headmaster of the school. A high school also meant a heavier burden on his resources but he was determined to carry on. "I feel that our only justification for making our home in these hills is service rendered. That constitutes our right to be here."[42]

While the school's reputation had spread and private individuals and government officials appreciated the value of the school, its recognition was withheld. This was apparently due to "political considerations."[43] Although Stokes was no longer politically active, his sympathies were with the nationalist cause. His school was also clearly a nationalist school bringing up young men and women who were loyal to their country and proud of their heritage. However, Stokes persisted with his efforts. The following year he invited the education minister of Punjab to the school. During the minister's visit, the students staged Shakespeare's *Julius Caesar* at a special school function. Though the minister was very impressed with the school and was full of praise for the work that was being done, recognition was still not granted.[44] The British did not want Stokes to run the school in the way he was running it. "They wanted him to close down the school because it was a national school and they created all kinds of trouble for Father," said Prem Chand. "When the first batch of students was to appear for matriculation the Education Department withheld their roll numbers even though full fees had been paid."

In 1930, students of the ilaqa appeared for the first time in the Punjab Matriculation Board Examination as private candidates. Among these was Grace, daughter of Agnes' sister Ada, who became the first girl from the region to ever pass the examination. Prem also matriculated that year with a first division. Two more batches appeared for matriculation from Tara School in 1931 and 1932 after which Stokes was compelled to revert the school back to the secondary level. This time it was not the British who instigated the move but the economic depression in the U.S.A. and the fall in share prices which reduced his foreign income considerably. The high school had meant a heavier burden but somehow he had managed to carry on. Now he not only faced an alarming fall in his American income but also the prospect of an uncertain Indian income which had not increased as expected. Though the income from the orchard in the initial years had showed promise, the profits were now being depleted by the steep rise in the cost of transportation, and his hope of meeting the growing expenses of the school from the orchard income remained unfulfilled. There was no way he could run a high school without a substantial, assured income. The closing of the high school was a loss not only to the ilaqa, but also to his own children. While Prem and Pritam were able to pass their high school from Barobagh, the education of his daughters who were in junior classes suffered, as did that of his youngest son, Lal Chand.

Despite this setback, it was a matter of great satisfaction for him to see that many students who passed out from Tara School could go on to study at St. Stephen's College in Delhi or in other leading colleges of Lahore, and that many others devoted their time to developing apple orchards on their lands. He was all for village boys going in for higher education in the plains. "The hills have laboured under a great disadvantage in these matters because of the difficulty our people have in facing the heat of the plains for their higher education, and we are in great need of a body of trained and educated men of our own who may form the nucleus for the educational upliftment of the tribes here," he wrote.

At one time he had hoped to send his children to Shantiniketan. That was before Tara School was conceived. Now he was happy that the little school at Barobagh had made it possible for his children to pass their childhood in the midst of other children from the neighborhood. "Your education, in the noblest sense, includes the lifting and ennobling of those about you," he reminded them. "God grant that you may prove worthy of the care and anxious thought which has been given to affording you the truest opportunity for growing to noble maturity."[45]

A highlight of this period for Stokes and his family was his mother's second visit to India in April 1927. She was in her eightieth year and had cancer, but she had an intense desire to see her son and his family. Year after year she used to send carefully selected Christmas presents for her grandchildren in India. Though thousands of miles away, she would try to picture their faces and visualize their lives. Knowing how much his mother missed them, Stokes tried to keep her informed with details of their lives in Kotgarh.

Suddenly in January 1927, Stokes received a letter from his mother expressing her desire to come to India even if it was for only a few weeks. "I do feel as if I must see you all—the dear boys and girls and Agnes before I go to my long home. The feeling has grown so lately I feel I must indulge in it."[46] She had hoped that either her daughter Florence or friend and companion Kate Miles, would accompany her, but when this became improbable she decided to take a doctor along. "It would only be about a month on the water to Bombay and I am a famous sailor you know—then two days in a sleeping car to Simla and from there a few days longer in a dandi—the easiest trip imaginable, and then about three weeks with you all and back to America as easily as I left it," she wrote.[47]

She set out from New York on 1 March and a month later was in Bombay. After spending four weeks in Kotgarh she sailed back from Bombay on 11 May and was home by mid-June, having celebrated her eightieth birthday on board the ship on 15 June. Her visit was wonderful. She was at last able to meet the grandchildren she had dreamed about. The apple trees were in bloom and she was amazed to see that they were proving so successful as a commercial enterprise. She was also glad to know that the little trees she had shipped from America were of help.

"How pleased your father would have been if he could have known what you have accomplished in your Indian life—in every direction. Agnes would have won his heart and his confidence and your wonderful house and marvellous outlook—the school, everything connected with it and your dear boys and girls, above all your ideals and the way in which you are carrying them out, would have so commanded his interest and his respect. Above all, he would delight over your apples—it is already proving such a success," she wrote on her return.[48]

Her visit to India was remembered long afterwards by her grandchildren (though at this time, except Prem, none of the others could converse in English) and the students of Tara School.* Fazl Ali recalled how Stokes took every care to make his mother comfortable. "When she found it difficult to walk on the uneven mountain paths he would carry her in his arms. 'She carried me when I was little—why should I not carry her now?' he would say."

Stokes and his mother had a very special relationship which strengthened with the passing of time. They were thousands of miles apart but their weekly letters kept them in the closest touch. "My nearness to you is a thing which transcends mere miles," he would tell his mother. Her visit to India was especially precious to mother and son. "The great joy—your joy and mine, dear—was the one month we had together—together in a very deep sense. We both knew that it was most improbable that it could ever be again in this world, but to me it was the great reality of each of our lives, of yours especially—the life I shall live over and over, as long as it lasts in this world."[49]

Florence Spencer Stokes was a remarkable person. Her outlook toward life was neither restricted nor insular. She had traveled widely, was an avid reader, and kept abreast of world affairs. When her son went to India, she began to read extensively about the country—its history, culture, and literature. She attended Tagore's lectures when he came to Philadelphia and New York, and did not miss any India-related events in the city. Though a dedicated Christian, her religious outlook broadened over time and she was able to comprehend and appreciate her son's interest in Indian philosophy. Stokes was very proud of his mother. Her influence on the development of his life and thought was deep and far-reaching. Her life has "ever been to me, an interpretation of the scriptures, and an inspiration," he wrote.[50]

When he saw her off on the ship at Bombay on 11 May, they both knew well that this was the last time they would see each other in this life. She died two years later, on 23 February 1929, of pneumonia without much suffering.

---

* Some recalled how Florence was keen for her eldest Indian granddaughter, Champa, to become a doctor and wanted to take her to America with her, but Stokes did not agree. If her grandmother's wish had been fulfilled, Champa would have been the first woman doctor of the hills.

CAME TO TEACH
AND STAYED TO LEARN

One of the most interesting aspects of Stokes' life was the evolution of his religious beliefs. Over the years he became increasingly interested in Hindu philosophy. He was first introduced to the subject at the Gujranwala Religious Conference of February 1907 where representatives from different religions spoke of their faiths. This was where he first heard the religious views of Arya Samajists who heavily influenced his thinking in later years. The assertion by representatives of the Arya Samaj that "the soul attains to mukti through karma and not by Grace" motivated him to study a translation of *Satyarth Prakash,* written by Swami Dayanand Saraswati, founder of the Arya Samaj.[1]

He then wrote a tract on the subject questioning the validity of this philosophy. The sole aim of his research was to seek the truth, he wrote. "To seek *the truth* and to impart that *truth* to others is the duty of every earnest and thoughtful man . . . To hear the opinions of those who think differently from us, and to hear these opinions with an open mind is the only wise and just way." In his first comparative study of Christianity and Hinduism he maintained that the paper was not against the Arya Samaj by a Christian, but might rather be called, "The difficulties which the philosophy of the Vedas as interpreted by Swami Dayanand Saraswati present to the mind of a Seeker after that Truth which the Vedas are intended to declare."[2]

He was impressed by the Arya Samaj, which had attracted a large number of progressive Hindus and with which he first came in contact during the Kangra earthquake, when the Punjab Arya Samaj did commendable work. Soon after the Gujranwala Conference he had met Mahatma Munshi Ram, the charismatic leader of the Arya Samaj and became interested in his gurukul system of education. In December 1907 he was present at the thirtieth anniversary of the

Arya Samaj celebrated in Lahore where Munshi Ram made a special mention of Stokes' interest in the gurukul and his intention to establish a gurukul for Christians. Stokes admired the dedicated spirit of the Arya Samajists, even though their religious viewpoints were new to him. In his anniversary address, Mahatma Munshi Ram urged the young men of India to "remove all enmity and jealousy and rear a big strength, in which you join Hindus, Mohemmedans, Jains and Christians to improve the world."[3] This all-encompassing philosophy of toleration clearly impressed young Stokes.*

During these early years Stokes continued to maintain contact with members of the Arya Samaj. He was a welcome guest of Mahatma Munshi Ram at the Gurukul Kangri in Hardwar. A letter sent by Rama Deva, editor of the gurukul magazine, on behalf of the Mahatma inviting Stokes to the anniversary celebrations of the gurukul in 1911, reflects the cordial relations between the two: "The gurukulites have very loving memories of your last visit to the institution and of the affectionate interest that you have ever since evinced in its progress. Mahatma Munshi Ram insists upon it that you must attend the forthcoming anniversary."

Stokes' contact with the Arya Samaj was re-established during the days of the begar struggle when he sought the help of Lala Lajpat Rai with whom he had become acquainted during one of the Arya Samaj functions. His later involvement in the national struggle led to long-lasting friendships with leaders of the Arya Samaj, including Lala Lajpat Rai, Madan Mohan Malaviya, and Lala Duni Chand. Stokes' admiration of the gurukul system was unwavering. "The Gurukul Kangri, and others like it stand as beacons in an age of material superficiality to remind us of the beauty of simplicity," he wrote many years later.[4]

Meanwhile Stokes' initial dissatisfaction with the Christian missions in India increased with the passage of time. The racist attitude of the missionaries troubled him. The missionaries had succumbed to the "fetish of racialism and colour-consciousness," despite the fact that it was the antithesis of the attitude of the early Christians. "The European missionary is divided by the colour bar from Christian natives just as acutely as from the pagan, and can organize his converts into a 'native church' which is still outside the pale of the European community," he charged.

He had also become extremely disillusioned with Christianity, especially as it

---

* Stokes and Andrews, both devout Christians, were attracted to the philosophy of Arya Samaj and the personality of its leader Mahatma Munshi Ram, later known as Swami Shraddhanand, at a time when the general feeling between Christians and Arya Samajists was one of hostility. Andrews was so devoted to the Mahatma that at one stage he even contemplated joining the Arya Samaj. Andrews was also the link between Gandhi and Mahatma Munshi Ram. (Gandhi used to call Tagore, Principal Rudra, and Munshiram, Andrews' "Trinity." [Gandhi in "Swamiji as I Knew Him," *Young India*, 6 January 1927])

was taught and practiced in India. Over the years he had become convinced that Christianity in India must change in its form and development and the Church in India, which was a foreign institution, should be replaced by a Church that was Indian in ethos. In an article he wrote on church unity in 1919 he rejected the movement of ecclesiastical unity. "No church can be expected to swallow whole the experience of another and yet thrive."[5]

Stokes did not want the Indian Church to have its life and thought cast in the mold of the West. "India must resist with all her power the tendency of the West to dominate her life and thought. Europe and America have not yet discovered a panacea for their own ills, much less for those of other nations." He felt the Indian Church should develop its own theology and tenets and if at some point it wished to enter the episcopal fold it should do so as an equal.* He insisted that the Indian Christian community must be true to India and must not allow its thought and life to be dominated, or its liberty curtailed, by even the most devoted and well-intentioned control of "aliens." He also wanted the Indian Church to free itself from Western financial help. The Westerners, he felt, were prone to measure success by the size of their plans and the amount of money spent on them, and many were involved in "Mission Drives" for vast sums to be collected and spent in further organizational work. But he was convinced that as long as the Indian Church was subsidized by the West, it could never grow freely into a life of its own.

Stokes was also critical of the attitude of Western missionaries toward Indian Christians. The mission system tended to develop a sense of superiority among Western missionaries and a sense of inferiority among Indian converts which outraged the self-respect of many Indians who saw "a bureaucratic spirit fully as strong among the missionaries as that evinced in the relations between the government and the people."[6] This prevented the best of Indians from becoming Christians. Andrews shared Stokes' views on the subject, observing that it was the "inconsistencies" of Christians that kept back the educated classes in India from accepting the Christian faith.[7]

The methods adopted by the missionaries in persuading Indians to convert were such that most conversions were of the poorest and the outcastes. The repelling feature of the transaction, Stokes believed, lay not so much in the fact that the converts were outcastes as in the knowledge that these people had changed their religion for economic gains without undergoing any spiritual experience

* Andrews, too, rejected the idea of superimposing the Christian ideal of the West on India which he thought would make the converts into hybrids. "We seem, somehow, to have missed our true Pentecost . . . we have in India a Church which is still a half-parasitic growth, too long clinging with all its tendrils to the West," Andrews wrote in an article, "The Indian Missionary Ideal," published in *The East and The West* in 1911.

which would justify such a step.[8] In a letter dated 3 January 1920, he wrote to his mother, "They tell you at home of the vast numbers of Indian converts. There are large numbers—nearly three and a half million. But what are they? Ignorant outcastes, mostly from the scavenger castes, with little of Christianity in them except the name, more worldly than the Hindus and less spiritual. That is the reality, and those of the better classes who have given up all for Christ are highly discontented. Western Christianity does not help, but hinders their advance in Christ. I am certain that the time has come to cease sweeping in vast numbers of nominal Christians and to work for the Christianizing of Hinduism—not the converting of Hindus."[9]

His criticism of the development of Christianity in India did not mean that he undervalued the missionary effort of the West or that he wanted it to cease at once in India. Nor was he hostile to missions; many missionaries were his personal friends. But he wanted their work in India to be educational and philanthropic. "I want it to cease to preach Christ by words but to continue for some years to incarnate His love, as the West has seen it, in labours of love."[10]

Apart from the form and work of missions in India and the attitude of the missionaries, it was in the acceptance of the basic principles of Christianity in which he also differed from fellow Christians. His study of theology led him to believe that Christ's message was "infinitely more" than what the Church had taught. While being a devout Christian, he was, from the beginning, unable to accept the "orthodox (so called) view of Christ's message."[11] For example, he had been unable to accept the theory of eternal punishment even as a schoolboy and was never comfortable with the practice of confessions. At one of the Christian conventions at Sialkot which he attended during his early years in India, he had been greatly distressed at the public confession of sin, so reminiscent of Hawthorne's *Scarlet Letter,* and had feared that the young novice who was accompanying him, Sundar Singh, would be utterly disillusioned by it.[12]

With the passage of time, Stokes' interest in Hindu philosophy grew. What had started as an exploratory study as a challenge to the Arya Samaj* resulted in his deep involvement in the thought embodied in the ancient Indian scriptures in which he was able to find answers to many of the questions that had preoccupied him. In Hinduism he found validation of his earlier rejection of the idea of eternal punishment, and his conviction that God had created no soul that He could not and would not save. An early letter he wrote from India shows that he had come to "appreciate that belief in universal salvation of *necessity* involved belief not only in 'another chance' but in many 'chances' if the lost sheep was

---

* The Arya Samaj believed in dialogue and debate on religious issues. Public discussions between Hindus and Christians were, therefore, held frequently.

to be sought until it was found."[13] In October 1906 he wrote, "If anyone is liberal in his views I may claim to be one who am a believer in universal salvation, transmigration of souls, the non-existence of sin as a power in opposition to holiness etc. Yet I have arrived at none of these views by not thinking about them, but rather by applying my whole mind to them with prayer."[14]

A letter two years later, in December 1908, shows that while he was still a "strong if not very orthodox churchman," his thought was shaping toward the philosophy manifested twelve years later in his book *Satyakama*. At the time of the great Messina earthquake in 1908 his parents and younger sister Florence were traveling in Sicily. Anxiety about their safety and the magnitude of the tragedy set him thinking once again about the philosophy of rebirth. "In the light of such catastrophes it seems to me impossible to look at the regenerating work of Christ as confined to one life in the world. The theory that only one short life is given as a time of development and testing for all eternity seems to me absurd when I see 200,000 men, women and children swept out of their earthly bodies in one short hour." Even before he had come out to India he had come to feel that this question found its true solution in the hypothesis of rebirth.[15]

In later years when writing about Christianity in India, Stokes admitted how he had come to India to teach not only about Christ, but Christianity in the garb in which he had received it from his forefathers. He had considered it axiomatic that the message he brought was the perfection of all truth—that anything beyond it was superfluous, that any truth taught by any other religion was better taught by his own.

In course of time he studied the propagandist literature of missions, and soon came to the conclusion that the Christianity it presented would be unacceptable to most. As a consequence he decided to study ancient Indian scriptures, and also to steep himself in the atmosphere of the later Puranic literature which so largely influenced the minds of the Indian masses. The object of his study at that time was to be able to "demonstrate to Indians how untrue to all experience, and unworthy of consideration, the whole Hindu attitude was." However, he found the results of his study to be "distinctly unsatisfactory." He discovered much that was "intellectually unacceptable, much that was demonstrably fallacious," as he would have found, he admitted, in the scriptures of his own or any other religious system. But gradually, over several months, it also dawned upon him that "these works contained the intellectual efforts of those who were seeking to grapple in the boldest and noblest manner with the deep problems of life, its meaning and its purpose." Before long, he discovered, to his astonishment, that in attempting to solve some of the problems the ancient thinkers of India had often shown "a finer spirit and a higher intellectual perception than the great minds of the early Church during the centuries when it was taking shape and evolving creeds."

At the same time he made another interesting discovery. He found that in the Hindu scriptures there were vast and important areas of thought and speculation on the meaning of life with which the Church had never dealt, or with which it had dealt most unsatisfactorily. In the Hindu scriptures he found "not so much in the actual solutions arrived at, as in the general tendency of thought and method of approach, the key to much that the Christian religion, as evolved in the West, has never attempted to explain, or about which its teachings have been frankly agnostic." As these new vistas opened out, it was a shock to him to discover that the Christianity taught in the West was "highly disconnected and fragmentary." It was defective because it consisted of "an array of mighty life-giving truths, each of them developing one-sidedly, laying vast stress upon certain aspects of life and entirely oblivious to others equally important."

His realization did not, however, diminish his faith; on the contrary, he felt that he now had a clearer understanding of Christianity. "The light from the Hindu scriptures had come to fill the gaps in Christianity" as he had known it, and to make it "a connected whole." In an honest appraisal, he wrote in an article in 1919, "This has been the writer's own experience. He came to teach and stayed to learn. He has found the idea at the back of the whole Hindu religious development of intense spiritual significance to his own spiritual progress, and has been deeply influenced by it. Yet, he is not less Christian—only more Hindu in his concept, and he humbly believes that in being more Hindu in his outlook upon life he is more Christian than he could otherwise have been."*

He was now convinced of the necessity of a synthesis between Christianity and Hinduism. "Christianity and Hinduism need each other. The best in each is incomplete without the other. The truths of each remain but half-truths without the light which each can shed upon the other. As men have learned to see with eyes unblinded by the age-old prejudices and preconceptions that shackle them today, they will come to understand that, when the divine synthesis has been affected, a true Christian will be able to call himself a Hindu, and a true and perfect Hindu will be able to say, 'I also am a Christian'."[16] In early 1920 he contemplated starting a monthly magazine in which he planned to discuss various concepts of Christianity and Hinduism and to see how one could be helped by

---

* Andrews expressed a similar sentiment in his article "Christ in India," which he wrote in 1924. "It is now more than twenty years ago since the time I started out on my first journey from England to India in order to teach as a missionary the principles of Christianity to the Indian people . . . Since then, the experience of India has been a strange reversal of all the things that I had anticipated. Instead of being a teacher I have had to be a learner, learning my lessons with great difficulty and perplexity. To narrate my story very shortly, I have been learning year after year to understand the true meaning of Christ from those who are not called Christians. I have found them often more truly Christians than those who are called by Christ's name" (*The Modern Review*, March 1924).

the other. The aim was to find in the synthesis something "more true to our intellect and our spiritual experience" than either Hinduism or Christianity alone had to offer. "For instance, the Vedanta and Christian conceptions of salvation if taken together must profoundly influence and modify each other. Christian experience will preserve individuality and the Vedanta will demonstrate the essential unity of spirit."[17]

"I am convinced that no matter what my feeble effort may be able to do toward solving the problem of interdependability of the two, still it is there and that there is a synthesis not yet fully seen by us, yet which will some day open to our eyes a vista of glorious realities than either the Hinduism or Christianity of the past have been able to give us," he wrote to Andrews. The writings in the magazine he planned to start would investigate these issues. He and other writers, divesting themselves as far as possible of their inherited preconceptions and prejudices, would look for that which was "neither 'Hindu' nor 'Christian,' but the truth." He did not plan to have a subscription price for the paper or to take money for its expenses. What he wanted to do was to carefully work out a mailing list of people in India, England, and America who would give the issues their patient attention. "In other words, I should like it for those who really matter in this respect." He had some correspondence on the subject with Kamakshi Natarajan, editor of the *Indian Social Reformer,* who seemed to take to the idea. Stokes was also keen to consult Andrews before venturing into the project.

The magazine was never printed, for soon afterwards Stokes got involved in more practical issues—begar in the hills and the Indian nationalist movement. While his involvement with the national movement diverted his attention from the role of Western missionaries in India, it brought him in close contact with some of the most eminent thinkers in India and helped in crystallizing his religious philosophy.

During the time Stokes was in jail, he had had the opportunity to put down his philosophical thoughts in writing. His book *Satyakama,* a "consideration on the *Meaning of Life,*" was "a system of speculative philosophy following original lines of vital importance in their relation to Hindu and Christian spiritual evolution." It represented an outlook upon life which had gradually been taking shape in his mind. The enforced solitude of the jail had enabled him to elaborate on his thesis.[18] But the rough first draft of 250 pages was a bare outline of his philosophy and he knew that it would take him several years to complete the work. On his release, he set aside the treatise for about a year so that he could approach it later with the "vision of an outsider."[19] But though his thought developed and became clearer in the course of subsequent years, it did not change in any important particulars. He had arrived at very definite conclusions. "It is old yet it is new. It is the product of the past and yet it is full of a new dynamic power . . .

I am sure it is both true to Christ and to the deepest in Hinduism, but it is neither Christianity nor Hinduism as commonly accepted by their followers."[20]

His philosophy of life sustained him in difficult times. The death of his son Tara in June 1924 was a time of fortitude and reflection and he drew courage from his philosophy. "It has brought me strength that I do not see in those about me. And the fortitude it has given me has not been that of despair but of hope and courage, and of confidence that I have lost nothing that really matters."[21] Answers in this time of personal sorrow came from the ancient scriptures, both Indian and Christian. "The Upanishads say, 'Not for the sake of the son is the son dear, but for the sake of the Atma' (the essential reality). I am coming to feel the truth of this, bearing out my philosophical outlook and confirming me in it. It is a profound conception and yet very beautiful in its humanity," he wrote a few days after Tara's death.[22] "A little while and I am with you, and again a little while and I am not with you—not only of Christ but of all men is this true. And rightly so," he wrote in another letter.[23]

Stokes always denied that he had become a victim of either Oriental or Occidental mysticism, "My philosophy of life has not been reached by wanderings 'on the blue' at all. It is the product of careful and earnest study of the nature of conscious experience, and an attempt to explain the phenomena of experience and understand them as an essentially connected whole," he wrote. The philosophy of Satyakama, a "divine synthesis" between Christianity and Hinduism, is summed up in a letter of 14 October 1924: "In certain particulars it is as far removed from Eastern thought as from that of the West, for I have had what so few have really had—a thought-life lived in the most intimate contact with two widely differing civilizations. I was born and brought up in the West, inheriting its traditions and points of view, and have maintained my close touch with the best thought of the West by constant reading and study as the contents of my library would bear witness. But at the same time the second half of my life has been lived in the very midst of an Oriental atmosphere and of the thought-currents that subconsciously influence the mental outlook of its people. I have also been absorbed in the books and philosophies of India for many years, yet without discontinuing my Western reading. Surely I am in a unique position to profit by both, which my temperament helps me to take fullest advantage of.

"From my Western temperament and thought-experience I have come to feel increasingly as the years go by the vital significance of personality and individuality. The evolution of personality toward the perfection of a multi-personal unity in which the oneness attained is the outcome of no elimination of the personal . . . that is not a product of 'Oriental mysticism.' It is an approach toward oneness, not by the path of gradual elimination of the individual but by the progressive inter-penetration of increasing sympathetic personalities . . .

"The East, on the other hand, has filled me with an overpowering sense of the essential oneness of existent reality. It seems to me that this has been attained in Eastern thought in a way that the West has failed to grasp. The West has lost the sense of oneness of life and has suffered terribly for it; its very true and proper recognition of the vital significance of individuality has made it almost completely lose sight of the essential oneness underlying all individualities. It is because it has come to take it for granted that each separate individuality is also a separately existent entity that it is able to take for granted that there can be a separate good or a separate salvation.

"The thought that I may be saved while my brother is damned, or that I may advance to an end in which my brother may not participate, is the consequence of this lack of the sense of the underlying essential oneness of life. And its evil results are not merely theoretical; it is the subconscious ground of the various conceptions which may be summed up in the idea of 'every man for himself'— every class for itself, every nation for itself—of these attitudes of mind that are the cause of most of the world's pain and evil. . . . As I see it the West and the East have each a vital contribution to make to the complete apprehension of the significance of human experience."[24]

While Stokes readily acknowledged the influence which Indian philosophy had on him, he did not believe that his viewpoint was totally Eastern. "The result of my twenty-four years in contact with the deeper life of India has not been to make me see all things exactly from the standpoint of Indian thought. That has profoundly influenced me, but my viewpoint as it has emerged at the end is neither completely Eastern nor completely Western, nor a 'mixture' of the two. Rather it is the result of the impact of the two . . . It is a new philosophy of life though it has its roots deep in the past of human experience and human thought. For me it is the Truth insofar as my spirit through years of deep experience and earnest thought . . . has been able to approach it."[25] However, he did not claim to have arrived at a final philosophy of life, for there could not be a "final" solution, but instead a progressive interpretation of experience with an ever clearer appreciation of its implications.[26]

Satyakama was not a book pertaining to any one religion. Christ was as much a part of it as Lord Krishna. While Stokes made extensive use of the Upanishads and the Gita which had played a profound part in shaping his philosophic position, he could not rest upon the authority of any scripture. "For me at least, the significance of the Upanishads, the Gita, or any other scripture, lies in its power to beget in those who study it deep far thoughts—to arouse responses and call forth powers for spiritual vision that before were latent. Whether the meanings and implications which I find are the ones which were present to those who composed the Upanishads and the Gita must remain a question of opinion . . . Yet my primary concern is neither with what these scriptures meant to those who first enunciated them, or to those who subsequently founded systems of philosophy or theology upon them. I am concerned with them principally because of the response they have called forth *in me* in the course of long years of loving study and earnest meditation. What we find in this 'scripture' or that is not so important as what it finds *in us*—gives rise to in us emotionally and intellectually. The power to evoke such responses in the deepest areas of our experiencing life constitutes, as I see it, the only authority to which any scripture may rightfully lay claim," he wrote in the foreword to *Satyakama*.

During the years of hectic activity and social commitment when he involved himself with community work, established the school, and developed apple orchards, Stokes was also occupied with *Satyakama* and was attempting to put together a final draft of the book. For years he had the strongest urge to complete the book and give it to others. Sometimes he wrote many pages in a day, and sometimes it took him a month to write a paragraph. At times he was so exhausted after his work that he could hardly speak. "I am conscious that I have written it with my very life—that it has probably come into form in exchange for years of my life."[27]

He cut himself off from the plains and rarely traveled to Simla. He did not even go down to see Gandhi or other nationalists. A few friends visited him at Kotgarh, among them Vithalbhai Patel, president of the Central Legislative Assembly, who came up to Barobagh in 1929. There were also occasional visitors like Paul Richard (husband of Mirra Richard, Sri Aurobindo's spiritual partner, who came to understand his philosophy). The studies he was engaged in were his swadharma, Stokes told Gandhi, and he would "not change it for another."[28] "I shall be able to have more quiet of mind when it is completed, for I have somehow felt it 'laid upon me'—to use Friendly language—to write it, and I shall have no real rest of mind until this is accomplished,"[29] he wrote in September 1928 when he had nearly completed the work. He expressed the same feelings to his wife when he explained to her why he wrote the book: "It is because I had to do so. It is not a question of whether others had any use for it, or whether any publisher will publish it. I could not rest until I had written it. Something within me constantly pressed me. The thought that I might die without having done so kept me awake at nights. When I shrunk from the burden of thought and felt the loneliness of thought I was unable to escape. The thoughts came to me, and with them always the feeling that they must be expressed. I could not escape."[30]

He tried to keep the book simple and close to the form and words in which it was first written in jail, but still feared that some might find it hard to grasp its underlying thought. "It is a tremendous task, for to see a vision is one thing and to make others see it is quite another."[31] The book was also long, almost 500 pages, and he was conscious that it contained far too much repetition. But despite such shortcomings, he had no doubt that the book embodied an outlook "worthy of the deepest consideration."

Stokes did not originally write *Satyakama* for publication. When he first undertook the work he wanted to explore what life had come to mean to him and to share his experience with his wife. But he was persuaded to change his mind after a visit from his old friend Andrews in the summer of 1926. Andrews felt that the book might be helpful to others and should be published. Gregg's interest in the book during the three years he spent with Stokes and his conviction that it should be published also influenced Stokes' final decision. There were few with whom Stokes could discuss his philosophical thoughts and Gregg's presence in Kotgarh during this period was helpful.

Gregg was a sympathetic listener. He found Stokes' book "exceedingly interesting, stimulating and helpful," and to be a "very valuable synthesis and development of the most important parts of Christ's teaching with the best and most essential parts of Hindu religious and philosophical thought."[32] Though he was the son of a congregational minister and his oldest brother was a minister, Gregg had increasingly become dissatisfied with the Christianity taught in most American churches. "In your son's philosophy I see the promise, for myself anyhow, of a spiritual road along which I can travel with a renewed sense of security, serenity, and enthusiasm. Around his central ideas I think I will be able to group other ideas and conceptions and feelings which hitherto have been fragmentary, disconnected, inconsistent and puzzling. Also I can discard some parts of my thinking which were useful as scaffolding, but are now in the way. Hence, as you can imagine, I am grateful to him," Gregg wrote to Stokes' mother. Another consideration in Stokes' decision to publish the book was that his philosophy had been a source of profound strength and comfort to him in times of trouble and difficulty. "The thought that to even a very few others it might be what it has been to me, naturally influenced me in favour of sharing it," he said.[33]

The personalized form of the book presented a problem. The book was written for his wife. It was in the first and second person and contained matter that was very personal. He was hesitant to share writings and experiences of so "intimate and personal a character," but was again influenced by Andrews who felt strongly that if the book was published no changes should be made which would eliminate "the personal element." Andrews believed this added greatly to its value to the ordinary reader, as it made "metaphysical philosophy a human affair, linking the great problems up with the deeper aspects of human experience."[34] He also did not agree with Stokes that the book should be published anonymously.

Both Andrews and Gregg hoped that the book would be published in the West. When Gregg returned to America in 1929, he tried to generate interest in the book but failed. Andrews too took the manuscript with him on his visit to England and America and tried to find a suitable publisher, but his efforts were also not fruitful. *Satyakama* was finally published in India by Ganesan of Madras in early 1931 and was well received. U. C. Bhattacharjee, professor of philosophy at the Presidency College, Calcutta, praised Stokes' efforts in the *Modern Review.* "He has thought well and thought vigorously and courageously, and his exposition is exceedingly happy and refreshing."

While Stokes was not committed to any particular interpretations of the Indian scriptures, Professor Bhattacharjee detected some very striking similarities between his system of thought and the Bengal Vaishnavas like Jiva Goswami. "He is a philosopher of Love like the Vaishnavas and it is no wonder that he has read the same meaning in the Vedanta as the Vaishnavas have done. In addition he is deeply versed in Christian teachings and this enables him to appreciate the Indian philosophy of love better than many." The similarity was interesting because Stokes did not have any acquaintance with these writers. (Gandhi too apparently saw a link between the Quakers and the Vaishnavas.)* Professor Bhattacharjee found the book excellent reading. "All may not agree with his conclusions and his interpretation; but no one who reads the book carefully can deny the author credit for earnest and clear thinking. In Mr Stokes we have the happy combination of a devoted husband, a loving father and an inspiring thinker—an ideal grhastha [householder]—'true to the kindred points of heaven and earth,' who keeps a house, founds a family, and yet has set his heart upon 'God who is our home.'"[35]

India's philosopher-president, S. Radhakrishnan, who was then vice-chancellor of Andhra University at Waltair, expressed his "deep thanks" to Stokes for writing the book. "I see that your conclusions though based on Indian scriptures are yet the result of personal reflection and experience. I may also say that I am in agreement with the greater part of the book; at any rate so far as your account of the individual soul and its progress goes . . . I am deeply touched by the references to your home life and congratulate you on it."[36] Dr. S. Kuppuswami Sastri, professor of Sanskrit at Presidency College, Madras, found the book "a very suggestive and interesting interpretation of Vedantic culture."[37]

That winter Stokes had copies of the book sent to leading British and American philosophers, both Christian and secular. The response from all of them

---

* "The history of the Quakers has been made glorious by non-violent non-cooperation. The history of the Vaishnavas in India bears testimony to the very same thing. The whole world can do what these people have been able to do" (Gandhi, "Did Ram Shed Blood?" *Navjivan*, 11.8.1929, *Coll. Works*, XLI, p. 278).

without exception showed that it did "appeal to thoughtful people as worthy of consideration."[38] Dr. J. H. Muirhead, professor emeritus at the University of Birmingham, general editor of the *Library of Philosophy*, and one of the leading secular philosophic scholars of Britain, found the book of great value as a personal interpretation of the best in Indian philosophy, in a form that did not confuse the Western reader with details of unfamiliar systems and Sanskrit terms.

"It is the first book of the kind I have read in which a writer who is familiar with Western methods of thought, and has immersed himself in Eastern spiritualism and religion, gives an interpretation of the latter from within. I should not be surprised to find that it was unique in this respect, and I hope it will have a circulation far beyond the country out of whose heart you may be said to have written it," Muirhead wrote to Stokes. He felt the book was specially suited to promote deeper understanding between the Eastern and the Western mind which was needed if the existing political and other problems were to find a peaceful solution. He also felt the book would be helpful in healing the religious differences which blocked immediate progress toward national unity in India.[39]

The well-known British thinker Lloyd Morgan, then very old and in failing health, described the book as arresting. "I hope it will kindle live coals. I am but a smouldering spark in the decaying embers, still I hope to be able to glow a little with sympathy as strength permits me to read more," he wrote to Stokes.[40] Dr. Alfred E. Garvie, principal of Hackney and New College, University of London, read Stokes' book with growing appreciation. "Again and again, as I read your book, I felt in touch with a kindred spirit, and recognized 'old friends' in the way of thought. Doubtless the one Spirit of God is leading us both into the truth."[41]

Although Dr. Garvie did not fully agree with Stokes' views, he was full of praise for the book. "I want a wider circle to share the treasure I have unexpectedly found." In a five-page review of *Satyakama* in the *Congregational Quarterly* of July 1932, Dr. Garvie wrote that the book proved to be a "treasure-trove" to him. "Seldom have I come across a book that has so gripped my mind and heart alike. It is no abstract philosophical discussion, although it deals with speculation regarding ultimate reality—deity, duty, destiny; but it is a 'human document' (to use the current phrase) palpitating with life."[42] In his theological book, *The Christian Belief in God*, published a few years later, Dr. Garvie acknowledged the value of some of Stokes' precepts and described *Satyakama* as a book in which "East meets West, and a Christian theosophy appears in an Indian mythological dress."[43]

Dr. H. R. Mackintosh, professor of philosophy at New College, Edinburgh, and moderator of the General Assembly of the Church of Scotland, was moved by *Satyakama* to "sincere reverence and admiration . . . I can salute in you a spirit and mind whose sincerity and penetration we may all covet."[44] Professor W. G. DeBurgh of the University of Reading who had always felt that Western language and philosophical terms were incapable of rendering Indian thought found the book particularly helpful. "In reading your book I was more helped than I have been by reading books by Indian writers, for you have been able to effect a synthesis of Western and Indian thought, knowing both from within."[45]

Stokes' old friend Dr. J. O. F. Murray, former master of Selwyn College, Cambridge, who had encouraged him to publish his religious poems more than twenty years earlier, and with whom Stokes had lost touch in recent years, was enthusiastic about his new book. "C.F. Andrews has certainly been a true friend both to England and to India in encouraging you to publish it—and to publish it in its intimate personal form." Murray felt that the book ought to be made easily accessible in England. "We in the West need to be brought into closer contact with the age-long seeking of the Indian sages after God. Dr Westcott used to say always that we needed the help of India to enable us to understand St. John, and I can see how true that intuition was from hints that have flashed out in page after page of your book."[46]

Response from America was slow but when it came it was from one of the leading philosophic thinkers, Professor James B. Pratt of Williams College, Williamstown, Massachusetts. Professor Pratt found *Satyakama* "extraordinarily" appealing. "Very few books of a deeply philosophical sort have I ever found so absorbing. You did well to leave in the personal touch, which adds greatly to its charm. But of course the great value of the book lies in the great conceptions which it expresses . . . The total world concept which you leave your readers, with the application which you make to human destiny, bring to me that kind of solemn joy that only great philosophy and great poetry—and sometimes great music—ever rouse."[47] In an article published in the *Journal of Philosophy* on "Recent Development in Indian Thought," Professor Pratt praised Stokes' efforts and wrote of "the ingenuity, persuasiveness, and charm with which the author has woven into the rather technical outlines of his philosophy many of the finest conceptions of Hinduism and of Christianity, and many of the deepest insights of human life, idealistic love, and religious experience."[48]

Professor Pratt's response was heartening to Stokes. While he had received a few very appreciative letters from England, this was the first letter from a fellow American indicating that the book had even been read. "I was beginning to feel that my years in the Himalayas had cut me off so far from the outlook of America that I was no longer capable of expressing myself in ways that would mean anything there: your letter has been an encouragement to me in that it has partially at least removed that doubt."[49]

There were other thoughtful responses. Professor Egerton of the Department of Sanskrit at Yale wrote, "It is clear that the writer is an honest, earnest and sincere thinker, that he is highly intelligent, and very well read in Indian thought. His system is in large part based on Indian philosophy, and where he diverges from it he does so quite consciously and intelligently . . . But the real purpose of the book is, obviously, not to expound Indian philosophy, or a synopsis of Indian philosophies, but to set forth the author's own system. I am naturally interested in the abstract fact that Indian thought has the power to stimulate a modern Occidental to develop such a system."[50]

But despite the appreciative response from many eminent scholars, Stokes was disappointed that the book did not receive the attention of critics in the West. Publishers too did not consider it a sufficiently good risk. Those who showed an interest wanted him to cut it down in size, which he was unwilling to do. A reviewer for Allen and Unwin described *Satyakama* as a beautiful and helpful book, with "gold nugget" of sentences, "consoling to the bereaved, very spurring," but pointed out that its "treasures" had to be dug for by ordinary non-philosophic readers like him. "Whether it would commercially be a success in England it is difficult to say . . . In India it is entirely suitable; for the English reading public it is more doubtful, being such an extraordinary mixture. Those who would be informed and helped by it might feel unable to wade through the welter of strange terms and abstractions. Yet as a presentation of a possible blending of Hindu and Christian (of course wholly unorthodox) religious thought it deserves re-publication."[51]

The book was not published in the West and could not be reprinted in India as its publisher, S. Ganesan, had closed down. But it continued to be of interest to a small but appreciative number of people both in India and in the West, and as one inspired reader in England wrote, "Everything is so finely-tuned and vivid. I know few people who would be able to write about the deepest things with such deep-felt simplicity. That is because the whole book has flowed directly out of his soul and out into the soul of his wife. It has been my morning reading during the weeks when I was forced to take my breakfast in bed and I felt myself inwardly comforted and stronger for the day after having read a few of those chapters. And the curious thing is that it is at the same time as captivating as a good novel. One is always desirous to read further."[52]

Andrews, who often studied the book and found more "truth and beauty" in it than he had at first discovered, was particularly disappointed that the book could not be published in the West. "For there are few things more needed today than mutual understanding between East and West with regard to that essential and fundamental philosophy from which each side of the human world starts and on the grounds of which it makes its own assumptions," Andrews wrote in an article, "Satyakama," published in the *Modern Review* in September 1933.

Stokes himself was convinced of the significance of the book. "The era of isolation in the relations of mankind is drawing to its close. Day by day the contact between the East and the West is becoming more intimate. As a consequence the influence of the East upon Western thought and of Western thought upon that of the East must steadily grow. Where will this ultimately lead us? Surely here is a question of vital interest to us all.

"Viewed purely from this angle *Satyakama* should be significant, for it embodies the reaction of a speculative Western mind to the spiritual outlook and atmosphere of the East. In it will be found what happened in the case of one Westerner who nearly twenty-eight years ago set out to live as an Indian and has lived almost exclusively among Indians ever since," he wrote in the preface to the book. "He might add that he is profoundly grateful for the experience these years have brought him, and feels that his life has been immeasurably enriched by it."

21 SATYAKAMVADI

Ever since Stokes had married and settled in Kotgarh he and his family had identified themselves totally with the interests and problems of the local people. They had sought to be as close to their neighbors and to be of as much service to them as was possible. As a result there was an ever-growing sympathy and understanding between them and their mainly Hindu neighbors. They respected Stokes and were happy and proud to have him live in their midst. They invited him to their weddings and other social functions and accepted the customary daan (gift) on such occasions. When Stokes' son Tara Chand died, his neighbors all shared in his grief. Not only Christians, but a large number of Hindu men and women, some from miles away, came to offer condolences. They insisted on digging the grave themselves and even attended the burial service.[1]

Despite these mutual gestures of friendship, Stokes and his family were still treated as outsiders, albeit benevolent outsiders, as far as the Hindus of the ilaqa were concerned, who would not admit them to their inner family. Being Christians, there was a limit beyond which Stokes and his family could not interact with them. This was due to the rigid caste system prevalent in the hills which did not allow people of higher castes to mix freely with either the lower-caste Hindus or with Christians. It even forbade high-caste Hindus from eating food cooked by the hands of Christians and low-caste Hindus. Full social interaction between families of the same caste, locally called hookah-pani, implied eating in each other's homes and permitted marriage between their members. The Hindu community in Kotgarh was so sensitive about this issue that many people boycotted families that maintained closer social relations with Stokes' Christian family.

These progressive families accepted Stokes in their midst as they had accepted no other Westerner or even an Indian Christian. They wanted Stokes' wider acceptance in their society but were conscious of the restrictions imposed on their social interaction because of his religion. In order to remove this barrier a few of them, led by Devi Das Bhalaik, approached Stokes in early 1932 wanting to know if he would be prepared to join the Hindu community.[2]

For Stokes, the proposal presented no special religious difficulty. In the past fifteen years he had been increasingly influenced by Vedanta and his attitude toward religion had at this time become such that a step of this nature involved no violation of conscience or belief. "My debt in spiritual experience to Christ is profound . . . but philosophically I am far nearer to the general Hindu position than to the Christian." During this period he had, in any case, moved away from the orthodox Christian standpoint. Not being satisfied with Christianity as it was believed and practiced then, he had found it difficult to adhere to it even in its outward form. With the passage of time, it had become even more difficult for him to take part in the Christian religious service and sacraments whose whole language and tradition was saturated with concepts he did not believe in.[3]

At one time church service was an important part of his life. He had even intended to build a chapel in Barobagh. The site was identified and he had meant to put in it the beautiful stained-glass windows which he had bought in England in 1910. The chapel was never built, but every Sunday he went to the church in Kotgarh accompanied by his wife and all their children. However, by 1920 he had stopped going to church even though he remained a Christian by allegiance. "As long as I was able to take an active share in a large part of the service I clung to it and since then have missed it." But now his conscience did not permit him to take part in so much of the service that it was not practical for him to attend it. "It is not merely the direct statements in the creeds, but in all the beloved and beautiful prayers there is present by implication so much that is opposed to my own spiritual experience that I could only repeat them in a most mutilated form, more and more so as the years go by."[4] It was many years since he had been to a church or taken part in common worship. But his family had continued to do so and he was glad that they could.

Stokes' mother had found it difficult to accept his views; she wanted that he and Agnes should be able to share in the spiritual life and service of the church and in the spiritual education of their children together. But Stokes could no longer do so. "I am not one of those who take religion so lightly that I can repeat with my lips that to which my spiritual experience does not give assent . . . Would it not be a joy for me to be able to go with her. I did so just as long as I conscientiously could."[5]

However, he also believed that what was right for one was not necessarily so for another. "I have lived too long and had too many difficulties of my own to feel in a position to judge any other man who tries honestly to settle the questions which face him in the struggle of life."[6] He had found much light in Hinduism, and much that he could not accept. The same was true of Christianity. "I have advanced far beyond the broadness of even the most liberal churchmanship that exists in the West, and I fear that my views would greatly shock many of my friends in Europe and America," he had written in a letter of 1924. "Yet I can say with even greater and I think more justifiable faith than in my younger days that I find all life the work of a divine and guiding Love, and the two 'great commandments' of Christ . . . great and splendid inspirations."[7]

In view of the sentiment and the practical considerations that had led to the controversial proposal, Stokes felt that not to respond to the majority Hindu community would be wrong on his part. Having outgrown the confines of individual religions, it was not significant for him whether he was a Christian or a Hindu, but joining the Hindu fold would have many important implications for his family, both religious and social. He was in fact already facing a dilemma as far as the religious guidance of his children was concerned. He could not bring them up in the Christian mold himself without being guilty of hypocrisy, nor, feeling as he did, could he deliberately arrange to have them brought up to such an outlook by another person.[8] The change in religious affiliation would enable him to feel far more free to discuss his philosophical thoughts with his children.

Stokes approached the question from two angles—its relevance to the Hindu community of Kotgarh, and its significance to his family. As far as the Hindus were concerned, he was governed by the same consideration that twenty years ago had impelled him to marry outside his race—the thought that the deepest and most dynamic influence was always that which came from within. As a sympathetic outsider, he had been able, within limits, to exert an influence in the development of the ilaqa. But, by becoming a member of the community which comprised the vast majority of the population of the hills, he felt certain that he would be able to do much more for them. The step would also enable his children, both sons and daughters, to marry within the hills. If his family was united by marriage and tied in the closest bonds of relationship with the local people, it would bring about changes in the rigid social order of the area. "This is a service we can render, but as members of the Christian community it would not be possible in Kotgarh."[9] He was aware that this step would mean a deliberate choosing of the hard and simple life of a poor hill farmer for his family but he was prepared for it. "The urge is rather to service than a betterment of worldly status."

As for the significance of conversion to his family, his position was fairly clear in the circumstances. The handful of families of heterogeneous antecedents which comprised the Christian community of Kotgarh were looked upon as outsiders by the people of the ilaqa. They were so few in number that they had to look largely to Simla or the plains for matrimonial alliances for their children. If his family were to remain identified socially with this little group, it would mean that they would be condemned permanently to be outsiders to the hill community as a whole.

"We feel that our family exists peculiarly for the service of these hills, the population of which is almost exclusively of Hindus. To render that service properly ours should be in the truest sense a mountain family, associated by the closest social ties with the mountain people. But unless it is socially a member of the local community there is no possibility of this; we should have to marry our girls out of the hills and bring brides for our sons from non-hill families. This would mean that our social trend would be always away from the hills toward the plains, and before long we should become by blood, relationship and interest a plains family even though our home remained here . . . If then, we wish our family to be fully identified in the years to come with the larger life of these hills it would seem that our social relations should be with the community which almost exclusively composes it."[10]

Though Stokes had no doubt that converting to Hinduism was clearly in the interest of his family, it was still not an easy decision for him to make. It presented no difficulty on a religious front to his two older sons Prem, now twenty, and Pritam, nineteen, who were studying at St. Stephen's College in Delhi, both of whom after a couple of days' consideration favored the step. But it was different for his wife. While Agnes was willing to have her husband and sons join the Hindu community, the thought of doing so herself was painful to her because it would cut her off from those she loved and looked upon as "her people."[11] Yet she was prepared to join the rest of the family if such a step was taken provided she was "free to work out her own religious life—her private life of the Spirit—without let or interference." Once convinced that the conversion would have an important bearing upon the future development and destiny of his family, Stokes decided to accept the offer as long as it was clearly understood that he was and would remain a satyakamvadi—one who is truthful—and that his wife would take the step because she felt it her duty to stand with him, and that she would be free in her own personal spiritual life.

In the meantime, word that Stokes was considering conversion spread and there was much resentment and misunderstanding among his Christian friends. Bishop A. B. Chandu Lal of Simla wrote to him for permission to categorically deny the news. In reply, Stokes gave him a frank appraisal of his position. "From the point of view of a Christian and a churchman I know that such a decision must seem shocking. You must, however, bear in mind that for those who approach it from our viewpoint it is not so." He also assured Chandu Lal that there would be no change in his relationship with the Christian community. He would not lose interest in its members and would be willing to help them as he had always done. "In the past changes over from one community to another have been accompanied by bitterness and resentment and mutual recrimination. It seems to me the time has come for us to face such situations in a more Christ-like spirit."[12]

Stokes' reply was of no comfort to Chandu Lal. In an emotionally charged letter, he informed Stokes that he had decided to come and see him and his wife and try to do what he could to save him from the calamity that he was contemplating to bring upon his family, and warned him that he would reap his action "abundantly." "We shall not take it complacently and feel we have obligations of friendship owing to you and your family . . . I hope to follow you to death until I bring you back to the shepherd of your soul . . . You have decided to stab your friends as if they were nothing to you but we shall not give you up in a hurry."[13]*

Stokes could understand Bishop Chandu Lal's feelings, but he was not prepared to accept the harsh language used by him, and urged him to use less extreme expressions when discussing the subject. "I would remind you that between you and me it is not a question of difference in faithfulness to the light that each of us sees, but of differing understanding of the implications of our respective lights." He was willing to meet him but only if they could discuss their differences in a "Christ-like spirit of mutual forbearance and patience," not if such a meeting was merely to rebuke him for being "unfaithful." "Remember that you are talking to one who has thought long and earnestly, and who has not throughout his life hesitated to attempt following where his light seemed to lead. As he respects your sincerity and the pureness of your motive in trying to save him from a step which you honestly believe to be wrong, so he is entitled to the same attitude upon your part . . .[14] Do not pray that God may guide us to your light, and that we may be guided in accordance to your own or the church's conception. 'To his own master every man standeth or falleth,' and I fear I shall not be able to walk by any light save that which seems vouchsafed to me."**

On 4 September 1932, Stokes, along with his wife and children, except for Prem, who was away at college, embraced Hinduism at the Chattarpur temple in Mehlan village in the presence of Sanyasi Ramanand Shastri of the Sadhu

* The propagandists, too, had a field day in creating a hype over the issue and giving uncalled-for publicity to it. Objectionable and inaccurate reports and notices were published in Punjab's vernacular newspapers, *Pratap* and *Milap,* which caused ill-feelings. One such unfounded notice that Madan Mohan Malaviya was going to perform Stokes' shuddhi resulted in great misunderstanding (*Extracts from Letters*).

** Almost all Christians were against the conversion and many wrote to him in the same tenor as Bishop Chandu Lal's letter. Stokes replied to as many as he could, explaining his reasons.

Ashram, Hoshiarpur. The conversion ceremony or shuddhi was performed by Pandit Govardhan Das of Nirmand, known as the Kashi or Banares of the hills.

The news that Stokes and his family had become Hindus was reported widely in the press. Stokes himself issued a statement saying, "We hope and believe that time will demonstrate the rightness of the step as we see it . . . Implications of our actions are not that we consider Christianity a false religion and Hindu religion a true one. To our understanding there is a deep underlying truth in all great religions of the world . . . Only in our case the path has led differently and each of us must follow the light as it shines for him."[15]

Though Stokes' action surprised many, few questioned his sincerity of purpose and his "courageous and steadfast devotion to his peculiar ideals of service, and his unquestionable spiritual aspirations." Stokes had hoped to confine his remarks to his brief statement, but misunderstandings about his motives impelled him to state his position more clearly. In a lengthy rejoinder published in the *Indian Social Reformer,* he explained that his decision to join the Hindu community was a result of his increasing conviction that his family could work out a more honest place for themselves in that community than they could hope to retain in the Christian.[16] "For Christianity is allegiance to at least a few basic beliefs. In details there is doubtless scope for wide difference of opinion, but as regards the divinity of Christ, for example, or the unique claims which the Church and the Gospels make for Him, no one has a right to claim for himself membership in the Christian community who does not hold these. And indeed I cannot imagine any one leaving the Church or joining another community who held these beliefs."

He did not feel that Hinduism was a religion in the same sense as Christianity or Islam. It was a *way of life* that many groups of individuals had in common, even though their spiritual and intellectual outlooks differed widely. It imposed a social discipline upon its members but left them the broadest latitude for their personal beliefs. While it had its imperfections too, he found its attitude of deep reverence and sympathy with all that manifested itself as a truly spiritual experience, quite irrespective of whether held among Hindus of the day or not, very wonderful. "I have felt of recent years that I could be honestly a Hindu, whereas I have not for a long time felt that I had the right to call myself a Christian. I am not so presumptuous as to claim that my position is the correct one and that of the Church mistaken, yet as the Church must follow its light so I must be as true as I can to what light I see."[17] But he also admitted that he was doubtlessly influenced by mixed motives as most people were. "Yet I am not conscious of any that is ignoble or entirely selfish."

Stokes' detailed statement, published under the heading, "Mr Stokes' Declaration of Faith," received special accolades from the magazine's editor, Kamakshi

Natarajan, who, describing Stokes as "the well-known American friend and so-cial servant of India," wrote, "These words coming from an earnest soul who has steadily pursued his ideals of service at all costs for over thirty years in this land, bear striking testimony to the truth of the famous message delivered a few years ago by another earnest soul, the Swami Sri Shankaracharya of Kasvir Peetha—'To admit Christians and Mohameddans to Hinduism is not to ask those who seek it to give up their faith, but rather to enable them to enlarge their outlook and widen their horizon and live a broader and more tolerant life, doing what lies in one's power to promote the happiness and content of the world.'" This won-derful message, Natarajan wrote, "deserved to be borne in mind and pondered over by earnest men of all religions."[18]

Professor James B. Pratt of Williams College, Massachusetts, who was then visiting India, read the account of Stokes' public acceptance of Hinduism and his explanation of his decision with great interest. "I thoroughly approved of your act because of the reasons you gave," he told Stokes. A year later, while dis-cussing *Satyakama* in the *Journal of Philosophy*, Professor Pratt wrote how Stokes had made a serious study of Indian thought and had found much in it of great philosophical and religious appeal and that he had become a Hindu in order to "break down the last wall of separation between him and his Indian fellows" to whom he was devoting his life.[19]

Andrews was in England at this time. He himself had been greatly influ-enced by the Arya Samaj and its leader, Mahatma Munshi Ram, and sympa-thized with his friend's position. Gandhi's views on Stokes' conversion are not known. A fragment of his letter to Stokes dated 25 November 1932, which reads, "What a joy it would be when people realize that religion consists not in out-ward ceremonial but an ever-growing inward response to the highest impulses that man is capable of . . ." possibly alludes to the subject.* Writing on the sub-ject many years later, Stokes admitted that as a Vedantist there was no need for him to have changed his religion. But he was a grhastha too and as such had a duty to his family which not only justified but made it necessary for him to take the step. "Had it been only a question of myself the question need not have arisen, neither the Upanishads nor the Gita are concerned with religious or so-cial affiliations or names, nor am I personally interested in them. If I were alone I should have been quite happy to have been free from all such names as 'Hindu' or 'Christian' or 'Muslim,' and to have gone about recognizing as my own, all

* Gandhi was against conversion whether it was known as shuddhi by Hindus, tabligh by Muslims, or proselytizing by Christians and questioned the use of conversion in this age of growing toleration and enlightenment. But, "Shuddhi," he said, "was entitled to the same toleration that is claimed for tabligh so long as either remains within moral and legitimate bounds" ("Swamiji as I Knew Him," *Young India,* January 1927).

that called forth responses from the depths within me, wherever I might find it. Freed from names and with such an outlook I feel I should have been meeting life in the very spirit that runs through the Upanishads; their concern was with 'the real' not with the fleeting forms that veiled it. But I had my children to consider."

Kotgarh residents believe that the Arya Samaj had played an important role in Stokes' conversion. The shuddhi movement was started by the Arya Samaj in the late nineteenth century to bring back to the Hindu fold those who had converted to Christianity or Islam. The Arya Samaj opened its first school in the hills at Dhada in Kotgarh in 1920. The school, called the Himalaya Anglo-Sanskrit Middle School, was inaugurated by the well-known Arya Samaj scholar and leader Mahatma Hans Raj, who gave a religious discourse on the occasion. Stokes welcomed the opening of this school in the ilaqa. He had already studied in depth the life of Maharishi Swami Dayanand, founder of Arya Samaj, and had been greatly impressed by the principles of the Samaj. According to Ram Dayal Singha, a prominent member of the Kotgarh Arya Samaj, Stokes was influenced by scholars and sanyasis of the Arya Samaj who started coming to Kotgarh after the school was opened there. Among these was Pandit Rishi Ram with whom Stokes often held religious discussions and who was instrumental in encouraging and arranging his shuddhi. Some of the teachers at Stokes' Tara School also had strong leanings toward Arya Samaj and had an influence on Stokes.

Stokes' conversion had many implications. The Christians were, of course, unhappy with the situation but many Hindus of the ilaqa, too, found it unacceptable. While they were not unfamiliar with the conversion of Hindus to Christianity, the conversion of a Christian to Hinduism was unheard of and posed problems. Even before a final decision to convert was taken, there was opposition from some quarters. The shuddhi itself was not without incident. A large number of people had gathered at Mehlan to participate in the ceremony. But when the ceremony was over and Stokes started to distribute the charnamrit, Babu Bishan Das, one of his longtime friends and supporters, withdrew his hand and declined to accept it. This caused a great deal of confusion for following his example a majority of the people assembled did not take charnamrit from Stokes, implying that they did not accept his conversion. Those that did accept included Sham Sukh of Shatla, Manohar Das of Delan, Shyamanand of Shamtala, Gangadas of Shatla, and Devi Das Bhalaik of Thanedhar.[20]

Sham Sukh found the reaction of the others inexplicable. "The people had reached an agreement and Stokes had met with all the requirements of the ceremony. His shuddhi was complete according to the shastras. He had worn a new dhoti and worn the janeyu (sacred thread). To then refuse to take the charnamrit from his hand was wrong—it was an insult to him. If anyone had any doubts they should have spoken earlier. He should not have been humiliated in this way."

It was customary among the Hindus of Kotgarh to obtain the permission of the Temple of Chatramukh, the area's oldest and most important temple, situated in Mehlan, before making any decision of importance relating to their religion or community. Since the Rana of Kotkhai was the hereditary trustee of the temple all permissions were obtained from him. The supporters of Stokes had accordingly sent a petition to the Rana for a chhaap (the king's stamp and seal) to perform his shuddhi. The Rana had agreed to grant permission but the chhaap did not arrive on the day appointed for the ceremony. Since all arrangements had already been made it was decided to go ahead with the ceremony and obtain the chhaap immediately afterwards. On this basis many considered the shuddhi improper and refused to accept it. They were not against the conversion but were opposed to the way in which it was carried out. They contended that this would become a precedent and could have an adverse affect on the community. The entire ilaqa got divided into two factions on this issue—the minority Shuddhi Party numbering about 250 people who supported the shuddhi, and the majority Shuchi Party consisting of more than 750 people who were against it.[21]

Sentiments ran so high that the Shuchi Party decided to ostracize all those who had supported Stokes and were now interacting with him socially. Those who had taken part in Stokes' shuddhi were now called Christians and derided as ramtelia (outcastes) and barred from entering Mehlan Temple. The privilege of using musical instruments of the temple on occasions like marriages and deaths, which was customary, was also refused to them. When representatives of the Shuddhi Party asked the deputy commissioner of Simla to intervene on their behalf, he expressed his inability to pass any orders and advised them to approach the courts for relief.

In July 1934, the Shuddhi Party finally took their case to civil court asking for the right of worship in the Mehlan Temple, which had been founded by, among others, their ancestors, and was now being maintained by the entire Hindu community. They also asked for restoration of the privileges they had enjoyed earlier, including use of the temple's musical instruments. The case was decided in favor of the Shuddhi Party on 20 September 1935. But the Shuchi Party appealed against the judgment. It was three years before the case was finally concluded. The Shuchi Party not only lost but were also asked to pay all legal costs.[22]

Although the issue was legally settled, ill-feelings persisted in the ilaqa. There was opposition to the shuddhi in the adjoining states, both from their rajas and the people and Bhai Parmanand, President of the Hindu Maha Sabha, had to make a special effort to persuade them to accept it. It soon became apparent that the whole question had taken the shape of a political issue between two groups and had nothing to do with religion. Families took sides upon the lines of old enmities and friendships.

Finally there was a reconciliation, largely due to the initiative of Stokes, who strove to find a solution which was acceptable to both sides without hurting the pride of either party. It was ultimately agreed that the entire ilaqa would accept Stokes' shuddhi, provided he took chandrayan (special holy water used at the time of shuddhi) in the Mehlan Temple. The Shuddhi Party also agreed not to claim legal costs from the Shuchi Party.[23]

The ceremony at Mehlan Temple, attended by representatives of rajas of Kotkhai, Bushair, Kumarsain, and Khaneti, marked his final acceptance by the Hindu community of the hills. The more orthodox elements in it were now appeased, but insisted that Stokes must rigidly observe all local customs in his relations with Christians and other castes, which he had to accept.

Many people were personally affected by this. Members of the Christian community closest to the Stokes family suffered most, especially since they were neither able to denounce Stokes' step like other Christians had done, nor could they be comfortable with the situation. Among these were Dhan Singh and his family, and Agnes' immediate relatives.

Dhan Singh who was Prem Chand's God-father, was exceptionally close to Stokes. He was "confused" by the turn of events and apprehensive of the future. However, after he and Stokes talked the whole issue over they firmly made up their minds to remain close to each other even if their differing religious outlooks led to their being members of different communities.[24] Finally Dhan Singh came to terms with the situation, even though he sometimes felt that Stokes had abandoned him. He remained a prominent member of the Kotgarh community, loved and respected both by Christians and non-Christians. He was the principal of the Mission School at Kotgarh and a padre for many years. He was president of the Nagri Pracharini Sabha and also encouraged the learning of Sanskrit in the ilaqa.

Agnes' sister Ada lived at Kharori, a stone's throw from Harmony Hall. Her Ladakhi husband, T. Nasib Ali, who was a close associate of Sadhu Sundar Singh and had traveled with him to Tibet several times, was very angry with Stokes and even threatened to kill him, though later his attitude softened. Ada's children, especially Fazl-ud-Din Ali and Grace, were distraught. Grace, at seventeen, was inconsolable. Fazl Ali continued to be tormented by his loyalty to the Church on the one side, and his regard and faith in Stokes on the other, but ultimately he reconciled to the change. Gris Chand, Lachhi, and Rachel, children of Agnes' brother Emmanuel, were also deeply affected. Having lost their parents at an early age, all three had lived with Stokes and Agnes at Harmony Hall during their childhood and had studied at Tara School.

Stokes was sensitive to the feelings of the Christian community. When Ram Dayal Singha suggested a big function to celebrate the occasion of his shuddhi, he would not hear of it. "I do not want to hurt the feelings of my Christian brothers," was his immediate reaction.[25] Yet there was an irrevocable breach with the Christians.[26] Some were so antagonized that they were prepared to kill him and were pacified with difficulty by Dhan Singh and Nasib Ali. Matters were made worse by the vow which Stokes was compelled to take at Mehlan restricting him in his social interaction with non-Hindus. Earlier, as a Christian he could not have full social relations with the Hindus. Now the situation was reversed—as a Hindu he could not freely interact with the Christians. The result was that while he was able to continue to provide monetary help, he could not maintain close relations with the Christian community as he had hoped. This was the hardest test for Stokes, especially as he watched Agnes follow strictly the rules with her immediate relatives.

Agnes courageously set about the painful task of readjustment. Stokes knew that the ordeal might well have resulted in disaster for one of less strength of character than her. She was not sustained as he was by the strength of conviction in the rationale of the step. Therefore, during the trying years that followed, she suffered in ways that he did not, except that he saw clearly the pain she was going through and suffered with her. "Had I not known what she was I should never have dared to ask of her the sacrifice I did, involving her so cutting herself off from the community in which she was born and which she loved. Had I known her for less than what she was I should not have ventured the step. Knowing her I asked of her what I know would bring her pain, convinced that in doing so I was moving for her and (our children's) eventual good."[27]

Whatever her personal pain and suffering, Agnes always defended her husband's action. According to her, he followed the traditions of local Hindus so strictly because he felt that he owed it to those who had invited and later supported him. He did not want to embarrass them in any way. He was, however, convinced, she said, that the hill people would in due course of time become more liberal in their thinking and in their relations with the minority and low-caste communities of the area.[28]

When Stokes' children expressed their distress over his position in following the local customs, his answer was, "We have made a promise and cannot break it." According to his son Prem, Stokes had converted to the Hindu intellectual philosophy and not to rituals, but afterwards his effort was directed toward becoming part of the community. "There were some people who took advantage of this. Even the servants became our teachers."

"He could never go back on his word; *woh vachan ke pakke thhe*," said Ram Dayal Singha who was then principal of the Arya Samaj School at Dhada and was close to Stokes. "At the time of shuddhi, people had taken an undertaking from him at Mehlan Temple that he would follow the local custom and traditions which implied that he would not allow any untouchable or Christian in his kitchen.* He kept this promise and did not make an exception even in the case of Dhan Singh for whom he had a special affection."

Stokes' granddaughter Urmila feels that an important reason for his succumbing even against his own wishes was because he was an outsider. "The problems arose because he really wanted to belong, he wanted to be accepted by the people. If it was a local person in his place he may have refused to accept all these customs." Dhan Singh's youngest son, Yashvir Singh Rathore, too, feels that Stokes had to surrender to the system—that being a foreigner he felt the pressure from the orthodox section of the people. According to Yashvir, the conversion did affect his father but it did not make him angry or bitter. Dhan Singh could understand Stokes' situation. Though he himself did not believe in casteism and had even dropped the distinctive Rajput name of Rathore, as a first-generation Christian, Dhan Singh, too, was obliged to follow certain customs. For instance, whenever his sister and her husband, both Hindus, visited him, a high-caste was called in to cook food for them. Knowing Stokes' compulsions and to avoid embarrassing him, Dhan Singh reduced his visits to Barobagh.

Stokes' children, however, did not follow these strictures. Pritam Chand, who worked closely with Dhan Singh in the Hindi Pracharini Sabha and who was F. J. Western's godson, said, "Dhan Singh and I used to always sit and eat together. We told Father—'you have made the promise to abide by the people's code, we have not.'"

Stokes' position was unenviable. But it was evident to him that the family could never be fully integrated into the majority community of Kotgarh unless it fully adhered to their rules. The rigidity of caste would not allow for any compromise. He was, however, confident that there would be progressive changes in the community in due course of time. He was hopeful that their joining it would serve as a catalyst in bringing about these changes especially because of his affinity with the people of the ilaqa.**

* The kitchen which used to be in the seclusion of an attic of a home in the hills in earlier days was the most sacrosanct place in it. High-caste Hindus did not allow Christians or low castes to enter their kitchens. The Christians of Kotgarh also practiced social untouchability. They did not fully interact with low-caste kolis and also did not allow them in their kitchens.

** In Stokes' case people had sometimes made exceptions. For example in 1924 when the wife of a poor laborer died in childbirth the villagers accepted Agnes' offer to take care of the baby. Normally it would have posed a problem since the baby was Hindu and could not be brought up in a Christian home—it could not even be handled or fed by a Christian. But after some consultations the villagers accepted her offer gratefully. Agnes looked after the baby till it was almost a year old, with no objections from anyone about any caste violations. (*Extracts from Letters*)

He also believed that being one with the larger Hindu community, being loyal to the discipline and feelings of the community, he and his family would play a role in finding solutions to the problems which confronted their neighbors. The fact that leading Rajput families of Kotgarh had taken the initiative in inviting him to join their community gave him hope for future changes. "We have become convinced that a new spirit is awakening, especially among the younger members of the community, and that we can serve best as one of the many families of the community in which new hopes and aspirations are moving."[29]

Those who supported Stokes' conversion were liberal in their outlook. They did not believe in dogma. It was this section of the people that was responsible for the unprecedented inclusion of Christians in traditional Hindu festivities during the marriage of Stokes' daughter Savitri in 1935. Christian friends were invited to the wedding, recalls Savitri's husband, Lakshmi Singh Sirkeik. People of his village welcomed them and did not discriminate between them and other guests. For the first time in Kotgarh ilaqa, Hindus and Christians ate together. It was the same at Prem's marriage ceremony a few months later. The three-day festivities in Barobagh were attended by Hindus and Christians who shared accommodation and sat together for the dhaam (wedding feast).*

Stokes' acceptance into the Hindu community marked the beginning of disintegration of caste-ridden communal prejudices in the area. Once people adjusted to the fact that a non-Hindu could become a Hindu they, over time, became more broad-minded in their relations with Christians and lower castes. "The people began to think in new terms and orthodoxy reduced. Our community is now very flexible as compared to other areas," said Prem Chand. Stokes' son-in-law Lakshmi Singh has no doubt that the conversion had far-reaching consequences: "*Jaat-paat dheela par gaya*" (the caste system loosened its grip). Earlier, people could not intermingle with each other in public places. After his conversion, Hindus and Christians began to mix more freely. People themselves reduced the chhuut-chhaat. Today jaat-paat is non-existent; everyone drinks water from the same well; everyone goes to the temple and all go to weddings together. They have been doing it for years. This is not so in the surrounding areas where people still follow caste discriminations.** According to Lakshmi Singh, "Stokes did not want to do anything which would hurt the people. He himself was following the reet-rivaz [customs] because the people had accepted him."

Stokes' conversion, however, had a deep impact on Christianity in the Simla

---

* This liberalization in attitude was, however, not universal. A few orthodox Hindu families continued to have reservations about Stokes' conversion. They did not eat with his family and kept their distance during weddings and festivities even till as late as 1944.

** Caste prejudices are common in other hill areas. Even nurses belonging to lower castes are not permitted to enter the homes of high-caste patients. Similarly at public functions high caste and low castes cannot even have tea together.

Hills. New converts lost confidence and many reconverted to Hinduism. Conversions to Christianity also came to a standstill: "It limited the growth of the Church in the area," said Rev Nihal Paul, son of Stokes' adopted children, Rupi and Fazal Din,* who now lives in England. While not wanting to pass judgment on Stokes, Nihal felt that whatever may have been Stokes' considerations, the step was wrong. He recalls how he and other members of his family were never invited to the main upstairs quarters of Harmony Hall but were entertained downstairs in the guest room. Agnes maintained the practice even after her husband's death, he said. It was many years later that they were invited upstairs but never to the kitchen.** "He practised chuut-chaat in order to be a Pahari Hindu," said Nihal. He described Stokes as an "American pragmatist"—"He wanted to live in the mountains and wanted to have a say in the affairs of the community."

It is apparent that when Stokes initially considered joining the Hindu community, he did not foresee the extent to which it would affect his relations with the Christian and other minority communities. His insistence, prior to the shuddhi, that he would maintain the same relations with the Christians as he previously had indicated that he did not fully realize the changes that the shuddhi could bring about in his social life. There is no denying that his hope, that once he joined the Hindu community, caste restrictions and customs would diminish resulting in more interaction between Hindus and Christians, remained largely unfulfilled during his lifetime. The infighting within the Hindu community over his shuddhi demanded all his attention and the issue of defining their relations with the Christians was sidelined. However, the situation did improve gradually over time.

* Of all the children he adopted, Rupi was the closest to Stokes and his family. She helped Agnes in many ways and even nursed the infant Lal Chand when Agnes was sick and unable to do so. Rupi, a pretty and cultured woman, fondly remembered the visits of Stokes and his wife to her home; of how they always brought traditional gifts on special occasions; of the time when Stokes sent her a grinding machine when he saw how difficult it was for her to grind wheat and corn by hand for her large family.

** Granddaughter Urmila confirms how her grandmother felt compelled to follow all rules imposed on her even after she became a widow. When her sister Ada used to come up to her house, she was treated differently. Urmila recalled one such visit when tea was served downstairs in the guest room. Afterwards when Urmila took the teacups back to the kitchen for washing, the family cook threw a tantrum. He wouldn't touch the dishes because they had been used by a Christian and was very angry that the cups had been brought into the kitchen, which he now declared as polluted. The dishes were supposed to go straight to the chhain (a small out-house) to be washed by the koli washer-woman and then only could they be brought into the kitchen. Urmila argued with the cook over his unreasonable stance, reminding him that when he and other kanaits (high castes of the hills) went to Simla they ate in all kinds of places without ever bothering to find out if the food had been cooked by a kanait, a Christian, or a koli. "The rules don't apply beyond Narkanda," retorted the cook. One had to follow the rules once one crossed to the Kotgarh side of Narkanda-ki-dhar.

Stokes did not resent the inimical positions taken by friends or relatives during this period. "My own experience is that as we grow older we tend to learn to respect the views of others more, even if they differ radically from our own," he wrote in reply to a letter from Fazal. "The real thing that matters for you, for me, and for everyone, is that we be true to the light we have. At this stage in our respective journeys our light is not the same—or, we may say, that standing at different points upon the same road the view revealed to us is not identical. Yet, as in the process of our journey we both draw near to the same goal, we shall find our views gradually approximating—until at the end of our journey they are identical."[30]

There was little change in the life of Stokes after he became a Hindu. The family had in any case always lived as an Indian family and not as a Western Christian family. They had fully adopted the pahari culture and their lifestyle was no different from that of their Hindu neighbors. Shoes were not allowed inside the house. There were no tables or chairs. Everyone sat on the ground. Food was eaten in the kitchen sitting on durrees. There was no European crockery or cutlery. Food was served in thaalis (brass plates) and eaten with one's hand. Since Stokes was a vegetarian—he had remained so since the days of the Brotherhood, he was also the only vegetarian in the family—rules in the kitchen were very strict. A ladle used for non-vegetarian curry could not be used for a vegetarian one. There was a strict code of hygiene or suchha-jootha which implied that no one could touch a clean utensil or pick up a roti with the right hand—the hand with which one was eating his or her food.* After finishing the meal everyone carried their thaali out of the kitchen and put it away for washing. It was not correct to expect the cook to pick up used plates or joothi thaalis.

Since the family lived in the midst of other Hindu homes, Stokes' children had developed close friendships with the children of their neighbors. They dressed like them and spoke their language and they all had Hindu names—Prem Chand, Pritam Chand, Tara Chand, Champavati, Savitri Devi, Satyavati, and Lal Chand. Now Stokes, who looked like a Kashmiri pundit in his buttoned-up coat and Gandhi cap, also changed his name to Satyanand (one whose joy is in "the Real" or in Truth) and his wife became Priya Devi. His children were well-versed in the tenets of Christianity and now to teach them the basic Hindu scriptures he engaged the services of Pandit Padam Dev, a well-respected scholar from Rohru in Bushair State.**

Stokes' position regarding Christianity in India had lost him many Christian

---

* Indians generally followed a strict code of succha-jootha or clean-unclean with regard to food. Rules for this were observed throughout the country, by the rich and the poor, by the orthodox and the modern.

** Pandit Padam Dev became Home Minister of the State after India's independence.

friends, a fact he regretted but accepted stoically. He did not consider his action a denial of Christ whom he now considered as "one of the greatest of Jagatgurus." No doubt it was a denial of the conception of the meaning of Christ which had been slowly evolved in the West since apostolic times, but he was convinced that it was no denial of the "profound significance and meaning of Christ to the growing spiritual experience of man." "I have found in Christ another meaning than the Christian does, and a meaning which fits in better with the general outlook of Hinduism than with the outlook of the Church. It may be an utterly mistaken one, but it has grown out of long years of very earnest meditation, and one can but follow His light."[31]

In a tender note to his thirteen-year-old daughter Savitri, the most devout of all his children and godchild of C. F. Andrews, he wrote, "*Satyakama*—if you read it understandingly, and again and again till you enter fully into its meaning—will not make you love Jesus less, or trust Him less, or be less loyal to Him, though it does not teach Him in the terms that the Church accepts . . . And after all what is the message of Jesus, save to love God with all your heart and your neighbour as yourself, and by so doing to work for the coming of the 'Kingdom of God' . . . This too is the message of my book."[32]

Stokes was not prepared to discuss his conversion any more than was necessary. But misunderstandings continued to arise, especially because of propaganda carried out by some Christians in North India who consistently went about claiming that he had joined the Hindu community as a method of converting Hindus to the Christian religion. Normally he ignored such comments, but an account in the *Harijan* of a conversation between Dr. Pierre Ceresole and Mahatma Gandhi, in which Gandhi was reported to have stated that Stokes had become a Hindu in order "to deliver the message of Jesus to the Hindus," disturbed him.[33] He now rarely wrote for publication but the report prompted him to clarify his position to the editor of *Harijan*, Mahadev Desai—"Each of us who takes spiritual matters seriously finds in the course of time the path wherein his spiritual aspirations and needs find their truest satisfaction. It was because I found mine in the spiritual outlook of the Upanishads and the Gita more completely than anywhere else that I wished to be a member of the Hindu community and thus afford those I loved the opportunity to develop freely and naturally in the midst of the atmosphere that had these great scriptures as their basis.

"Religious developments are the products of age and environment, but the true spiritual life is something that is the common treasure of individuals of every religion, and is not Hindu or Christian or Muslim—at least that is my feeling."[34]

He saw Christ as the *ishta-devta* (one's deity) for those who had faith in Him as their savior. "Christ is obviously yours," he told an ardent young Christian who sought his advice, "and in giving Him your loyal love and service you will doubtless obtain strength and comfort for the path that lies before you. The fact that you find your comfort and courage in Him is an indication that you should advance through Him."[35]

Stokes, however, was not keen to publicize these developments in his life among his people in America. "I have a lot of Quaker and other relatives for whom I entertain a great affection, and I know this is a side of my life that would only worry them." His own family in Germantown, of course, knew all about his conversion. But he tried to avoid publicity of the subject in deference to his sister Anna's wishes, more so after her death a few years later, and tended to agree with the family that the subject need not be unnecessarily talked about. "It is not a deadly secret which we go out of our way to hide, but we are gratified insofar as it does not become a matter for discussion," he wrote to a cousin in America.[36]

THE BURDENS INCREASE

Stokes' health, which had been steadily declining for a number of years, became precarious after a badly mishandled operation of the gall bladder in the winter of 1934 in Delhi. It resulted in greater suffering and loss of strength. In a checkup the following winter by his friend and physician Dr. Ansari, it was found that he needed another urgent operation. Dr. Ansari was reluctant to entrust the task to any local surgeon and strongly urged Stokes to go to Vienna, which then had the best experts in the field, and promised to make necessary arrangements for him.

Both Stokes and Agnes knew that the operation was critical and that "chances of his not returning were very definite." At the same time Ansari had made it clear to them that there was no hope of recovery and that without the operation his life would be one of increasing weakness and pain. The decision was made more difficult because they knew that he must make the trip by himself. It was quite out of the question for Agnes to accompany him, leaving their children to the care of others. Nor could he afford to take a friend along. Finally they decided that he should go to Vienna alone and Agnes and the children should remain in Delhi for the winter. Agnes fully appreciated the gravity of the situation, and as in various other crises of their married life, she rose to the occasion with the finest spirit during what Stokes described as the "most poignant period of [their] married life," and sent him off "uplifted by her brave smile and the firmness of her self-control which refused to break down" at a parting they both knew "might well be final, so far as this world was concerned."[1] For Stokes it was even harder because of the circumstances in which he was leaving his wife and children. Socially, this was a trying time for the family. Alienated from the Christians, they were yet to be fully accepted into the Hindu community.

The operation in Vienna on 2 March 1935 by Austria's leading gall-bladder specialist, Dr. Kanz, turned out to be more serious than expected. In a two-and-a-half-hour operation, the doctor removed not only the gall bladder and numerous adhesions but also almost half of Stokes' stomach. During the night following the operation, he collapsed. Dr. Kanz and his team rushed to his side at three in the morning and spent several hours resuscitating him.*

Three days after the operation, when Stokes was still in pain and without food or water, he wrote to his wife, "It is a joy to be able to put pen to paper again . . . when I was by no means sure if I should ever be able to do so again. . . . Somehow I feel it is God's will that I should serve our hills for some more years; therefore I have been able to come safely through the ordeal."[2]

He arrived back in Bombay on 24 April feeling better in health than he had done for years and determined to follow his doctor's instructions faithfully. He wanted to be sure that there would be no carelessness or recklessness this time.

On his return home one of his chief concerns was to get his children settled, which meant getting them suitably married. Though his eldest son, Prem, was then just twenty-two years old, according to the hill tradition he was already of marriageable age, as were Pritam, twenty-one, and Champa, eighteen. As far as the elder two boys were concerned, there was no need to search for brides for them, for Devi Das Bhalaik, who was a leading Rajput of Kotgarh and who had played an important role in Stokes' conversion, was eager to have an alliance with them for two of his daughters—Shakuntla and Shanti—an arrangement which was satisfactory to both families.**

But when Stokes selected Lakshmi Singh, the son of Manohar Das of Delan, another powerful Rajput of the ilaqa, for his daughter Champa, there arose a problem. The happy-go-lucky, beautiful, and spirited young girl did not feel she was cut out for the life of a hill farmer's wife. Not having the courage to disagree face-to-face with her disciplinarian father, she wrote him a note saying that she did not wish to marry in the hills, but would be willing to marry "anyone" from the plains that he would select for her.[3] Stokes was not happy but did not try to change her mind. Instead he placed the proposal of Lakshmi Singh before his younger daughter, Savitri. Being the most docile and pious of all his children, Savitri was willing to comply with her father's wishes. At sixteen, she became the first of Stokes' children to be married. The marriage took place in 1935 and was solemnized in the Vedic tradition. It was also registered under the Special Marriage Act which provided for marriage between people of different religions.

---

* Stokes had a near-death experience at the time of the operation and recounted afterwards how during the operation his spirit hovered over his body, unable to resolve whether it should go back to the body or not and ultimately deciding to return to it. Doctors were surprised when he described to them the details of the surgical procedure. He related this experience to Savitri in a letter he wrote her from Vienna. The incident was often talked about in the family.

** Shakuntla had endeared herself to Stokes when, a few years earlier, she rescued four-year-old Lal Chand from a runaway donkey he was riding.

This was a precautionary step which Stokes took because of the many misunderstandings over his shuddhi. A year later Champa was married to Manmohan Nath, a struggling young lawyer living in Quetta, in British Baluchistan on the North West Frontier, who had once attended Stokes' Gita discourses in Simla.* The youngest daughter Satya married Onkar Nath Dang, another city man who was an officer in the Royal Air Force. Stokes was impressed with Manmohan and Onkar because they were both self-made men.

All three of Stokes' sons-in-law were of modest means. In arranging matches for his daughters, Stokes devoted special attention to their personalities, temperament, and character and gave their financial position a secondary place, turning down several offers from other families of considerable means and position. He had prepared his daughters for a hard life. "It was not fair to girls to bring them up in a manner that would make them unfit to live happily in the homes in which they must marry. If they had to bear burdens, it was for parents to train them that they could do so."

His daughters' marriages were performed traditionally, but he did not give them any cash dowries as was the prevailing custom. Instead, he arranged to give them each Rs 1,000 a year, in quarterly installments, from his American income. This was not only because he disapproved of dowries as ordinarily given, but because he also felt that this was a better way for a father to help his daughter and her husband. Nor did he give them a large number of customary fine clothes and jewelry, though he did give them household and utility items. And, to avoid any misunderstandings in the future he took great pains to make his financial position and obligations clear to the families of each of his prospective sons-in-law.[4] It was evident that he was concerned about the future happiness of his daughters, admitting, "It is a hard job getting our girls husbands to whom we feel happy to entrust them." Soon after settling Satya's marriage he wrote to a friend, "We do hope it will turn out a happy marriage. As far as we can see it should, but who can tell. At any rate we have done the best we could."[5]

In the years after joining the Hindu community, Stokes became embroiled in yet another issue with the government of Punjab. This was regarding his family's statutory rights as agriculturists. A peculiar situation arose when the revenue department refused to register some plots of land measuring about five bighas in his name, which he had bought in Chuan near the river Sutlej, on the grounds that after conversion he had lost his right to buy land in the ilaqa as he was now no longer an agriculturist under the Land Alienation Act.

The Act, passed in June 1919, was aimed at excluding outsiders who were mak-

---

* The Arya Samaj in Lahore took a keen interest in the marriage. Professor Sain Das, former principal of D.A.V. College, made arrangements for the engagement in Lahore.

ing inroads into the ilaqa by lending money to poor farmers and then acquiring their land in default. Under the Act, all sections of the Kotgarh community engaged in farming as an occupation were put together as a single agricultural group with the exclusive right to buy and sell land among themselves. The Stokes family was previously classified with the Christians, who, under the terms of the Act, constituted one subsection of the main agricultural group of Kotgarh. But now that Stokes and his family were no longer Christians, according to the administrative officials, they did not fall into any of the eligible categories.

The principle upon which the agricultural group had been constituted in the ilaqa was that it should include all those who lived by farming there. But in spite of the fact that the Stokes' family was the largest farming family in the ilaqa, not merely owning farm land but actually working on it themselves, and Stokes had already been in possession of statutory rights at the time of the enactment of the Land Alienation Act, the authorities would not yield to his representations. It was an incredible situation that only an unthinking bureaucracy could create. After all that Stokes had done to become one with the Kotgarh community, to now lose their statutory rights as agriculturists was the greatest calamity that could befall the family. It would mean great hardship for them as they could not give up farming life. The family had intermarried into the local Hindu agricultural community and, as a consequence, was not in a position to leave the ilaqa even if they could afford to do so.

"It is obvious that a farmer who was not able to purchase land would sooner or later be placed in an impossible position," Stokes wrote to the deputy commissioner, Simla, urging him to restore the family's "statutory rights" as agriculturists. "The situation as it stands seems extraordinary. We can lose our statutory rights because we cease to be Christians. We could acquire them by becoming Christians again. Yet it may be pointed out that in so far as we have changed our social affinities in Kotgarh it has been to another section of the same agricultural group—a section with which we were entitled to do purchases and sales of land before we ceased to be Christians."[6]

In 1936, mutation of the land in question was sanctioned by Simla's deputy commissioner, W. G. Kennedy, under a discretionary section of the Land Alienation Act. But when Kennedy forwarded the case to the government with the recommendation that it might be treated as a special case, the request was turned down by the financial commissioner. In private, Kennedy told Stokes that the only course open to him would be to obtain a declaration from a civil court that he was a Hindu kanait of Kotgarh ilaqa as he would then fall under one of the agricultural groups listed in the Act.

While successive deputy commissioners of Simla were sympathetic, the position of the financial commissioner, Ambala division, who was the final authority on the subject, was that, because Stokes was listed as a member of an agricultural tribe in Kotgarh as a Christian, he could not be shown as an agriculturist once he had ceased to be a Christian. When there was no satisfactory settlement of the case for many years, Stokes' friends in the Indian Civil Service, including Simla's former deputy commissioner, G. M. Brander, advised him to seek the assistance of a good pleader and apply for a court review of the order against him. Brander especially was quite clear that once having acquired the status of a statutory agriculturist he could not lose it by "change of religion," and considered his case to be "an absolutely cast-iron" one.[7]

The issue was finally resolved in Stokes' favor after several years and took up much of his time and attention. It also gave him many anxious moments for the sake of his children, particularly his sons.

Another cause of worry for Stokes was his diminishing income, which left him constantly short of money. His income from America had reduced considerably during the past years due to the Depression and its after-effects. It came down further when, in 1937, the U.S. government passed a law under which persons living outside the U.S. and drawing incomes from America had to pay an extra 10 percent tax on their American income. The outcome of all this was that, whereas in 1929 Stokes had an annual income of about Rs 20,000 from America, his income in 1938 fell to almost half of that.[8] He was not hopeful of an improvement in the near future either, for though the family's estate had come through the Depression very well, the returns from it were not what they used to be.*

The income from his orchards also did not increase as much as he had expected. Transportation costs had more than doubled during the previous decade. To make matters worse, there were times when Simla fruit agents would not pay up the committed amount due to their own monetary difficulties. Consequently, while the yield of apples from his orchard had increased manifold, the profit remained limited.

Meanwhile his expenses had grown. Apart from the school, on which he was spending a minimum of Rs 3,000 a year even now, there were many other commitments. He was sending money to a number of educational institutions, including D.A.V. College, Lahore, and taking care of local emergencies like famines, failure of crops, and epidemics. There were expenses connected with the publication of religious books and the building of a temple at Barobagh. His personal expenses had increased due to his own ill-health, including the operations in Delhi and in Vienna, and the education and marriages of his children.

---

* By 1941–42 Stokes' American income had reduced to $2,600, the equivalent of Rs 8,600 approximately.

He had also decided to build separate houses for his sons close to Harmony Hall so that each of them could live independently. One house was built in 1936, and he had plans to build another one soon.

It was his usual practice to keep aside in advance a certain sum of money to be given in charity each year and he was not prepared to compromise on this.* There were no reserves either, for at the end of each year whatever extra money was left over was again given away in charity. It was gupt daan (charity in secret) and no one, not even his family, knew where this money was sent. "That was his business," said his son Pritam Chand. "He gave a lot in charity but we do not know to whom he gave and what amounts. I don't think even my mother knew all the details of it."**

Despite his failing health and monetary problems, Stokes remained committed to the cause of education. He was president of the management committee of the Dhada school. While he made a monthly contribution to the school it was still in dire need of funds. Before he left for Vienna in 1935, he had made a special visit to Lahore to introduce the principal of the school, Ram Dayal Singha, to a number of eminent men like Bakshi Tek Chand, Dr. Gokul Chand Narang, and Thakur Datta Sharma from whom he could expect to get help for the school.[9]

A day before his operation in Vienna, when he was unsure of the outcome, a major concern in his mind was for the schools back home. In a letter to Agnes he wrote, "Obviously you will not be in a position to carry a middle school or even a lower middle school (should I not return) . . . You will have to see what you can do. You will, I know, keep in view my ideal of service, and if you cannot run any kind of school, will contribute what is possible to the school at Dhada."[10]

When the Dhada School was raised to high school in anticipation of getting permission from the education department, the British director of education took disciplinary action against the school and ordered it to be closed. As its closure affected a large number of children, Stokes pleaded with the authorities to re-open it. There was a need for at least three schools in the area, covering Kotgarh, Dhada, and Barobagh. Not only were there enough students to fill the rolls of three schools, but the logistics of the ilaqa, with valleys and moun-

---

* He insisted that his children did the same. When they were young each of them was given two apple trees. They tended the trees and the income from them was theirs at the end of the year. Each child, however, was expected to first give 25 percent of his or her income in charity. For many years the children gave this money to an old destitute woman who lived in Kotgarh.

** While he donated money to educational institutions and for relief work he did not believe in giving charity in the ordinary sense. He wanted people to be independent and maintain their self-respect. Many people, however, took loans from him for purchase of land or in emergencies. These were always paid back.

tains separating each area, made it necessary that children of each large locality have a school of their own. The Dhada School, however, remained closed for ten years.

Meanwhile, his beloved Tara School, too, was beset with problems. The school, then till the sixth class, was still not recognized. A new regulation of 1937 providing that students from unrecognized schools would be admitted into recognized schools only after they had, with the sanction of the inspector of schools, been examined by the headmaster of the school into which they sought admission, created complications. In the normal course, children of Tara School automatically proceeded to the seventh class of the Mission School at Kotgarh. The new stipulation meant that the headmaster of the Mission School could not now admit children from Tara School without first obtaining permission from the inspector of schools. There was thus the possibility of the students of Tara School being denied further education.[11]

The new circumstances placed Stokes in a difficult situation but he was determined to persevere and, while none of his own children were now in the school, he had no intention of closing it. The school was giving vidya daan (gift of education) to children who would have found it hard to get to any other school—especially girls who constituted over a quarter of each class—and he did not have the heart to deprive them of this facility. But faced with these unforeseen complications he felt compelled to further reduce the classes, and in 1939 the school went back to primary level with sixty-nine children, seventeen of whom were girls.

In the meantime, Stokes' health, which had improved after the operation in Vienna, regressed and he found it difficult to take part in active teaching. With time thus spared he turned his attention to a subject that had interested him for a long time—the writing of short stories in English for Indian children as a means of helping them learn English easily and naturally.

He believed that such literature would help a child master simple foundations of the English language in a manner that enabled him to derive the most benefit from his class studies. The idea was novel, and Lahore's well-known publishers Messers Uttam Chand Kapur and Sons agreed to bring out a book of stories under the title *Stories for the Children from Many Lands, Retold by Satyanand Stokes*.[12]

Stokes also now found time to delve into genealogical research of his family. He had been greatly interested in the subject at one time but was unable to pay attention to it for many years. A chance letter in August 1935 from Milton Rubincam, corresponding secretary, National Genealogical Society of the United States and himself a descendent of Thomas Stokes, the progenitor of the Stokes family in America, revived his interest. He was suddenly keen to see any new facts that came to light. "I shall never lose my feelings for the subject," he wrote.[13]

Fresh information on the family before it left England, contained in a new book, *Notes on My Stokes Ancestry,* published in 1937 by his cousin Dr. Joseph Stokes, an eminent physician of Moorestown; the valuable research of Helen and Anson Phelps Stokes, both renowned genealogists; and Milton Rubincam added to his renewed interest in the subject. Consequently, during the winter of 1942, he set out to trace Thomas Stokes' ancestry in light of new information now available. This formed the third and final part of his earlier genealogical study—*Stokes of Harmony Hall and Some Allied Ancestry.* "The real and proper interest in family history arises, I think, from a sound instinct—an appreciation of the value and significance of continuity."[14]

Dr. Joseph Stokes, the family genealogist for almost five decades, was delighted with Stokes' study, which he described as "a monumental contribution to the genealogy of the Stokes family."[15] Stokes was himself surprised at the keen interest he still felt in these matters. "I was amused to find how interested I still am able to become in a genealogical problem. One might have thought that as a Vedantist, almost the whole of whose interest is concentrated in philosophy, such questions would no longer interest but that is not the case," he wrote to Rubincam. "I indeed look upon a family as an instrument that Spirit may be said to be fashioning through the ages for its experience . . . the family is in a very real sense the product of custom—but no less real on that account. If it develops fine traditions of idealism and a code of honour, and learns to hand on from generation to generation the memory of the best that has been achieved through and in terms of it then it becomes something of real value and significance. Unless its members learn to do this a family is practically meaningless. Every family in the world is as 'old'—in mere years—as any other."[16]

He was conscious of the fact that many people were inclined to look upon genealogical research as "a useless and rather trifling occupation, only suitable for those who had discovered nothing more valuable in which to engage their energies." But this was not his own experience, nor did he find an interest in the ideals and activities of his ancestors inconsistent with having ideals and activities of his own. "On the contrary I can say with the utmost sincerity that the knowledge of what those who have long since passed away, endured and dared for their ideals, and the thought of the difficulties they faced and surmounted, has been a very real inspiration to me."[17]

That year, he also compiled extracts from his letters to his mother, a companion volume to a similar collection of extracts he had made earlier from his mother's letters to him. Entitled *Harmony Hall Letters,* it was made primarily for his wife—"Should the time come when you have to walk part of the way alone may it be a source of comfort to you."* It contained his dreams of service and the ideals and traditions of the family, a true legacy to his descendents. "That is the 'wealth' that I leave my dear ones—far more truly riches than any property or material means I can pass onto them, and something of which no robber can deprive them if they truly make it their own."[18]

The following year he compiled his important political articles and correspondence. The *Collected Essays, Memoranda and Letters* consist of a selection of his writings since 1913. "These are employments of the old age," he wrote to his son-in-law Manmohan Nath in Quetta. "Just as at the end of a day we put the room in which we have been working in order, so it seems to me that in the closing years of a life it is good to review what one has done and thought and stood for during the years, and try to arrive at an understanding of the meaning of one's birth. One should not take away with one an impression lacking in all clarity of one's life and a mere accumulation of odds and ends, otherwise one's birth lacks significance . . . So you see the room has been largely tidied up for the close of the day."[19]

In the winter of 1943 he made his last Will. This was prompted both by the changed conditions in the world and a fresh ruling of the financial commissioner against the family's status as "statutory agriculturists." Being greatly concerned about the implications of the ruling, he decided to transfer his land to his children immediately. He kept the Chuan property and a small new orchard in Dugar Jubbar in his own name to retain his status as a landholder. He had already put in Agnes' name the small house adjoining Harmony Hall along with a small orchard and some fields.[20]** This was the house in which Stokes and Agnes had first started their married life thirty years before.

In an earlier Will of 1937, which he had made keeping in mind the Hindu law of succession and local custom of the hills, he had bequeathed his entire property in Kotgarh in equal shares to his three sons to be cultivated jointly till the time they wished to separate the ownership. The Will provided that in the event of any of his sons predeceasing him, the son's share would be equally divided among his male heirs. In the new Will, he included his daughters as well. This

---

* The original *Harmony Hall Letters*, referred to in the introduction of this biography, is not traceable. It was not with Agnes for several years before her death. A copy of these letters is in the Nehru Memorial Museum and Library, New Delhi.

** He made special provision for his wife as he did not want her to be in a position of complete dependence on anyone, not even her sons. The provision of his father's Will creating the family estate in America were such that no one who was not his direct descendent could receive income from it nor any share of the principal at the conclusion of the trust. As a result, after his death, Agnes would have no income from this source. This had always been a matter of great regret to him and he wanted to be sure that she was compensated.

was because one of them was in a very hard situation and he realized that they too might need support. He now gave each of them a plot of land sufficient for a small orchard so that if, for some reason, they had to fall back upon their own resources, "they would have a place they could call their own, and where with grit and industry they could bring up their little ones or spend their old age near their brothers' homes without feeling they had to depend upon the charity of anyone."[21]

The land given to each of his daughters was twenty-five pahari bighas (about five acres) as against approximately 350 pahari bighas given to each son. In addition, he gave to the daughters collectively what he described as an "almost worthless little field lying below Nainidhar within the boundaries of Shatla." Since the daughters would have no rights in Barobagh, they could use this field for grass-cutting and wood-collecting which were essential for a farming family. Several years after Stokes' death, when land ceiling was likely to be introduced in the area, Agnes gave an additional fifteen bighas to each of her daughters in Dugar Jubbar on the advice of her son Lal Chand.

Though he gave his daughters only one-fourteenth the share of his sons, he still felt the need to justify his action to his sons, as is evident in an accompanying note he wrote to them. "You may be surprised that I have provided a small plot for each of your sisters. You know that if I were following the American custom—as all my inherited conceptions urge me to do—I should leave all our property in equal shares to all of you, boys and girls alike. But after long years of consideration I have decided against this. Yet as you know, I have the same affection for your sisters as I have for you, and I do not think therefore that you will grudge me my leaving them a little standing-ground out of the many hundreds of bighas I leave to each of you. We are living in strange times, and we do not know what the conditions will be in the coming years. I am not prepared to contemplate the possibility of their being left with no income from the American estate and possibly in straitened circumstances while you and yours enjoy all that I have to leave. I want each of them to be able to feel that if all else fails they still have a little property to which they can turn in times of difficulty. Twenty-five bighas each is not very much, but if they are properly built up, and there is room for the orchard business, each of your sisters and their children will be able to derive a sufficient income to live on from a little orchard. Possibly circumstances may be such that this will make all the difference between actual poverty and modest security."[22]

Sometime earlier, in a separate Will pertaining to his share of the family estate in America, Stokes had exercised the option open to him under the terms of his father's Will to redefine the mode of distribution of interest and principal among his children. His father did not bequeath his estate to his children, but left all his assets in a Trust providing for the interest on the principal to be divided among his wife, children, and grandchildren. The Trust was to be dissolved on the death of his children, and the principal then distributed equally among all his grandchildren. However, the Will provided that his children could, if they desired, change the distribution among the grandchildren. All others in the family followed the Will in its original form, but Stokes exercised his option so as to provide a greater share for his sons at the cost of his daughters. His daughters would get two-thirds of what the sons inherited, both of the income and the principal, when the trust dissolved. In addition, he made analogous provisions for his grandchildren, that in case any of his children died without making a Will, the same principle would be followed for their heirs, that is, the daughters of his children would get two-thirds of what the sons received.[23]*

Family sources say that after he became a Hindu he did not initially intend to give any property to his daughters. It was the difficult circumstances of his daughters that prompted him to change his mind and make some provision for them. None of his daughters was sufficiently educated to fend for herself in case the need arose. Some members of the family now feel that he was unfair to his daughters, both in respect to their inheritance and in their education. They argue that the justification, that he was following Hindu traditions in this matter, is not valid as many progressive Hindu families, especially those influenced by the Arya Samaj, believed in and practiced equal rights for women. His proponents on the other hand give him credit for being the first in the hills to include daughters in his inheritance. Since then giving land to daughters has become far more common.

While making these changes he urged his sons to always give consideration to the family and not merely look at matters from the viewpoint of individual gain. Warning them against internal quarrels which so often resulted in the breaking up of a family unit and the consequent fall of its position in society, he urged them to "stand together; help each other and each other's children. Never part with what I have left you to outsiders. Give your family a chance. In strengthening the family you strengthen your own children and their children."[24]

While settling the affairs of his estate, one of his chief concerns was also to ensure that the land which he had given to different people from time to time was legally transferred to them. Stokes had gifted land to a number of people— to friends, family, children he had adopted, associates from the Brotherhood days and to those who worked for him. In Khilon village he gave land to Sheenkru, who had come to work for him at age ten and remained with the family all his

---

* When Stokes died in 1946, newspapers in Philadelphia commented pointedly on this division of the family's inherited wealth between sons and daughters.

life, and also to his brothers. While much of the land had been legally transferred to the beneficiaries, some was still in his name and he now began to take steps to transfer it to the concerned families. "I have always looked on them as theirs—not as ours, apart from the legal technicality," he told his sons. "Should I not for any reason be able to do so, remember that this is an obligation of honour, and I charge you, as soon as your own names are entered as owners of these properties, to immediately effect the transfer. My honour is involved in this."[25]*

* The names mentioned in this connection were those of Lachhi and Gris Chand, Isaac John's sons, Bodh Raj, Isa Das' son, and Rupi. He gave land to various other people but the matter has never been publicized.

MARKETING THE FRUITS OF LABOR

Stokes remained concerned with the difficulties of transporting apples from Kotgarh. The road project on which he was depending was stalled when Sir Malcolm Hailey, the governor of Punjab, who had sympathized with the apple growers was transferred. Under the circumstances, Stokes now discouraged further expansion in apple plantation as he felt that even if more trees were not planted, farmers who had already used part of their land for apples would still be able to generate sufficient income to be reasonably prosperous.

But the situation was soon reversed when the Punjab Agricultural Department decided to step in to promote apple cultivation in a big way. Seeing the success of Delicious apples in Kotgarh, the department initiated a massive campaign to popularize the fruit in the entire hill territories under its jurisdiction. By the early thirties, traditional cereal crops were replaced by apple orchards in many areas and people looked forward to the time when their trees would start bearing fruit and their life of penury would change to that of plenty.

However, the Punjab Agricultural Department did not simultaneously address the transportation issue. As a result, once new orchards began to bear fruit, the problem of transporting the produce became acute. Mules, which had barely managed to carry the fruit of early growers could not now cope with the increased volume. Also, the gap between demand and supply became so wide that mule-men raised their rates exorbitantly, cutting into the apple growers' profit margin.

When Stokes had first sent his fruit to the market, mules were there for the asking and their rates at five to six rupees a pair were fairly reasonable. But now the rates had almost doubled, and when the crop was a large one and the mules were few, mule-men demanded as much as sixteen to twenty rupees a pair.[1] This resulted in large amounts of fresh fruit being left to rot in the orchards. Stokes himself saw his profits from the orchard plummet and faced substantial loss. The cost of carrying a case of apples from Kotgarh to Simla was more than the cost of transporting the same case from Simla to Calcutta and he no longer found it practical to send his fruit beyond Simla.

Stokes was distressed to see that apples which he had dreamed would bring prosperity to the people were now turning into a burden for them. Though all fruit growers suffered, the worst affected were small farmers who had no money to transport their produce. They were thus forced to sell their fruit in the fields to buyers from Simla who were prepared to pay only nominal prices. In 1934, farmers had to dispose of their apples for as little as twelve annas a mound.

In September that year, when the new governor of Punjab, Sir Herbert William Emerson, was camping at Thanedhar, Stokes made an official representation to him on behalf of fruit growers explaining the difficulties people of Kotgarh were facing due to lack of transport facilities. But Emerson was not enthusiastic about introducing motor transport on the Hindustan–Tibet road. His position was that since large quantities, up to three or four lakh mounds of produce, came in to Simla over this road, a large number of trucks would be required to carry it and the whole length of the road would have to be paved. It entailed an expenditure of at least two or three lakh of rupees, which he felt the provincial government could not afford.

Stokes met the governor several times and tried to convince him that the motor-road project was both economically worthwhile and financially practical, and that, once the road was opened, revenue from it could recover the expense incurred in a reasonably short period and thereafter yield a substantial profit. The motor transport, he suggested, could be used only for the more expensive perishable produce such as fruits and vegetables, and the hardier goods like potatoes and wool would be handled by mules to avoid undue pressure on the road. But Emerson was not convinced. He also did not favor the construction of a circular road around Simla to link the Hindustan–Tibet road at Sanjauli with the Cart Road to Kalka, a proposal Stokes had been recommending so that traffic congestion at the Simla end of the road could be reduced.[2]*

To solve the problems of the apple industry, Stokes, with help and encouragement from S. B. Lal Singh, then fruit officer of Punjab, decided to get the farmers together and form an association which could take up their case at various levels. The Kotgarh Fruit Growers' Association was established in 1936 and Stokes, as

---

* The circular road around Simla town was eventually approved. The road acts as a divider between the up-going traffic into the hills and the down-coming traffic to the plains passing through Simla. Thanks to this road, the heavy traffic of goods from the interior and the congested local traffic of Simla town can be regulated and organized.

its secretary, worked to bring about changes for the welfare of orchardists in the ilaqa as well as in the state. He also met all expenses of the association from his personal funds.[3]

The new orchards planted and extended following the government's encouragement also began to bear substantial fruit in 1936. So much fruit was produced that growers almost came to blows in their efforts to obtain mules, and their desperate need drove the prices of transportation up to astronomical levels. Stokes approached Simla's deputy commissioner, K. V. F. Morton, and apprised him of the desperate situation of the growers, including himself, who were all faced with ruin unless authorities took drastic measures to help them.

Anticipating that the yield would double with every crop during the next few years, Stokes urged Morton to take up the fruit growers' case with the provincial and central governments and convince them to make the road fit for a limited number of trucks to carry the surplus fruit which mules could not carry. "Four or five trucks to start with would not put so heavy a strain on the road that it would have to be completely metalled." He insisted that the central government should be induced to take a practical interest in the transport problem facing fruit growers. "It seems to me that now we growers have shown the way, this one vital necessity to economic uplift might be considered by them. Our people are not in a position to bring much political influence to bear but it would be a fine achievement to raise the economic life of the people of an area which at present suffers from every kind of economic disability. My thirty-three years of practical knowledge of the hills and their potentialities convinces me that their condition can be materially raised if a chance is given. Kotgarh is only a part of the area, but what is possible there is possible throughout."[4]

He also discussed and explained to other senior officers in the government, including the secretary of Simla Municipality and the engineers in charge of the Hindustan–Tibet road, the problems faced by fruit growers. So far the road had been a matter of convenience for the general public and an added facility for potato growers but now, with apples having become an important produce of the region, motor-transport facilities became an issue of vital importance upon which the livelihood of a large number of farmers depended.

While Stokes' efforts did not bear immediate results they did bring the matter to the fore and many officials were sympathetic to the fruit-growers' cause as a letter by Major. A. Beatson Bell, secretary of the Municipal Committee, demonstrates. "I have been approached by the fruit growers in the Kotgarh area, through Mr Stokes with a suggestion to lower octroi on road-borne fresh fruit, brought in via Sanjauli," Bell wrote to the deputy commissioner, Simla. "As you will appreciate, however, even a total abolition of octroi would be but a 'flea bite' for these people (who are so disadvantageously placed, in competition for Simla's fresh-fruit trade) in comparison with the really substantial reduction in transportation charges, which the opening of the road wholly or even one or two stages towards Kotgarh, for motor transportation, would confer on them. I am further prompted to point out that all efforts to ameliorate the lot of coolies and animals on that road deserve encouragement both from a humanitarian and SPCA point of view."[5]

During the following months, Stokes continued to seek support for fruit growers. He stressed again and again—in private conversations, official discussions, in representations to the governor of Punjab and to the Viceroy of India—that unless a means could be found which would enable growers to get their fruit to the market on time and at reasonable rates the industry would collapse. People could not cope with transport so costly that it left no profit for them. "Our produce is perishable and we must be able to depend upon its getting to the market on time," he reiterated. "The road is there already; the market is at the other end of it, eager to absorb our fruit. The public of Simla appreciate and profit in health by our produce. All that is needed is that the way be opened for us to get it to its market at an economic cost."[6]

At the Hill Fruit Show in Simla in September 1937, the transport problem was uppermost in the minds of participants and organizers as well as of those who spoke at the prize-giving ceremony. Placards on the subject were hung on walls. One after the other speakers spoke of the lack of cheap transport to serve the pressing needs of an increasing output while stressing that the days of pack mules or human backs for transport of heavy goods were past. Stokes' orchards received the first prize for quality, but for him there was little joy in this recognition. In an emotionally charged speech he spoke of the utter impossibility of improvement or expansion of the fruit industry under existing conditions. "At this very moment splendid dessert apples are rotting in Kotgarh. We need, and we believe we have, the moral support of the people whom we serve to the best of our ability, but we need also the practical support of those who have power to alter the present strangling conditions."[7]

Stokes' unsparing efforts drew the attention of the media, and the transportation of apples soon became a subject of public debate and a matter of discussion in the provincial and local press. The *Civil and Military Gazette* wrote of the serious handicap under which fruit growers of the Simla hills were now laboring. If apples from Simla Hills could be marketed properly they would displace inferior Japanese apples from the market, it asserted. "These Japanese apples are at times shipped as far as Simla, the next-door neighbour of one of the finest fruit-growing areas in the world."[8]

Simla's popular weekly, *Liddells*, devoted much space to the subject of fruit-growing in the Simla Hills, asserting that it had been "clearly proved, after years of experimenting, that in this part of the Himalayas there can be produced as good apples, pears and kindred fruits grown in temperate and cold climates as can be found in any of the more famous fruit-growing areas of the world."[9] It sought support for transport facility for the fruit growers: "A sufficiency of motor transport, at reasonable rates at which it can be made available, would save and foster this industry as well as supply the territories further south served by the railway with an ample supply of the finest fruit."

Stokes himself gave detailed accounts in the regional press of the problems faced by apple growers. "It is as producers, to whom the question of prompt and reliable transport facilities has become as one of life and death, that we make our appeal," he wrote. He argued that the opening of motor transport on the Hindustan–Tibet road would not only benefit the fruit growers in Kotgarh, but would open many avenues for the development of the region. Besides potatoes, green peas, too, had become an important crop in recent years, and great quantities of it were sent from Simla to all of north India. Other green vegetables such as cabbage and cauliflower grew in the hills at a time when they could not be grown to advantage in the plains. "The whole of this mountain area back of Simla stands ready to be developed into an economic asset to the province and the country if proper transport facilities are afforded."[10]

Stokes' relentless efforts resulted in eventually winning over the sympathies of the Punjab government and many senior officials favored providing some relief to the growers of Simla hills, but by now the road had passed from under the control of the Punjab government to the government of India. The road remained under the Public Works Department (PWD) only for purposes of maintenance and it was for the central government to decide whether it was to be opened for motor transport of fruit or not.[11] Even the governor of Punjab expressed his inability to take any action, pointing out that in the final resort it was for Delhi to decide, as the larger part of the funds needed had to be supplied from there.

In the summer of 1938, Stokes prepared a detailed memorandum restating the problem of transport faced by fruit growers and stressing that the financial viability of the orchards rested as much on the production of fruit as it did on marketing it. The memorandum, which was presented to the government of India and circulated widely, received the sympathetic attention of many officials. The managing committee of the Provincial Cooperative Fruit Development Board at Lyallpur even approached members of the Punjab Legislative Assembly to take up this matter in their next session.[12] Stokes' old friend Duni Chand, who now was representing Kotgarh ilaqa in the Punjab Assembly, made every effort to help and impressed upon the provincial ministers the dire circumstances faced by fruit growers of Kotgarh.[13] A resolution passed by the Kotgarh Fruit Growers' Association in June, embodying the reasons for opening of the Hindustan–

Tibet road for motor transport of fruit to Simla, was presented to the Punjab governor, Sir Henry Duffield Craik. Copies of the resolution were also given to the minister for Development, the minister for Public Works, and the Local Self-government as well as to some members of the Legislative Assembly. The issue was subsequently raised in the Punjab Assembly.

But despite Stokes' concerted personal efforts and the persistent and numerous representations made through the Fruit Growers' Association, no headway was made. At the same time there was greater pressure to plant apple trees in other areas of the hills. The maharaja of Patiala put in a big orchard and even the Simla municipality considered going into the fruit business.[14] The government's decision to greatly curtail its summer migration to Simla both in terms of numbers and the duration of their summer stay there, bode ill for fruit growers. The most appreciative purchasers of their fruit in the past were government officials and members of the Assembly in Simla, who consumed large quantities during the season and took thousands of cases with them on their return to the plains. Now if this migrant segment of Simla's population was confined to Delhi, growers would have to take their fruit to the more distant markets of Delhi and Calcutta.

Anticipating a grave crisis for the growers, Stokes now appealed to the Viceroy, the Marquess of Linlithgow, who was known to have an interest in fruit cultivation and was also familiar with the Simla Hills where he had traveled extensively. In a representation made to him on 18 June 1939, Stokes highlighted the gravity of the situation. "If we needed motor transport before it has now become a matter of life and death for us. Our chief market is moving hundreds of miles further from us down into the plains, and at present transport rates all our margin of profits will have been consumed by the time we reach our patrons." The growers could not wait for an expensive, perfectly constructed road. To be saved from ruin they needed something immediate even though it was modest. "Delay means the destruction of the industry; a modest start *now* will save us."[15]

The outbreak of the Second World War brought more problems for growers as the army began purchasing mules on a large scale for their needs. Faced with this new complication, Stokes sought the help of the political officer for Simla Hills, Major W. F. Webb, and urged him for his consent to run four half-ton trucks for a couple of months during the height of the apple season. Though there was a lot of sympathy for the growers, no steps were taken to mitigate their suffering. The attention of officials was turned to more pressing matters during the war and while military trucks plied on the Hindustan–Tibet road with heavy loads, not even marginal interim relief was provided to growers whose condition continued to deteriorate with the increasing disparity between apple production and the means of available transport.

Mule rates, which had risen from eleven rupees per pair in 1938 to thirty per pair in 1942, jumped to fifty-two rupees per pair in 1944.[16] While prices of apples had also increased in the market, nearly one-third of the income from sales was being taken up merely in taking them as far as Simla. These high transportation costs made it impossible for the growers to send their fruit further into the plains even though government offices had by now shifted to Delhi. Stokes feared a glut in the Simla market which could consume no more than six to seven thousand large cases of apples annually, whereas the output of Kotgarh apples was twice that and was expected to grow three or four times in the next few years.[17] Kotgarh fruit growers also faced competition from the Kulu growers who paid less than two rupees a mound for transportation over a sixty-four-mile stretch of road as against ten to thirteen rupees which the Kotgarh growers were paying for a distance of forty-nine miles to Simla.[18]

The year 1944 was a particularly difficult one. Market prices of potatoes were exceptionally high resulting in a greater demand for mules for their transportation. For apple growers mules had simply become unavailable at a price that they could afford. The situation was so desperate that growers were sending boxes to Simla on coolie backs at the rate of ten rupees per box, yet a great amount of fruit lay rotting in the orchards.[19] The result was that though the crop had touched a record high of 12,000 to 13,000 boxes, growers suffered financial loss.[20]

In September that year, Stokes once again took up the case of fruit growers with the governor of Punjab, Sir Bertrand Glancy. In a meeting with the governor on 30 September at Barnes Court in Simla, he apprised him of the critical situation faced by apple growers and the travails they had faced all these years and appealed to him for interim measures of relief. If the growers could only get permission to ply three one-and-a-half-ton trucks daily between Thanedhar and Simla from early September to the end of November it would help them to overcome their immediate difficulties. The demand of fruit growers was neither impossible nor impractical and this very modest step would not add any cost to the government.[21] In a follow-up letter he again pleaded for an interim arrangement to save people from disaster. "To wait to give us relief some years hence, when we can be given a first class motor road, would be like refusing a patient emergency treatment because the facilities for a complete and ideal treatment were not to hand. But the best delayed treatment will not avail if the patient is permitted to die before it can be applied."[22]

Sir Bertrand Glancy was sympathetic in his approach and promised to do whatever he could for the next year. Stokes also took up the matter with Sir Kenneth Mitchell whom he had known for many years. Mitchell, who was earlier with the Department of Communication, was familiar with the Hindustan–Tibet road and its problems and had always sympathized with Stokes in his efforts to find a solution to the transport problem. Now that Mitchell was the chief controller of Road Transport and Development at Delhi, Stokes hoped that he was in a position to help.[23] "What we plead with your department is a good motor road as soon as possible after the war, and *in the meantime* some measure of relief," he wrote to Mitchell. "The one question for us is the Hindustan–Tibet Road and transit facilities on it. Upon this our future hangs . . . Do help us to keep our heads above water until you can give us the kind of a road we really need, and I believe deserve."[24]

Support also came from other senior government officials, the most important among whom was Lieutenant-General Hutton who was now head of the post-war rural development plans of the central government. During his visit to Kotgarh the previous summer, Hutton had been deeply moved by the growers' difficulties and had told Stokes that he would do everything in his power to help them in getting motor facilities. He now once again reassured him.[25] Trevor Jones, the chief engineer of PWD, who had visited Kotgarh, was sympathetic too.

The executive and superintending engineers of PWD found Stokes' request for sanction for three one-and-a-half-ton trucks to ply daily for only three months from September onwards as interim *emergency* measures, "moderate and reasonable," and were prepared to recommend their use after the rains as a temporary measure of relief until the road had improved.[26] The Civil Supplies Department offered to buy 4,000 boxes of apples directly from the growers at Kotgarh for the military. The offer was especially welcome since the terms of purchase included transportation of fruit by truck from Kotgarh to Simla by the buyer, and was one which would ease the pressure on mule transport and consequently bring about a fall in mule rates. Stokes saw an added advantage in this arrangement. The military contract could be a means of, at last, getting the haulage of fruit by truck started on the Hindustan–Tibet road.[27] He had now every reason to be at last hopeful of an early solution to the growers' problems.

After the trials of 1944, prospects brightened for the growers in 1945. The governor's sympathetic approach together with a more amenable attitude of the officials, at last set things moving. The end of the war resulted in a decrease in demand of timber by the military and consequently a lesser demand of trucks. Kotgarh was included in the scheme for the government's post-war policy for extensive road development,[28] and the interim relief of the limited facility of motor transport for three months was finally granted. Once the trucks started moving, Stokes could foresee other important developments. So far the fruit was packed in wooden boxes. The growers had to apply each year to the forest department for trees they needed to cut for their boxes. This arrangement was far from satisfactory as it meant not only the destruction of valuable trees, but uncertainties and delays in getting sanctions. It also involved a high cost in the cutting and haul-ing of trees as well as in making boxes. But with better transport facilities, the need for wooden boxes would diminish as growers could then pack their fruit in nirgal (bamboo) baskets which would serve equally well. Also, motor transport would make it more practical to return wooden boxes to farmers for reuse. All this in turn would stem the depletion of forests.

Stokes was confident that once transport facilities were given to people, sub-stantial revenue would be generated for the Simla district. Income taxes on ag-ricultural income would come in time and transporting of the fruit itself would become a very profitable business. So far as the upkeep of the road was con-cerned, he saw no reason why a minimum road-tax on every case of apples should not be levied for this purpose. All these factors could change the face of the hills in a few short years.

Stokes' family was then the wealthiest in the region. Whether it would con-tinue to be so remained to be seen. "But if it does I charge you to keep it as a trust," he advised his sons, "a means to the common good. In the deepest sense it is not yours; you, our family, are its custodians for the common good."[29]

WORLD WAR II AND AFTER

For many years, Stokes kept away from active politics and refrained from writing on political issues. The last time he had expressed his political views was in 1929 after the Gandhi-Irwin talks on whether the Congress should have anything to do with the Round Table Conference in London.

The general opinion was that Indians should not participate in it but Stokes felt that India should support the Viceroy in his plan for the conference. Since the British government had formally stated that their final goal was "equal" dominion status for India, he felt India should participate in the conference and should strive for a commitment to a definite date, when, irrespective of the conditions then prevailing, full dominion status would be granted to the country, even if the date was ten or fifteen years in the future.

"What do ten or fifteen years matter provided genuine progress is being made? What does matter is that we should not stand still, as we are undoubtedly doing on the present basis so far as our hopes for Swaraj are concerned,"[1] he had written in a long memorandum to Jawaharlal Nehru on 25 November 1929. He was convinced that if such a date was fixed, British officials would exert themselves to help prepare the Indian people for self-government during the interim period. It would also lead to real and wholehearted cooperation on the part of the British with Indian nationalists. Without this he could see no path to self-government save the one that led through "violence and disorder and at least temporary chaos."

Nehru studied his proposal carefully but did not agree with his viewpoint. "I think the course you suggest will be injurious for us and will delay the day of our freedom," he wrote.[2] Nehru's feelings were shared by many others. In its Lahore session of December 1929, the Congress had declared complete independence as its goal and resolved to boycott legislatures and the Round Table Conference. A few months later Gandhi launched civil disobedience, a political method with which Stokes was still not in agreement.

That was almost ten years previous, a period during which Stokes deliberately distanced himself from politics and devoted his time to philosophy and community development. Now when war seemed imminent, his attention once again turned to world affairs. After much thought he came to very clear conclusions. If there was a war, it was imperative that Britain and her allies win it and to ensure their victory it was essential that India give its wholehearted support to the war effort.[3] In three important letters written on 30 March, 31 March, and 4 April of 1939 to Subhash Chandra Bose, who was then Congress president, Mahatma Gandhi, and Jawaharlal Nehru respectively, he outlined the reasons that had led him to these conclusions and urged the leaders to draw up a line of action for the country if a war broke out.

The existing world conditions, resulting from imperial exploits, were such that another war was more or less a certainty, he maintained. He could see no way out of the impasse by which the empire-holding powers and aspirants to empire-building could come to a settlement without a war. All the leading nations of the world wanted to enjoy their empire and a war would be for an empire, not for the ending of it.[4] It would be a war in which Britain and her allies would be fighting to keep imperial domination as it existed and Germany and her allies to secure a share in that domination.[5]

He felt certain that future peace in the world and prevention of another world conflagration lay in "the termination of the whole imperial system and (in) self-determination for all peoples, large and small, weak and strong." He was also convinced that to bring imperialism to an end at the earliest practical opportunity, it was essential—if there was a war—that Britain and her allies should come out victorious. "This is not because I trust the British in this respect or believe for a moment that the Imperial government contemplates relinquishing its hold on the non-European peoples, but because even if the British and her allies come out victorious they would be in such a state of exhaustion and war-weariness that they will be unable to resist the demands of the subordinated peoples for complete self-determination. On the other hand if Germany and her allies win there will be powerful rejuvenation of imperialism and on a basis even more objectionable than the present," he wrote to Subash Chandra Bose urging him to decide on a plan of action for the Congress.

It was some time since he had been in touch with Gandhi, but could not now desist from expressing his concern to him. "I do not write any more for the papers but I have felt I could not keep silent, for it seems to me that the fate of the world for quite a long time to come hangs in the balance today," he wrote, advocating that, in the event of a war, there should be complete and nationwide support for the British, with the Congress leading it. "I am certain that it is in the interests of the subjugated peoples of the earth that she and her allies defeat the new aspirants to empire. By so doing they will break the onrush of this fresh wave of imperialism that is surging towards us and threatens to submerge us for heaven knows how long."[6] He feared the new imperialism that was threatening the world. Should Germany win the war, India and the other subjugated nations would become mere "hewers of wood and drawers of water" to a nation whose "conscience would not be wounded by directing all our activities to subserve its ends," he warned. "A new caste system, based on race and power, would become firmly established with the German 'Aryan' as Brahman and Kshatriya, the other European races as Vaishya, and the non-European peoples as the Shudras of the world."

Knowing Gandhi's views on ahimsa, Stokes knew that such a solution would not be easily acceptable to him. But he still tried to convince him that under the present circumstances a war would be justifiable, that for many ahimsa meant "a freeing of the spirit from hatred and anger and a desire to harm others," that there was a distinction between the dharma of individuals and the duty of nations, and whatever may be the dharma of individuals, it would be right for the country to go to war to fight the evil of imperialism.[7] He expressed the same sentiments to Jawaharlal Nehru—a victory for Germany and her partners in the impending war "would mean a fresh wave of imperialism developed with a ruthlessness and thoroughness such as we have not experienced."

He anticipated that a war was going to be very difficult for Britain and her allies and they would need every ounce of strength they could muster to be able to win. "If we all support them they can, I feel almost sure, but if India hangs back or remains floundering in a sea of divided counsels, I am more doubtful. Therefore I think Congress should be ready to come to the country with a clear lead to support Britain in such a war, and that everyone in this country should be urged to throw his full strength on her side . . . Her aims and ours would be different. She would be fighting for the retention of empire, we to bring about the end of imperialism."[8]

There was no reply from Subhash Chandra Bose who was very unwell at that time and Stokes doubted whether he had read his letter at all. Both Gandhi and Nehru were prompt in replying even though they did not agree with him. "As to the great question raised by you, my reading of the Gita and interpretation of ahimsa are different from yours. I do not believe that killing in war can ever be done without anger. As I believe in unadulterated ahimsa I am groping as to India's duty . . . I am shirking the national solution. My own individual conduct is determined but I quite agree with you that the national can be quite the opposite," Gandhi wrote.[9] Nehru was in general agreement with Stokes' analysis of the situation. "I feel, however, that we cannot, under present circumstances, go so far as you suggest, that is, agree to support any war against fascism. If we fight for democracy we must have democracy to fight for . . . It is a very difficult situation where we are pulled in two different directions and it is not possible to say how one would function at a particular moment."[10]

Stokes himself never thought of the British Empire as a "democracy"; it was certainly not so as regards its non-European peoples and he believed that it never would be. It was not because he thought of the British as champions of democracy that he urged the necessity of throwing the country's weight behind them in the event of war. "I am not interested in the victory of the British but the defeat of the threat that a victory of the Axis powers would offer to the exploitable peoples of the earth . . . This may be a mistaken view but it is not one which I have reached lightly. Above all I feel it is vital we should have achieved unity and a clear-cut policy if and when the crisis breaks upon us," he wrote in a second letter to Nehru on 22 April 1939.

When Britain declared war on Germany in September 1939, it did not have India's support, though it did make extensive use of Indian men and supplies throughout the duration of the war. The Congress, however, passed a resolution calling on the British to define their objectives, especially as regards the subordinated peoples of the Empire, and India in particular. Stokes was pleased to see that the Congress had put the moral issues squarely up to the Imperial government. But as expected the British failed to give a straightforward answer and attempted to sidetrack the question.

Stokes wrote to Gandhi again reiterating that a German victory would be the greatest catastrophe for the world. "For the non-Europeans it would be a case of 'out of the frying-pan into the fire.'" He insisted that taking a chance with an all-out victory for the Nazi government could not be justified and that if there was a certainty of the Allies ultimately winning then he himself would favor India's withholding all aid but there was no such certainty.

"We, the exploited and subordinated peoples of the world, cannot afford to have the Germans win, and I fear that if she should, as a result of our refusing to do our share in obstructing her at this time, we could not escape our moral responsibility for the consequences to the world, especially to the militarily weak non-European peoples of Asia and Africa, despite the fact that we are innocent of producing the situation which has brought about the war . . . I feel that the future demands of us that we do not remain inactive at this critical time, waiting for the British to give way to our just demands. The outcome of the war may depend on the line this country takes now—not what line she may ultimately take."[11]

But Gandhi had felt that considered from the nonviolent standpoint, which in his opinion was the only point worth considering, it would be immoral for the Congress to give her moral support to Britain unless the latter's position was made clear. "I do not lay down the law as you do about Nazism. Germans are as much human beings as you and I are. Nazism like other 'isms' is a toy of today. It will share the same fate as the other 'isms' . . . I fancy I see the distinction between you and me. You, as a Westerner, cannot subordinate reason to faith. I, as an Indian, cannot subordinate faith to reason even if I will. You tempt the Lord with your reason; I won't," he wrote in reply to Stokes.[12]

The war years kept Stokes busy. Government officials in Simla turned to him for help—whether it was for raising money for the war fund or obtaining more recruits for the army or ensuring an equitable distribution of controlled consumer items—they knew they could depend upon him.[13] It was largely due to his efforts that Kotgarh remained in the lead in every field. It was smaller than the Kotkhai tehsil of Simla district but it sent a larger number of its men to the army in this war, as it had done in the previous one. Kotgarh men were on active service in Africa, the Middle East, Europe, and on the Burma Front. Many were wounded in action and some became prisoners of war at Japanese hands. The people of Kotgarh also purchased a greater number of National Security Certificates than those of other areas.[14] Stokes' own financial position was constrained but he willingly put in his share, though his contributions were strictly for the Red Cross.[15] On a personal level, Stokes tried to ease the burdens imposed on the people by various restrictions and scarcities of the war. As chairman of the Civil Supplies Committee, he ensured just distribution of the limited supplies of essential items like kerosene, sugar, grains, and seeds to every resident of Kotgarh by personally supervising their sales.[16] He traveled frequently to Simla to arrange for essential articles for fruit growers—nails for apple boxes, wrapping paper, insecticides, and so forth, all of which had become scarce.

However, as the war progressed he became more and more disillusioned. The Allied powers were beginning to talk of reverting to the pre-war status as far as the empires and their subjugated peoples were concerned, and Stokes like other educated Indians began to feel more and more that if England wanted full support from India, promises for the future would not be enough and it would have to consider giving India a genuine national government immediately. The position which the Allies were now taking was of great concern to him. "If this is all the Allies are fighting for, then all this bloodshed and destruction is in vain, the beautiful new world for which we are asked to give the lives of ourselves and our children a dream, and the future a nightmare of progressive brutalization for the spirit of man."[17]

He was convinced that conquering the Axis powers would accomplish nothing unless the evil system that was the cause of these ever recurring catastrophes was uprooted. "This can never be done by hanging on grimly to what we all had . . . Nor could it be accomplished by a re-division of the spoils of empire over the non-European world by the great nations of the West. The only practical solution is the foregoing of all empire by every nation, and an honest attempt to work out a scheme which gives every people, strong or weak, an equal share in the world," he wrote to his cousin Warrington Stokes in America in early 1943.[18] "If you want a happy world, it must be a world in which you do not seek for special privileges and try to keep special advantages cornered for your own nation. You cannot have them both. And after this present terrible business you certainly cannot have the same world you had before, whatever choice you make. It is either to be a much juster—and consequently happier—world, or it will be one with all the past evils and dangers and hardships immensely accentuated. It is not merely a question of a world you are ready to accept for yourselves but what fate you are prepared to hand to your children."

Warrington Stokes and his friends in America were so impressed with the presentation of Stokes' views that they sent copies of his letter to President Roosevelt and other American leaders, and gave parts of it for radio broadcasts and for publication in newspapers. Stokes then wrote on similar lines to Lord Wavell, the Viceroy of India, as well as to Anthony Eden, the British foreign secretary. The letters were duly acknowledged, but as he had expected there was no fruitful result. Lord Wavell's secretary conveyed the Viceroy's full appreciation of Stokes' "motives in writing." On the other hand, Anthony Eden felt that the "suggestion that the peoples of Asia have been forgotten in our aims is not supported by the declarations of our policy which are on record." To Stokes, their replies seemed "a conspicuous example of the blindness of those at the helm of human affairs to the basic issues."[19]

All this while the possibility of a victory of the Axis powers continued to make him anxious. He was haunted by the prospect of what such a victory would mean for India and the other subjugated nations. He spent sleepless nights, pacing anxiously, thinking of the sorrows that had been brought upon the peoples of the world.[20] "No one can tell what is going to happen in these lunatic times," he wrote to his cousin Dr. Stokes in Germantown.[21] He became more and more concerned as the ravages of war increased. "The great sin against humanity has been perpetrated. The selfishness and the short-sightedness of the great nations that cling to imperial domination, and the ambition of those other great nations who desire to replace them, are brutalizing and destroying our race. What will be left when the madness is over we cannot say." One thought which comforted him greatly, however, was that his ancestors had never been party to the outlook and activities which had brought as their fruit the present terrible conditions in the world. "We have always—for centuries—opposed those attitudes which are responsible for the present havoc, and have stood for the only ideal that can save humanity. And we have been ready when necessary to suffer for our dreams."[22]

Although Stokes was not now actively involved in politics, he was still a suspect in the eyes of the government. That his sympathies were with the nationalists was an established fact. Simla authorities were also peeved at his insistence on walking with an umbrella on the Mall in a khadi kurta-pyjama in violation of the Simla municipal by-laws.* While he was not charged for the offense, he was one of the few exceptions who got away with it. He, however, was kept under close watch and came under greater scrutiny after the Quit India movement was launched by Gandhi in August 1942 and which resulted in the arrest of all the Congress leaders and the declaration of Congress as an illegal body. He and his family were kept under strict surveillance and each time anyone of them passed through Kalka, either while coming down to the plains or returning to the hills, the matter was reported to the police. There was every possibility of his being arrested and, although his health was poor, he was quite prepared for the eventuality. All his important papers were quietly tucked away with Lakshmi Singh and he was ready to go any time they came for him.[23]

As it was after World War I, the end of World War II also brought with it great disappointment. There was resentment among the Asian countries at an attempt by the imperialistic powers to re-impose their domination in East Indies and Indo-China, and Stokes like other Indians was particularly outraged with the British for making use of Indian troops to re-establish the French and Dutch in their pre-war positions. "Nothing that the British can say about their true intentions toward Indian independence carries the slightest weight in the face of what they are seen to be doing," he wrote.[24]

Post-war events clearly indicated that Britain and her allies had not changed heart, that they still were determined to retain for themselves a dominant position in the world. He did not hate the British, on the contrary he admired their many magnificent qualities. But he did feel intensely bitter with them for expecting to be allowed, and being ready, to sacrifice the interests of the world at large for their own selfish advantage. He also no longer trusted them. "Never believe the British when they talk of such large numbers of the highest posts in India being held by Indians as proof that India is being given self-government. It is true that Indians are in such posts but they are carefully hand-picked men upon whom Britain can depend to forward her ends," he wrote to his sister Florence Coleman in America. The British were past masters at pretending that they intended to give India independence, he charged. All this talk of handing over the moment the Hindus and Muslims were prepared to agree to a single

---

* A Simla municipal traffic by-law banned coolies and job-porters from carrying any loads or loitering on the Mall. Later, ill-dressed Indians and khadi-clad Congressmen were also told to keep away from the Mall. They were not allowed even the use of an umbrella. (*Imperial Simla*, p. 202)

program was whitewash. They knew that Hindus and Muslims would never reach agreement on this basis, and they knew how to keep the Hindus and Muslims so divided that such an agreement could not be reached. "Had such a proposition been placed before the American colonies before the war of independence it would not have been possible for them to have reached the necessary agreement . . . indeed one of the assertions in Britain at that time was that the different colonies could never reach a common policy. Nor were they in fact ever in agreement until *after* the revolution was ended. In the same ways Hindus and Muslims will agree to a modus operandi when they must depend on themselves to do so, and not before. And they will find it then, as the colonists did when thrown upon their own resources," he contended.

And yet, neither for Britain's nor for India's sake did he wish to see the Indo-British connection severed overnight. For years he had insisted that the only way for it to be satisfactorily terminated was for a specific date to be settled upon—some years hence, a period during which the British would join wholeheartedly with Indians in evolving administrative and governing machinery that would give the country an ordered government and economy. Ten or even fifteen years would not have been too much at one time, but India was now not prepared to wait that long—and he was convinced beyond doubt that, irrespective of the situation in the country, India should now be left to her own resources.[25]

25

THE VEDANTIST

Stokes continued to spend long hours in study and meditation and strove to cultivate a spirit of humility. In a letter of 1939 he wrote, "There was a time when I too thought that I was worthy to be a teacher of others, but as I grow older and look at myself possibly with clearer eyes I lose all confidence in any fitness that I once thought I had to teach others, for I find in myself a thousand spiritual weaknesses and faults which show me that it is for me to learn not to teach—to humbly strive for even a little of the spiritual treasure of which I have been talking and writing most of my life. More and more I feel the urge to be silent and to learn in silence what I may, trying as best I can to win a communion in which there will be no place for littleness and unworthiness."[1]

He was also unwilling to enter into religious discussions in which he had once delighted, or to embark upon a comparison of the merits of Hinduism and Christianity. "That time is however past," he told Fazl Ali. "Follow your light; if you do so faithfully it will lead to more light. It is faithfulness that matters. Truth is a boundless ocean and the wisest of us is like a little child playing with the shells on the shores of it. The best that each of us can do is to be as utterly faithful as in us lies to the highest light that we see at each given step of our journey.

"Think of all your life as a sacrifice—something, each detail of which is to be shaped humbly and lovingly as the best that you are capable of making it, to be offered up to the best and the highest that you know, for love, in gratitude, with humility, seeking no reward. Learn to accept pain and pleasure, honour and contempt, victory and defeat, as blessings—capable of making your soul if you accept them in the spirit, not of mere resignation to the will of God, but willing acquiescence. If you—and I—can learn to do this we need not bother about the relative merits of this theology or that, for we shall grow spiritually and as we grow the eyes of our spirit will open to ever wider vistas. God is to be seen with the eyes of the spirit by the pure in heart—no more to be grasped by these puny human brains of ours than the ocean is to be held in the shell of the child who plays on the shore. Nor is it to be found in Jerusalem nor in Samaria but in the heart of him who seeks to worship Him in spirit and in truth . . . to worship Him with his work and in his life, and with all his love . . . let each of us be lit with the light that we see."[2]

He received letters from different parts of the country—from Hindus, Muslims, and Christians. They wrote to him, sharing their thoughts and religious concerns. He was addressed as Reverend Stokes; many called him Brother Stokes or Swamiji. Badrudin Khan, whose father was an Afridi Pathan and mother a Brahmin and who was born and educated in the U.S.A. and now called himself a bhakt, wrote from Calcutta: "Your life is wonderful . . . When I think of you all the way at Kotgarh, and another great soul, Verrier Elwin, up amongst the Gonds in Central Provinces it shows how God draws some people in directions never anticipated by them."

Christians wrote to him expressing their differences of opinion with him in matters of religion and seeking clarifications. Many turned to him for help and valued his advice and opinion. "I cannot claim that I have understood everything which you have written, still I admire your way of illustrating spiritual things in clear and simple words," wrote Joseph Moses from Sabathu. While Moses was skeptical about Stokes' faith, yet he longed to meet him personally, wanted to read his books, and urged him to "pray" for him. Since little was known of Stokes' life to outsiders, there were misconceptions too. "Are you running an ashram?" he was asked.[3]

Stokes continued to be intensely absorbed in the study of scriptures, especially the Vedas and the Upanishads, and encouraged others to do the same. While he believed in and had great respect for the Indian Guru-shishya tradition he himself had no Guru. For him life, and the experience it brought with it, was the great teacher. He learned Sanskrit largely on his own so that he could study the original Vedic texts. From 1920 onwards, much of his time and all his thought were taken up in an effort to understand these scriptures and meditate upon them.

In his personal life he was very much detached. He lived as a recluse in the hills and had little interaction with the outside world. A very private person, he shunned publicity. He had few friends and there was no one in Kotgarh or elsewhere with whom he was in very close communication and to whom he could express his deepest thoughts. His old friend Andrews, who often visited him at Kotgarh during the earlier years, was now too involved with Gandhi and his work even for regular correspondence. When his mother was alive he penned down his philosophical ruminations in his weekly letters to her even though she sometimes found it difficult to understand his "mystical orientalism." After her death there was a distinct void in this respect.

There were, however, many Sanyasi guests at Harmony Hall. The Sadhus who passed by Kotgarh on their way to the holy Mansarovar Lake in Tibet looked for a night's shelter after a long trek and were invariably directed to Stokes' home. Eager to hold discussions with these learned men and to learn something from them, Stokes not only welcomed them but was reluctant to let them go and urged them to spend more time with him at Barobagh. Local residents remember instances when Sadhus went up to Barobagh for a night's shelter and did not emerge from there till three or four days later.

In 1935, he published a little collection of verses from the Upanishads which he had prepared for his family and which he had been using in his own morning and evening devotions as a basis for meditation. The collection was titled *Devupasana.* It was mostly in Sanskrit but there was an English translation too.[4] The same year he published a selection of shlokas from the Gita with the hope that the collection would lead his friends and neighbors in the mountains to an appreciation of this great scripture and that it would be a means of awakening the community to "a deeper spiritual life." The book, which included a little less than a fourth of all the verses comprising the Gita, consisted of those shlokas that he had himself found most helpful and inspiring.

The Gita had the most profound influence on Stokes' thought and life. For years he studied the book, first in English and then in Hindi. He was not satisfied until he had finally made himself fully at home with it in Sanskrit, and in Sanskrit he went through it literally hundreds of times.[5*] During the years of his political involvement, he often cited the Gita in his writings and also in his speeches. The power of the Gita lay in its permanent relevance and universal appeal, he wrote. "Any scripture that is really great has not only a message for one time but for all times, and not for the individual only but for all peoples and humanity as a whole. If we can enter into its spirit deeply enough we shall find light to guide us in whatever circumstances we find ourselves and no matter with what difficulties we may be confronted," he wrote in an article titled "The Message of the Gita."[6] In later years, whenever he was in Simla for a sufficiently long period he would give discourses on the Gita in his home.

He did not think that in India's vast religious literature there was any single work that had such a profound and universal appeal to the spiritually minded as the Gita. "To what countless thousands in all ages has it been a solace in times of

* For his study of the Gita he turned to the large number of critical works both in Hindi and in English and felt especially indebted to the editions of S. Narayan Swami Chidghanand and Lokmanya Tilak in Hindi, and those of Pt. Sitanath Tattvabhushan, K. T. Telang, D. S. Sharma, Swami Swsrupanando, and that of Mrs. Annie Besant and Babu Bhagwan Das in English. He also relied on commentaries of Sri Shankara and Sri Ramanuja on the Gita.

trouble, a guide on the path of life and an inspiration in the midst of difficulty! The voice that speaks through it speaks to the deepest that is in us, and from our inmost being draws forth a response of love and joy and confidence. We rise from reading and meditating upon the message it sets forth calmed from the fervour of earthly ends, strivings and anxieties, clothed in a new fortitude to meet what life may bring of joy and sorrow, honour and dishonour, failure and success. To me this seems the clearest indication of its spiritual validity and entitles it to its acknowledged place as one of the great scriptures of the world."[7]

"Nor does it speak only to the hearts of those who belong to one particular sect or school of thought. Men and women of the most diverse religious outlooks have found in it that for which their souls were longing. This wideness of its appeal is a further indication of its spiritual significance."

He had reached his position regarding the Gita after long study and contemplation. In a rejoinder to Professor Pratt's assertion that to him it was the Buddha rather than Sri Krishna who stood almost side by side with Christ, he clarified his position as regards the Gita and Sri Krishna. He admitted how, for a long time, it worried him because he could not separate it from Sri Krishna, prince of the Yadavas and friend of Arjun, or see in the activities of that prince anything of such outstanding spiritual significance as to place him upon a spiritual par with either Christ or Buddha. "But gradually there dawned upon me the truth that in the Gita it is not Sri Krishna who is speaking to us, but the *Atman*—that deepest, truest *self* of us all. Over and over again through the mouth of Krishna that Atman—the inner self of Krishna, of you, of me—stresses the fact that if it is known, *tattvatah*—if we come to really truly know it—we shall attain it, and in doing so find our salvation."

The teaching of the Gita, he realized, was "the teaching of salvation in the Atman, and in the Atman alone. Those who cannot as yet grasp it think that the Gita teaches the worship of Sri Krishna. Some even think it teaches that *Krishna* is the supreme Purusha, i.e. the supreme Atman. This is as though Mahatma Gandhi should deliver a religious discourse on the radio, and some one should take the radio box as his guru or God, falling down before it, offering flowers to it, bathing it, worshipping it.

"As I see it, Sri Krishna, Buddha, Christ, Nanak and all the great jagatgurus were the wonderfully-attuned radio instruments, especially fitted to 'pick up the wave' of the Atman—one and only 'broadcaster.' That is why we hear through the mouths of various of them phrases the gist of which is, 'Only through Me—only in Me—can you find salvation'; 'I am the Way; no man cometh to the Father but by Me'; 'I am the Path and the Supreme Goal.' *I the Atman*—not 'I the Christ' or 'I Krishna.' I the Atman—the great Deep—am calling to the deep in you. In finding what you are—*tattvatah*—you will find Me; in finding Me you will know what you really are, and the infinite richness within you that remains for you to realize in the terms of your own individuated personality . . . So you see, I am no follower of Krishna, or Christ, or Nanak or Buddha; I am profoundly grateful for these wonderfully-attuned radio instruments of the spirit because through them I can hear *the Atman* calling—Atman completely manifesting itself personally as God, as Father—and calling to the Atman in me, revealing Myself to me. This is what I find in the Gita."[8]

In 1937, Stokes started building a small temple in Barobagh which had been his dream for many years. He wanted to decorate the temple with mantras from the Vedas and the Upanishads and shlokas from the Gita which together would reveal the deep meaning of the scriptures to the seeker—a collection of such mantras, if studied with devotion, would give strength to the suffering to bear their sorrow and would help the seeker to reach his goal. His dream temple was to be like a "beautiful book in stone and wood," on whose walls would be inscribed the ancient adhi-atmik (spiritual) wisdom which would be a source of solace to his neighbors who reflected upon them and to any visitors who came to Barobagh in future years. He wanted the temple to be "truly beautiful and long-lasting," but was not sure whether he could meet the entire cost of building it. He knew that if he had had such doubts about any other project he might not have started it, but he had set his heart on the temple and was determined to carry it through. It was an inner compulsion—"It seemed to me that I would not be at peace till I had started the project," he wrote.

Perplexed with these doubts, one day he suddenly thought of confiding in his old friend Jugal Kishore Birla, scion of India's leading business family and a philanthropist. In a letter to him, Stokes explained his difficulties and requested that if on reading the letter he was willing to help then he would gratefully accept two and a half thousand rupees for this work (this was approximately half the cost of building the temple). When Stokes wrote to Birla he was not only thinking of financial help from him; he also felt that if Birla's reply was sympathetic it would mean that he wholeheartedly supported Stokes' idea and that itself would be a source of encouragement to him. However, he made up his mind that no matter what happened he would not ask anyone else for help.[9] Birla had great regard for Stokes and had incorporated verses from his *Devupasna* in the Birla Mandir in Delhi.[10] He concurred with Stokes' plan and immediately sent a telegram asking him to start the work on the temple. Birla's response removed all doubts from Stokes' mind.

The money sent by Jugal Kishore Birla was of great help, but the final cost of construction of the temple turned out to be more than double of what Stokes had anticipated, and it was with difficulty that he was able to complete the task. But he always felt that without Birla's help, and more than that his graciousness and support, he may not have had the courage to take up the project.[11]

The *Paramjyotir Mandir* (temple of eternal light) in Barobagh—as Stokes named the temple—is exceptional in many ways. The wood-paneled temple walls have Sanskrit shlokas, also in wood, impressed on them. Hindi translations of the shlokas are also displayed so that anyone with even basic knowledge of the language can understand and contemplate them. This was done with the aim of making the temple a source of light and inspiration for the learned as well as for the ordinary person. Stokes hoped that the temple would become a means to show the way to those looking for peace and internal strength, more so during times of difficulties and trials.

Stokes designed the temple building himself and meticulously followed its progress till it was completed. The family kitchen in Harmony Hall became his work-place where, after meals, he would spread out his sketches and drawings and pore over them diligently, working out every detail with careful precision.[12] He not only made the selection of the shlokas, he also painstakingly calligraphed their translations in Hindi himself. The characters in wood for the shlokas were crafted by the local carpenter Naari. The stone and the slates for the temple were quarried from and brought over long distances, and the Burma teak came all the way from Calcutta.[13] The simple beauty of the temple is striking. The small square structure made of gray stone and broad teak beams with a slate roof, though basically following the hill architecture, is unique in its conception. There is no idol in the temple; it is dedicated to the Dev (Lord) "who is beyond all names, words and forms and is yet present in the hearts of all men, to that Atman who is the light of all lights." A beautiful painting of Lord Krishna and Arjun by the renowned painter Nand Lal Bose and gifted to Stokes by the artist adorns one wall with a couplet from the Gita inscribed below it.[14]

Stokes was keen to put a gold kalash atop the temple as was customary, but Agnes did not think they could spare the money for it. He finally decided against it, not because of her resistance to the idea, but because of the devastating famine in nearby Mauni where all his attention and resources were soon directed.

The Paramjyoti Mandir, a fulfillment of Stokes' dreams, also created some tensions for him. The caretakers of the powerful local Dom Devta took exception to the fact that Stokes' temple was not dedicated to any local deity or Devta. This was unprecedented in the history of the ilaqa as, according to hill tradition, it was mandatory for every temple to be under the jurisdiction of a Devta without whose permission and blessings no religious ceremony could be sanctified.

It was a long-standing practice that on the first of the month the Dom Devta was taken in a procession to the Mehlan Temple from his abode in Suld village.

En route to Mehlan the Devta and his entourage stopped in every village, where people danced and sang. There was much excitement on the occasion and people in every village looked forward to it. Barobagh village, close to Suld, was on the procession route and there was much merriment whenever the Devta arrived. When Stokes built Paramjyoti Mandir without any Devta or a deity, it was regarded as an affront to the prestige of Dom Devta, and his caretakers decided to boycott Barobagh from their monthly itinerary. This was a great disappointment to Stokes, especially as it implied that the people were not willing to accept the Mandir.

But then the caretakers changed their mind. Stokes' daughter Satya remembered how, for many months, the Devta did not come to Barobagh and then after a long gap he was suddenly brought there with a lot of fanfare. There was much happiness all around, as it meant that the Barobagh temple was now accepted by the people of the ilaqa. Not only this, but since Stokes was the administrator of the Barobagh temple, his status was elevated and he was honorably taken to the prestigious annual Sharog ka Mela, a privilege which until then was accorded only to local Rajas and Ranas.

In a little book containing the eighty-two shlokas in the temple, he wrote, "It is my prayer that the temple and this little booklet may be a source of peace to many." Pandit Lal Chand of Manama village, a much-respected teacher of Hindi and Sanskrit at Tara School, became the temple priest.

With the passing of years, there were more changes in Stokes' philosophical thinking which led him to a purely advaitic position. This did not mean that he had rejected the philosophy of *Satyakama* which he had arrived at after long years of study and introspection. On the contrary, he maintained that *Satyakama*'s philosophy was a "long step" removed from the dvaita or dualistic Christian position under the influence of which he had been brought up, and a step nearer to what he felt to be pure advaitic or monistic position at which he now found himself.[15]

Satyakama, in its final shape, embodied a hypothesis that had completely satisfied him as "the most reasonable interpretation of the implications of our deepest spiritual experience." For many years after its publication, he continued to feel that it set forth the only possible hypothesis for one who was convinced of the profound and permanent experiences of personality and conscious relationships. But this changed in the winter of 1939. In a brief allusion to how this profound change came about in his thinking, he wrote, "No advaitic position was a possible one for me until 1939 as I believed that a pure monism was essentially inconsistent with any reality or significance for individuated personality. My awakening to the understanding that this is not so—an awakening that came like a flash and wholly unlooked for—opened up a path of thought which leads to what I am certain is real advaita without turning personal relationships into an illusion, or doing away with meaning and significance for the 'world' and finite experiencing."

In 1944, he set out to write about his philosophical journey of more than forty years that took him "from the dvaita Christian position to the pure advaitic or monistic position." His intention was to trace, if possible, the "transitions in thought and philosophic outlook" that had gradually led him to his present position and to leave a record of the "modifications in outlook (or inlook?)" that had taken place since he wrote *Satyakama* in jail twenty-two years before.[16] His health had deteriorated much since then, but there was an inner urge impelling him not to leave things where they stood. "I am conscious of being able to see deeper than I could then, and of an awareness of aspects of spiritual experience that I was not then conscious of along with a growing disinclination to talk of them even with those most dear." The book was never completed but the introductory pages touch upon the crucial "spiritual awakening" which led him to the path of advaita, and "trace the development of a line of thought which, starting from purely Christian experience, first arrived at the outlook set forth in *Satyakama* and then—with that as a transitional position—passed on to the advaita."[17]

The philosophy contained in *Satyakama*, however, remained of vital importance to him and he believed that it "hung together perfectly" as a possible explanation of the significance of finite experience. "At the time it took its final shape I thought of it as my final conception—at least for the present stage of the journey—of the meaning of life, and indeed it is still final for a large part of that vision," he wrote. It was this conviction which led him to include relevant excerpts from *Satyakama*, which was now out of print, in his latest work. He also included in it quotations from letters received from British, American, and Indian philosophers, not because he needed assurance that the lines of thought he had been exploring were worthy of consideration, for he knew they were so, but because he felt that "to others the fact that men of different lands, standing high as philosophic students in their own countries, find *Satyakama* worthy of attention may serve as an inducement to read what they might otherwise pass by."[18]

In tracing the path by which he had arrived at the advaitic conception, he considered two experiences—one belonging to his childhood and the other to his early boyhood—which had a lasting effect on him, and which he felt together exercised a profound influence upon the evolution of his thought. His first sense of infinities had come to him in the framework of the childish experience of a little boy of five or six which he thus described: "Our summer home was by the sea and I had been playing by myself not far from it. The day was clear, with a blue and cloudless sky. I remember lying on my back looking up into it. Suddenly the thought came to me, 'Suppose I should fall off the ground up and up into the sky, where would I fall to?' I was gripped by the idea that there was nothing out there and that I should go on falling for ever and ever, and always there would be the same emptiness ahead. Terrified, I shut my eyes, holding frantically to the grass on either side in fear I should find myself starting on that endless journey. I remember my breath coming in gasps and that finally I managed to get up and run to my mother, burying my face in her lap. The experience made a deep impression on my childish mind and for months after it I used to wake up in terror at night and creep for safety into my mother's bed. In the course of time the first vividness of this adventure in thought faded away, yet the heart-shaking impression of endlessness—boundlessness—undoubtedly remained."

The second experience of an overwhelming magnitude was one from his school days—the thought that those of his friends and others who did not follow the Christian religious path would burn in eternal hell. He emerged out of the agony of this thought with the help of the parable of the lost sheep, but the impression of that experience relating to an everlasting hell remained in his mind.

"It is thus apparent that the two most soul-shaking experiences I had undergone by the time I reached young manhood grew out of the sense of timelessness. The first was the childish terror at the thought of falling forever onward into space that had no end. The second was sheer horror at the thought of a fearful retribution and vengeance that would go on forever through endless time.

"And just as both impressions were profoundly real when they first presented themselves to me—the one driving me in blind terror to shelter in my mother's arms, and the other almost driving me to madness—so I believe it was the sense of endlessness left by the earlier impression that prepared my mind to grasp the full horror of endlessness in the latter. Together they made the sense of infinities a reality and rendered it impossible to all my subsequent thought-life for me to remain contentedly absorbed in the finite."[19]

The long foreword to the book contains extensive quotations from his letters and other writings, showing how while step by step there was a change in his thought and development, there was no marked change in his basic faith and beliefs and he had not gone too far out from the path of his Quaker ancestors. "The purpose of this Foreword," he wrote, was "not to give an account of the details of my life, but to show the path of experience by which I was gradually led away from the orthodox faith of my forefathers toward vistas that would have indeed seemed strange to them. And yet they are vistas which, though in an unfamiliar setting, contain much that would have appealed to my Quaker ancestors—the followers of 'the inner light.'" In an earlier book, *The Traditions and Ideals of Our Family* completed in 1942, he had written: "For the Quakers were indeed Christian Yogis and Yogins, seeking ever in the long silent meditation of their public meetings and private devotions the divine illumination from within, and abandoning completely all external ritual acts as means to salvation."[20]

It was not surprising, therefore, that his spiritual journey took him to the path of advaita. Like his Quaker ancestors he was a follower of "the inner light." To him, the Quaker principles of looking within and of silent meditation were akin to the Vedantic principles. "It is almost identical with some of the most beautiful teachings in the Upanishads. They too tell us to look *within* if we would find the divine principle of our lives. And the path that our forefathers pointed out was a path of Dhyan Yog. 'Often retire into thy own heart . . . in the silence of all the roving of thy natural will,' as Isaac Evans advised his son. There is a great deal in common between the way of the Friends and the way of the Upanishads."[21]

Whatever might have been his misunderstandings with the Christian community, there was now no conflict in Stokes' mind about Christ just as there had been none even when he had entered the Hindu fold. "If I mistake not, the implications of much of Christ's teaching, especially as set forth in St. John's gospel, are clearly advaitic, and I have a feeling that He Himself would have viewed my quest and its present culmination with vastly greater sympathy and understanding than would most of his followers."[22]

In more recent years one can perceive a parallel in the spiritual quest of Stokes and that of Dom Henri le Saux, the French Roman Catholic priest who later became famous as Swami Abhishiktananda (Joy of the Anointed). The parallel is all the more remarkable since Stokes was a grhastha (a family man) and Abhishiktananda, sanyasi (a monk). Dom Henri le Saux went to India in 1948 at the age of 38 and was greatly influenced by Indian spiritual thought and philosophy. He lived with monks and hermits and was in close contact with Ramana Maharishi.

Both Stokes and Abhishiktananda wrote about their advaitic experience and viewed the Vedantic way as superior. However, Abhishiktananda, who remained a Catholic priest, attempted to integrate the Hindu advaitic experience of the Self with his beliefs as a Christian. "There is neither opposition nor incompatibility between Christianity and advaita, but rather two different levels," he wrote. "Advaita is not in opposition to anything; it is not a philosophy, but rather an anubhava—existential experience."[23]* Eminent British Quaker author, educationist, and social worker Marjorie Sykes felt that Stokes' leaning toward Vedanta

---

* Abhishiktananda wrote about his experiences in detail. Though his writings were powerful and eloquent, his manuscripts were found to be unpublishable. It was only in the sixties after the Vatican Council brought about vast changes of outlook, in particular the opening of the Church vis-à-vis the world and the other great religious traditions, that Abhishiktananda's path-breaking books were published.

was not surprising in view of his Quaker heritage. "It was natural for him to move in the direction that he did," she said.[24]

According to Rev W. W. Jones, historian of Christianity in India, Stokes, like Andrews, Verrier Elwin,* and Keshub Chandra Sen** was too big—intellectually and spiritually—to fit into any "slots" in the Christian community of his time. "He evolved out of formal Christianity, much as Luther evolved out of the Catholic Church; and he was willing to make the necessary sacrifices for that. All these 'heretics' of their time made profound contributions to India, and they have to be recognized and treasured; just as theologians have to study the doctrinal heretics of the past. For the problems they dealt with never go away, and the answers they devised for their own stance in life are no less instructive and inspiring, just because the orthodox majority declared them 'wrong.'"[25]

Though contemporary Christians may not have sympathized with Stokes' religious views, the liberalization of Christianity in subsequent years and its revised views about other religions indicate that Stokes' philosophy would have been more acceptable to the Christian community of latter-day India—an India in which a Catholic sanyasi, Swami Abhishiktananda, could have OM on his cross and the Christa Prema Seva Ashram in Poona could teach Christian beliefs through Indian religious thought. Indeed, as theologian Rev. R. W. Taylor of the Christian Institute for the Study of Religion and Society said, "Stokes was at least fifty years ahead of his time as far as his religious views are concerned."[26]

* Verrier Elwin, a bishop's son, studied theology at Oxford and was ordained in the Church of England. He came to India in 1927 to join Poona's Christa Seva Sangh. Soon he became disillusioned with the Sangh and its objective of converting people to Christianity and eventually gave up his Christian faith. From 1932 onwards Verrier worked with adivasis in Madhya Pradesh.

** Keshub Chandra Sen was a nineteenth-century social reformer and leader of Brahmo Samaj. Known as the Apostle of Harmony of Religion, his molding of the Brahmo Samaj into a church heavily influenced by Christian doctrines and the devotional practices of the Hindu Vaishnva cults were not appreciated by other Brahmo Samaj leaders.

EVENTIDE

The last years of Stokes' life brought him much pain, anxiety, and nervous strain caused by a complication arising from the marriage of his youngest son, Lal Chand. Both Stokes and Devi Das Bhalaik, whose two elder daughters were already married to Prem and Pritam, had looked forward to the probability of Lal marrying a younger daughter of Devi Das. But twenty-year-old Lal Chand developed ideas of his own on the subject and made a proposal of marriage to the charming daughter of Thakur Amin Chand Singha of Kotgarh, the very girl Devi Das had in mind for one of his sons.

Stokes knew that such an alliance would cause bitterness but suddenly found himself confronted with a most difficult situation. Even though Lal Chand had asked for the girl's hand without the knowledge of his parents, the girl's mother accepted his proposal. Stokes felt he could do nothing but honorably accept the situation. "To have opposed it would have placed the girl in a most humiliating position as the result of the initiative of a member of my family." He profoundly disapproved of the way in which the proposal was made, but since it had been made and accepted, he felt strongly that his family's honor, "*dharma—not merely izzat* [respect]," required that they stood by it. As he told his family, "Only one path was in honour open to me, and I have taken it."[1]

The marriage of Lal Chand on 15 December 1944—this was a civil marriage in Simla, the traditional wedding took place in Barobagh a few months later— resulted in grave misunderstandings and bitterness between his family and that of Devi Das Bhalaik with whom he had had very cordial relations over the years. A concerted effort on his part to resolve the differences in this extremely delicate situation did not meet with success. His hope that over time there would be a reconciliation remained unfulfilled.

This turn of events brought bitter disappointment to Stokes. The Kotgarh community had hardly recovered from the differences over his shuddhi, and here was a situation which could embroil the entire ilaqa in another feud with people divided over support either to Devi Das Bhalaik or to Amin Chand Singha, two leading and powerful families in the area. During the following months, he tried to handle the situation in such a way that people were not forced to take sides. "Our ilaqa has suffered sufficiently in recent years from that," he said. There was a rift within Stokes' own family, too, with his two elder daughters-in-law taking an uncompromising position in this matter. With these forces now at work, the organic unity of the family was weakened, and the carefully nurtured harmony of Harmony Hall, lost. "The position is hardly a bed of roses for either my wife or me, and the efforts to evolve the least unsatisfactory modus operandi in the circumstances has put a heavy strain upon both of us," Stokes wrote.

The split in the family had severe repercussions. Up to this time the entire family had lived together harmoniously. Though, for the last four or five years, Stokes and his wife had moved out of Harmony Hall and were living in their old, smaller house as they found the constant racket created by energetic grandchildren rather overpowering, the family all ate together in the same kitchen. (The old home was connected to Harmony Hall with a wooden bridge.) But when this new situation arose they altered this arrangement. Now Stokes and Agnes started living exclusively in their smaller house and eating there as well. Prem's and Pritam's families shared the Harmony Hall facilities. Lal and his new bride moved into a separate house which Stokes had built for him.* "It seemed very strange at first but we are gradually getting used to it as the young people would have to do (this) in any event at the time of our death."[2]

Sadly, there was no change in the situation despite Stokes' best efforts to bring about a rapprochement. "As for us two old people, we are learning to take the position calmly, though we had always been so used to harmony in our family that this type of relationship bore—and still to a somewhat lesser extent bears—upon our spirits. My dear wife has been wonderful throughout, and I do not know what I would have done without her strong common sense and self-control, for at times things have been very trying," he wrote to his brother-in-law Marshall Truitt.

Two years earlier he had transferred his lands to his three sons keeping a very small portion for himself and Agnes. It had, however, not been divided individually but he was giving them a share of its income. He now felt it imperative to make a legal division as early as possible. The winter of 1945 was taken up in this task.[3]

Stokes faced much financial hardship too during these years. After transfer-

---

* He bequeathed Harmony Hall to Prem Chand, his eldest son. Pritam and Lal Chand were each given new houses which he built for them next to Harmony Hall. Lal Chand built a modern home for himself in his lower orchard a few years after his fathers' death and later dismantled his house in Barobagh.

ring the land to his sons, he was not taking any income from their share of the orchards except the sum of Rs 500 which each of them gave him every year. Consequently his income was now substantially less than what it had been. In 1945 the income of Prem and Pritam from their respective orchards was Rs 15,000 each and of Lal Chand, Rs 12,000. The combined income from Stokes' small orchard in Dugar Jubbar and his wife's in Barobagh was only about Rs 7,000.[4] From this the running expenses of the orchard had to be paid, which had also grown considerably after the war, leaving little to him by way of profit. Though his income from America continued, it was also not much.

He had never built up financial reserves and there was little to fall back upon. As a result, he was burdened with monetary constraints and more so since he was not prepared to cut down on what he considered were his social obligations. Finding themselves with such limited resources for the first time in their married life and not knowing what the future would bring, Stokes and Agnes tried to cut down on every personal expense. He reduced buying books and discontinued subscribing to American journals. He was always careful in spending money but now he became a stickler for accounts, even asking his daughter Champa who was visiting him to pay for the postage stamps she needed to send letters to her husband in Quetta. The shortage of money affected his home life. Kitchen expenses were kept to a minimum and the family fare became even simpler than what it had always been.[5] "*Hum bahut greeb ho gaye hain* [we have become very poor]," he would often say, recalled Champa. The only luxury he allowed himself was his hookah or water-pipe which he first started smoking when he was living as a Sadhu. He was also very particular about how his hookah was prepared. The chillum or coal container had to be filled in a special way. During these last years it was his cook, Shalotar, who had the privilege of cleaning and filling his chillum.

His life had come full circle to the old days of the Brotherhood. Again unable to afford to pay for a car or a rickshaw, he and Agnes made the journey in stages between Simla and Kotgarh on foot, and this when his wife was not too strong and his own health frail.[6] Yet he did not hesitate to give Rs 1,000 for the endowment fund of the DAV Intermediate College started in Simla in 1945, nor fail to send Rs 500 to the Ramakrishna Mission.[7] Prem was upset and urged his father to take a larger share from the orchard income for himself. "After paying out all from the money you get from America you have hardly anything left . . . And it is wrong. Why can't you also get a share in the apple crop. After all, it is yours."[8] But Stokes was not willing to compromise. He did not wish to take any money from his sons. Nor did he complain. "Our wants are very modest, and after meeting them we have enough to give to our various activities that interest us."[9]

In these last years he had become neglectful of writing home. When his mother was alive the weekly letters that went to and fro between Kotgarh and Philadelphia had kept the family in close touch, but after her death the link was broken and a special effort had to be made to maintain contact. Though his brother Spencer came to Kotgarh a number of times, the exchange of letters with him and with his sister Florence had become occasional. Their affection for each other, however, remained unchanged.

His correspondence was more regular with Marshall Truitt, his sister Anna's husband. Marshall was not only a friend but also the executor of his father's will and one on whom Stokes greatly depended. In the winter of 1946, he wrote a detailed letter to Marshall telling him all about his affairs in India, the state of the orchards, sent pen-sketches of his children and their spouses, and included the details of Lal's marriage and its effect on the family unity. "It has seemed to me wise, since you are the family link with our American affairs, that I should give you a full understanding of how we stand out here." In a rare admission of the overwhelming demands upon him, Stokes wrote, "When one is not very strong and various responsibilities for the local public, as well as family complications accumulate it may not be a proper excuse but at least it furnishes a reason for having been so neglectful about my duty to write and keep you informed."[10]

Stokes was not involved in active politics, but as far as the Kotgarh ilaqa was concerned, he was still putting into practice the concept of vigilance committees which he had advocated to the Congress many years earlier. In a way, he was a true representative of the people. Having lived for well over forty years in Kotgarh he had become an institution and people turned to him for help, advice, and for necessary correspondence with the authorities for the solution of their many difficulties. "The fact that our people up here have some confidence in me is a responsibility for me to consider their interests."[11]

People knew for certain that if the cause was just they could expect all help from him. Officials, too, were aware of his determination to protect the rights and privileges of the people. "You are more powerful than an average member of the Punjab Assembly and I wish you to raise your powerful voice against the doings of the government from time to time," Duni Chand, who was now a member of Punjab Legislative Assembly, wrote to him while seeking his support for the 1946 elections.

During these elections, Stokes' efforts were to get the whole district to vote together only for one candidate. If people did not vote together, part of the vote would cancel out the other part, and the hill votes would have no impact. This, he knew, would not be in the interest of the hill people. "The Simla district rural vote can only be of any influence if we, of Kotgarh, Kotkhai—and if possible,

Bharauli, first settle among ourselves who to vote for, and then all of us vote for the same man."[12] Also, he tried hard to see that every person whose name was on the electoral list cast his or her vote. He himself came up to Kotgarh from his winter home in Chuan to cast his vote.[13]

The problems of Indo-British relations, imperialism in its broader aspects and the perils of racialism were also issues that continued to preoccupy him. "What line the Western peoples take in the next year or two—even in the next few months—regarding imperialistic domination of the nations of Asia and Africa, the colour question and kindred problems will determine the kind of world that we will hand over to our descendants."

He held the British and other empire-holding nations ultimately responsible for both world wars and the deaths and suffering that had resulted from them. "I have grown old in India—it is almost forty-three years now since I came here—and I have been pondering this question without rancour but with deep feeling for all but the first three or four years of this period. My conclusion is that there can never be continued peace in the world or satisfactory relations between its peoples—either of Western nations among themselves or of the West with the East—until these imperialistic nations have been compelled to disgorge their empires and give up the positions of unfair advantage . . . Now, if ever, was the time when America and Russia could have insisted upon the acceptance in principle of the liquidation of all empires, and the taking of the initial steps in that direction. It would have taken some time if it was to be done in an orderly manner and with minimum loss to all, but it would have to follow an agreed definite time-table, with unalterable dates set for each stage," he wrote in a letter of 15 January 1946.

All his life he had grappled with the basic problems of imperialism and racialism, pondered over the subject and written extensively about it. His writings, he said, were in a sense, "a testament" that he had "kept the faith" with his Quaker ancestors. "The struggle for right and fair play in the relations of men is a fight worth fighting. I shall never regret such part as I have been able to play in it . . . One only hopes that the 'beautiful new world' towards which all freedom-loving people have been aspiring since times immemorial will one day become a reality."[14]

In the winter, he sent a copy of his *Essays, Memoranda and Letters* to his cousin Warrington Stokes in America in the hope that it might serve a useful purpose. "The issues dealt with throughout the book are living issues—especially at this juncture when the world is in the melting pot . . . In a world of hand to mouth and day to day expediencies, it deals with the great questions with which it is concerned upon the sound basis of principles of true equity—the only basis upon which the relations of men and nations can find a true and lasting solution . . . I am not an extremist, or a starry-eyed visionary . . . Nor am I a socialist . . . Only I am convinced that no human relations that are not based upon true equity can give any hope for 'the brave new world' about which we have heard so much," he wrote.[15] In a brief foreword to the collection he reiterated, "In the solution of the problems involved in the relations existing between Great Britain and India lies the capacity to solve world-wide problems that will otherwise destroy the world."

Though Stokes did not live to see the historic day of India's independence from Britain which heralded the disintegration of empires and the building up of a more equitable world, it proved that his hopes and dreams were founded on practical realities. His prediction of 1930 pertaining to the future relations of people from different countries is a reality today. The key to material prosperity of humanity as a whole might not be politics, he had suggested, but the new industrial outlook of big business—an outlook for which America was largely responsible, and which he believed future generations would view as one of the major contributions of that country. The lines on which Western industrialism was developing necessarily required a more prosperous and less poverty-stricken world. The new industrialism depended for its continued growth and expansion on a growing buying-power over a constantly expanding area. "I look to see it actively engaged before long in forwarding such a growth—not out of philanthropic sentiment but because its very existence depends on it."[16]

This new industrial outlook was increasingly unpolitical in its attitude toward races and peoples, "It does not in fact see them as people at all, but rather as trade-areas." This future industrial domination of the world, he was convinced, would turn out to be "super-racial." "It will have its factories where they will pay best—not in a particular country because that is the country of a particular people toward which it has emotional inclinations. It will employ those whose employment is most paying, whose employment best ensures the cutting down of costs so that the output may be sold at prices within the reach of an ever larger number of people. It will increasingly refuse to put up with backwardness and incapacity to buy in any of the areas of the world." The change would not come overnight. "But it will come inevitably, blindly impersonal, having no reference to race or nation or colour—and the more beneficial for that reason," Stokes had predicted with prophetic foresight.[17]

One of the last tasks of Stokes' life was to hand over Tara School to the Punjab Education Board. The school had been his greatest joy and when, in early 1946, he finally decided to close it, it was not only due to financial compulsion, but because he knew that he did not have long to live. It was for the same reason that he was unable to go ahead with his plans to establish a public library in Mangsu village, something on which he had set his heart.

During all his years in Kotgarh, Stokes had had a sustained interest in education. He had started his life there as an English teacher at the Mission School. He constantly strove for the development of educational facilities for the children of Kotgarh. He opened new schools at Khunni, Nainidhar, and Barobagh and started the first middle and first high school in the ilaqa. He could have sent his children to the best schools anywhere in the country but he chose to educate them with their neighbors. At Tara School he was able to put into practice his ideals of education. The school provided education with a purpose and cultivated a spirit of national pride in the children. He was prepared to make any sacrifice for the school, putting in long hours of work at the cost of his health. He was not wealthy, but over the years had spent more than one lakh rupees on the school, cutting down on personal expenses and foregoing many important requirements of the family.

In March 1946, when the assistant inspector of schools was camping at Kotgarh, Stokes told him of his intention to close the school and suggested that the District Board could perhaps run it thereafter. He also offered the Board rent-free use of one of the school's blocks of five classrooms together with a small playground.[18] On 6 May, Stokes sent a formal confirmation of his offer for the school accommodation, affirmed by his wife and his sons, to the Board. He also undertook the responsibility of repairing and repainting the rooms before handing them over. The offer was valid for five years and binding on his heirs in case he died before that period. He was hopeful that during this time alternative accommodation would be available, or quite possibly his heirs would be ready to let the Board authorities continue to use the buildings rent-free.[19] It was a matter of great satisfaction to him that the school would carry on even though he himself would be disassociated from it. At least children of the neighborhood who were too far off from the nearest schools—at Kotgarh, Mehlan, Dhada, or Bhutti—would not be deprived of basic education.

His health had not been stable ever since he developed stomach ulcers in the months preceding his arrest in 1921. He suffered from almost continuous stomach ailments during the following years. Doctors first suspected cancer of the stomach but once that was ruled out there was no definite diagnosis. The operation in Vienna had seemed to help initially, but it provided only temporary relief. Removal of the gall bladder led to digestive problems. Doctors were unable to determine the root cause of the trouble except to conclude that it was related to his stomach. He had been steadily losing weight for the past few years and became progressively frailer and tired easily. He could eat no meal, however simple, without throwing up unless he lay down immediately afterwards for an hour or more, and often even that did not help.[20]

He had become so weak that any labor required very conscious effort on his part—even the writing of letters was a strain at times. His condition deteriorated from year to year. By 1945 he had begun to stoop and his feet remained swollen. The swelling increased and he found it difficult to climb stairs and had to shift from his living quarters on the first floor to the guest room downstairs. Soon he found it difficult to even walk up the few stairs to the guest room. He then decided to move into one of the school rooms which had only a couple of steps. His daughter Champa, who came to Kotgarh every summer from Quetta, recalled his suffering, as well as his discipline and spirit of endurance. The swelling had spread to his legs and he was in great pain. The nausea and throwing up of almost every meal did not keep him away from his reading and writing, nor did he ever complain. He was generally cheerful and retained his sense of humor, often joking with the younger folk. He also continued to smoke his hookah, something he had never attempted to give up. He went to the temple twice a day, accompanied by Agnes. He usually performed a simple hawan in the morning and aarti in the evening when he also read from the Gita and meditated.* The only indication of his intense suffering, Champa remembered, was that he stopped going to the little baithak (office) down in the orchard, close to Tara's grave, which he had used as his study for almost twenty years.

During the last three or four years he used to often say that it was time to leave his choga (clothing). The body, he always said, was like clothing which gets worn out with use and has to be changed. It is like a mount given to us to traverse the journey through life—the land of experience. Once we reach the last stage of the journey and the mount is tired and weary, it is time to change it and embark on the next stage of our journey, he said.[21] In the summer of 1945, when Prem came up to Kotgarh from Shahbad where he was working with the Associated Cement Company, he found his father very thin. "It is time to change the vehicle of life, one can't carry on with a vehicle like this," he told Prem while raising his thin wasted arms. Prem believed that he probably stopped trying because he knew that the doctors could not do anything about his health.

His thoughts now often turned to the distant past. "I am not really old, but the combination of ill health and accumulating years makes me feel so, and with it comes an increasing tendency to recall one's early life and those who were so near in those early years. They are more vividly present than they were to me a dozen years ago," he wrote in his last letter to his sister Florence. During the next few months his condition worsened. He was overcome with a great physical weariness which made it at times an effort even to lift his hand. He found it dif-

* Some of his grandchildren recall how in the evening the temple bells would ring without fail and then all would be quiet in Barobagh. After Lal Chand's marriage, his young wife, Vidya, used to accompany them to the temple occasionally. On days when he was too unwell to go he would ask Vidya to go to the temple in the evening and light the lamp.

ficult to sit because of the swelling in his legs and did his writing while standing. "I am really on my 'last legs,' and should not be at all surprised if I cannot meet you at all unless I can do it soon," he wrote to a friend on 7 May.[22]

On Friday, the 10th of May he left Kotgarh for Simla with Agnes. It was a routine visit to arrange for material for the coming apple crop. The Cabinet Mission was then holding its discussions at Simla and he hoped, too, that he might get to hear some good news about the country's future during his visit. In Simla he chanced to meet a doctor who was in Vienna at the time of his surgery and who advised him to take some medicine to alleviate his suffering. The medication did not suit him. He had a severe reaction and had to be rushed to the hospital for acute diarrhea.[23] His admission to the government Ripon Hospital was ominous. Firstly, it was with great difficulty that Agnes was allowed to stay with him. Then the doctors, both British and Indian, were negligent. The loss of fluid had left him dehydrated and he was in great pain, but, despite his precarious condition, he was not put on a drip or given a morphine injection as was the practice then.

Pritam Chand came down to Simla soon after his parents left Kotgarh. There was no apparent reason for his coming, perhaps it was a premonition. Stokes himself was certain that he had very little time left, but he tried to carry on with his daily routine of reading the newspaper, going through his mail, reading the Gita, and saying his prayers. He also anxiously awaited the news of the outcome of the Cabinet Mission and inquired about it several times.

On the 13th morning he called his lawyer and made his last Will leaving his personal effects to his wife. He also willed her the small Dugar Jubbar orchard which was still in his name.[24] He charged her with no special responsibility. "You will, I know—keep in view my ideal of service . . . I do not bind you to any line of action for you will know what truth and honour dictates," he had told her when he had gone to Vienna.[25]

All of that day he waited for Lal Chand, his youngest son, who was away in Kulu on shikar (a hunt), asking for him many times. At 12 o'clock at night, Lal Chand and Lakshmi Singh arrived. They had rushed down as soon as they heard of his illness, marching nonstop all the way. After talking to them briefly, he asked them to rest for some time. "Go eat, rest and sleep," he told Lal, "Your mother will need all your strength tomorrow." He never liked Agnes to be out of his sight even for a moment, but now he told her to go to the other room and read the Gita. "You have a very difficult day ahead of you tomorrow," he said.[26] Pritam Chand, however, sat with him through the night.

The end came on the following morning, 14 May 1946, a Tuesday, at five o'clock. Agnes, Pritam Chand, Lal Chand, and Lakshmi Singh were all by his bedside. Despite the suffering, he was at peace. He asked Agnes to help him sit up and said his morning prayers. "He was in pain, *par dhyan men thhe* [but was in meditation]," Lakshmi Singh recalled. Like the yogis of yore, he breathed his last in a sitting posture, his hands folded in prayer, reciting shlokas from the Gita.[27]

The news of his death flashed across the country. In a poignant note to Agnes, Gandhi wrote, *"Ab tum kiya karogi?* [What will you do now?]"[28]

His had been a life of service. He sometimes felt that few of his dreams of service had come to full fruition. "Very few of them have had more than the most imperfect realization," he wrote. "Yet the dreams were something . . . They were not ignoble dreams, no matter how imperfectly they found fulfilment."[29] Like Artahan, the Other Wise Man, from whose life he had drawn inspiration as a young boy, he had done the best he could from day to day. "He had been true to the light that had been given to him . . . he knew that even if he could live this earthly life over again, it could not be otherwise than it had been."[30]

He was indeed a member of the "Brotherhood of the Free Spirit," one who, like Tagore and Andrews, had "upbuilt" the Fairy Arch from the East to the West. An arch perceived by Romain Rolland as "not altogether broken down amid the vicissitudes of human history. Poets, philosophers and thinkers had upbuilt it in the past . . . The men of sword had often pulled it down. But it had remained, half suspended in the air—the 'Fairy Arch from the East to the West.'"[31]*

In a way Gandhi's words written more than twenty years earlier—"So long as we have an Andrews, a Stokes, a Pearson** in our midst, so long will it be ungentlemanly on our part to wish every Englishman out of India"—best sum up India's tribute to Stokes.[32]***

---

* Romain Rolland spoke of a "Fairy Arch from the East to the West." He started a Brotherhood of the Free Spirit in Europe and invited Rabindranath Tagore to become one with them in this new Brotherhood.

** W. W. Pearson was close to Gandhi, Rabindranath Tagore, and C. F. Andrews. He came to India in 1907 as a representative of the London Missionary Society but later resigned from his mission. He then became associated with Tagore's work at Shantineketan. He was also actively involved with the Indian problems in Fiji and South Africa. Willie Pearson as he was called was held in great affection by people who knew him. "We loved him at first sight," Gandhi said of Pearson. Tagore's testimony was, "We seldom met with anyone whose love of humanity was so completely real" (*A History of the London Missionary Society, 1895–1945,* Norman Goodall, p. 37).

*** A few months before Stokes' death, Gandhi was asked if it would not be better for Englishmen not to attempt to come to work in India just then, when the atmosphere in India was so poisoned, but to wait for better times, Gandhi cited the example of Andrews, Stokes, and Pearson, all of whom had been distrusted but had lived down the distrust of both the government and the people. "If even a C.F. Andrews and a Stokes and others had to labour under distrust, for you to be distrusted may not be wondered at," he said ("Discussion with a member of Friends Ambulance," *Harijan, Coll. Works,* p. 154. 31.3.1946).

EPILOGUE

Over the years, the ilaqa of Kotgarh became synonymous with the name of Stokes. This was so during his lifetime and holds true today, more than fifty years after his death. There are still people in Kotgarh who remember Stokes and his work and nostalgically recall their association with him.

When you speak to people who knew Stokes you get a vivid picture of the man they loved, respected, and accepted as their own. They talk of the free dispensary which he ran from his house and the way he tried to educate people about basic health care. They tell you of instances when he rushed the critically ill to Simla in his own dandi or in hired rickshaws, or brought in specialist doctors from the plains to fight epidemics in the ilaqa, all at his own expense. You will be told how Stokes freed many small farmers from the clutches of money-lenders by helping them pay off their loans and how he never turned away a needy person. They tell you of his love for the children of the ilaqa, his untiring concern for their education, and the way he inculcated the dignity of labor among them. They tell you of his passion for Hindi, his devotion to the Hindi Nagri Pracharini Sabha, and his arranging to move its circulatory library from village to village in small wooden cupboards.

People still recall the time of famines and shortages when Stokes would open his grain store to the needy, the time he spent the greater part of his year's income on buying blankets for the famine-stricken villagers of Mauni, and of the time during the war when he took up the task of distributing scarce essential commodities to villagers with his own hands so that everyone got a fair share. Harry John, son of Stokes' colleague at the Kotgarh Mission School, Isaac John, describes how Stokes sat on a bench in the bazaar from morning till evening measuring twill cloth and pouring out kerosene oil. "I got half a bottle of kerosene from him myself."

Guru Dhian of Pamrai village, who was the chief organizer at Stokes' centenary birthday celebrations, clearly remembered the time when, as a little boy, he was stricken with typhoid fever and Stokes came to visit him and told his father that the boy should be given milk. "But we have no milk, the Cows are all dry," bemoaned the father. Stokes did not reply but from the next day, till Guru Dhian fully recovered, Stokes' milkman brought a lota of milk for the child every day.

"How can we forget Stokes Sahib?" said Jiwand Lal of Shatla. "When my sister-in-law fell seriously ill in Kotgarh, he personally went to the political agent in Simla to secure permission to get a car up to Kotgarh, hired the car and took the old lady to Lady Reading Hospital in Simla and saw to it that she was given proper attention and treatment."

There are other traits of Stokes which people remember: his insatiable curiosity, his sense of humor, and his emphasis on following one's dharma. Guru Dhian remembered how Stokes could get very angry at times and his face would become red. "But not with the poor and downtrodden with whom he was always sympathetic. Whenever I saw him angry, it was with the officials. He could not tolerate any injustice and his temper would flare up if he saw any wrong-doing." Others, particularly family members, often bore the brunt of Stokes' temper. Stokes was aware of his shortcoming and would sometimes say that in his next life he would wish to be born without such a temper. Some also believe that Stokes was not practical and worldly wise and that some of the predicaments he faced were due to his trusting nature.

More than anything else, it is the apples which have kept the memory of Stokes alive among the people. Apples have affected the life of every person who lives in Kotgarh. When Stokes died in 1946, apple production in the province had already reached 15,000 boxes per year, about a third of which was from Harmony Hall orchards.[1] In subsequent years, land under apple cultivation expanded rapidly and as the young orchards started bearing fruit, production grew. With the spread of the Delicious variety, which came to be known as Kotgarh apples, to the surrounding hill areas, the seeds of an economic revolution in Himachal were sown, bringing undreamed-of prosperity to the people. The orchards, started by Stokes as a lifeline for the poor, served as a nucleus for the development of horticulture in the state, which is now a leader in this industry in India, and whose orchard management and fruit production compares favorably with the best in the world.

Stokes' contribution was not only the introduction of American Delicious apples to India, but his scientific experimentation in identifying the variety best suited to the region. Delicious apples flourished naturally in the region—it was almost as if the Himalayas were their natural habitat. Equally important were the scientific methods of cultivation and the modern ideas of marketing used by him which resulted in increased production of good quality apples and their commercial success.

Although other fruits like peaches, plums, apricot, and pears as well as citrus and other sub-tropical fruits are now grown in plenty in the state, apples remain the premier crop of the region and the apple industry continues to grow. Each year several hundred acres of additional land is brought under the fruit, raising the income of landowners as well as providing employment to people. When Stokes first introduced the Delicious variety in Kotgarh the total area under apple cultivation was only 25 acres. It gradually extended to 150 acres in 1930, to 250 acres in 1940, and 1,500 acres in 1950.[2] Today it is approximately 235,000 acres, almost one-eighth of the total cultivated area in Himachal Pradesh.

The state has the highest per capita production of apples in India and also the highest percentage of cultivable area under apples. The total annual production, depending on weather conditions, is now between fifteen to thirty million boxes of eighteen kilograms (forty pounds) each, which brings in revenue of about 200 million rupees to Himachal's fruit-based economy. Significantly, the Delicious apples were ultimately identified as the most promising variety, and remain the most popular apples with growers and consumers alike. Ninety percent of the present plantation of apples in Himachal Pradesh is made up of the Delicious variety, which also fetches the highest price in the market.[3] The fact that the average size of apple orchards in the state is less than one hectare and that 80 percent of the orchardists are marginal farmers, indicates the degree of Stokes' success in influencing the common man to improve his economic condition.

Cultivation of Delicious apples has spread not only throughout Himachal Pradesh, but to the entire Himalayan apple-growing belt extending from Jammu and Kashmir in the West, to Arunachal Pradesh in the East. An incredible 90 percent of all Delicious apples are derived from the progeny of the original stock imported and planted by Stokes.[4] These apples are not only the best in India, but are comparable in quality to the best produced in America, the country of their origin. Kotgarh, however, remains the heart of apple industry in Himachal Pradesh. The lessons in methods of cultivating apples which the Kotgarh farmer learned from Stokes have not been forgotten and have been passed on to the next generation, and Kotgarh continues to produce the finest quality of apples with the highest average yield. Shimla district, where apples were first introduced by Stokes, produces about 80 percent of the total apples grown in the state.

Apples and the attendant prosperity of growers have made Kotgarh unique in many respects. As an administrative area, Kotgarh, which once was the poorest in the region and where villagers surrendered their land because they could not afford to pay the revenue, now boasts of being one of the richest in the country. In a study of the human factor in Indian development, anthropologist Kusum Nair discovered that in all other areas in the country, education had brought about a change in the standard and outlook of the people except in Kotgarh where "transformation in the economy and way of life of a people, the primary cause (if any single factor can ever bring about a socio-economic revolution of any substance) was not education—but apples. Education has followed the apples. It did not precede them."[5]

Stokes also introduced a work culture which remains unique to the region. His stress on dignity of labor, by setting a personal example, changed the local people's attitude to work. The result was that even when the region became prosperous and people could afford to hire help, they preferred to work with their own hands. "This attitude to work pervades the entire population," Nair observed in her noted book, *Blossoms in the Dust,* "and marks it out as clearly distinct from the adjacent areas and from most areas elsewhere in the country . . . There is no evidence of any contempt for the work. It is not considered incompatible with enlightenment, education or social and caste status, though of course, it is a new kind of work, as distinct from routine kind of agricultural operations, and the distinction is probably important."[6]*

There were sociological changes too. Economic independence brought about rapid changes in the status of low castes. They were no longer mute and submissive, but became aware of their rights and asserted themselves. According to Nair these changes and trends were, however, not true of other areas in Himachal Pradesh where not only did many of the lower castes continue more or less in the same depressed conditions as of old, but even peasants of other castes were often steeped in poverty and backwardness. Also, whereas in Kotgarh no one now worked as a casual, unskilled laborer, villagers in other parts of the state still continued to work on daily wages.[7]

Today, Himachal Pradesh is called the Apple State of India, and Stokes, the Johnny Appleseed of India. He is remembered as the economic emancipator of the hills.** Apples have changed the lives of hill people who for generations had been compelled to work as baithus (the equivalent of bonded laborers)*** and as

---

* While the older generation in Kotgarh continues to have the same attitude to work even today, the younger generation now tends to shy away from manual work and depends more on hired labor.

** In appreciation of Stokes' contribution to the state, the Himachal Pradesh government opened a Satyanand Farmers' Community Centre in Kotgarh in 1976 and announced that Himachal Pradesh University's new horticultural complex at Khaltoo (now renamed Nauni) near Solan would be named after Satyanand Stokes. The complex was not ultimately named after Stokes, only its library was. (*The Tribune*)

*** Stokes devised a means to do away with the system of baithu by insisting that laborers who took loans not work for free but be paid back part of the capital from each day's wages.

begarees when Stokes first came to Kotgarh, and those who could hardly eke out a living for their families are now well-to-do orchardists with surplus incomes. They live in modern homes having all amenities and can afford to educate their children in the best institutions. Economic prosperity has brought health and happiness to hundreds of Kotgarh families. People cannot forget the debt they owe to the American who decided to make Kotgarh his home at a time when most Westerners chose to keep their distance from the "natives." Stokes was truly a hill-man. "We have to create an ideal Pahari family life—not an American or European or even plains life," he told his children.[8] "No country is so lovely, so grand, so beautiful as our lovely Himalayas,"[9] he would say.

The interests of the hill people were always foremost in his mind. People's appreciation of Stokes, whom they still fondly remember as *Saabji*, was evident on his centenary birthday celebrated in Thanedhar on 16 August 1982. People walked in rain from long distances to pay their respects to one who gave them economic prosperity, self-esteem, and restored their confidence, who accepted their lifestyle, customs, and traditions as his own, who shared equally in their joys and sorrows, fighting for the rights of the villagers at every step and striving till the very end to better their lives. One for whom the good of the community was always of greater importance than any personal consideration, and who, in the best spirit of the founding fathers of the country of his birth, made the poor people of the hills aware of their "rights as men."

As the state's chief minister, Ram Lal, paid tribute to this "Messiah of the Hills," an unprecedented crowd listened in rapt silence. But the highlight of the festivities were the Stokes geet or folk songs composed almost sixty years before and sung in accompaniment to the local baja by a party from Khilon, the village which had provided many of Stokes' workers and to whom, in turn, he had given land, education, and livelihood. As the singers broke into the lyric— "*Sahiba amriki mahre herano gaaye* . . . [We sing the song of our American Sahib . . .]," the villagers, mostly the older ones, stood up for naati, the Pahari dance which Stokes so enjoyed, reveling in the memories of a lifetime spent in the company of this remarkable man.*

Twenty-five years later, in August 2007, Stokes' 125th birthday was celebrated in Narkanda, ten miles from Kotgarh, where a statue of Stokes was unveiled by His Holiness the Dalai Lama. Praising Stokes' immense contribution to the development of the hills, the Dalai Lama—who has made Dharmasala town in Himachal his home after leaving Tibet in 1959—said, "It is proof of how a single person can bring about an economic revolution in an entire state."

---

* Two poems in Hindi were composed for the occasion. One by Shyamlal Sharma, former teacher of Virgarh School (earlier known as Dhada school) and the other by Hari Singh Parmar of the nearby Bhutti School.

Ram Dayal Singha's remark, *"Main in sebon ke pakne par jab yeh vriksh par chamakte hain Mr Stokes ko dekhta hun* [When the apples ripen and shine on the trees, I picture Mr. Stokes in them]," and the sensitive appraisal of Shamanand, Stokes' cook for thirty years and the proud owner of a small apple orchard, *"Amir or gareeb ko ek jaisi roti khilai; hamare lekhe to jeeta hai, noton ki barish hoti hai* [He gave food to the rich and the poor alike, for us he is still alive, for there is a rain of currency notes]," not only sum up the sentiments of the people, but epitomize the legacy which Stokes left behind. As one looks around at the prosperous Kotgarh ilaqa, the Hindi couplet he so often quoted comes to mind—*"Ho-kar ke mar gaye sab koii; ho-kar kar gaya hai kuch, jeeta hai ek woh hi* [Many have come and gone, but he who has accomplished something in his life has really lived]."[10]

POSTSCRIPT

Agnes lived alone for thirty-seven years after her husband's death, in the small house adjacent to Harmony Hall where she had first come as a bride in 1912.* She became a victim of the feuds that continued to plague her family after Lal Chand's marriage in 1944. Her efforts to start a Stokes Memorial Library at Thanedhar did not succeed even though she erected a building for the purpose and purchased a large number of books. She, however, continued her husband's practice of purchasing medicines from Simla and distributing them free to the villagers. Like her husband she too was always willing to give interest-free loans to villagers to purchase land or build a home.

There was a rapid deterioration in her health after Lal Chand's sudden demise in 1973. She died in the Snowdon Hospital in Simla in 1983. For days she hung between life and death. Oblivious of her surroundings, she would suddenly start singing Christian hymns she had learned as a child—they were in Urdu: *"Sun aasmani fauj shareefe . . .* [Hark the Herald angels sing . . .]."** Her daughter, Champa, who nursed her, was distressed and arranged to hold special prayers in the hospital—both by a Hindu priest and a Christian padre.

During a visit to Barobagh some years ago, I found that my grandparents' first home had almost crumbled and there was talk of pulling it down. At one time there were also plans to convert Harmony Hall into a guest house to keep

---

* The house, which was falling apart due to lack of care, was demolished after Pritam Chand's death in 2003.

** Agnes used to often sing such hymns during the last years of her life. On the other hand, Dhan Singh, who as a Christian would have been buried after his death, as was the local custom, left instructions in his will to be cremated instead. His family had to seek special permission from the church to fulfill his wishes.

it in use, but these were later dropped. The hillock on which the temple stands was sinking on one side. It was obvious that unless timely steps are taken, the temple will soon become a monument of the past. It was distressing, too, to see a tall telecommunications tower erected next to the temple, dwarfing the beautiful landmark and violating its sanctity.* Going down on the eastern side of the property I passed by the little office with its majestic view of the Himalayas and the river Sutlej, where Stokes did so much of his writing. The small wooden structure looked old and forlorn. I looked in the vicinity for Tara's grave, around which I had played as a child. It was not there. Gone with it were the beautiful country violets his mother planted around it and tended with loving care for many years. All that remained were serried rows of apple trees.

Agnes had wanted to make a samadhi for her husband beside the temple. Though work on it was started, her dream remained unfulfilled. Stokes' ashes lie buried near the office building, marked only by a small heap of stones surrounded by wild shrubs. The place once teemed with the perennial narcissus planted by Agnes. Most have withered; a few still manage to bloom each year, rebelliously, braving the neglect and ravages of time!

While the hills abound with apples propagated by Stokes, Barobagh wears a desolate look. There is no happy laughter of children at play nor loud talk of village folk. All the sons of Stokes' sons have left their village and returned to America, the land of their forefathers. According to Prem Chand, his father wanted to have a Stokes village here but he had not reckoned with the possibility of the younger generation moving away. An old legend has it that no one has ever really lived in Barobagh: people come and go, say the locals.

SUBSEQUENT FAMILY HISTORY

Of Stokes' three sons, Prem Chand, the eldest, became an engineer and worked in the plains while his wife looked after their orchard at Kotgarh. Pritam Chand and Lal Chand continued to live on the farm with their wives. Later Lal Chand joined the Congress and was elected to the state legislature. After his death in 1974, his wife, Vidya Stokes, took his place in politics and became a minister in the Himachal government. Of the daughters, only Savitri lived in Kotgarh. Champavati moved to Simla from Quetta with her family after the

---

* During Stokes' lifetime a hawan used to be performed in the temple on all important occasions and neighbors were invited to participate in it. After his death Agnes followed the practice for some years but then gave it up due to lack of support. The temple was in disuse and in a state of neglect for many years till of late, as Pritam Chand's daughter Santosh Khindaria began taking an interest in it. She arranged to have a hawan performed in the repainted temple every Sunday during the summer months. As of this writing, this practice has again been suspended.

partition of India, where her husband, Manmohan Nath, established his law practice. Satyavati also came to Simla with her two daughters after her husband's death in 1952. She joined the Congress and became a member of the Indian parliament.*

While the orchards were well taken care of by different members of the family, it was largely Stokes' son-in-law Lakshmi Singh Sirkeik who was his torchbearer in this respect. Recipient of the prestigious Udyan Pandit award, Lakshmi Singh experimented with different varieties of apples and other fruit and was the first in the region to start a large nursery of apple saplings. He kept abreast of developments in fruit-growing, shared his experiences with fellow farmers, and continued to advise and guide the younger farmers. He acknowledged Stokes as his mentor.

The third generation of the family, consisting of twenty-nine cousins (five are now deceased), are spread far and wide. None bearing the name Stokes, however, live in India. The sons of Stokes' three sons, Prem, Pritam, and Lal Chand, have migrated to America. Only their daughters remain. Of Stokes' daughters' children, all but one remain in India. Few have married in the hills.

Stokes' grandchildren view him differently. Grandson Vijay Kumar Stokes, an alumnus of Princeton University, does not consider apples to be the main contribution of his grandfather. "That was an accident," he says, "no one knew that apples would make such a difference. It is the other big changes—educational, social, and cultural—that he brought about in society that are of greater significance."

It is Vijay's dream to restore Barobagh to the old vibrant and expansive estate that it was during his grandfather's time. He is making efforts to preserve Harmony Hall for posterity, promising to keep it open for all of Stokes' descendents. He is also collecting artifacts for a museum he plans to open in some of the old buildings of Tara School.

Grandson Surendra Mohan Kanwar, of the Indian Administrative Service (IAS), felt that apples were the "most lasting" contribution of his grandfather. "Other social changes in the hills would have come about sooner or later but no one could have brought and propagated the Delicious apples in the region as Stokes did."

Surendra, a keen horticulturist and the author of a comprehensive book on apple cultivation, *Apples: Production Technology and Economics,* and of a companion volume in Hindi for the common farmer, pioneered the cultivation of dwarf varieties of rootstocks in the Simla Hills that had been evolved and popularized in Europe. Inspired by his grandfather, he experimented with different methods

---

* Satyavati later married Y. S. Parmar, chief minister of Himachal Pradesh.

of pruning and training and studied their effect on the Malling series of M-9, M-7, and M-104, which he planted in his orchard in Rohanda in 1972. These dwarf varieties, which he found to be most adaptable to the Himalayan environment, proved to be very successful in terms of production and regularity of crops and are now fast becoming the popular choice of farmers in Himachal Pradesh.

The American and Indian branches of the Stokes family have kept in touch with each other. Stokes' mother came to India twice. His brother Spencer Stokes visited Kotgarh a number of times. The family maintained contact after Stokes' death. His sister Anna Truitt's son, Dr. Marshall Truitt, who had many Indian friends, visited Kotgarh a couple of times. Anna's daughter Florence Meigs also visited the family in India, as did her granddaughter Anna Meigs. Dr. Donald E. Stokes, a cousin of Samuel Stokes who was Dean of the Woodrow Wilson School of International Relations at Princeton University for several years made special efforts to remain in touch with the family. From the Indian side, a number of family members including Prem Chand, Pritam Chand, Lal Chand, Satyavati, and several of Stokes' grandchildren have been welcome guests at the Philadelphia homes of their cousins.

THE DESCENDENTS OF S. E. STOKES

S. E. Stokes b. 16 Aug. 1882 in Germantown, Pennsylvania, m. Agnes d/o Babu Benjamin of Kotgarh (orig. from village Sarun Bargain in Mandi State) on 16 Sept. 1912. (d. 14 May 1946)

1. Prem Chand Stokes 7 Dec. 1913–24 Oct. 1998, m. Shakuntla Devi nee Narain Dasi d/o Devi Das Bhalaik of Thanedhar, Kotgarh, Dec. 1935.

> Uma Stokes b. 8 Sept. 1936, m. Mahavir Singha (Kotgarh); children Rajiv, Radhika, and Sandip.
>
> Vijay Kumar Stokes b. 26 Aug. 1939, m. Prabha Singha (Kotgarh); daughters Chitra and Anuradha.
>
> Indra Stokes b. 3 Aug. 1941, m. Praveen Moudgil (Uttar Pradesh); sons Mayan and Milan.
>
> Ashok Stokes b. 11 Sept. 1944, m. Rauna Dorothy Fernandes (Goa); children Shamona and Shanil.
>
> Vinod Stokes b. 2 Oct. 1947.
>
> Deepak Stokes b. 1 Oct. 1949, m. Kusum Gangadhar (Delhi); children Arvind and Sonia.

2. Pritam Chand Stokes b. 13 Jan. 1915 (during parents' visit to America), m. Shanti Devi nee Niranjan Dasi d/o Devi Das Bhalaik of Thanedar, Kotgarh, July 1938. (d. 27 July 2003)

> Vijay Lakshmi Stokes 4 Mar. 1941–31 Oct. 2005, m. Swarup Chauhan (Himachal); daughters Deepika, Jyotsna, and Rashmi.
>
> Santosh Stokes b. 4 May 1941, m. Vinod Khindaria (Punjab); daughter Gauri.
>
> Anil Stokes b. 17 May 1948, m. Louise Moya (USA); children Arjun, Sanjay, and Anjali.
>
> Sushma Stokes b. 7 Jan. 1951, m. Sudhir Chandra (Uttar Pradesh); children Kapil and Nalini.

3. Tara Chand Stokes 23 July 1916–June 1924.

4. Champavati 22 July 1917–13 Oct. 1990, m. Manmohan Nath s/o Jagan Nath Kanwar of Lahore, Oct. 1936.

> Surendra Mohan Kanwar 9 July 1937–11 July 2005, m. Pamela Nangia (Punjab); children Kartik and Madhurima.
>
> Usha Kanwar b. 28 Oct. 1938, m. K. V. Malhotra (Punjab); children Sonia, Jyotika, and Gaurav.
>
> Asha Kanwar b. 28 Feb. 1940, m. Vishnu Datta Sharma (Uttar Pradesh); children Ankur Datta and Nandini.
>
> Sheila Kanwar b. 6 Feb. 1943, m. Sutikshan Malhotra (Punjab); children Simi and Sudhir.
>
> Jatinder Kanwar b. 8 Feb. 1945, m. Radha Kashyap (Himachal); children Ritu, Sunaina, and Ajay.
>
> Shabnam Kanwar b. 28 May 1949, m. Brij Gossain (Uttar Pradesh); daughters Upasana and Niharika.
>
> Rakesh Kanwar b. 28 Sept. 1950, m. Neelam Chandel (Himachal); daughters Navita and Sheetal.

5. Savitri 30 Mar. 1919–2 Sept. 1989, m. Thakur Lakshmi Singh s/o Manohar Das of Gopalpur in Kotgarh, Sept. 1935.

> Chander Mohan Sirkeik b. 10 Jan. 1937, m. Satya Priya Chauhan (Himachal); children Yamni and Raman.
>
> Jagmohan Sirkeik 31 Dec. 1939–30 Aug. 1970, m. Pushpa Jaret (Himachal); sons Vinay and Pradeep.
>
> Kamla Sirkeik b. 22 Oct. 1941, m. Jatinder Singha (Himachal); children Ujwala, Ruchita, Ajay, and Bhavna.

Vimla Sirkeik 20 Jan. 1943–2001, m. Suresh Bhalaik (Himachal); children Anup and Anita.

Promila Sirkeik 4 Apr. 1945 –4 Oct. 1980, m. Hans Raj Singha (Himachal); children Vivek and Shruti.

Madan Sirkeik b. 4 July 1951, m. Godavri Metha (Himachal); children Preeti and Prashant.

Brij Sirkeik b. 2 July 1951.

6. Satyavati b. 10 Apr. 1920, m. Onkar Nath Dang s/o Kirpa Ram Dang of Delhi, 1939.

Urmila Dang b. 1 Feb. 1944, m. Narinder Kanwal (Punjab); daughter Diya.

Premila Dang b. 29 Mar. 1948, m. Adolf Vincent Condillac (Goa); children Brinda and Kunal.

7. Lal Chand Stokes 17 Mar. 1925–12 Sept. 1973, m. Vidya Devi d/o Amin Chand Singha of Kotgarh, Dec. 1944.

Sudhir Stokes b. 6 Dec. 1946, m. Ranjan Man Singh (Punjab); daughter Shilarana.

Sudha Stokes b. 20 Feb. 1949, m. Deep Puar (Punjab); sons Dhruv and Rahul.

Sanjiv Stokes b. 11 Oct. 1950, m. Anita Malhotra (Punjab); daughters Shelilah and Shyamoli.

ACKNOWLEDGMENTS

I thank the numerous people of Kotgarh who spared their time to reminisce about the life and work of Satyanand Stokes. My meetings with them unraveled many aspects of Stokes' personality, gave me a host of anecdotal information, and were of great help in developing the story.

Much as I would like to it is not practically possible to include all their names in these pages. I do, however, want to mention a few. Among these are Stokes' son-in-law Lakshmi Singh Sirkeik, and Agnes' nephew, Fazl ud-Din Ali. Both were close to Stokes and could, with their remarkable memories, reconstruct Stokes' life with ease. Stokes' sons Prem Chand and Pritam Chand (Lal Chand, the youngest son, died in 1973), also provided me with important details, as did Ram Dayal Singha of Kotgarh and Sham Sukh of Shatla. I also thank my brother Jatinder Kanwar for helping me to conduct the innumerable interviews in Kotgarh.

I am indebted to Agnes Stokes, Champavati and Manmohan Nath, Lakshmi Singh Sirkeik, Fazl ud-Din Ali, Ram Dayal Singha, Gris Chand, Lachhi Kumar, Sudhir Stokes, Eugenia Mange Bennett, George Gillespie, Donald E. Stokes, Milton Rubincam, and the Rev. Daniel O'Connar for letting me make use of material in their possession, and to Prem Chand Stokes, Rakesh Kanwar, Premila Condilac, and Dr. Marshall Truitt for letting me make copies of photographs which they had.

I appreciate the assistance and encouragement I received from Rev. Wilzbacher, Rev. James Stuart, Rev. R. W. Taylor, Surinder Suri, Stephen Alter, B. R. Grover, T. R. Metcalf, and G. Berriman. I also acknowledge John Beasant, Mark Tully, Peter Bernstein, Megan Holt, Kailash Joshi, Raj Kanwar, Anna Meigs, Sybil Stokes, Vidya Stokes, Vinod Stokes, Ruth Stokes, Peter Truitt, Eleanor Szanton, Kitty Streitwieser, and Tenzin N. Teethong, all of whom have touched the book in one way or another.

I am thankful for the support received from the Indian Council of Historical Research, Ford Foundation New Delhi, and the Center for South Asia Studies, University of California at Berkeley.

I want to express my special thanks to Penguin India's editor, Ravi Singh, who read my manuscript and never doubted the story or its future. A reprint of the book within three months of publication proved him right.

Eminent author Khushwant Singh helped with the first publication of the book and has been a source of strength. "A book on Stokes was waiting to be written," he told me with his intuitive sense of history when I first met him ten years ago. Although he had never met Stokes, he knew of him and was at college with his sons at St. Stephen's. My very special thanks to him for his valuable support, suggestions, and advice. At 92 he is enthusiastic about the American edition and I am grateful. "The book is of perennial interest and should be readily available in India and abroad," he insisted when I saw him in Delhi last April.

Susanne and Lloyd Rudolph have been of special help with this edition. I thank them for their interest, patience, and enthusiasm.

Working with Rebecca Tolen at Indiana University Press has been a pleasant experience and I thank her for making it so.

One person whom I remember with gratitude on this occasion is Shri Gurdial Mallick, who was close to Stokes' friend C. F. Andrews at Shantiniketan. Mallickji, as he was known to one and all, never met Stokes but knew of him from Andrews and always talked exuberantly about him. I can never forget his visits to our home in Shimla in the sixties—a beaming old man who delighted in everything and everybody and the reverence with which he spoke to my mother because she was Stokes' daughter.

I am indebted to my great-grandmother Florence Spencer Stokes for the record she left of her son's life and whose detailed and descriptive letters made the personality of my grandfather real to me in a way nothing else could have. Knowing that it would be two months before her son would receive a reply to his letters, she often quoted from them when she wrote to him, which greatly helped me to weave the early years of Stokes' stay in India with authenticity.

I also acknowledge with respect my father, Manmohan Nath, a well-known lawyer of Simla and my mother, Champavati, the eldest daughter of Stokes, both of whom encouraged my interest in my grandfather's life. The unswerving faith of my parents in their children has held us in good stead. Having moved almost 1,000 miles to Simla from Quetta in the aftermath of the partition of India in 1947 with five small children and only the clothes on their backs, they did not dwell on how they were going to feed, clothe, and educate us; they were just determined to do it. Not having had the advantage of a higher education, my mother was especially keen that her daughters should get the best education. If I have one regret, it is that this book was not completed during their lifetime.

My older brother, Surendra Mohan Kanwar of the Indian Administrative Service, who was an avid horticulturist, was generous with his advice. A walking encyclopedia on Himachal Pradesh, he was always there to answer my many questions on the social history of Himachal and my queries related to apple production. I miss his presence but am grateful for what we shared. I also want to thank my sister Usha Malhotra for her constant help and her irrepressible joy in the book.

I thank my son, Ankur, for transcribing my manuscript on the computer and for encouraging me to stay on with the project and to become more computer literate.

Finally my deep appreciation to my daughter, Nandini, the co-author of this book, without whose inspiring support and unfailing help this book may not have become a reality. Nandini acted as my sounding board over several years with great patience. She was also the first editor of this book. The prologue was her idea and her composition. In many ways this book is her and my combined effort.

I am grateful that my children have been a part of this book—for it is as much their heritage as it is mine.

And with what words can I express my thanks to Saahil, Arjun, and Neha for providing all the excitement in my life and for helping to keep the lamp burning, and to Vishnu for being the person he is and for so ungrudgingly letting me spend the time I did on this book.

Lastly and most importantly I express my profound gratitude to His Holiness the Dalai Lama for blessing my work by writing a foreword for the book. It is a precious gift which means much to me, my family, and the people of our hills.

APPENDIX 1.

FOLK SONG COMPOSED ON THE OCCASION OF STOKES' MARRIAGE

(Translated from the local dialect by Pt. Ram Dev Shastri of Kotgarh)

Let us gather and dance with our dear American Sahib,
We are fortunate to have him with us.

We commence with the song of Kali of Hattu* and the Dev of Mehlan,**
Then we will sing about our Sahib and his love for us.

O Lounkur Veer,*** I am sitting at your feet.
Inspire me to compose and sing for Sahib, as he is as precious to us
    as the Ganges water.

O dear Sahib, you came from America where you lived like a Lord,
People rushed to Thanedhar when you came to live amongst us.

This American has removed our poverty and brought us gold and
silver, and lorries and motor cars.

With his coming horse carriages have come to the hills.
People of nearby districts are wide-eyed with wonder at our prosperity.

Dear Sahib has visited many places of importance,
but this Barobagh of ours has fascinated him.

Fortunately he has come to us to live in Barobagh for good.
Now Rai Sahib Amin Chand has begun to think that Sahib should be
    married soon.

We will invite the Dev of Mehlan with his team of drummers,
as Mem Agnes gets ready to marry our Sahib.

* Nearby Hattu mountain, known for its natural beauty and its famous temple of the
  goddess Kali.
** Widely worshipped deity of a temple in Mehlan village.
*** Lonkour Veer is the local devta of Thanedhar area.

O brothers, come to Barobagh,
and join us in arranging a grand feast to celebrate his wedding.

He will bring his bride home
and will weave his thread of life amongst us.

APPENDIX 2.

STOKES' WRITTEN STATEMENT

TEXT OF STOKES' WRITTEN STATEMENT AT HIS TRIAL BEFORE
MAJOR M. L. FERRAR, DISTRICT MAGISTRATE, LAHORE, ON 17 DECEMBER 1921.

I. I have been arrested upon the ground that my recent speeches and writings have been of a nature to bring about a breach of the peace. I am charged with so speaking and writing that the people of India are thereby incited to hatred for the present Government.

This charge is, broadly speaking, based upon (a) reports received of my lectures, (b) two articles entitled respectively "Oppression in the Simla Hill States" (Nov. 24th & 25th) and "The Acid Test of Loyalty" (1st, 2nd & 4th of December), (c) the general tendency of my articles, notably "Differences of Opinion" (Oct. 15th) and "The Price of Swaraj" (Nov. 16th).

II. The object of this Statement is not to evade imprisonment, for which as a non-cooperator I am prepared. I make it in order to deny categorically the charge that I have ever given a lecture or written an article that tended to provoke hatred upon the part of the hearer or reader. I have not shrunk from telling the truth as I see it; I have used every effort of late to persuade the people of this land to strengthen by their support and obedience the great leader who has been granted to India at this time of crisis. And yet I have lost no opportunity of making the people feel that their most sacred duty was to start the work of reformation in their own hearts by cleansing them of hatred and violence. Were I defending myself I could call witnesses from every place where I have lectured to vouch for the truth of what I say.

As to my writings, they are before the public in book and pamphlet and newspaper, and I have every confidence that not one can be found which may be justly said to promote hatred for government or for the Britishers. On the contrary, while seeking to arouse the aspirations of the people of this land, they have consistently pointed out that our path must be one of self-sacrifice, never of hatred or violence. The last paragraph of my book entitled *National Self-Realization* written in 1920 expresses my position clearly:

Not by hatred, not with anger, can we gain our end, if our end be worth the gaining. These are of "Ahamkara" and lead to darkness. Where we see evil, selfishness, injustice, let us stand unflinchingly against them, regardless of personal consequences, hating the deed and not the doer, for the doer is but our other self. This is the Satyamarg (the path of truth); there is no other.

That my views have not changed on the subject the last lines of the last article sent to the press by me before I was arrested demonstrate. Speaking of "The True Non-cooperator" and what his attitude towards his opponents should be, I concluded:

These are high counsels and hard for weak and sinful men burning under a bitter sense of wrongs inflicted. Yet it is not by low counsel that any Swaraj will be won that is worth the having. If we fight with the ignoble weapons of pride and hate and prejudice we are undone, even if we win a sort of unmoral victory. If we fight in the spirit of true nobility God and eternal Justice fight with us and the victory is certain. So fighting even defeat is victory.

I have not the slightest hesitation in saying that this has been what I have said to the people constantly in my lectures. Those who have heard me throughout the Punjab will recognize the truth of this assertion.

III. In this section I desire to show how undependable the reports are upon which the authorities have to rely when they trust to ignorant subordinates for information about the movements and activities of non-cooperators. The Deputy Inspector General of Police when bringing his charge against me said, "On the night of Friday, the 2nd December, I received a letter brought me by special messenger informing me that Mr Stokes was travelling up to Lahore and was reported to be conveying instructions from the Central Congress Committee to Lala Lajpat Rai in regard to civil disobedience, directing him to resort to such disobedience and to hold a mass meeting in Lahore in contravention of the Seditious Meetings Act. Mr Stokes was arrested on the morning of the 3rd December and taken to the District Police Lines."

In the first place, the above shows an astonishing ignorance of the constitution of the Congress and its organization. What is this "Central Congress Committee" that sends instructions to Lala Lajpat Rai? That, however, is by the way. My object in quoting the above is to show how manifestly incorrect the information was upon which the authorities acted. I was reported to be bringing instructions from a "Central Congress Committee"; was it assembled in Simla or in Kotgarh, from which I was returning to the plains after a visit to my family? Lala Lajpat Rai had himself just returned from the South, while I was fifty miles above Simla at my home—yet I was reported to be bringing him instructions. Coming down from Simla I had reached Ambala in the evening, spent the next day quietly with a friend; left at five in the morning for Ludhiana where I remained all day with an old friend who is an ardent cooperator. In the evening I went out for an hour by tonga to see a loom and took the night train for Lahore. I was arrested on the way during the early hours of the morning—presumably to prevent my carrying the "instructions" to Lahore!

Again I desire to draw attention to the following report sent with reference to my tour in the Ferozepur district. I do not blame the Deputy Inspector General of Police for making it, but I should like him to consider it an example of the kind of reports we are subjected to. The Deputy Inspector General said: "The Superintendent of Police in reporting these meetings drew attention to the mischief done by Mr Stokes. During the war Mr Stokes was given a Commission and employed on recruiting duty in the Ferozepur District. His appearance there in association with disloyal agitators created a bad impression on the villagers."

Surely before making such a report as the above, the Superintendent of Police should have been sure of his facts. *I never was employed on recruiting duty in the Ferozepur district.* I have in fact only once been there before, and then for but half a day. When even a Superintendent of Police can fall into such errors, what is to be expected of his less educated subordinates?

In this connection I shall refer to one other statement I am reported to "have asserted that formerly famines were unknown in India." Actually what I did say, and have said upon other occasions when referring to ancient Indian civilization, was that Megasthenes had written "it is affirmed that famines have never visited India and that there has never been a general scarcity of nourishing food." This sentence is but a link in a chain of evidence by which I have often sought to demonstrate that the Indians of the past were able to maintain the prosperity of their land from the earliest times practically up to the occupation of the country by the Company.

I give the above merely to illustrate how the ignorant police agents etc., report our lectures. We deliver them in the vernacular, they are reported in scraps and bits by persons quite incapable of taking verbatim reports, and are thereafter turned into English sometimes with quite remarkable results.

Of course where such agents have taken down the complete lecture in shorthand there is no reason why it should not be used as evidence; otherwise such reports, as I have shown in specific instances, are apt to be highly misleading. Where, as in my own case, there is a long and fairly consecutive series of articles over my own signature there is no justification for making use of the very unreliable and fragmentary information (or misinformation) furnished by police and other agents. The same applies to irresponsible reports sent to newspapers, which the writer may or may not see. When our views are on record in them from our own pens there is surely no justification for making use of such reports.

Yet it will be seen that, in charging me under Section 108, only general allegations about the "tendency" of my signed articles are made and support is mainly sought from these reports of subordinates which I have shown to be in several instances quite unreliable.

Though denying that any of the articles in question have the tendency to spread hatred or arouse a spirit of hatred against any person or group of persons, I admit that not only I but every other Congressman is labouring for an entire rectification of the relationship at present obtaining between "the rulers and the ruled." We are doing this by entirely peaceful means, yet in order to accomplish it we have undoubtedly sought to create a profound dissatisfaction with various aspects of the existing relationship, and with it a nation-wide aspiration for one that is consistent with national self-respect. We have sought to help the Indian people to retrieve their self-confidence, and in order to do so have held constantly before their eyes the achievements of the past Indian civilization, pointing out various particulars in which it excelled the present. We have tried to demonstrate that India has in the past shown herself fully capable of managing her own affairs, and to prove how the common assumption that the country was in a state of anarchy and ruin when the British arrived, is a gross exaggeration.

I personally have devoted much attention to this, for I am convinced that the view commonly taught naturally leads to the position that Indians are unfitted by temperament to control their own destinies. Such a position is highly demoralizing both to the nation teaching it and to the nation which accepts the teaching as true. Yet I would point out that in disputing it I have constantly supported my assertions by quotations from well-known statesmen, travellers and historians. The police are in possession of my collected notes, and if they study them carefully they will see what an amount of evidence I might bring forward to support my position.

Surely I am not the only man who has ever asserted the prosperity of India at the time of the advent of the Company. Here in jail I have no large library at my disposal, but I can still quote some paragraphs from the pen of the former Commissioner of Assam (HSL Cotton) who wrote in 1890:

> The manufactures of India were once in a highly flourishing condition. The various native courts encouraged large towns and urban enterprise. European traders were first attracted not by the raw products but by the manufactured wares of this country. The fame of the fine muslins of Bengal, her rich silks and brocades, her harmonious cotton prints had spread far and wide in Asia as well as in Europe. "The Bengal silk cloth," writes Mr Verelest, one of our earliest Gov-

ernors, "were dispersed to a vast amount, to the west and the north, inland as far as Gujrat, Lahore and even Ispahan."

The Indian cities were populous and magnificent. When Clive entered Murshidabad, the old capital of Bengal, in 1757, he wrote of it, "This city is as extensive, populous and rich as the city of London, with this difference that there are individuals in the first possessing infinitely greater property than in the last city."

All the arts then flourished, and with them urban life—I will cite an example, the city of Dakka. It was during the time of the Mogul Government that this city reached the highest degree of prosperity. But even less than a hundred years ago, the whole commerce of Dakka was estimated at one crore of rupees, and its population at 200,000 souls. In 1787 the exports of Dakka muslin to England amounted to thirty lacs of rupees; in 1817 they had ceased altogether. The art of spinning and weaving, which for ages afforded employment to a numerous and industrious population, have now become extinct. Families which were formerly in a state of affluence have been reduced to penury. This decadence has occurred *not in Dakka only, but in all districts.* Not a year passes in which the commissioners and district officers do not bring to the notice of the government that the manufacturing classes in all parts of the country are becoming impoverished.

On the other hand agriculture is everywhere expanding at the expense of manufacturing industry. Every exertion is being made to increase the area under cultivation with staple crops. The area under cultivation is increasing by leaps and bounds, and the increase in the amount of the agricultural produce exported from the country is pointed to as irrefrangable evidence of increased national prosperity. *This is a vain delusion.* The Indian foreign trade has, indeed, been developed, but while the soil of the country has been impoverished by over-cropping, foreign competition has filled the Indian market with the produce of foreign manufacturers. The most profitable Indian industries have been destroyed and the most beautiful Indian arts have greatly deteriorated or died out.

The development of petty industries, the establishment of the jute and cotton mills to which I have already alluded, even the accumulation of gold and silver, the increased use of ornaments, brass pots, cotton cloths and umbrellas among the people, afford but a poor compensation for the variety of social life once spread through the country.

The resources of India will vie almost with those of America itself. The dimensions of Indian trade are already enormous and yet no country is more poor than this. The expansion of trade is at the expense of manufacturing industry. *The economic conditions upon which material prosperity depends are lacking.*

An India supplying England with its raw products and in its turn dependent upon England for all its important manufacturers is not a spectacle which
is likely to reconcile an Indian patriot to the loss of the subtle and refined oriental arts, the very secret of which has passed away—or to the loss of that constructive genius and mechanical ability which designed the canal system of upper India and the Taj at Agra.

I hold the same views, and have become convinced that those who hold the vital
interests of India in their hands should be made accountable to the Indian people
for their policies and activities. It seems to me that this is the only way in which
India will be able to safeguard her interests and defend herself from exploitation.
For this reason I have attempted to expose the defects of the present relationship
existing between Government and the people. Of course, if we may be said to
create hatred for Government when we expose its defects, then I am guilty. In
that event the only alternative would be *silence* or *sedition*.

I do not propose to defend myself with regard to the charge made against my
articles. When the proceedings of this trial have been published, with the full
text of the articles themselves, I have every confidence in the verdict of the public
both here and in England. I assert, however, that it is not just to take a portion of
any article out of its context; the *whole article* must be considered. That entitled
"The Acid Test of Loyalty" is *one* article, appearing in three parts, and from start
to finish forms one consecutive argument.

I admit the quotation from my article of May, 1919, upon the necessity of
maintaining law and order. I hold the same opinion now and consider that there
are occasions when even martial law may be necessary. Yet I would point out that
the title of the article from which the Deputy Inspector General quoted was "The
Duty of Government and Englishmen" and it was a criticism of the martial law
methods then being used, which it said should immediately be put a stop to "if
the government is to maintain that relationship with the people which will alone
render its position a possible one in the new era which is dawning on the world."

With regard to the maintenance of order, I would add that no group of people
in this land at present is more anxious for this than Mahatma ji and those associated with him. While still at large, the greater part of our thought and effort
was devoted to insuring that order was kept; and since being jailed, probably our
greatest anxiety is that the masses remain true to Mahatma ji's injunctions as to
perfect non-violence.

At the same time I submit that order is not the *only* necessity for the Indian
people. A deal man is the most orderly and peaceful man possible. We have
striven to infuse new life and aspiration into the people, and yet teach them to
be non-violent and free from hatred.

The Deputy Inspector General of Police quotes from a letter found among my papers, undated and addressed to "Swamiji." I would merely remark with reference to this letter that it marked a period several months ago when some of us felt the need of a greater definiteness in our plans. We put the questions proposed in the letter to Mahatma ji and he satisfied us that we had no grounds for anxiety. In fact one of the opinions then put forward was that most of us should be in jail by the latter part of December and so it is falling out. This letter gives my own view of the supreme duty of the moment to strengthen Mahatma ji's hands by our obedience, that the great dynamic inspiration of his personality may be able to unite the whole Indian people in their struggle for national self-realization. For I am convinced that he alone can make all India feel that this is a spiritual movement,—not a mere political campaign.

I would close this statement with one other observation. It is wrong to think of us as irreconcilables; we are many of us the same men who worked wholeheartedly with the authorities in the days of the Great War. I personally not only joined the Reserve but gave the use of my estate freely and sent every available man into the Army. We have taken our present position because we have come to feel that the Government is *not* prepared to co-operate with the people of India. We stand where we do because we have come to feel that the Government's only idea of co-operation is that the people of India should submit to its decisions. The authorities say, "here is a plan which we have made; assist in making it a success." This is not "cooperation." The very nature of the invitation implies a point of view contrary to the spirit of co-operation. There was no "coming halfway" upon the part of those in power. Had they said, "Help us to devise a method by which India can attain to a position in the Empire consistent with her interests and her self-respect," and had they been prepared to take up the problem in the true spirit of cooperation without any idea of merely persuading Indians to accept their views on the subject in toto, can we imagine that there would have been any non-cooperation movement in India today? I do not think so.

S.E. STOKES

APPENDIX 3.
VERSES WRITTEN IN JAIL

Stokes wrote the following verses in the Central Jail, Lahore a few weeks after he began serving his sentence of six months. The poem was sent anonymously for publication in the papers—as a message from those within the jail to those outside.

HIND

As I stand in my prison courtyard
And look up into the sky,
Where the small birds wheel and flutter
And the eagle soars on high—
Where bank upon bank the white clouds
Hang bright in the azure blue—
Where the winds of heaven blow freely
And life shines clean and true.

Then over my restless spirit
There settles a peace divine;
And I can feel Thy presence,
My hand seems clasped by Thine—
Away fade the walls that enclose me
And hushed is the sordid din
Of clanking fetter and clinging gate
That oppressed and hemmed me in.

The drooping wings of my spirit
Grow strong in Thy strength sublime
And I rise and soar in Thy power
O'er the changing fields of Time;
The Future lies spread before me
And Ah! I can clearly see
The web that Thy hand is weaving,
The things Thou hast said shall be.

My heart with rapture is thrilling
For there spreads before my eyes
A vision of self-devotion—
A vision of sacrifice.
And Hark! down the wind is carried—
Its notes all clear and free—
The song of the sons of the Future—
The song of Equity.

They sing as they march of Thy Justice,
Oh Source and Goal of Life!
They hymn the end of the selfish—
The end of war and strife.

And they march with hearts undaunted
By fetters or prison bars,
With their loins girt up for Justice
And their eyes fixed on the stars.

Gone is my dream, but my prison
Erks me no more. Behold!
Its walls are as walls of marble,
Its bars as bars of gold;
And I joy that God in His mercy
Hath granted this boon to me—
To march with the sons of the Future—
To suffer dear Hind for thee.

GLOSSARY

AARTI: A form of prayer performed by the waving of light and incense, usually accompanied with chanting.

ACHKAN: A long, formal, high-necked coat usually worn in North India.

ADVAIT: Non-duality. Also, the name of a school of Vedanta philosophy that teaches the oneness of God, the soul, and the universe.

AHIMSA: Doctrine of refraining from harming anyone.

ARJUN: A hero of the epic *Mahabharata* and the recipient of Krishna's teaching in the Bhagavad Gita.

ASHRAM: Hermitage.

ATMAN: The Self or Soul. Also denotes the Supreme Soul, which according to Advaita Vedanta, is identical to the individual soul.

AVATARA: An incarnation of God.

BAJA: Musical band mainly consisting of drummers and trumpeters.

BANDE MATRAM: Salutations to the Motherland.

BHAGAVAD GITA: Lit., the "Song of God." One of the most important scriptures of the Vedanta philosophy consisting of the teachings of Sri Krishna to Arjuna on how to realize God while carrying on the duties of life. The eighteen chapters of this work are a part of the Indian epic *Mahabharata*.

BRAHAMACHARYA: The first of the four stages of life, the life of an unmarried student.

CHAITANYA: A sixteenth-century Hindu saint of Bhakti Yoga, well known for his devotion to Krishna.

CHAMAR: People considered low-caste because they skinned hides of cows to make shoes.

CHARKHA: Spinning wheel.

CHARNAMRIT: Holy water distributed at the end of a prayer meeting or religious ceremony.

CHHUUT-CHHAAT: Special regulations which forbade interaction with people of lower castes.

CHURIDAR: A fitted pyjama worn by both men and women.

CRORE: The sum ten million.

DAL: Lentils, basic Indian food eaten with roti or rice.

DANDI: Similar to a palanquin carried by four men, but more basic; used for transporting people in areas where there is no other means of transportation.

DARBAR: Court of a king.

DHARMA: Individual's duty.

DHYANA: Meditation.

DHYAN-YOG: Yoga of Dhyana; meditation.

DHOTI: Loin cloth, short or long.

GAYATRI MANTRA: The most famous Vedic mantra—"Let that adorable, full of light [God] enlighten us, who meditate on him."

GHEE: Clarified butter.

GITA: Short for the Bhagavad Gita.

GURU: The spiritual teacher. *Gu* means darkness, and *ru* means destroyer. He who destroys the darkness, or ignorance, of the disciple is a guru.

GURUDWARA: Place of worship of the Sikhs.

HALWA: A popular Indian dessert generally made with semolina; usually served on special occasions such as sacred ceremonies or marriages.

HAWAN: Religious ritual in which offerings are made through the fire.

HOOKAH: Water pipe.

ISHWARA: The supreme personal God of Hinduism.

JAAT-PAAT: Regulations for interacting with people of different castes.

JAGATGURU: Spiritual teacher of the world.

JAI-JAI-KAR: Slogan of victory.

KAMANDAL: A special wooden bowl used by mendicants.

KARAMYOGI: One who works selflessly. From Karma yoga, the path of selfless work. One of the four main yogas, or paths to union with God.

KARMA: Action which yields results to the doer, or which is the effect of his previous deeds.

KHAD: Stream, usually at a lower level from where villagers fetch water.

KHASH: Non-scheduled castes.

KRISHNA: One of the most widely worshipped Incarnations of God in Hinduism. Sri Krishna delivered the message of the Bhagavad Gita to his friend Arjuna on the battlefield of Kurukshetra.

KURTA-PYJAMA: A loose, long, full-sleeved shirt and loose pants.

LADDU: A popular ball-shaped Indian sweet.

LAKH: The sum one hundred thousand.

MAHANT: Spiritual and administrative head.

MAHATMA: Great soul, great man, or saint.

MAIDAN: Flat ground, like a playing field.

MANTRA: A sacred word, verse, or vedic hymn. Also the name of God that a guru gives to a disciple at the time of initiation.

MURGI: Lit., hen, but usually used for fowl.

NARKANDA-KI-DHAR: Dhar used for mountain or ridge.

OM: Sometimes written as Aum. The most sacred word of the Vedas. It is a symbol of both the Personal god and the Absolute.

PADRE: A Christian clergyman, priest.

PAHARI: Of the hills; Pucca pahari—total hill-man.

PAISA: A coin of small denomination. Before the introduction of metric currency one rupee was equal to sixteen annas and one anna was equal to four paisa.

PANCHAYAT: Local self-government.

PASHAM: Pashmina.

REZTA: A full-length, long-sleeved dress gathered at the waist; worn by the women of Kotgarh with a colorful head-scarf called a "dhatu."

RISHI: A seer of Truth to whom the wisdom of the Vedas was revealed. Also, a general name for a saint or ascetic.

ROTI: Indian bread made of whole wheat and cooked on a griddle.

SAABJI: Saab for sahib. A word of respect used for someone who is considered superior. The suffix "ji" expresses respect.

SABZI MANDI: Vegetable market. Sometimes used as a proper noun as in this case.

SALAAM BABA, SALAAM MAHARAJ: Salaam—greetings. "Baba" and "Maharaj" used here as words of respect to a spiritual person.

SANATANA DHARMA: Lit., the "eternal religion." The religion of the Hindus, formulated by the rishis of the Vedas.

Sastras: Scriptures.

Sat Sri Akal: Truth is God.

Shaloka: A verse in a Sanskrit scriptural work.

Shuchi: From sacchi for true; also pure.

Svadharma: One's personal duty.

Swamiji: A term of endearment and respect by which a Swami is addressed.

Tehsil: Administrative unit.

Tehsildar: Head of Tehsil.

Upanishads: The well-known sacred Hindu scriptures containing the philosophy of the Vedas. They mainly deal with the knowledge of God and record the spiritual experiences of the sages of ancient India. Of the one hundred and eight Upanishads, eleven are called major Upanishads.

Vedanta: Lit., the "end of the Vedas." A metaphysical philosophy derived from the Upanishadic texts.

Vedas: The most sacred scriptures of the Hindus and the ultimate authority of the Hindu religion and philosophy.

Yogi: A person who practices Yoga; an adherent to Yoga philosophy; a markedly reflective or mystical person.

Zamindar: Feudal landlord in British India who paid the government a fixed revenue. Today, big landowners.

Zaridar: Brocade.

NOTES

1. A JOURNEY OF NO RETURN

1. Florence Stokes, *A Sketch of the Life of Samuel Evans Stokes* (The Biddle Press, Philadelphia), p. 72.

2. Florence S. to Stokes, 5 January 1924.

3. Stokes, *The Letters of Nancy Evans Stokes with a Historical Note by Samuel Evans Stokes,* 1916, private publication, p. 4.

4. Ibid.

5. Florence Stokes, *A Sketch of the Life of Samuel Evans Stokes,* pp. 5–6.

6. Ibid., pp. 18–21.

7. Stokes, *The Traditions and Ideals of Our Family,* pp. 122–26. *Public Ledger,* Philadelphia, 25 March 1836.

8. Florence S. to Stokes, 7 January 1908.

9. Florence Stokes, *A Sketch of the Life of Samuel Evans Stokes,* p. 31.

10. Ibid., pp. 39–42.

11. Ibid., p. 63.

12. Stokes, *Introductory Notes on Advaita,* 1944, unfinished manuscript.

13. Ibid.

14. Ibid.

15. Florence Stokes, *A Sketch of the Life of Samuel Evans Stokes,* p. 72.

16. Florence S. to Stokes, March 1904, n.d., and 12 December 1904.

17. Cyril Davey, *Caring Comes First, The Leprosy Mission Story* (UK: Marshall Pickering, 1987), pp. 25–26.

18. Laura Platt to Florence S. as quoted in Florence S. letter to Stokes, 8 February 1904.

19. Florence S. to Stokes, 26 December 1904 and letter of end 1906, n.d.

2. THE QUEST BEGINS

1. Florence S. to Stokes, 30 March, 3 April and 9 May 1904.

2. Draft of Will made by Stokes, 1904, Stokes Papers.

3. Marion Carleton as quoted in Florence S. letter to Stokes, 18 September 1905.

4. Florence S. to Stokes, 19 August 1906.

5. Florence S. to Stokes, 3 April 1905.

6. Florence S. to Stokes, 24 and 6 June 1905.

7. Florence S. to Stokes, 28 February 1904.

8. Florence S. to Stokes, 20 March and 27 May 1904. Southwark House Day Nursery, Fifth Annual Report, 1915. Reports for Southwark Neighbourhood House, 1907 and 1918.

9. Florence S. to Stokes, 17 April 1905.

10. Florence S. to Stokes, 18 June and 16 October 1905.

11. J. O. F. Murray, Introduction to Stokes' *The Love of God: A Book of Prose and Verse.* First published by Roffey and Clark, Croydon, 1908. Also Stokes to F. J. Western, Appendix, *The Love of God,* 5th ed. (Longman's, Green and Co., 1912).

12. Stokes, "An Opportunity for Layman of the Brotherhood of Imitation," *The Love of God.*

13. Ibid.

14. Florence S. to Stokes, 6 March 1905.

15. Florence S. to Stokes, 22 May 1905. The books he asked for were *Life of St. Francis of Assisi, The Mirror of Reflection,* and *Mrs Oliphant's Francis of Assisi.*

16. Florence S. to Stokes, 22 May and 12 December 1905.

17. Florence S. to Stokes 25 July and 18 September 1905.

18. Florence S. to Stokes, 6 March and 18 June 1905.

19. Florence S. to Stokes, 22 May 1905.

20. Stokes to Florence S., undated letter of end 1905. Also Florence Stokes, *A Sketch of the Life of Samuel Evans Stokes,* pp. 74–75.

21. Stokes to Florence S., 1 October 1905.

22. Ibid.

23. Florence S. to Stokes, 4 November 1905.

24. Florence S. to Stokes, 2 January 1906.

25. Florence S. to Stokes, 9 November 1905.

26. Florence S. to Stokes, 9 January 1906.

27. Florence Stokes, *A Sketch of the Life of Samuel Evans Stokes,* p. 75.

28. Florence S. to Stokes, 26 December 1905.

29. Ibid.

30. Stokes to Florence S., 7 February 1906.

3. THE ASCETIC

1. Florence S. to Stokes, 10 July and 19 August 1906.

2. Florence S. to Stokes, 6 August 1906.

3. Stokes, "Interpreting Christ to India: A New Departure in Missionary Work," *The Love of God.* The article was first published in *The East and the West* in April 1908. It was also published in *The Missionary Review of the World* in September 1908.

4. Florence S. to Stokes, 22 May 1905.

5. Stokes to Florence S., October 1906, undated.

6. Eugene Stock, *The History of the Church Missionary Society,* vol. 2, CMS, London, p. 202; Julius Richter, *History of Indian Missions* (Edinburgh and London: Oliphant Anderson and Ferrier, 1908), pp. 192–93. K. N. Thakur Das, *Himalaya Mission of CMS and Spiritual Movements in Simla Hills* (1840–1947), Research Paper.

7. *The Missionary Review of the World,* October 1910.

8. Stokes, "Interpreting Christ to India."

9. Stokes, "An Opportunity for Laymen," *The Love of God.*

10. Stokes, "Interpreting Christ to India."

11. Friedrich Heiler, *The Gospel of Sadhu Sundar Singh* (George Allen and Unwin, 1927), p. 54.

12. C. F. Andrews, *North India* (London: A. R. Mowbray and Co., 1908), pp. 154–55.

13. C. H. Robinson, Preface to Stokes' *Arjun, the Story of an Indian Boy* (Westminster: Society for the Propagation of the Gospel in Foreign Parts, 1910), pp. vii–viii.

14. Florence S. to Stokes, 7 January 1908.

15. Florence S. to Stokes, 25 September 1906, referring to Stokes Sr.'s talk with Dr. Chapman of New York.

16. Stokes, "Interpreting Christ to India."

17. Ibid.

18. Stokes, "An Opportunity for Laymen."

19. Stokes, *Scheme for a Christian Gurukul,* pamphlet, undated.

20. Ibid.

21. C. F. Andrews to D. H. D. Wilkinson, 24 November 1908, Stokes' Candidate Papers, CMS Archives. Also D. O'Connor, *C.F. Andrews, The Development of His Thought, 1904–14,* Ph.D. thesis, University of St. Andrews, Scotland, 1981, p. 215.

22. C. F. Andrews, "Is Sadhu Sundar Singh Living?," *The Christian Century,* November 1931.

23. C. F. Andrews, *The Renaissance in India: Its Missionary Aspect* (London: Church of England Zenana Missionary Society), pp. 242–43.

24. C. F. Andrews, "Is Sadhu Sundar Singh Living?"

4. VISIT HOME

1. Florence S. to Stokes, 12 February and 30 July 1907.

2. Florence S. to Stokes, 4 November 1905.

3. Florence S. to Stokes, 19 August 1906.

4. Florence S. to Stokes, 20 August 1907.

5. Florence S. to Stokes, 3 January 1908.

6. Stokes to Florence S. December 1907 n.d.

7. Ibid.

8. Florence S. to Stokes, 3 and 7 January 1907.

9. C. F. Andrews, *North India,* pp. 180–81.

10. C. F. Andrews, *The Renaissance in India,* pp. 242–43.

11. *Delhi Mission News,* January 1908.

12. *The Nation,* "In the Driftway," 15 February 1922.

13. Stokes to F. J. Western, 1911, n.d., Appendix, *The Love of God;* Charles M. Robinson to Randall C. Davidson, Archbishop of Canterbury, 4 April 1908, Davidson Papers, Lambeth Palace Library, Westminster 149/150.

14. Stokes, "Interpreting Christ to India."

15. Stokes to Western, Appendix, *The Love of God.*

16. Charles M. Robinson to Davidson, 4 April 1908, Davidson Papers, 149/150.

17. Davidson to Charles M. Robinson, 6 April 1908, Davidson Papers, 150/150.

18. Bishop of Lahore at SPG Annual Meeting, as reported in the Mission Field, July 1908.

19. Pan-Anglican Congress, Section D, *Report to Lambeth Conference,* 1908, pp. 28–29, Lambeth Palace Library.

20. Ibid.

21. *The Church Abroad,* "Sympathy, Sympathy, Sympathy," August 1908.

22. As quoted in Florence S. to Stokes, 25 February 1910.

23. Stokes to Davidson, 27 August 1908, Davidson Papers, 151/150.

24. E. Grose Hodge to D. H. D. Wilkinson, 27 July 1908, Stokes' Candidate Papers. CMS Archives.

25. D. H. D. Wilkinson to P. Ireland Jones, 5 August 1908, Stokes' Candidate Papers.

26. Stokes to D. H. D. Wilkinson, 19 August 1908, Stokes' Candidate Papers.

27. D. H. D. Wilkinson to P. Ireland Jones, 5 August 1908, Stokes' Candidate Papers.

28. Davidson to Stokes, 10 September 1908, Davidson Papers, 160/150.

29. P. Ireland Jones to D. H. D. Wilkinson, 20 August 1908, Stokes' Candidate Papers.

30. P. I. Jones to D. H. D. Wilkinson, 16 September 1908, Letter No. 342 O, CMS Archives.

31. C. F. Andrews to D. H. D. Wilkinson, 24 November 1908, Stokes' Candidate Papers.

32. Pocket Diary of Davidson, 1908, Vol. 632. Lambeth Palace Library; Stokes to Davidson, 16 October 1908, 170/150.

33. Note by Davidson, 29 October 1908, Davidson Papers, 173/150.

34. G. B. Durrant to P. Ireland Jones, 30 October 1908, Letter-book, 1907–1910, p. 261, CMS Archives.

35. J. O. F. Murray, Introduction, *The Love of God.*

36. Hannah P. Morris as quoted in Florence S. letter to Stokes, 10 April 1908.

37. Marjorie Sykes in revised manuscript of *Quakers in India,* Stokes Papers.

5. THE BROTHERHOOD IN INDIA

1. C. F. Andrews, *What I Owe to Christ* (London: Hodder and Stoughton, 1932), p. 176.

2. C. F. Andrews to E. S. Talbot, Bishop of Winchester, undated but of mid-1914.

3. C. F. Andrews, "The Indian Missionary Ideal," *The East and the West,* p. 46.

4. Ibid., pp. 48–49.

5. *Delhi Mission News,* October 1909.

6. 22nd Report of the Cambridge Committee, 1909.

7. There is a discrepancy about the number of persons interested in joining the Brotherhood. The *Mission News* of August 1909 incorrectly reported that four Englishmen had joined the Brotherhood. Apart from Western and Branch, Sellers of London wanted to join the Brotherhood but did not do so finally.

8. William Branch to P. Ireland Jones, 27 November 1909, Letter No. 329, CMS Archives.

9. Resolution proposed by Stokes at the Himalaya District Mission Council, 9 April 1909. Precis 5:204, 1909, CMS Archives.

10. G. B. Durrant to P. Ireland Jones, 31 January 1908, Letter-book, 1907–1910, p. 151, CMS Archives.

11. Stokes to P. Ireland Jones, 5 April 1910, Letter No. 157 O, CMS Archives.

12. P. Ireland Jones to G. B. Durrant, 5 November 1908, Letter No. 169 O, CMS Archives.

13. Resolution proposed by Stokes, Precis 5:204, 1909.

14. Ibid.

15. *Delhi Mission News,* July 1909.

16. Stokes' appeal for funds dated 3 February 1910, Hosten Papers, Vidyajyoti Library, Delhi, Vol. 38, pp. 518–24.

17. Ibid.

18. Ibid.

19. Florence S. to Stokes, 17 and 24 May 1910.

20. P. Ireland Jones to G. B. Durrant, 15 March 1910, Letter No. 133 O, CMS Archives.

21. Stokes to P. Ireland Jones, 5 April 1910.

22. Florence S. to Stokes, 6 September 1910.

23. C. F. Andrews, *What I Owe to Christ,* p. 170.

24. C. F. Andrews to Bishop Montgomery, 27 October 1911, Lahore Letters received CLR-40, Vol. 5, p. 18, USPG Archives.

25. Florence S. to Stokes, 6 May 1910.

26. F. J. Western to H. Hosten, 23 May 1923, Rule of the Brotherhood, Hosten Papers.

27. *King's Messengers,* January and April 1909. Preface to *Arjun, The Story of an Indian Boy.*

28. World Missionary Conference, 1910. *Report of Commission IV, The Missionary Message in Relation to Non-Christian Religions* (Oliphant, Andersen and Ferrier), pp. 313–14.

29. W. H. T. Gairdner, *Edinburgh 1910: An Account and Interpretation of the World Missionary Conference.* Published for the Committee of the World Missionary Conference by Oliphant, Anderson and Ferrier, 1910, p. 223.

30. Florence S. to Stokes, 21 January 1910.

31. Florence S. to Stokes, 3 July 1910 and 7 May 1911.

6. ALTERNATE PATH

1. S. K. Rudra to F. J. Western, 20 August 1910, Stokes Papers.

2. H. F. Beutel to P. Ireland Jones, 8 August 1910, Letter No. 325 O; C. F. Hall to H. E. Fox, 2 August 1910, Letter No. 325 O, CMS Archives.

3. Rudra to Western, 20 August 1910.

4. C. F. Andrews, *What I Owe to Christ,* p. 163. Also C. F. Hall to H. E. Fox, 2 August 1910.

5. M. Grime to P. Ireland Jones, 4 August 1910, Letter No. 325 O, CMS Archives.

6. Interview with Sham Sukh.

7. C. F. Andrews, *What I Owe to Christ,* p. 163.

8. Stokes to Florence S., 25 August 1910.

9. *The Mission Field,* December 1910.

10. Stokes to Florence S., 25 August 1910.

11. Account of event by Sham Sukh of Shatla village, Kotgarh, who was then studying in the sixth class and was himself taken out of the school and sent to study in Rampur. Also Mission Field of November and December 1910.

12. Interview with Sham Sukh.

13. Florence S. to Stokes, 25 April 1910.

14. Florence S. to Stokes, 18 June 1911.

15. G. B. Durrant to P. Ireland Jones, 28 October 1910, Letter-book, 1910–1913, p. 48.

16. Florence S. to Stokes, 13 June and 3 July 1910.

17. Florence S. to Stokes, 21 January, 3 May, and 10 October 1910.

18. Florence S. to Stokes, 10 October 1910.

19. *New York Times,* 6 January 1911.

20. Ibid.

21. Ibid.

22. Stokes to C. Bardsley, 28 August 1911, Appendix to *The Love of God.*

23. E. F. Wigram to G. B. Durrant, 16 March 1911, Letter No. 152 O, CMS Archives.

24. C. F. Andrews to Wigram, 2 June 1911, Letter No. 152 O, CMS Archives.

25. Stokes to Wigram, 10 June 1911, Letter No. 185 O, CMS Archives.

26. F. J. Western to Wigram, 10 June 1911, Letter No. 185 O, CMS Archives.

27. C. F. Andrews to Wigram, 2 June 1911, Letter No. 152 O, CMS Archives.

7. AN INNER STRUGGLE

1. C. F. Andrews, *What I Owe to Christ,* p. 171.

2. C. F. Andrews in *Evening Ledger,* Philadelphia, 3 July 1922.

3. Stokes to Florence S., quoted in Stokes' letter to F. J. Western, Appendix, *The Love of God.*

4. *The Tribune,* 16 June 1921.

5. Stokes to F. J. Western, n.d., Appendix, *The Love of God.*

6. "The Pan-Anglican Congress—Summary of the Sectional Debates with Notes and Comments," The *Church Times,* 26 June, 1908. Bishop Montgomery's paper, p. 893; USPG, x-series 1327, SPG Archives.

7. C. F. Andrews, "Race with the Christian Church," *The East and the West,* vol. 8, July 1910.

8. Stokes to A. W. Nott, 16 February 1911 in Note to the 4th edition of *The Love of God.*

9. Stokes to C. Bardsley, 28 August 1911, Appendix, *The Love of God.*

10. Florence S. to Stokes, 11 May and 18 June 1911.

11. Florence S. to Stokes, 16 May 1911.

12. Stokes to C. Bardsley, 28 August 1911, Appendix, *The Love of God.*

13. Stokes to F. J. Western, 1911, n.d., Appendix, *The Love of God.*

14. Stokes to Agnes, personal notes, Stokes Papers.

15. C. F. Andrews, *What I Owe to Christ,* p. 172.

16. Ibid.

17. C. F. Andrews, *Evening Ledger,* Philadelphia, 3 July 1922.

18. C. F. Andrews, *What I Owe to Christ,* p. 177.

19. C. F. Andrews to Mahatma Munshi Ram, 11 June (probably of 1913), Benarsi Das Chaturvedi Papers, Acc. No. 315, National Archives.

20. Stokes to F. J. Western, 1911, n.d., *The Love of God.*

21. Stokes to C. Bardsley, 28 August 1911, *The Love of God.*

22. Ibid.

23. Preparatory Paper for Commission I, World Missionary Conference Edinburgh

1910 as quoted in *C.F. Andrews, The Development of His Thought, 1904–14.* Ph.D. thesis, 1981, D. O'Connor, p. 220.

24. C. F. Andrews, *What I Owe to Christ,* p. 173.

25. Davidson to Bishop Lefroy, 26 March 1912, Lahore Letters Received, CLR 40, Vol. 5, p. 35, SPG Archives.

26. Florence S. to Stokes, 7 November 1911.

27. E. W. Biscoe to Stokes, 23 October 1911, Stokes Papers.

28. As quoted in Florence Stokes to Stokes, 1 October 1912.

29. B. K. Cunningham to Stokes, 6 October 1911, Stokes Papers.

30. W. E. S. Holland to Stokes, 21 December 1911, Stokes Papers.

31. W. Henderson of Christian College, Madras, to Stokes, 20 September 1912, Stokes Papers.

32. Arthur W. Davies to Stokes, 17 October 1911 and Arthur Sunkesles to Stokes, 23 October 1911, Stokes Papers.

33. Bihari Lal to Florence Stokes, 30 October 1911, Stokes Papers.

34. S. K. Rudra to Stokes, 24 October 1911, Stokes Papers.

35. C. F. Andrews to Bishop Montgomery, 27 October 1911, Lahore Letters Received CLR-40, Vol. 5, p. 18, SPG Archives.

36. C. F. Andrews to Bishop Montgomery, 27 October 1911.

37. Davidson to Bishop Lefroy, 26 March 1912.

38. F. J. Western to Hosten, 23 May 1925, Hosten Papers.

39. B. Chaturvedi and M. Sykes, *Charles Freer Andrews—A Narrative* (London: George Allen and Unwin Ltd., 1949), p. 74.

40. C. F. Andrews, *What I Owe to Christ,* p. 179.

41. C. F. Andrews to E. S. Talbot, Bishop of Winchester, undated but of mid-1914.

42. C. F. Andrews, *What I Owe to Christ,* pp. 171, 176.

43. C. F. Andrews to E. S. Talbot, undated but of mid-1914.

44. Stokes to Agnes, personal notes of 1921.

45. Marshall Truitt Jr. to Florence S., n.d., but of 1928.

46. Proceedings of the Punjab Central Mission Council, 29 September 1911; Precis 1911, pp. 273, clxxx. CMS Archives.

47. F. J. Western to Stokes, 2 February 1912, Stokes Papers.

48. C. F. Andrews to Stokes, 21 July 1912.

49. F. J. Western to Stokes, 2 February 1912.

50. Sudhir Rudra to Stokes, 11 February 1912.

8. HOME AT LAST—A FAMILY MAN

1. Interview with Savitri Devi, daughter of Stokes.

2. Interview with Rupi Paul, one of Stokes' adopted children.

3. Florence S. to Stokes, 27 August and 18 September 1911.

4. Florence S. to Stokes, 24 September 1911.

5. Florence S. to Stokes, 13 July 1911.

6. Florence S. to Stokes, 24 September 1911.

7. Florence S. to Stokes, 30 October 1911.

8. Florence S. to Stokes, 24 September 1911.

9. Copy of Sale Deed, 6 February 1912, Stokes Papers; Final Settlement Report of the Simla District 1915–16.

10. Florence S. to Stokes, 26 August 1912.

11. Florence S. to C. F. Andrews, 11 August 1926, Stokes Papers.

12. Florence S. to Stokes, 26 May 1912.

13. Florence S. to Stokes, 14 September 1913.

14. Stokes to Florence S., 5 June 1912.

15. Stokes to Florence S., June 1912, n.d.

16. Ibid.

17. Stokes to Florence S., 17 July 1912.

18. C. F. Andrews to Stokes, 12 July 1912, Stokes Papers.

19. Florence S. to Stokes, 16 September 1912.

20. Stokes to Florence S., 3 September 1912.

21. Ibid.

22. Stokes to Florence S., 27 December 1912.

23. Elizabeth Wistar to Florence S., 1 January 1913, Stokes Papers.

24. Stokes to Florence S., January 1913, undated.

25. Stokes to Florence S., 20 August 1913.

26. Stokes, "The India of the Future," Collected Essays, Memoranda and Letters.

27. Stokes to Florence S., 28 January 1914.

28. Stokes to Florence S., 18 December 1913.

29. Stokes to Florence S., 15 January 1914.

30. W. A. Kelk to Stokes, 10 September 1928, Stokes Papers.

31. *Philadelphia Record,* 9 April 1914; *North America,* 9 April 1914; *The Germantown Guide,* 11 April 1914.

32. Warrington Stokes to Florence Coleman, 2 June 1963, Stokes Papers.

33. Stokes, *Stokes of Harmony Hall and Some Allied Ancestry,* Introduction, 21 September 1923.

34. Stokes to descendants of Dr. Hinchman Stokes I and Nancy Stokes, 21 May 1916, Stokes Papers.

35. Stokes to Florence S., 3 November 1915.

36. Stokes to Florence S., 27 November 1915.

37. Agnes to Florence S., 14 March 1916.

38. Stokes, *Letters of Nancy Evans Stokes,* 1916, private publication, p. 12.

39. Stokes to Florence S., 24 July 1917.

40. Stokes to Florence S., 16 December 1923.

9. WAR ON TWO FRONTS

1. Stokes to Florence S., 9 May 1916 and 12 September 1917.

2. Stokes to Florence S., 10, 17 April and 7 May 1917.

3. Stokes to Florence S., 7 May 1917.

4. Stokes to Agnes, 25 October and 8 November 1917.

5. Stokes to Florence S., 21 February 1919.

6. Stokes to Florence S. 19 March 1919.

7. Stokes to Florence S., 21 February 1919.

8. Stokes, "Unsatisfactory Peace," Collected Essays, Memoranda and Letters.

9. Stokes, "The Rowlatt Bills," Collected Essays, Memoranda and Letters.

10. Ibid.

11. Stokes to Florence S., 5 June 1919.

12. 24 February 1919.

13. R. C. Majumdar, H. C. Raychaudhuri, and Kalikinkar Datta, *An Advanced History of India,* 3rd ed. (Macmillan, 1967), p. 981.

14. Stokes to Florence S., 5 June 1919.

15. Stokes, "The Situation in the Punjab, Duty of Government and Englishmen," *National Self-Realisation* (Madras: S. Ganesan, 1921), pp. 37, 41.

16. Stokes, "Letter to Sir Michael Francis O'Dwyer," 3 May 1919. Also Note to the above in Collected Essays, Memoranda and Letters.

17. The *Modern Review,* October 1921.

18. Stokes to Florence S., 4 September 1919.

19. Stokes to Florence S., 5 June 1919.

20. Ibid.

21. Ibid.

22. Stokes, Postscript to "The Rowlatt Bills," Collected Essays, Memoranda and Letters.

23. Stokes, Note to "Some Thoughts on the Yellow Peril," Collected Essays, Memoranda and Letters.

24. Stokes to Florence S., 5 June 1919. Mandates—a system of international supervision of colonial areas. The peace treaty provided for a mandatory surrender of subjects' territories by the vanquished nations to the victor. The Intimate Papers of Colonel House, Vol. 4, "The Ending of the War," June 1918–Nov. 1919 (London: Earnest Berm, 1928), pp. 299, 505–506.

25. Stokes to Florence S., 5 June 1919.

26. Stokes to C. F. Andrews, 16 August, n.d. but of 1920, Benarsi Das Chaturvedi Papers, National Archives.

27. Stokes to Florence S., 28 January 1914.

28. Stokes to Florence S., 21 August 1920.

10. FOR THE RIGHTS OF MEN—BEGAR

1. C. F. Andrews, *The Tribune,* 19 February 1921.

2. Representation of the Agricultural Community of Kotgarh to Deputy Commissioner, Simla, 26 August 1920, Stokes Papers.

3. C. F. Andrews, *The Tribune,* 19 February 1921.

4. Representation of 26 August 1920.

5. Ibid.

6. Tract submitted by William Edwards, 1850, Final Report of the First Regular Settlement of the Simla District in the Punjab, 1881–83, Lt.-Col. E. G. Wace, Calcutta, 1884.

7. Pamela Kanwar, *Imperial Simla* (Oxford University Press, 1990), pp. 29–30.

8. Stokes to H. P. Tollinton, 16 April 1919, Stokes Papers.

9. Stokes to H. P. Tollinton, 8 May 1919.

10. Lt. Col. A. Elliot to Stokes, 10 April 1920, Stokes Papers.

11. Stokes to H. P. Tollinton, 8 May 1919 and 7 March 1921, Stokes Papers.

12. Stokes to Florence S., 15 October 1921.

13. Representation of 26 August 1920.

14. Stokes to Lt. Col. A. Elliot, 1 September 1920, Stokes Papers.

15. Stokes to H. M. Cowan, Deputy Commissioner, Simla, 10 October 1920.

16. Ibid.

17. Stokes to Florence S., 30 October 1921.

18. S. E. Stokes, "The Viceregal Trip to Baghi," Editors Note, Collected Essays, Memoranda and Letters.

19. C. F. Andrews, "Forced Labour in the Hills," *The Modern Review*, December 1920.

20. C. F. Andrews, *The Tribune*, 8 and 19 February 1921.

21. As quoted in Hugh Tinker, *The Ordeal of Love* (Delhi: Oxford University Press, 1979), p. 172.

22. Benarsi Das Chaturvedi and Marjorie Sykes, *Charles Freer Andrews, A Narrative* (George Allen and Unwin, 1949), p. 159.

23. C. F. Andrews, *The Tribune*, 19 February 1921.

24. C. F. Andrews to W.W. Pearson, 12 November 1921 as quoted in Chaturvedi and Sykes, *Charles Freer Andrews*, p. 159.

25. C. F. Andrews, "Forced Labour in the Hills," *The Modern Review*, December 1920.

26. C. F. Andrews, *The Tribune*, 24 February 1921.

27. C. F. Andrews, *The Tribune*, 8 February 1921.

11. JOINING THE FREEDOM STRUGGLE

1. Stokes to C. F. Andrews, 16 August (year unmarked but of 1920) Benarsi Das Chaturvedi Papers, National Archives, Acc. No. 315.

2. Ibid.

3. C. F. Andrews in Introduction to Stokes', "Failure of European Civilization as a World Culture," 1921; P. C. Roy Chaudhury, *C.F. Andrews, His Life and Times* (Bombay: Somaiya Publications, 1971), p. 6.

4. Stokes to Florence S., 23 November 1920.

5. Ibid.

6. Stokes, "National Self-Realization," Collected Essays, Memoranda and Letters; *The Bombay Chronicle*, 7, 9 and 15 December 1920.

7. Ibid.

8. Ibid.

9. Ibid.

10. Stokes to Florence S., 13 December 1920.

11. Ibid.

12. Gandhi on Congress Resolution as quoted in *The Ordeal of Love*, pp. 172–73.

13. Stokes to Florence S., 5 March 1921.

14. C. F. Andrews, "Modern Slavery in Rajputana," *The Tribune*, 24 April 1921.

15. *The Modern Review*, August 1921.

16. Stokes to Florence S., 5 March 1921.

17. "In a State of Suspense," *The Indian Social Reformer*, 22 May 1921.

18. Stokes to Florence S., June 1921, n.d.

12. THE FIGHT CONTINUES

1. Stokes to M. S. Williamson, 7 March 1921, Stokes Papers.

2. Stokes to A. Langley, 8 March 1921, Stokes Papers.

3. Stokes to M. S. Williamson, 7 March 1921.

4. Stokes to Florence S., 5 March 1921.

5. Stokes to Florence S., 5 June 1921.

6. Stokes' Note on "Forced Labour in the Hills," Collected Essays, Memoranda and Letters.

7. M. S. Williamson to Stokes, 19 April 1921, Stokes Papers.

8. Stokes to M. S. Williamson, 28 April 1921, Stokes Papers.

9. Stokes to J. D. Boyd, 28 May 1921, Stokes Papers.

10. Stokes, "Oppression in the Simla Hills," *The Tribune*, 24 November 1921.

11. Stokes to Florence S., 1 July 1921.

12. C. F. Andrews, "Letters on Non-cooperation, IV," *The Leader*, 22 August 1921.

13. Stokes, "Begar in Simla Hills," *The Tribune*, 23 July 1921.

14. Stokes to Agnes, 12 July 1921.

15. *The Tribune*, 23 July 1921; also Stokes to Agnes, 12 July 1921.

16. Stokes to Agnes, 12 July 1921.

17. Stokes to Florence S., 1 July 1921.

18. Stokes to Florence S., 1 July 1921.

19. *The Tribune*, 29 June 1921.

20. *The Tribune*, 2 July 1921.

21. *The Tribune*, 13 July 1921.

22. Ibid.

23. Gandhi to Stokes, 16 July 1921, Stokes Papers.

24. *The Leader*, 18 August 1921.

25. Stokes to Florence S., 1 July 1921.

26. Stokes to Agnes, 2 July 1921.

27. *Young India*, 21 July 1921.

28. *The Bombay Chronicle*, 27 July 1921.

29. *The Tribune*, 25 August 1921.

30. The *Modern Review*, September 1921.

31. The *Modern Review*, December 1920.

32. Stokes to Florence S., 3 September 1921.

13. IN KHADI

1. Gandhi to C. F. Andrews, 13 August 1921, *Collected Works*, XX, p. 499.

2. Stokes to Agnes, 1 August 1921.

3. *The Tribune*, 7 August 1921.

4. *The Tribune*, 10 August, 1921.

5. *The Tribune*, 11 August, 1921.

6. *The Leader*, 14 August 1921.

7. *The Tribune*, 12 August, 1921; Gandhi to C. F. Andrews, 13 August 1921.

8. *The Tribune*, 19 August 1921.

9. Ibid.

10. *The Tribune*, 17 August 1921.

11. *The Tribune*, 19 August 1921.

12. Interview with Fazl-ud-Din Ali.

13. Stokes to Agnes, 1 August 1921; Stokes to Florence S., 13 August 1921.

14. Stokes, "Unity Our Supreme Duty," *The Tribune*, 21 August 1921.

15. Ibid.

16. *The Leader*, 14 August 1921.

17. Stokes, "Unity Our Supreme Duty."

18. *The Tribune*, 16 September 1921.

19. *The Tribune*, 11 September 1921.

14. FOLLOWING THE NATIONAL TRAIL

1. Stokes to Florence S., 21 September 1921.

2. Stokes to Florence S., 1 August 1921.

3. Stokes to Florence S., 21 September 1921.

4. Stokes to Agnes, 3 September 1921.

5. Gandhi to Stokes, 20 September 1921, Stokes Papers. Also Gandhi, "Circular Letter," 20 September 1921, *Collected Works*, XXI, p. 138.

6. "A Manifesto," *Young India*, 6 October 1921, *Collected Works*, XXI, p. 235.

7. Home Political, Telegram No. 1021, dated 9 October 1921, Simla Records 4, File 303/1921, National Archives.

8. Home Political, File 303/1921.

9. W. K. Waddell to Stokes, 5 June 1911, Stokes Papers.

10. Home Political, Appendix to Notes, p. 31. W. M. Beach, 7 October 1910. Home Political Simla Records 4, File 303/1921.

11. *The Tribune*, 24 June 1921.

12. Home Political, report by S. P. O'Donnell, 6 October 1921, Simla Records 4, File 303/1921.

13. Stokes to Florence S., 30 October 1921.

14. *The Tribune*, 6 and 8 November 1921.

15. Stokes to Florence S., 30 October 1921.

16. Stokes to Florence S., 25 February 1924.

17. Stokes to Florence S., 30 October 1921.

18. Stokes to C. F. Andrews, 21 October 1921, Collected Essays, Memoranda and Letters.

19. Stokes to Agnes, 19 October 1921.

15. ARREST AND TRIAL

1. Stokes, "The Acid Test of Loyalty," November 1921, Collected Essays, Memoranda and Letters.

2. Ibid.

3. Nehru, *An Autobiography* (Allied Publishers), p. 79.

4. Home Political, Delhi Records 2 and 3, File 18/1921.

5. *The Tribune*, 4 December 1921.

6. *The Tribune*, 8 December 1921.

7. Home Political, Telegram No. 30285-J, dated 3 December 1921, File 459/1921. *The Tribune*, 4 December 1921.

8. *The Tribune*, 8 and 9 December 1921.

9. Gandhi, "Reward of Adoption," *Young India*, 8 December 1921, *The Tribune*, 14 December 1921.

10. C. F. Andrews to Benarsi Das Chaturvedi, 11 December 1921, Benarsi Das Chaturvedi Papers.

11. During December and January about 30,000 people were sentenced to prison because of their involvement with the non-cooperation movement. Nehru, *An Autobiography,* p. 81.

12. Gandhi, "Has Das Been Arrested?" *Navjivan,* 11 December 1921, *Collected Works,* 1921–22, XXI, pp. 564–65.

13. Gandhi, Notes, "In the Absence of a President," *Young India,* 15 December 1921, *Collected Works,* XXII, pp. 7–8.

14. "Whither Are We Drifting?" *Searchlight,* Patna, 9 December 1921.

15. Dhan Singh to Agnes, 5 December 1921, Stokes Papers.

16. Stokes to Florence S., 2 December 1921.

17. Gandhi, "A Wife's Faith," *Young India,* 9 March 1922, *Collected Works,* XXIII, p. 53.

18. Dhan Singh to Agnes, 5 December 1921, Stokes Papers.

19. *The Tribune,* 8 December 1921.

20. Stokes to Florence S., 5 December 1921.

21. Stokes to Florence S., 9 December 1921.

22. *The Tribune,* 10 December 1921.

23. *The Tribune,* 17 December 1921.

24. "Statement of S.E. Stokes of Kotgarh," *The Tribune,* 17 December 1921.

25. *The Tribune,* 23 December 1921.

26. Ibid.

27. Lala Duni Chand to Florence S., 10 December 1921.

28. Florence S. to Agnes, 27 January 1922.

29. Florence S. to Agnes, 28 February, 9 and 19 April 1922.

30. Florence S. to Agnes, 9 April 1922.

31. Florence S. to Agnes, 28 February 1922.

16. GUEST OF THE BRITISH EMPIRE

1. Stokes to Florence S., 3 January 1922.

2. Ibid.

3. C. W. Gough to Agnes, 14 January 1922, Stokes Papers.

4. Gandhi to Stokes, 1 March 1924, Collected Essays, Memoranda and Letters; Stokes to Gandhi, 24 February 1924, National Gandhi Museum and Library, SN 8371.

5. Gandhi to Agnes, 4 March 1922, Stokes Papers.

6. *The Modern Review,* January 1922; Maulana Abul Kalam Azad, *India Wins Freedom* (Orient Longman, 1988), p. 11.

7. Algoo Ram Shastri, *Lala Lajpat Rai,* Lok Sewa Mandal, 1957, p. 384. The visitor was S. Nihal Singh of the *Literary Digest.*

8. Gandhi to Agnes, 4 March 1922, Stokes Papers.

9. Gandhi, *Young India,* 9 March 1922, *Collected Works,* XXIII, p. 53.

10. Stokes to Gandhi, 18 January 1922, S.N. 7804.

11. Ibid.

12. Stokes to Florence S., 3 May 1922.

13. C. F. Andrews to Florence S., 8 August 1922, Stokes Papers.

14. Stokes to Florence S., 3 May 1922.

15. Ibid.

16. Ibid.

17. Stokes to Florence S., 29 May 1922.

18. Stokes to Florence S. 13 June 1922.

19. Stokes to Florence S., 28 November 1922.

20. Report of the All India Congress and the Central Khilafat Committee at Lucknow, June 1922, Home Political, File 941/1922, National Archives.

21. Home Political File 914/1922 NAI; Khushwant Singh, *A History of the Sikhs,* vol. 2 (Princeton University Press, 1966), p. 204.

22. Stokes, Note to Memorandum submitted to the All India Congress Committee at its Calcutta session in November 1922, Collected Essays, Memoranda and Letters.

23. Ibid.

24. Ibid.

25. Stokes to Florence S., 8 November 1922.

26. C. F. Andrews to Florence S., 8 August 1922, Stokes Papers.

27. *The Tribune,* 26 November 1922.

28. Stokes to Florence S., 28 November 1922.

29. *The Tribune,* 29 November 1922.

30. Stokes to the Editor, *The Tribune,* 16 December 1922.

31. Stokes, "What Is Non-cooperation?," Collected Essays, Memoranda and Letters.

32. Stokes to Florence S., January 1923, undated.

33. Stokes, Confidential Memorandum to Pandit Motilal Nehru, 2 February 1923, Collected Essays, Memorandum and Letters.

34. Ibid.

17. DEBATES WITH GANDHI—TEST OF FRIENDSHIP

1. Stokes, "The Spinning Franchise, Introductory Note," Collected Essays, Memoranda and Letters.

2. Stokes to Gandhi, 24 February 1924, National Gandhi Museum and Library, SN 8371.

3. Ibid.

4. Gandhi to Stokes, 1 March 1924, Collected Essays, Memoranda and Letters.

5. Gandhi to Stokes, 18 March 1924, Collected Essays, Memoranda and Letters.

6. Ibid.

7. Stokes to Gandhi, 25 March 1924, National Gandhi Museum and Library, SN 8581.

8. Gandhi to Stokes, 18 March 1924, Collected Essays, Memoranda and Letters.

9. Stokes to Gandhi, 25 March 1924.

10. Ibid.

11. Ibid.

12. Stokes to C. F. Andrews, undated letter of October 1924, Collected Essays, Memorandum and Letters.

13. Stokes to Gandhi, 25 November 1924, Gandhi Museum and Library, SN 11738.

14. Stokes to Andrews, October 1924.

15. Gandhi, "Is It Compulsion?," *Young India,* 13 November 1924, *Collected Works,* XXV, pp. 316–317.

16. Stokes to C. F. Andrews, 23 October 1924. "On the Unity Conference and the proposal for a Spinning Franchise," Collected Essays, Memoranda and Letters, Nehru, *An Autobiography,* p. 126.

17. Gandhi, "Not Even Half-Mast," *Young India,* 4 December 1924, *Collected Works,* XXV, p. 391.

18. Stokes to Gandhi, 25 November 1924.

19. Stokes to Florence S., 13 August 1921.

20. Stokes to his cousin Eliza Nicholson in America, 30 April 1924, Stokes Papers.

21. Stokes to Florence S., 30 October 1921.

22. Stokes to Gandhi, 25 March 1924.

23. Gandhi to R. B. Gregg, 27 November, 1926, *Collected Works,* XXXII, pp. 377–378.

24. Stokes to Eliza Nicholson, 30 April 1924.

25. Stokes to Gandhi, 24 February 1924.

26. Ibid.

27. Stokes to Gandhi, 28 February 1924, National Gandhi Museum and Library, SN 8386.

28. Stokes to Gandhi, 7 March 1924, National Gandhi Museum and Library, S.N. 8458.

29. Gandhi to R. B. Gregg, 2 October 1926, *Collected Works,* XXXI, p. 469.

30. Interview with Champavati.

31. Stokes to Gandhi, 10 February 1924, National Gandhi Museum and Library, SL 8315.

32. Gandhi to Stokes, 1 March 1924, Collected Essays, Memoranda and Letters.

33. Gandhi to Stokes, 1 September 1926, *Collected Works,* XXXI, p. 343.

34. Stokes to Gandhi, 25 November 1924.

35. Gandhi, "A Gospel of Hate," *Young India,* 29 December 1920, *Collected Works,* XIX, p. 172.

36. Gandhi, "The Shadow of Simla," *Young India,* 21 July 1921, *Collected Works,* XX, p. 408.

37. Gandhi, "English Learning," *Young India,* 1 June 1921, *Collected Works,* XX, p. 158.

38. Gandhi, "Speech at Indian Majlis," 1 November 1931, *Collected Works,* XLVIII, p. 265.

39. Gandhi to Mahadev Desai, 28 June 1929, *Collected Works,* 1929, p. 132.

40. Gandhi to Stokes, 8 June 1939, *Collected Works,* LXIX, p. 332.

41. Gandhi to M. R. Jayakar, 23 March 1932, *Collected Works,* XLIX, p. 230.

42. Gandhi to Stokes, 15 December 1939; *Harijan,* 23 December 1939, Collected Essays, Memoranda and Letters.

18. JOHNNY APPLESEED OF THE HIMALAYAS

1. Interview with Mahavir Singha, Kotgarh.

2. Stokes, "The Kotgarh Orcharding Situation," Stokes Papers.

3. Florence S. to Stokes, 6 March, 15 June and 7 July 1921.

4. Florence S. to Stokes, 20 October 1921.

5. Florence S. to Stokes, 7 July 1921.

6. Stokes to Florence S., 31 August and 8 September 1926.

7. Stokes to Florence S., 6 August 1924.

8. Stokes to Florence S., 31 August 1926.

9. Stokes to Florence S., 27 July, 31 August, and 1 November 1927.

10. Stokes to Florence S., 27 July 1927.

11. Stokes to Florence S., 27 July, 8 September, and 19 October 1927.

12. Stokes to Florence S., 17 December 1928.

13. Stokes to Florence S., October 1927, undated.

14. Interview with Ram Dayal Singha of Kotgarh and with Fazl-ud-Din Ali.

15. Kusum Nair, *Blossoms in the Dust, The Human Factor in Indian Development* (New York: Frederick A. Praeger, 1962), p. 166.

16. "Fruit Growers in Simla Hills," *Civil and Military Gazette,* 25 September 1937.

17. A plea for adequate transport facilities by the Fruit Growers' Association, Kotgarh, 1938, Stokes Papers.

18. Stokes to Florence S., 27 June 1928.

19. S. E. Stokes to K. V. F. Morton, Deputy Commissioner Simla, 15 February 1937, Stokes Papers.

20. Stokes to Florence S., 12 July 1928.

19. A SCHOOL IN MY GARDEN

1. Stokes to Florence S., 27 March, 13 November 1923, and 24 March 1924.

2. Stokes to Florence S., 10 March 1924.

3. Stokes to Florence S., 6 May 1925.

4. Stokes to Florence S., 1 December 1924.

5. Richard B. Gregg to Florence S., June 1926, Stokes Papers.

6. Interview with Fazl-ud-Din Ali.

7. Richard Gregg to Florence S., 11 July 1925, Stokes Papers.

8. Interview Fazl-ud-Din Ali.

9. Stokes to Florence S., 26 May 1926 and 10 August 1927.

10. Stokes to Florence S., 13 November 1923.

11. Stokes to Florence S., 24 March 1924.

12. Stokes to Florence S., 13 November 1923.

13. Stokes to Florence S., 7 September 1925.

14. Interview with Fazl-ud-Din Ali.

15. Interview with Prem Chand Stokes, Stokes to Florence S., 7 September 1925 and 26 May 1926.

16. Ram Dayal Singha, Notes on S. E. Stokes, Stokes Papers.

17. Gandhi to Stokes, 1 September 1926, *Collected Works,* XXXI, p. 343. Also Gandhi to V. Sundaram, 6 June 1926, *Collected Works,* XXX, p. 543.

18. *The Tribune,* 8 June 1921.

19. Gandhi to Richard B. Gregg 23 May 1926, *Collected Works,* XXX, p. 472.

20. Stokes to Florence S., 16 June 1925.

21. Stokes to Florence S., 27 January 1927.

22. Stokes to Florence S., 27 March 1923.

23. Stokes to Florence S., 22 November 1926.

24. Stokes to Florence S., 4 March 1928.

25. Ibid.

26. Stokes to Florence S., 22 June 1927.

27. Stokes to Florence S., 4 March 1928.

28. Stokes to Florence S., 12 September 1923.

29. Stokes to Florence S., 6 May 1925 and interview with Prem Chand Stokes.

30. Richard B. Gregg to Florence S., 11 July 1925.

31. Stokes to Florence S., 7 September 1925.

32. Interview with Fazl-ud-Din Ali.

33. Richard B. Gregg to Gandhi, 14 May 1926, National Gandhi Museum and Library, S.N. 10728.

34. Stokes, *Background of History,* Manuscript, p. 1; Stokes to Florence S., November 1926, undated.

35. Richard B. Gregg to Gandhi as quoted by Gandhi in his Notes, "Indian Textbooks," *Young India,* 16 September 1926, *Collected Works,* XXXI, p. 409.

36. Richard B. Gregg to Florence S., June 1926, Stokes Papers.

37. Stokes to Florence S., 19 August 1925.

38. Account with Prof. Khub Ram 1926, Stokes Papers.

39. Interview with Fazl-ud-Din Ali; School accounts 1926, Stokes Papers.

40. Stokes to Florence S., 17 August 1927.

41. Gandhi to Richard B. Gregg, 23 May 1926, *Collected Works,* XXX, p. 472.

42. Stokes to Florence S., 21 February 1928.

43. Stokes to Florence S., 31 August 1927.

44. Stokes to Florence Stokes, 31 August 1927.

45. Stokes, *The Traditions and Ideals of Our Family,* Stokes Papers.

46. Florence S. to Stokes, 12 January 1927.

47. Florence S. to Stokes, 5 January 1927.

48. Florence S. to Stokes, 22 October 1927.

49. Florence S. to Stokes, 9 October 1927.

50. Stokes, *The Traditions and Ideals of Our Family;* Stokes, *The Love of God,* 1908, Dedication.

20. CAME TO TEACH AND STAYED TO LEARN

1. Stokes, Pamphlet on *Arya Samaj,* n.d., Stokes Papers.

2. Ibid.

3. *The Tribune,* 5 December 1907.

4. *Vedic Review,* April 1921 as quoted in *The Indian Social Reformer,* June 1921.

5. Stokes, "Church Unity," *National Self-Realisation,* S. Ganesan 1921, Madras, pp. 84–85.

6. Ibid.

7. C. F. Andrews, "Race Within the Christian Church," *The East and the West,* Vol. 8, July 1910.

8. Stokes, "Church Unity," *National Self-Realisation.*

9. Stokes to Florence S., 3 January 1920.

10. Ibid.

11. Stokes to Florence S., 7 August 1920.

12. Hervey De Witt Griswold, *Studies in Religion and Culture, Insight into Modern Hinduism* (New York: Henry Holt and Co., 1934), p. 172, footnote.

13. Stokes, *Introductory Note on Advaita,* Stokes Papers.

14. Stokes to Florence S., October 1906, n.d.

15. Stokes to Florence S., n.d. but of early 1909.

16. Stokes, "The Problems of Christianity in India," *National Self-Realisation,* 1921, pp. 111–12.

17. Stokes to C. F. Andrews, 16 August, n.d. but of 1920, Benarsi Das Chaturvedi Papers.

18. Stokes, Foreword to *Satyakama,* S. Ganesan, Madras, 1931.

19. Stokes to Florence S., 27 November 1923.

20. Stokes to Florence S., 3 February 1924.

21. Stokes to Florence S., 8 July 1924.

22. Stokes to Florence S., 1 July 1924.

23. Stokes to Florence S., 23 July 1924.

24. Stokes to Florence S., 4 October 1924.

25. Stokes to Florence S., 19 September 1928.

26. Stokes to Florence S., 26 November 1928.

27. Stokes to Florence S., 17 December, 25 September and 26 November 1928.

28. Stokes to Gandhi, 10 February 1924, National Gandhi Museum and Library, S.N. 8315.

29. Stokes to Florence S., 25 September 1928.

30. Stokes to Agnes, 1932, n.d.

31. Stokes to Florence S., 27 November 1923, and 20 October 1926.

32. Richard B. Gregg to Florence S., 11 July 1925.

33. S. E. Stokes, Foreword to *Satyakama*.

34. Stokes to Florence S., 22 September 1926.

35. *The Modern Review*, May 1932.

36. Dr. S. Radhakrishnan to Stokes, 29 March 1932. Extracts from Letters.

37. Dr. S. Kuppuswami Sastri to Stokes, 26 September 1932. Extracts from Letters.

38. Stokes, *Introductory Note on Advaita*, Stokes Papers.

39. Dr. J. H. Muirhead to Stokes, 9 March 1932. Extracts from Letters.

40. Dr. L. Morgan to Stokes, 13 March 1932. Extracts from Letters.

41. Dr. A. E. Garvie to Stokes, 27 March 1932. Extracts from Letters.

42. *The Congregational Quarterly*, July 1932, X, no. 3.

43. Alfred E. Garvie, *The Christian Belief in God, in Relation to Religion and Philosophy* (London: Hodder and Stoughton, 1932).

44. Dr. H. R. Mackintosh to Stokes, 11 April 1936. Extracts from Letters.

45. Dr. W. G. De Burgh to Stokes, 2 May 1932. Extracts from Letters.

46. Dr. J. O. F. Murray to Stokes, 23 February 1932. Extracts from Letters.

47. Prof. J. B. Pratt to Stokes, 7 June 1933. Extracts from Letters.

48. J. B. Pratt, "Recent Developments in Indian Thought," *The Journal of Philosophy*, 14 September 1933.

49. Stokes to J. B. Pratt, 12 July 1933. Extracts from Letters.

50. Prof. Egerton's comments as quoted in Extracts from Letters.

51. Unnamed Reviewer. Extracts from Letters.

52. Excerpt from letter of Mrs. Roland Host, 19 July 1935, Stokes Papers.

21. SATYAKAMVADI

1. Stokes to Florence S., 16 June 1924.

2. Stokes to Bishop Chandu Lal, 17 July 1932. Extracts from Letters.

3. Stokes' personal letter of 7 December 1939 to K. Natarajan, editor of *The Indian Social Reformer*. The letter was published in June 1946, two weeks after Stokes' death, under the heading "Why Change Religion?"

4. Stokes to Florence S., 18 March 1924.

5. Stokes to Florence S., 21 May 1924.

6. Stokes to Florence S., 29 April 1924.

7. Stokes to Florence S., 3 February and 8 April 1924.

8. Stokes, "Why Change Religion?," *The Indian Social Reformer.*

9. Stokes to Chandu Lal, 17 July 1932.

10. Ibid.

11. Ibid.

12. Ibid.

13. Chandu Lal to Stokes, 9 August 1932. Extracts from Letters.

14. Stokes to Chandu Lal, 11 August 1932. Extracts from Letters.

15. *The Indian Social Reformer,* 17 September 1932.

16. "Mr Stokes' Declaration of Faith," *The Indian Social Reformer,* 8 October 1932.

17. Ibid.

18. "Conversion to Hinduism," *The Indian Social Reformer,* 29 October 1932.

19. Prof. J. B. Pratt, *Journal of Philosophy,* 14 September 1933, p. 312; Pratt to Stokes, 7 June 1933, Extracts from Letters.

20. Interview with Sham Sukh of Shatla village.

21. Civil Appeal in Courts Sub-ordinate to the High Court, 26 November 1935, Stokes Papers.

22. Decree of 20 September 1935, Stokes Papers.

23. Note on the Temple question, n.d., Stokes Papers.

24. Stokes to Chandu Lal, 17 July 1932. Extracts from Letters.

25. Interview with Ram Dayal Singha of Kotgarh.

26. Interview with Iris Jamila, daughter of Ada and Nasib Ali.

27. Stokes, *The Traditions and Ideals of Our Family,* pp. 150–53.

28. Interview with Agnes.

29. "Mr Stokes' Declaration of Faith," *The Indian Social Reformer,* 8 October 1932.

30. Stokes to Fazl-ud-Din Ali, 10 October 1935, Stokes Papers.

31. Stokes to Mahadev Desai, *Harijan,* 15 August 1936.

32. Stokes to Savitri, 7 April 1932, Stokes Papers.

33. *Harijan,* 18 July 1936.

34. Stokes to Mahadev Desai, *Harijan,* 15 August 1936.

35. Stokes to Fazl-ud-Din Ali, 4 February 1939, Stokes Papers.

36. Stokes to Milton Rubincam, 28 March 1939, Stokes Papers.

22. THE BURDENS INCREASE

1. Stokes' Note of 1935 with reference to his operation in Austria. Extracts from Letters.

2. Stokes to Agnes, 6 March 1935.

3. Interview with Champavati.

4. Stokes to Kirpa Ram Dang, 28 June 1938, Stokes Papers.

5. Stokes to Chand Mal, 1938, n.d., Stokes Papers.

6. Stokes to Deputy Commissioner, Simla, 15 November 1938, Stokes Papers.

7. G. M. Brander to Stokes, 8 May 1941, Stokes Papers.

8. Stokes to Kirpa Ram Dang, 28 June 1938, Stokes Papers.

9. Interview with Ram Dayal Singha.

10. Stokes to Agnes, 1 March 1935.

11. Stokes to G. M. Brander, 23 August 1939, Stokes Papers.

12. Stokes to Rup Krishan of Lahore, 18 February 1938. Rup Krishan's artist wife agreed to do the sketches for Stokes' book. Stokes Papers.

13. Stokes to Milton Rubincam, 13 August 1935, Stokes Papers.

14. Stokes to Rubincam, 17 April 1939, Stokes Papers.

15. Dr. Joseph Stokes to Stokes, 19 August 1942, Stokes Papers.

16. Stokes to Rubincam, 15 May 1942, Stokes Papers.

17. Stokes, Introduction to *Stokes of Harmony Hall and Some Allied Ancestry,* 21 September 1923, Stokes Papers.

18. Stokes, "Forenote," Harmony Hall Letters, 16 September 1942.

19. Stokes to Manmohan Nath, 3 February 1943, Stokes Papers.

20. Stokes to Registrar of Wills, 16 December 1937, Stokes Papers.

21. Stokes to Marshall Truitt, 4 January 1946, Stokes Papers.

22. Stokes to his sons, 24 February 1943, Stokes Papers.

23. The Last Will and Testament of Stokes, 23 February 1943, Stokes Papers.

24. Stokes to sons, 24 February 1943.

25. Ibid.

23. MARKETING THE FRUITS OF LABOR

1. Representation to H. W. Emmerson, Governor of Punjab, 26 September 1934, Stokes Papers.

2. Stokes to K. V. F. Morton, Simla, 15 February 1937, Stokes Papers.

3. Stokes to Pritam Singh Deol, Marketing Officer, Punjab, 5 May 1946, Stokes Papers.

4. Stokes to K. V. F. Morton, 15 February 1937, Stokes Papers.

5. Major A. Beatson Bell, Secretary Municipal Committee, Simla to Deputy Commissioner, Simla, 21 October 1936, Stokes Papers.

6. A plea for transport facilities by the Kotgarh Fruit Growers Association, 1938, Stokes Papers.

7. *Civil and Military Gazette,* 26 September 1937.

8. Fruit Growing in Simla Hills, The Lack of Transport, *Civil and Military Gazette,* 25 September 1937.

9. *Liddell's Simla Weekly,* 25 September 1937.

10. Stokes, "Motor Transport on the Hindustan-Tibet Road," 5 October 1937, Stokes Papers.

11. S. G. Stubbs, Secretary, P. W. D. Punjab to Stokes, 22 July 1938, Stokes Papers.

12. Secretary, Provincial Cooperative Fruit Development Board, Lyallpur to Stokes, 14 December 1937, Stokes Papers.

13. Duni Chand to Stokes, 29 June 1938, Stokes Papers.

14. Stokes to K. V. F. Morton, 15 February 1937.

15. Stokes to the Viceroy, 18 June 1939, Stokes Papers.

16. Plea for transport facilities by the Fruit Growers Association, Kotgarh, 1944, revised.

17. Stokes to Rai Sahib Narsingh Das Chopra, Honorary Magistrate, Sutar Mandi, Lahore, 26 January 1946, Stokes Papers.

18. Stokes, "The Kotgarh Orcharding Situation," 12 June 1945, Stokes Papers.

19. Stokes to Amin Chand, 20 November 1944, Stokes Papers.

20. Stokes to Rai Sahib Narsingh Das Chopra, 26 January 1946.

21. Military Secretary to Stokes, 18 September 1944; Stokes' appeal to Sir Bertrand Glancy, Governor of Punjab, 24 September 1944, Stokes Papers.

22. Stokes to Sir Bertrand Glancy, 14 October 1944, Stokes Papers.

23. Stokes to Amin Chand, 20 November 1944.

24. Stokes to Kenneth Mitchell, Chief Controller of Road Transport and Development, Government of India, n.d. but of end 1944, Stokes Papers.

25. Lieut. Gen. I. J. Hutton to Stokes, 25 July and 15 August 1944, Stokes Papers.

26. Stokes to Amin Chand, 20 November 1944.

27. Stokes to Harnam Dass, Managing Partner, Lehnu Mal Thakur Dass, Mashohra, Stokes Papers.

28. Stokes to Trevor Jones, Chief Engineer, PWD, 18 January 1944, Stokes Papers.

29. Stokes, *Traditions and Ideals of Our Family,* p. 154.

24. WORLD WAR II AND AFTER

1. Stokes, "Memorandum to Jawaharlal Nehru," 25 November 1929, Collected Essays, Memoranda and Letters.

2. Jawaharlal Nehru to Stokes, 5 December 1929, *Selected Works of Jawaharlal Nehru,* vol. 3 (Orient Longman), pp. 574–575.

3. Stokes to Subhas Chandra Bose, 30 March 1939, Collected Essays, Memoranda and Letters.

4. Stokes to Gandhi, 31 March 1939, Collected Essays, Memoranda and Letters.

5. Stokes to Subhash Chandra Bose, 30 March 1939.

6. Stokes to Gandhi, 31 March 1939.

7. Ibid.

8. Stokes to Jawaharlal Nehru, 4 April 1939, Collected Essays, Memoranda and Letters.

9. Gandhi to Stokes, 8 June 1939, Collected Essays, Memoranda and Letters.

10. Jawarhalal Nehru to Stokes, 18 April 1939, Collected Essays, Memoranda and Letters.

11. Stokes to Gandhi, 6 December 1939, Collected Essays, Memoranda and Letters.

12. Gandhi, "The Moral Issue," *Harijan,* 23 December 1939. Gandhi published Stokes' letter and his own reply as correspondence between a Western friend and himself.

13. D. R. Budhwar, Deputy Commissioner, Simla to Stokes, 8 August 1941; Tandon, Deputy Commissioner Simla to Stokes, 31 May 1943, Stokes Papers.

14. Stokes to C. N. T. Henry, D. C. Simla, 10 October 1945, Stokes Papers.

15. Stokes to D. R. Budhwar, 2 September 1941.

16. Stokes to Messrs Bishamber Mall Gujjar Mall, 27 December 1944, Stokes Papers.

17. Stokes to Warrington Stokes, 18 February 1943, Collected Essays, Memoranda and Letters.

18. Ibid.

19. Stokes' note on his correspondence with the Viceroy and the British Foreign Secretary, Collected Essays, Memoranda and Letters.

20. Interview with Vidya Stokes.

21. Stokes to Dr. Joseph Stokes, 31 March 1942, Stokes Papers.

22. Stokes, "Forenote," Harmony Hall Letters, 16 September 1942.

23. Interview with Lakshmi Singh Sirkeik; Stokes to Pandit Rishi Ram, 18 November 1943, Stokes Papers.

24. Stokes to Florence Stokes Coleman, 15 January 1946, Stokes Papers.

25. Stokes to Florence Stokes Coleman, 15 January 1946, Stokes Papers.

25. THE VEDANTIST

1. Stokes to Fazl-ud-Din Ali, 4 February 1939, Stokes Papers.

2. Stokes to Fazl-ud-Din Ali, 20 February 1939, Stokes Papers.

3. Joseph Moses to Stokes, 10 April 1942, Stokes Papers.

4. Stokes to Milton Rubicam, 13 August 1935. The book was edited and seen through the press by Prof. Raghu Vira of the Sanatan Dharma College, Lahore. Note to *Devupasana*.

5. Stokes *Introduction to the Gita,* 29 October 1935, Stokes Papers.

6. Stokes, "The Message of Gita," 1939, Collected Essays, Memoranda and Letters.

7. Stokes, *Introduction to the Gita,* 29 October 1935.

8. Excerpts from Stokes' reply to Prof. J. B. Pratt's letter of 7 June 1933, undated. Extracts from Letters.

9. Stokes, Introduction to *Collection of Mantras in the Barobagh Temple.*

10. Interview with Vidya Stokes.

11. Stokes, Introduction to *Collection of Mantras in the Barobagh Temple.*

12. Interview with Shamanand, Stokes' family cook for many years.

13. Stokes to Prem Chand, August 1939, Stokes Papers.

14. Interview with Vidya Stokes.

15. Stokes, *Introductory Notes on Advaita,* 1944, Stokes Papers.

16. Ibid.

17. Ibid.

18. Ibid.

19. Ibid.

20. Ibid.

21. Stokes, *The Traditions and Ideals of Our Family,* p. 80.

22. Stokes, *Introductory Notes on Advaita.*

23. J. Glenn Friesen, *Abhishiktananda: Hindu Advaitic Experience and Christian Beliefs;* Hindu-Christian Studies Bulletin II, 1998, p. 32.

24. Interview with Marjorie Sykes.

25. Letter from Rev. W. W. Jones to author, 14 October 1997.

26. Interview with R. W. Taylor of the Christian Institute for the Study of Religion and Society.

26. EVENTIDE

1. Stokes to Pritam Chand, 7 December 1944 and Stokes' Memorandum on Lal Chand's marriage, Stokes Papers.

2. Stokes to Marshall Truitt, 14 January 1946, Stokes Papers.

3. Stokes to Pritam Chand, 7 December 1944.

4. 1945 contract with Sheikh Barkhat Ullah, Fruit Agent, Stokes Papers.

5. Interview with Champavati.

6. Prem Chand to Stokes, undated letter, Stokes Papers.

7. Stokes' correspondence with DAV College Management and Ramakrishna Mission, Stokes Papers.

8. Prem Chand to Stokes, undated letter, Stokes Papers.

9. Stokes to Marshall Truitt, 14 January 1946.

10. Ibid.

11. Stokes to Duni Chand, 19 November 1945, Stokes Papers.

12. Stokes to Surat Ram, 5 January 1946, Stokes Papers.

13. Stokes to C. N. T. Henry, Deputy Commissioner Simla, 2 January 1946, Stokes Papers.

14. Stokes' Foreword to Collected Essays, Memoranda and Letters, 20 July 1943.

15. Stokes to Warrington Stokes, 5 February 1946, Stokes Papers.

16. "Civil Disobedience as a Political Method," Stokes to Richard B. Gregg, 25 December 1930, Collected Essays, Memoranda and Letters.

17. Ibid.

18. Stokes to Das, Inspector of Schools, 9 April 1946, Stokes Papers.

19. Stokes to Das, Inspector of Schools, 6 May 1946.

20. Stokes to Florence Stokes Coleman, 15 January 1946, Stokes Papers.

21. Stokes to Florence S., 12 August 1926.

22. Stokes to Lal Singh, Fruit Development Adviser to Government of India, 7 May 1946, Stokes Papers.

23. Interviews with Pritam Chand and with Champavati.

24. Interview with Lakshmi Singh Sirkeik.

25. Stokes to Agnes, 1 March 1935 from Vienna, Stokes Papers.

26. Interview with Pritam Chand.

27. Interviews with Pritam Chand and with Lakshmi Singh Sirkeik.

28. Information from Champavati, Vidya Stokes, and other family members. Letter not traceable.

29. Stokes, "Forenote" to Harmony Hall Letters, 16 September 1942.

30. Henry Van Dyke, *The Story of the Other Wise Man* (New York: Harper and Bros., 1899).

31. C. F. Andrews "The Arch from East to West," *The Modern Review,* January 1921; also "A Letter from Romain Rolland to Rabindranath Tagore," *The Modern Review,* July 1919.

32. Gandhi, "Plea for Cool-headedness," *Collected Works,* XXIII, p. 41.

EPILOGUE

1. Stokes, "A Plea for Adequate Transport Facilities by the Fruit Growers Association," Kotgarh, Stokes Papers.

2. The Land of Delicious Apples, *The Tribune,* 27 June 1966.

3. *Apple Cultivation in Himachal Pradesh,* official pamphlet, 1974.

4. Interview with Surendra Mohan Kanwar.

5. Kusum Nair, *Blossoms in the Dust, The Human Factor in Indian Development,* p. 163.

6. Ibid., p. 167.

7. Ibid., pp. 167–69.

8. Stokes, *The Traditions and Ideals of Our Family,* p. 156.

9. Stokes to Satyavati, 21 March 1935. Letter written from Austria. Extracts from Letters.

10. Interview with Shamanand.

BIBLIOGRAPHY

PRINCIPAL SOURCES

STOKES PAPERS

Stokes' personal correspondence with family members, friends, and colleagues.

Stokes' correspondence with government officials on begar, the Hindustan–Tibet road, education, and relief work.

Stokes' manuscript books and collections.

NATIONAL ARCHIVES OF INDIA, NEW DELHI

Benarsidas Chaturvedi Collection. Letters, C. F. Andrews to Munshi Ram (Swami Shraddhanand) 1913–16.

Home Political, Simla Records, 1921–1922.

Home Political, Delhi Records, 1921–1922.

NEHRU MEMORIAL MUSEUM AND LIBRARY, NEW DELHI

Satyanand Stokes Papers consisting of:

    a. Extracts from Letters, Principally arising out of the Life and Thought at Harmony Hall, Kotgarh, together with Other Relevant Letters (1905–1935), 1942.

    b. Collected Essays, Memoranda and Letters (1913–1943), 1943.

NATIONAL GANDHI MUSEUM AND LIBRARY, DELHI

Copies of letters from Stokes to Gandhi.

Copies of letters between Richard B. Gregg and Gandhi.

PUNJAB STATE ARCHIVES, PATIALA

Guru-ka-bagh Congress Inquiry Committee and related papers.

CAMBRIDGE BROTHERHOOD, DELHI

Stokes' printed letters about his change of plans.

Delhi Mission News and other relevant journals.

VIDYAJYOTI INSTITUTE OF RELIGIOUS STUDIES, DELHI

Hosten Papers.

CHURCH MISSIONARY SOCIETY ARCHIVES, UNIVERSITY OF BIRMINGHAM, BIRMINGHAM

Stokes' Candidate Papers, 1908.

Punjab and Sind Mission Precis books, 1906–1912.

Original letters received, 1908, 1909, 1910–1912.

Letters sent, 1907–1913.

United Society for the Propagation of the Gospel Archives, Rhodes House Library, Oxford

Letters received and letters sent by Bishop H. H. Montgomery, SPG Secretary, 1908–1911. Relevant CMD papers.

Lambeth Palace Library, Westminster

Correspondence of Archbishop Randall Davidson (1908, 1911). Pocket Diaries of Archbishop Davidson, 1908.

Urban Archives, Temple University, Philadelphia

Records of Southwark Neighbourhood House, Philadelphia (1904–1915).

New York Theological Seminary Library, New York

Stokes' pamphlet on a Scheme for a Christian Gurukula.

Genealogical records of the Stokes family and newspapers reports have been taken from Historical Society of Pennsylvania, Philadelphia; Trenton Public Library, New Jersey; Germantown Historical Society, Philadelphia; Free Library of Philadelphia, Philadelphia.

SECONDARY SOURCES

Select Bibliography

Andrews, C. F. *North India*. London: A.R. Mowbray and Co., 1908.
——. *The Renaissance in India: Its Missionary Aspect*. London: Church of England Zenana Missionary Society, 1912.
——. *What I Owe to Christ*. New York: Abingdon Press, 1932.
——. *Sadhu Sundar Singh: A Personal Memoir*. London: Hodder and Stoughton, 1934.
——, and Mookerjee, Girija. *The Rise and Growth of the Congress in India*. London.
Appasamy, A. J. *Sundar Singh: A Biography*. London, 1958.
Azad, Maulana Abul Kalam. *India Wins Freedom*. Madras: Orient Longman, 1988.
Berreman, G. D. *Hindus of the Himalayas: Ethnography and Change*. Berkeley: University of California Press, 1972.
Bhasin, Raja. *Simla: The Summer Capital of British India*. Delhi: Penguin Books, 1992.
Chaturvedi, B., and Sykes, M. *Charles Freer Andrews. A Narrative*. London: George Allen and Unwin, 1949.
Chaudhury, P. C. Roy. *C.F. Andrews, His Life and Times*. Bombay, 1971.
Chetwode, P. *Kulu—The End of the Habitable World*. New Delhi: Time Books International, 1989.
Davey, Cyril. *Caring Comes First, The Leprosy Mission Story*. United Kingdom: Marshall Pickering, 1987.
Dyke, Henry Van. *The Story of the Other Wise Man*. New York: Harper and Bros., 1899.
Gairdner, W. H. T. *Edinburgh 1910: "The Preparation of Missionaries. An Account of the Interpretation of the World Missionary Conference*. Edinburgh: Oliphant, Anderson and Ferrier, 1910.
Gandhi, M. K. *The Collected Works of Mahatma Gandhi*. The Publications Division, 1978.
Gandhi, Rajmohan. *Mohandas: A True Story of a Man, His People and an Empire*. India: Penguin Viking.
Garvie, Alfred E. *The Christian Belief in God, In Relation to Religion and Philosophy*. London: Hodder and Stoughton.
Gibbs, M. E. *The Anglican Church in North India 1600–1970*. Delhi: ISPCK, 1972.

Goodall, Norman. *A History of the London Missionary Society 1895–1945*. London, 1954.

Gregg, Richard B. *The Economics of Khadi*. Triplicane: S. Ganesan, 1928.

———. *The Power of Non-violence*. London, 1936.

Grisword, Hervey De Witt. *Insights into Modern Hinduism, Studies in Religion and Culture*. New York: Henry Holt and Co., 1934.

India's Struggle for Independence, Visuals and Documents. New Delhi: National Council of Educational Research and Training.

Haines, Richard. *Genealogy of the Stokes Family, Burlington County, N.J.* Camden, N.J.: Sinnickson Chew and Sons, 1903.

Heiler, Friedrich. *The Gospel of Sadhu Sundar Singh*. London: George Allen and Unwin, 1927.

Horniman, B. G. *Amritsar and Our Duty to India*. London: Allenson and Co., 1920.

House, Col. *The Intimate Papers of Colonel House, Vol. IV, The Ending of the War, June 1018–Nov 1919*. London: Earnest Benn, 1928.

Hoyland, John S. *C.F. Andrews. Minister of Reconciliation,* 1940.

Jones, Kenneth W. *Arya Dharam*. Berkeley: University of California Press, 1976.

Jordan, Wilfred. *Genealogical and Personal Memoir*. Lewis Historical Publishing Co., 1939.

Jordens, J. T. F. *Dayananda Saraswati, His Life and Ideas,* 1978.

———. *Swami Shraddhananda, His Life and Causes*. Delhi: Oxford University Press, 1981.

Kanwar, Pamela. *Imperial Simla, The Political Culture of the Raj*. Delhi: Oxford University Press, 1990.

Kanwar, S. M. *Apples: Production Technology and Economics*. Delhi: Tata McGraw-Hill, 1987.

Kipling, Rudyard. *Plain Tales from the Hills*. London, 1930.

Lyon, Jean. *Just Half a World Away, My Search for the New India*. New York: Thomas Y. Crowell Co., 1954.

Majumdar, R. C. *History of the Freedom Movement in India*. Calcutta, 1963.

———, H. C. Raychaudhuri, and Kalikinkar Datta. *An Advanced History of India*. London: Macmillan and Co., 1967.

Malden, R. H. *Foreign Missions*. London: Longmans, Green and Co., 1910.

Mansingh, Surjit. *Historical Dictionary of India*. New Delhi: Vision Books, 1998.

Moorestown New Jersey Tricentennial. 1982.

Nair, Kusum. *Blossoms in the Dust: The Human Factor in Indian Development*. New York: Frederick A. Praeger, 1962.

Nanda, B. R. *Mahatma Gandhi*. Delhi, 1958.

Nanda, V. S. *"The Stokes of Kotgarh."* SPAN, September 1970.

Natarajan, J. *History of Indian Journalism, Part II of the Report of the Press Commission*. Delhi: Publications Division, Government of India, 1955.

Nehru, Jawaharlal. *Selected Works of Jawaharlal Nehru*. Delhi: Orient Longman, 1977.

———. *An Autobigraphy*. London, 1936.

Pande, B. N. *Concise History of the Indian National Congress, 1885–1947*. Delhi, 1985.

Patel, P., and Marjorie Sykes. *Gandhi, His Gift of the Fight*. Hoshangabad: Friends Rural Centre, Rasulia, 1987.

Pennell, T. L. *Among the Wild Tribes of the Afghan Frontier: A Record of Sixteen Years' Close Intercourse with the Indians of the Native Marches*. London: Seeley, Service and Co., 1922.

Rai, Lajpat. *The Arya Samaj*. London: Longmans, Green and Co., 1915.

Reed, Stanley, ed. *A Statistical and Historical Annual of the Indian Empire: The Indian Year Books 1922–32*. Bombay and Calcutta: Bennett, Coleman and Co.

Richter, Julius. *History of Indian Missions*. Edinburgh: Oliphant, Anderson and Ferrier, 1908.

Rubincam, Milton. *A Little-known Adventure of Thomas Stokes—1665*, The Genealogical Magazine of New Jersey, Oct. 1937.

——. *A Critical Analysis of the Stokes Pedigree.* Proceedings of the New Jersey Historical Society, April 1941.

——. *Samuel Evans Stokes: A Pennsylvanian's Contribution to Modern India.* Pennsylvania Historical Junto Meeting, Washington, D.C., 30 May 1987.

Shabab, Dilaram. *Kullu—Himalayan Abode of the Divine.* Delhi: Indus Publishing Co., 1996.

Shastri, Algoo Ram. *Lala Lalpat Rai.* Lok Sewa Dal, 1957.

Singh, Harnam. *The Indian National Movement and American Opinion.* Delhi, 1962.

Singh, Khushwant. *A History of the Sikhs.* Princeton, N.J.: Princeton University Press, 1966.

Singh, Mian Govardhan. *History of Himachal Pradesh.* Shimla: Minerva Book House, 1981.

Stock, Eugene. *The History of the Church Missionary Society, Supplementary Volume.* London: The Fourth Church Missionary Society, 1916.

Stokes, Florence. *A Sketch of the Life of Samuel Evans Stokes.* Philadelphia: Biddel Press.

Stokes, Joseph. *Notes on My Stokes Ancestry.* 1937.

Stokes, Francis Joseph, Jr. *Stokes, Cope, Emilen, Evans Genealogy, 1682–1982.* Philadelphia, 1982.

Stokes, S. E. *A Scheme for a Christian Gurukula.* Pamphlet.

——. *Arya Samaj.* Pamphlet.

——. *Arjun, The Life-story of an Indian Boy.* Westminster: Society for the Propogation of the Gospel in Foreign Parts, 1910.

——. *The Love of God: A Book of Prose and Verse.* 5th ed. London: Longmans, Green and Co., 1912.

——. *The Gospel According to the Jews and Pagans, The Historical Character of the Gospel Established from Non-Christian Sources.* London: Longmans, Green and Co., 1913.

——. *Letters of Nancy Evans Stokes with an Historical Note on the Stokes Family of Burlington County.* New Jersey: Private publication, 1916.

——. *The Construction of the Hindu Family, and the Facilities It Would Afford for Genealogical Research.* The Genealogical Society of Pennsylvania, March 1916.

——. *National Self-Realization.* Madras: S. Ganesan, 1921.

——. *To Awaking India.* Madras: Ganesh and Co., 1922.

——. *Satyakama or "True Desires."* Madras: S. Ganesan, 1931.

——. *Barobagh Temple Mantras.* Private publication, 1942.

——. *Devupasna.* Private publication, 1935.

Stokes, Satyanand. *National Self-Realization and Other Essays.* Delhi: Rubicon Publishing House, 1975.

Stuart, James. *Swami Abhishiktananda: His Life Told through His Letters.* Delhi: ISPCK, 1989.

Sykes, M. *Quakers in India: A Forgotten Century.* London: George Allen and Unwin, 1980.

Talbot, Ian. *Punjab and the Raj.* Maryland, 1988.

Tinker, H. *The Ordeal of Love: C.F. Andrews and India.* Delhi: Oxford University Press, 1979.

Vable, D. *The Arya Samaj, Hindu without Hinduism.* Vikas Publishing House. Pvt. Ltd., 1983.

Walther, Rudolph J. *Happenings in ye Olde Philadelphia 1680–1900.* Philadelphia, 1925.

Whalen, William J. *The Quakers or Our Neighbours, The Friends.* Philadelphia, 1984.

World Missionary Conference, 1910, Report of Commission IV, The Missionary Message in Relation to Non-Christian Religions. Edinburgh: Oliphant, Anderson and Ferrier, 1910.

OFFICIAL PUBLICATIONS

Anderson, J. D. *Final Settlement Report of the Simla District 1915–16.* Lahore, 1917.

Development Profile of Himachal Pradesh. Shimla: Directorate of Economics and Statistics, Himachal Pradesh, 1985.

The Imperial Gazetteer of India. Vol. XVI. London: Clarendon Press, 1908.

Gazetteer of the Simla District. 1888–89, Calcutta, n.d.

Statistical Outline of Himachal Pradesh. Directorate of Economics and Statistics, Himachal
    Pradesh, 1981.

Wace, Lt. Col. E. G. *Final Report of the First Regular Settlement of the Simla District in the Pun-
    jab 1881–83.* Calcutta, 1884.

A Brief History of the Freedom Struggle in Himachal Pradesh. Language and Culture Department,
    Himachal Pradesh.

Freedom Fighters of Himachal Pradesh. Language and Culture Department, Himachal Pradesh.

INDEX

Italicized page numbers indicate illustrations.

Asha Sharma

is a granddaughter of Satyanand Stokes. A graduate of the Columbia University School of Journalism, she has been a fellow of the Indian Council of Historical Research New Delhi and a Research Associate at the University of California–Berkeley. Having lived in most parts of India as an army wife, she now divides her time between California, where her two children live, and Himachal Pradesh, India.